Words of Encouragement from Former Christian Leaders

I Shall Come Again, *Lord of Lords*, and *King of Kings* prove with astonishing clarity that our Lord has already fulfilled His promise, that He returned in 1844, a date that is confirmed 16 times in the Bible. Anyone who has a desire to see the Bridegroom and enter His heavenly Banquet must take this one step: read, with an open heart, the convincing evidence presented in these volumes. ***I encourage all Catholics to test "the Spirit" of Bahá'u'lláh, the Glory of God, to see if it is the Spirit of Truth*** (I John 4:1).

–LOU MEYER
Former Catholic Priest

For centuries Christians and Jews have pondered this glorious prophecy of Isaiah: "*For to us a child is born, to us a son is given, and the government will be on His shoulders. And He will be called Wonderful Counselor, Mighty God, Everlasting Father, Prince of Peace...He will reign on David's throne and over His kingdom, establishing and upholding it with justice and righteousness from that time on and forever*" (9:6-7).

The entire world is now encompassed with uncertainty and fear. The cry for peace is heard constantly, and yet there is no peace. These volumes set forth God's plan to remedy our greatest need at this critical juncture in history. ***The King of Kings*** has come and made His Kingdom available to all of us.

As one who has followed Him for more than forty years and experienced and witnessed His divine powers in transforming the hearts of humankind, I am pleased to recommend these volumes to any reader who will approach them with a seeking heart and an open mind. They present biblical evidence for the Advent of the only One who can save us from the impending dangers and calamities. ***In this work you will discover Bahá'u'lláh to be the King of Kings and Prince of Peace, who has come to establish God's Kingdom on earth as it is in heaven. I invite all Christians and Jews to participate in building this most glorious Kingdom***.

—DR JACK E. MCCANTS
Former Methodist Minister

By writing these volumes, Dr Motlagh has made a momentous contribution to our understanding of biblical prophecy. ***As a former Baptist minister, I urge all Christians to investigate the news of the Return of our Lord as presented in** I Shall Come Again, Lord of Lords, **and** King of Kings.* *"Arise, shine, for your light has come, and the glory of the Lord rises upon you"* (Isa. 60:1).

—MEL CAMPBELL
Former Baptist Minister

...a labor of love, and a work of over three decades of research. This is the most challenging and the best documented work on the fulfillment of a divine Promise uttered again and again since the dawn of history. Its message is timely, its proofs convincing, and its purpose divine—one that can lift and join the heart of humanity to the Heart of God. ***It should be read and reread by anyone gifted with an inquisitive and open mind—***

anyone who believes in reason, has faith in God's promises, and desires to see their fulfillment. "*Did I not say to you that if you would believe you would see the glory of God?*" (John 11:40).

—PAUL JACOBI
Former Catholic Priest

The message presented in these volumes should appeal to every Christian and every Jew. ***They prove the realization of a most glorious dream: the fulfillment of a hope and a promise affirmed more than a thousand times in the Bible***. They appeal to reason and apply scientific methods to scriptural prophecies to prove that once again God has spoken to humanity, that He has expressed His love and His grace by sending His Son in the Glory of the Father. Let me share this quotation from the Bahá'í Scriptures with all Christians and Jews: "*All the signs have been revealed; every prophetic allusion hath been manifested. Whatever hath been enshrined in all the Scriptures of the past hath been made evident.*"

—ELRICO EVANS
Former Baptist Minister

The Bahá'í Faith today presents the Christian Churches with the most tremendous challenge ever offered them in their long history: a challenge, and an opportunity. It is the plain duty of every earnest Christian...to investigate for himself with an open and fearless mind the purpose and the teachings of this Faith...O, Christian believers!...cast away your conflicting dogmas and interpretations which have caused such disunity...Recognize Christ in the glory and power of the Father, and heart and soul, throw yourselves into His Cause.

—GEORGE TOWNSHEND
Former Episcopal Minister

About this Work

Your work is the best I've seen on biblical prophecies and proofs of Bahá'u'lláh's Revelation. You offer so much information in relatively few pages. Your many references prove clearly the book's central claim. Your language is simple and exciting. You take the reader through a complete spiritual and prophetic adventure. Your approach is modest, yet dynamic. I pray it will excite all your readers as it has excited me.

—JOE KILLEEN
Bible Scholar with a Degree in Eschatology and Soteriology

There are few works by a single author that can rival Dr Motlagh's in their sheer scope, depth and thoroughness of scholarship. Without doubt, future Bahá'ís will thank Dr Motlagh for his achievements, that are, in my opinion, not only astonishing—they are heroic.

An important work that will be referenced by future Bahá'í scholars for millennia to come.

—ROBERT F. RIGGS
Aerospace and Marine Scientist, Inventor, and Author of The Apocalypse Unsealed

King of Kings

Volume III
Prophecies of the Second Coming

Hushidar Hugh Motlagh

Global Perspective
Mt. Pleasant, Michigan
www.globalperspective.org

King of Kings

ISBN 0-937661-23-6 (cloth)
ISBN 0-937661-24-4 (paper)
Library of Congress Catalog Card No. 98-94040

To order copies of this book and other works by this author, in the United States call or fax:

1-800-949-1863

If you prefer, order online from any country:

www.globalperspective.org

Our present address:

**Global Perspective, 1106 Greenbanks Dr.
Mt. Pleasant, MI 48858, USA**

For further information and possible change of our address, visit our Website or send us an E-mail to:

info@globalperspective.org

Dedicated to

'Abdu'l-Bahá, the Servant of Bahá, the Master, the Center of the Covenant, the Beautiful and Glorious Branch of the Lord

Behold, the Man
whose name is the Branch!
Zechariah 6:12

In that day the Branch
of the Lord will be
beautiful and glorious.
Isaiah 4:2 NIV

Here is my servant
...my chosen one in
whom I delight.
Isaiah 42:1 NEB

The messenger
of the covenant.
Malachi 3:1

I will now bring my
servant, the Branch.
Zechariah 6:12

About the Cover:

The two suns symbolize Bábu'lláh and Bahá'u'lláh, ***the Gate of God*** and ***the Glory of God***. The design of the cover was influenced by a dream. My original goal was to place a larger sun to symbolize Bahá'u'lláh, and a smaller one to symbolize the Báb. Later I decided to make the two suns equal, but a dream changed my plans.

October 28, 1995

In a dream, early in the morning, suddenly I saw a large beautiful sun in various shades of orange. It was facing me, as if looking at me from about 10 meters above the ground and 50 meters away. In this marvelous source of light I perceived a Being, as if it had a soul and wanted to communicate with me. It moved purposefully back and forth and in other directions as if trying to send me a message. This celestial scene inspired in my soul a sense of awe, joy, and ecstasy. The sun was so close, yet it did not hurt my eyes.

At this point I feared that gazing at the sun may damage my eyes, so I closed them. But nothing changed. I continued to see the sun exactly as I did before.

After a while, I decided to change my perspective. When I looked up and toward my left into the heavens, I saw another circle of light, another sun, with the same color but many times smaller, like a star visible in daytime. After a few moments, I turned my gaze back to the soft orange sun near me and once again beheld its beauty and splendor. This celestial sight so enchanted and inspired my soul, I began saying again and again, "O God how great art Thou!" "O God how great art Thou!" I continued to praise God in those words, each time louder and louder until I woke up. At that moment, I had no doubt about the meaning of the dream. I knew I was being guided to return to the original dimensions of the design.

The sizes of the two suns on the cover do not represent the exact dimensions I saw in my dream. The orange sun was about 25 to 30 times larger than the other source of light. But the cover still demonstrates ***the principle*** that I was taught in my dream: That the ***Revelation*** or expression of Bahá'u'lláh's glory is much greater than that of the Báb and indeed of any Messenger or Redeemer of the past and for a long time into the future. Equal suns would have violated the recognition of that prime principle.

Other Works by This Author

Books on Proofs and Prophecies

I Shall Come Again
Lord of Lords
Come Now, Let Us Reason Together

Introductory Books

One God, Many Faiths; One Garden, Many Flowers
Choosing Your Destiny
On Wings of Destiny

Compilations

The Glorious Journey to God
Unto Him Shall We Return

Others

Effective Teaching
Applied Psychology
A Messenger of Joy
Teaching: The Crown of Immortal Glory
Proclaim the Most Great Name

Forthcoming Books

The Glory of the Son
The Glory of the Father
Will Jesus Come from the Sky or as a Thief?
In the Clouds of Glory
The Spirit that Acknowledges Jesus Christ
By My Fruits You Shall Know Me
Heaven's Most Glorious Gift
Seek and Ye Shall Find
The News that Every Christian Should Know
The Remembrance of God
Does Your Fishbowl Need Fresh Water?

Contents

A Call to all Peoples of the World

Prophets have prayed since the dawn of history for the triumph of goodness and the demise of evil:

> O Lord…shine forth! Rise up, O Judge of the earth… Lord, how long will the wicked, how long will the wicked triumph? Psalms 94:1-3 NKJ

Humankind has been waiting for a Kingdom joined by love and ruled by justice:

> Thy kingdom come. Thy will be done in earth, as it is in heaven. Matthew 6:10

Bahá'u'lláh declares that the time for the promised Kingdom has come:

> All created things are heard exclaiming: "The Kingdom is God's, the Almighty, the All-Knowing, the All-Wise."[1]

Bahá'u'lláh declares Himself the promised one of all nations and religions. He claims to be the King of Kings and Lord of Lords, the world Savior and Redeemer promised in all sacred Scriptures to bring peace, love, justice, and order to this chaotic world.

> Lift up your heads, O ye gates; and be ye lift up, ye everlasting doors; and the King of glory shall come in. Who is this King of glory? The Lord strong and mighty...Lift up your heads, O ye gates; even lift them up, ye everlasting doors; and the King of glory shall come in. Who is this King of glory? The Lord of hosts, he is the King of glory. Psalms 24:7-10

Bahá'u'lláh invites all the peoples of the world, in the clearest and most emphatic terms, to investigate His divine Mission and to rejoice at the dawning of the new day:

> O My friends that dwell upon the dust! Haste forth unto your celestial habitation. Announce unto yourselves the joyful tidings: "He Who is the Best-Beloved is come! He hath crowned Himself with the glory of God's Revelation, and hath unlocked to the face of men the doors of His ancient Paradise." Let all eyes rejoice, and let every ear be gladdened, for now is the time to gaze on His beauty, now is the fit time to hearken to His voice. Proclaim unto every longing lover: "Behold, your Well-Beloved hath come..."..."Lo, the Adored One hath appeared arrayed in the fullness of His glory!" O lovers of His beauty! Turn the anguish of your separation from Him into the joy of an everlasting reunion, and let the sweetness of His presence dissolve the bitterness of your remoteness from His court.[2]

This book is written to help all seekers and lovers of truth to pursue their divine destiny, and to carry out their spiritual commitment and responsibility to God. It is written to help them discover if Bahá'u'lláh is indeed the Glory of God—the most awesome expression of divine Splendor.

Bahá'u'lláh has reiterated the proclamation of His divine Mission thousands of times in writings equal to 100 volumes. These are a few excerpts from those volumes:

> He Who is the sovereign Lord of all is come. The Kingdom is God's, the omnipotent Protector, the Self-Subsisting. Worship none but God, and, with radiant hearts, lift up your faces unto your Lord, the Lord of all names.[3]

> O Kings of the earth! He Who is the sovereign Lord of all is come...Wash your hearts from all earthly defilements, and hasten to enter the Kingdom of your Lord, the Creator of earth and heaven...

> Ye are but vassals, O Kings of the earth! He Who is the King of kings hath appeared, arrayed in His most wondrous glory, and is summoning you unto Himself...Arise, and serve Him Who is the Desire of all nations, Who hath created you through a word from Him...

> By the righteousness of God! It is not Our wish to lay hands on your kingdoms. Our mission is to seize and possess the hearts of men. Upon them the eyes of Bahá are fastened.[4]

> Say: This is the Voice of God, if ye do but hearken. This is the Day Spring of the Revelation of God, did ye but know it. This is the Dawning-Place of the Cause of God, were ye to recognize it. This is the Source of the commandment of God, did ye but judge it fairly. This is the manifest and hidden Secret; would that ye might perceive it. O peoples of the world! Cast away, in My name that transcendeth all other names, the things ye possess, and immerse yourselves in this Ocean in whose depths lay hidden the pearls of wisdom and of utterance, an ocean that surgeth in My name, the All-Merciful.[5]

A Call to Christians

Bahá'u'lláh claims to have fulfilled all the prophecies of the Gospel concerning the return of Christ:

> He, in truth, hath come unto the world in His most great glory, and all that hath been mentioned in the Gospel hath been fulfilled.[6]

Bahá'u'lláh, in His time, sent Epistles to religious leaders in general and to Pope Pius IX in particular. None of them responded to His call. Here are a few messages from His Epistles:

> O Pope! Rend the veils asunder. He Who is the Lord of Lords is come overshadowed with clouds, and the decree hath been fulfilled by God, the Almighty, the Unrestrained ...He, verily, hath again come down from Heaven even as He came down from it the first time. Beware that thou dispute not with Him even as the Pharisees disputed with Him (Jesus) without a clear token or proof. On His right hand flow the living waters of grace, and on His left the choice Wine of justice, whilst before Him march the angels of Paradise, bearing the banners of His signs. Beware lest any name debar thee from God, the Creator of earth and heaven. Leave thou the world behind thee, and turn towards thy Lord, through Whom the whole earth hath been illumined...Dwellest thou in palaces whilst He Who is the King of Revelation liveth in the most desolate of abodes? Leave them unto such as desire them, and set thy face with joy and delight towards the Kingdom... Arise in the name of thy Lord, the God of Mercy, amidst the peoples of the earth, and seize thou the Cup of Life with the hands of confidence, and first drink thou therefrom, and proffer it then to such as turn towards it amongst the peoples of all faiths...

> Call thou to remembrance Him Who was the Spirit (Jesus), Who when He came, the most learned of His age

> pronounced judgment against Him in His own country, whilst he who was only a fisherman believed in Him. Take heed, then, ye men of understanding heart! Thou, in truth, art one of the suns of the heaven of His names. Guard thyself, lest darkness spread its veils over thee, and fold thee away from His light...Consider those who opposed the Son (Jesus), when He came unto them with sovereignty and power. How many the Pharisees who were waiting to behold Him, and were lamenting over their separation from Him! And yet, when the fragrance of His coming was wafted over them, and His beauty was unveiled, they turned aside from Him and disputed with Him...None save a very few, who were destitute of any power amongst men, turned towards His face...
>
> The Word which the Son concealed is made manifest. It hath been sent down in the form of the human temple in this day. Blessed be the Lord Who is the Father! He, verily, is come unto the nations in His most great majesty. Turn your faces towards Him, O concourse of the righteous... 'Lo! The Father is come, and that which ye were promised in the Kingdom is fulfilled!...' My body longeth for the cross, and Mine head waiteth the thrust of the spear, in the path of the All-Merciful, that the world may be purged from its transgressions...[7]

This is a call to Christians who are waiting for the second Advent of their Lord. It is an invitation to all sincere followers of Jesus to open their hearts and minds to the most glorious news in human history. It asks all those who insist on the accuracy of their interpretation of prophecies to reconsider their assumption, to ponder the spiritual state of all those who made the same assumptions and held the same conviction at the time of the first Advent. They assumed that their Savior would come as a king to rescue them and restore their ancient glory and splendor. They dreamed of another David. That one unfounded assumption caused them to deny their Lord. Read this book with an open mind and respond to its most challenging and transforming message—a message that can change this planet into a veritable paradise.

Unfortunately, most Christians are unaware of Bahá'u'lláh's advent and the abundance of evidence He presents in support of His claim. Among Christian leaders and scholars perhaps one in a thousand has read even a single book about Bahá'u'lláh. If they take time and investigate the monumental evidence for His claim, they will see Him shine as brightly as the sun.

Consider this statement from a Christian leader and scholar, George Townshend, Canon of St. Patrick's Cathedral, who investigated the news of the coming of the Lord and recognized Bahá'u'lláh's Advent as the fulfillment of the most glorious promise in the Bible:

> Slowly the veil lifts from the future. Along whatever road thoughtful men look out they see before them some guiding truth, some leading principle, which Bahá'u'lláh gave long ago and which men rejected.[8]

"A little boy wandered away from his mother while she was shopping in the mall. A security guard found him wandering around by himself and took him to the mall's main office. There the guards bought him ice cream and told him jokes to keep him amused. Finally, his distraught mother showed up. Sobbing, she gathered the child in her arms. He blissfully kept eating his ice cream. In response to her questions the boy simply said, 'Gee, Mama, I didn't even know I was lost until I was found.'" Only when people are found by Bahá'u'lláh, will they realize what they have been missing.

So far, Bahá'u'lláh is largely unknown to the peoples of the world. He is still in the state of "a thief in the night."

> That is the day when I come like a thief! Happy the man who stays awake. Christ (Revelation 16:15)

For most people, the Sun is still concealed behind the clouds. I hope this book will scatter some of the clouds. I pray that it will awaken the conscience of Christians everywhere, for the cost of ignoring or denying the divine Call is too great to contemplate.

Whenever statements are made about Christians denying Bahá'u'lláh, the purpose is not to refer to ***all*** Christians, but only to ***some***. The great majority of Christians have never even heard the name of Bahá'u'lláh. I believe, if Christians seriously examine the evidence for Bahá'u'lláh's claim, the majority of them will recognize Him as the One they have been waiting for. The denial is not willful; it results mostly from misconceptions and a lack of knowledge.

1

Have Ye Shut Out Yourselves By Reason of My Name?

Bahá'u'lláh

Bahá'u'lláh has written a special Epistle for Christians. He reasons with them in the kindest and gentlest way and invites them to investigate His Message with an open heart.

He begins His Epistle by addressing Christians as the "followers of the Son" and asking them if they have deprived themselves of His glory because of His name. The new name is the first obstacle that prevents most Christians from investigating Bahá'u'lláh's claim. Often it casts fear in their hearts. To show His authority, Bahá'u'lláh begins His invitation by the word "Say," equal to "Thus saith the Lord," a phrase used frequently in the Hebrew Scriptures:

> ***Say***, O followers of the Son! Have ye shut out yourselves by reason of My Name?[1]

Bahá'u'lláh asks Christians to ponder why they would deny the very Redeemer for whose advent they have prayed day and night:

> Day and night ye have been calling upon your Lord, the Omnipotent, but when He came from the heaven of eternity in His great glory, ye turned aside from Him...[2]

Bahá'u'lláh then asks Christians to learn from the examples of history. In one of His works (*The Book of Certitude*), Bahá'u'lláh cites the story of the great Messengers and Redeemers of the past and shows how each time, without exception, people refused to open their hearts and minds to God's message. Bahá'u'lláh's purpose is to increase insight and awareness in seekers of truth. Most people ignore or underestimate the value of history in understanding human nature.

> The Lord, the God of their fathers, sent word to them through his messengers again and again...But they mocked God's messengers, despised his words and scoffed at his prophets... II Chronicles 36:15-16 NIV

Our two most reliable guides to truth are the Scriptures, and history. The Scriptures show God's side; history presents the human side. The Scriptures reveal God's mind; history tests and unveils the human mind. The Scriptures teach the divine principles; history shows how fallible people practice the principles. The Scriptures reveal God's perfection; history manifests human imperfection.

The metaphoric language of prophecies empowers the imagination. It allows people to soar freely through the splendid clouds of "the rapture," and bask in glamour, power, and glory. History brings the soaring bird of imagination and fantasy down to the earth of reality. History throws light on prevailing illusions and fantasies. The light prevents people from believing whatever they wish to believe. This apparent loss of freedom and power makes them feel uncomfortable. They prefer not to look back.

One of the lessons of history is that we seldom learn from history. No wonder history keeps repeating itself. We think the past is irrelevant to the present. We find it difficult to relate to peoples of ancient times, who lived a primitive life. Yet one of the lessons of history is that civilizations change but not the way people feel and behave. Kingdoms come and go but the kingdom of the human heart remains the same. Many authors have emphasized an urgent need to learn from the lessons of the past:

> History is not just the concern of historians and social scientists. It is not the lonely domain of political prognosticators and ivory tower academics. It is the very stuff of life. And, it is the very stuff of faith. In fact, the Bible puts a heavy emphasis on historical awareness...Again and again in the Scriptures, God calls upon His people to remember.[3]
>
> Remembrance and forgetfulness are the measuring rods of faithfulness throughout the entire canon of Scripture...In fact, the whole direction of a culture depends on the gracious appointments of memory: "Wonders cannot be known in the midst of darkness. Righteousness cannot be done in a land of forgetfulness" (Psalms 88:12).[4]

The great Christian historian of the last century, Lord Acton declared:

> History must be our deliverer not only from the undue influence of other times, but from the undue influence of our own, from the tyranny of the environment and the pressures of the air we breathe.[5]

And finally, English author and orator John Briggs encourages historical awareness as an essential step to the well being of both society and individual:

> Just as a loss of memory in an individual is a psychiatric defect calling for medical treatment, so too any community which has no social memory is suffering from an illness.[6]

When Jesus compared His coming and the world's conditions to those of Noah's times, He clearly predicted that history will repeat itself:

> The coming of the Son of Man will repeat what happened in Noah's time. Matthew 24:37 NAB

To inspire open-mindedness, self-understanding, and humility, Bahá'u'lláh asks Christians to pause and ponder, and to examine the story of their faith. He encourages them to put themselves in the position of the Jews at the time of Jesus. They too, like Christians of today, prayed hard and long for the advent of their Redeemer, yet when He came they rejected Him. ***They thought they knew the exact meaning of the prophecies about the advent of their Messiah, yet they saw no connection between Jesus and the prophecies they had read time and again. Could not the same happen today? What makes Christians of today different from the contemporaries of Jesus***?

Bahá'u'lláh asks Christians to remember the kinds of people who accepted Jesus. They were all ordinary people with no power. Bahá'u'lláh first cites the example of a fisherman, Peter, who recognized his Redeemer. Next He mentions the example of a prestigious and popular leader—the most learned Jewish theologian of his age—who did just the opposite: denied and demeaned his Redeemer. Bahá'u'lláh does not name the prestigious leader, but we can tell who he was. Very likely he was Annas, who occupied the highest spiritual position among the Jews. Bahá'u'lláh then asks Christians to take heed, to wake up from their dreams.

Every king and ruler who has ever lived would envy the Kingdom of Christ. Political leaders appear and disappear, but the star of Jesus shines high in the heavens with dazzling splendor. But how much effort and sacrifice were required and how long did it take to raise His star? How did people respond to His message and relate to His followers at the beginning? For the most part, the people ignored them. That is why we have very few references in the historical records of that time about Jesus and Christians. "Only one pagan writer in the century following Jesus' death [around 115 A. D.] offers us an explicit reference to him as a historical figure."[7] That writer is Tacitus, who wrote:

> To dispel the rumor, Nero...treated with the most extreme punishments, some people popularly known as Christians, whose disgraceful activities were notorious. The originator of that name, Christus, had been executed when Tiberius was emperor by order of the procurator Pontius Pilatus. But the deadly cult, though checked for a time, was now breaking out again not only in Judaea, the birthplace of this evil, but even throughout Rome, where all the nasty and disgusting ideas from all over the world pour in and find a ready following.[8]

Religious writers did no better. The following, one of the earliest Jewish references to Jesus, offers an example:

> It is taught: On Passover Eve they hanged Yeshu. For forty days beforehand a crier went out proclaiming, 'He is going out to be stoned, because he has practiced magic and led Israel astray. If anyone has anything to say in his defense, let him come and speak for him.' But they found nothing in his favor, so they hanged him on Passover Eve.[9]

Although the star of Bahá'u'lláh has risen to amazing heights, although in a span of a century and a half His followers have spread His faith to over 200 countries and territories, many continue to ignore rather than investigate His message of peace, harmony, and salvation.

It seems so natural to think that only the past generations could pass a misjudgment as tragic as ignoring or denying their Lord and crucifying Him. Just as young people often look down on old people, new generations look down on past generations. They live under the illusion that they are not as blind as their ancestors. As Jesus taught, it is easier to see a speck in someone else's eye than a plank in one's own (Luke 6:41). The people of Israel felt the same way. They thought they were wiser than their ancestors who persecuted the Hebrew prophets:

> Woe to you...you hypocrites! You build tombs for the prophets and decorate the graves of the righteous. And you say, ***'If we had lived in the days of our forefathers, we would not have taken part with them in shedding the blood of the prophets.'*** Christ (Matt. 23:29-30 NIV)

After reminding Christians of the most critical lesson in history, Bahá'u'lláh proclaims that He has come for their salvation and to this end He has suffered beyond measure. He asks them why they run away from Him.

> We, verily, have come for your sakes, and have borne the misfortunes of the world for your salvation. Flee ye the One Who hath sacrificed His life that ye may be quickened [receive life]?[10]

Of course, people run away mostly because of fear—fear of being deceived. Even ***the thought*** of a new religion triggers negative feelings in many a heart and soul. People are warned from childhood to watch out for deceivers, to protect their precious faith from intruders. They are told that only the most eccentric believer would look beyond the safe confines of his own faith. All these teachings and tendencies take their toll in creating fear and avoidance. Some people's faith is so fragile, they fear that even the sound of a new name may break it! Fear does not stay alone. It calls other compatible emotions for support. Guilt is among the first to respond. Guilt poses this question: are you being loyal to your own faith? Then it asks: why should you play with temptation? Fear also invites apathy, suspicion, and self-satisfaction. It says, if you have a secure house, why would you wish to go into the house of a stranger you have been told all your life not to enter?

What then can possibly overcome these immense obstacles: fear, avoidance, guilt, apathy, suspicion, and self-satisfaction? History shows that for most people the power that can overcome them is the fear of God, the fear of losing His favor.

If people are afraid of being deceived, they must be equally afraid of losing the One for whose sake they are afraid. The Scriptures ask us to fear no one except God. They also declare that fearing God is a sign of wisdom. If people remember these two instructions, they might say, "Since I fear God, I need not fear deception. He will guide me. He will give me the wisdom to choose my spiritual destiny. Perhaps with His help I can enter the house of a stranger, not with the intention of staying, but for the purpose of inquiring, observing, watching, and knowing him." This may be the reason why Bahá'u'lláh appeals to the believer's fear of God.

In His Epistle, Bahá'u'lláh then asks Christians not to follow such leaders as have strayed from the path of truth. In all ages, people prefer to follow their religious leaders without taking much responsibility for their own spiritual destiny. This tendency is so natural, so well-established, it prevents most Christians from even a cursory examination of the Bahá'í Faith. When they are invited to read a Bahá'í book or attend a Bahá'í meeting, they decline without hesitation. Often, their first thought is to ask their pastor. What would the pastor say? Any religious leader who encourages church members to look into another religion invites criticism and may even undermine his own security. If the pastor is adventurous he may suggest the studying of other faiths from the works of Christian authors or else within the confines of a Sunday school class.

After referring to the example of religious leaders, Bahá'u'lláh asks Christians if they think He is after His own self-interests. If that were the case, He intimates, why would He live constantly under the threat of His enemies? Would His true motive be the accumulation of wealth? If that were the case, He reminds them, why then would He live in the most horrible places?

> Do ye imagine that He seeketh His own interests, when He hath, at all times, been threatened by the swords of the enemies; or that He seeketh the vanities of the world, after He hath been imprisoned in the most desolate of cities? Be fair in your judgment and follow not the footsteps of the unjust.[11]

Suffering cannot be an absolute proof, but it can be a mark of distinction. It sets Bahá'u'lláh apart from the countless selfish leaders who use their powers for personal gain. This mark of distinction makes the task of investigation much simpler because no man of any wisdom exposes himself to pain and suffering for a lie.

Then Bahá'u'lláh asks Christians to observe fairness, for His life testifies to His unconditional self-sacrifice for God.

He then declares that He has opened to them the Gates of the Kingdom. Would they not open the door of their houses to Him? Can anyone think of a greater loss? Suppose someone asks you to open your eyes to a marvelous mansion. He says that by seeing and acknowledging it you can become a part owner, a permanent resident of that mansion. Would it be wise to reject such an offer?

> Say: We, in truth, have opened unto you the gates of the Kingdom. Will ye bar the doors of your houses in My face?[12]
> Bahá'u'lláh

Bahá'u'lláh's invitation to enter "the gates of the Kingdom" is in keeping with Jesus' promise that He would return to receive and take those who trusted Him to dwelling-places in His Father's house:

> Set your troubled hearts at rest. Trust in God always; trust also in me. There are many dwelling-places in my Father's house; if it were not so I should have told you; for I am going there on purpose to prepare a place for you. And if I go and prepare a place for you, I shall come again and receive you to myself, so that where I am you may be also...
> Christ (John 14:1-3 NIV)

Bahá'u'lláh then compares His own coming with that of Jesus. He reminds Christians of this biblical verse:

> I [Christ] have come down from heaven...
>
> Christ (John 6:38 NEB)

And then offers one of His own:

> He [the Spirit of Christ], verily, hath again come down from heaven, even as He came down from it the first time.[13]
>
> Bahá'u'lláh

No one has testified that Jesus came from heaven, except Jesus Himself. If Jesus' testimony about Himself is correct, could not Bahá'u'lláh's testimony also be correct? Bahá'u'lláh then warns Christians not to dispute with Him as did the people of past ages, when He appeared in the Spirit of Christ.

> Beware lest ye dispute that which He [Bahá'u'lláh] proclaimeth, even as the people before you disputed His utterances.[14]

Among those who argued with Jesus were the Pharisees, who strictly followed tradition and literal interpretation of the Bible. They loved to argue with just about everything Jesus said. Among their arguments was this:

> Surely this is Jesus son of Joseph; we know his father and mother. How can he now say, 'I have come down from heaven'?
>
> John 6:42 NEB

Are the theologians of our time not at least as able and zealous as the Pharisees in carrying out arguments? Are they less absorbed in their dreams and fantasies? Do people change that much? If Jesus lived today among the people of this age and made the same claim that He made to the Pharisees (that He has come down from heaven), would they not respond the same way? Would they not laugh at Him? From this observation alone, the seekers of truth can gain a sense of humility that may lead them and lift them to the kingdom of true knowledge.

Did people accept Jesus' testimony concerning His God-given authority to disclose the meaning of prophecies? They had difficulty accepting His testimony even about sensible and ordinary things, much less spiritual truths:

> I tell you the truth, we speak of what we know, and we testify to what we have seen, but still you people do not accept our testimony. I have spoken to you of earthly things and you do not believe; how then will you believe if I speak of heavenly things? Christ (John 3:11-12 NIV)

Human beings are not known for being open-minded. Psychologist Dr. Wayne Dyer makes this observation:

> I listen to talk radio for several hours each day in cities all over North America. It is my observation that virtually everyone who calls to a radio station to discuss a current topic is attached to his or her idea and to the notion of making someone else wrong. It seems to be unheard of for someone to listen to another point of view with an open mind. The callers almost always are quiet and polite for a few moments while the other party is talking, and then ignore everything that was said and state their own position. Seldom do I hear anyone say, "You make a good point. I'll rethink what I believed before I made this call."[15]
>
> This attachment to ideas and to making others wrong is the history of the being called Human Being, and it accounts for untold wars and misery since the beginning of recorded history...Seldom if ever do we change our minds based upon solid ideas presented by others.[16]

If people respond with closed minds to secular issues, what can we expect when religious issues are involved?

I am reminded of one of my students (Dawn) who described her father (David) as a brilliant lawyer. Several times she referred to his superior mental abilities. Before entering the law, David was a priest but fell in love, married, and resigned his priesthood.

Dawn had come to some Bahá'í meetings and wanted to tell her father about the Bahá'í Faith. She asked for a copy of ***I Shall Come Again*** and indicated that he would read it in no time. She said she highly respected her father's judgment and could not wait to hear his verdict. I gave her a copy of the book and then added, "Don't overestimate your father's open-mindedness. Few people have that kind of mind! Be gentle in expressing your enthusiasm about the Bahá'í Faith. Parents are instantly alarmed about what their daughters are discovering!"

Dawn assured me of her confidence in her father's fairness and openness to new ideas. She was all excited about what her father had to say. When Dawn went home, she gave the book to David and asked him to read it. Instead of reading the book, he simply checked the section in his encyclopedia about the Bahá'í Faith, but did not make any strong comment, for fear of alienating his daughter. (His purpose of checking the encyclopedia probably was to find out if her daughter was facing any danger.) But Dawn's mother could not keep her silence. After discovering that her daughter was seriously interested in investigating the Bahá'í Faith, she could not conceal her concern. In a state of utter anger she exclaimed, "I don't want to hear that word (Bahá'í) again!"

Dawn was taken by surprise. She could not believe her parents' emotional and irrational response. She had never tested them in this way. Later she stated that if her parents found out that she was continuing to investigate the Bahá'í Faith, they would cut off all financial support. Dawn's encounter with the Bahá'í Faith also had what psychologists call "halo effects." Next semester, when her parents discovered that she wanted to take a course in "Philosophy of Religion," they were highly alarmed. They warned her not to proceed. Once again, they feared, she would become mixed up in her beliefs. Prior to their daughter's spiritual adventure, they had never shown such a concern about what courses she would take. This example may be extreme, but it shows the supreme powers of emotion in preserving our ancestral beliefs, in preventing change, and in protecting a comfort zone that has been built and embellished over the course of centuries.

Many people worship ***the name*** Jesus Christ instead of the Spirit behind it. Jesus Christ means "***Deliverer, the Anointed One***." What is the significance of a word? Its l-e-t-t-e-r-s or its ***meaning***? Is Jesus' magnificence due to the unique combination of letters in His name or because of what those letters represent? In many languages the name Jesus and the title Christ are entirely different. If it is Jesus' mission—Deliverer—that matters, then cannot that same mission be found under a new title or a different arrangement of letters such as "Bahá'u'lláh," the Glory of God?

Some Christians say, "No name can save but Jesus." The same holds true with all other great Messengers and Redeemers. When Moses came, ***was there any "name" other than Moses*** that could save the people? When Abraham or Noah appeared, ***was there any name other than those names***?

Some Jewish theologians use the same line of reasoning to prove the superiority and uniqueness of their own Savior. They show that according to their Scriptures the only Savior is God, who was and is their Savior:

> Truly You are God, who hide Yourself, ***O God of Israel, the Savior***!...A just God and a Savior; there is none besides Me. Isaiah 45:15, 21 NKJ
>
> For I am the Lord your ***God***, the Holy One of Israel, ***your Savior***...I, even I, am the Lord, and besides Me there is no savior. Isaiah 43:3, 11
>
> See also Isaiah 49:26; 60:16; Psalms 106:21

After showing that their Savior is God, the Jewish theologians ask: "Which would you prefer to have as your Savior? Jesus or God?" To prove the superiority of his choice, a Jewish author has published a book called: *You Take Jesus, I'll Take God.*[17]

What about false christs? What about warnings such as this?

> Take heed that no one deceives you. For many will come in My name, saying, "I am the Christ," and will deceive many. Christ (Matt. 24:4-5 NKJ)

Surely no one wants to be deceived. But does this mean that no one should investigate? Should Christians ignore Jesus' numerous commandments that they should seek and search, that they should look for their Master? At the beginning of the Book of Revelation, which contains many significant prophecies about His return, Jesus said:

> Blessed is the one who reads the words of this prophecy, and blessed are those who hear it and take to heart what is written in it, because the time is near. Revelation 1:3 NIV

How can we "take to heart" the many signs Jesus gave in that incredible book if we fail to take time to see their clear and unmistakable fulfillment in the advents of the Báb and Bahá'u'lláh?

He who gave the warnings, also gave us definitive signs and reliable standards by which we can separate the false christs from the true One.

Fear of being deceived is a justifiable concern, but should it paralyze our sense of courage and curiosity? The topic of false christs and the Antichrist is considered to be so critical, it is covered in detail in two chapters in this volume. (See Chapters 4 and 5.)

To continue with Bahá'u'lláh's Epistle, after comparing His advent to that of Jesus, He declares:

> Thus instructeth you the True One, could ye but perceive it.[18]

Bahá'u'lláh calls Himself "the True One," perhaps because Christians remember these words:

> I am the way and ***the truth*** and the life. No one comes to the Father except through me. Christ (John 14:6 NIV)

Bahá'u'lláh intimates that He is ***the same Truth*** revealed again. Once more He repeats His claim, this time through the metaphor of the Burning Bush, a symbol of God. Thus Bahá'u'lláh reminds Christians of His great authority. He shows them that His Voice is indeed the Voice of God:

> ...and the Burning Bush calleth aloud: "He Who is the Desired One is come in His transcendent majesty."[19]

The divine Voice asks Bahá'u'lláh to declare that the Father has come. This too is prophesied:

> For the Son of man shall come ***in the glory of his Father***...
> Christ (Matt. 16:27)

> Say, Lo! ***The Father is come***, and that which ye were promised in the Kingdom is fulfilled![20] Bahá'u'lláh

Then the heavenly Voice calls Bahá'u'lláh "the Word" that Jesus concealed from the world. Most people consider themselves mature. They think they can "bear" the weight of any message. They forget this fact:

> I have yet many things to say unto you, but you cannot bear them now. Christ (John 16:12)

The claim Jesus made in His time was not difficult to bear, for He called Himself the Son. That title is not threatening, for all true believers are called the children of God. In spite of this, at the beginning very few could accept Jesus as the Son. What would have happened if Jesus, instead of saying the Son has come, had said the Father has come? Yet this is the Message that Bahá'u'lláh declares today. "Father" points to maturity. Now people are more capable—at least potentially—of understanding the meaning of that message. The disclosure of that "Word" (Father) was postponed until now. Bahá'u'lláh declares that when the Hour arrived, the hidden Word, the One Jesus concealed, was made manifest:

> And when the appointed time was fulfilled and the Hour had struck, the Word shone forth above the horizon of the Will of God.[21]

In Volume I, 16 biblical prophecies were presented to prove the exact year of the arrival of the Hour. It was made clear that all those prophecies were fulfilled by the Báb and Bahá'u'lláh. In sheer number alone those prophecies outnumber the time-prophecies of the first advent by more than five times.

Bahá'u'lláh warns Christians to accept His Word with full devotion and gratitude because such an acknowledgment is better for them than everything else they possess:

> Beware, O followers of the Son, that ye cast it [the Word] not behind your backs. Take ye fast hold of it. ***Better is this for you than all that ye possess***.[22] Bahá'u'lláh

Then Bahá'u'lláh introduces a message seemingly unrelated to the topic. He says that God stands near to those who manifest good deeds:

> Verily He is nigh unto them that do good.[23]

What are the distinguishing marks of those who "do good"? They act with courage, justice, detachment, and total devotion to the divine—deeds that are essential in the path of the search for truth.

After this brief statement, Bahá'u'lláh speaks again by declaring the fulfillment of still another prophecy:

> ***The Hour*** which We had concealed from the knowledge of the peoples of the earth and of the favored angels hath come to pass.[24] Bahá'u'lláh

Bahá'u'lláh's statement is in keeping with Jesus' pronouncement that the day and the hour of His return must be kept secret:

> No one knows about that day or ***hour***, not even the angels in heaven, nor the Son, but only the Father.
> Christ (Matt. 24:36 NIV)

> I will come on thee as a thief, and thou shalt not know what ***hour*** I will come upon thee. Christ (Rev. 3:3)
> See also Mark 13:32

Bahá'u'lláh then fulfills another prophecy:

> But when the Comforter is come, whom I will send unto you from the Father, even the Spirit of truth, which proceedeth from the Father, ***he shall testify of me***...
>
> Christ (John 15:26)

> Say, verily, He [Christ] hath testified of Me, and ***I do testify of Him***.[25]
>
> Bahá'u'lláh

The seeker of truth is assured that when Jesus said, "he will testify of me," He intended none other than Bahá'u'lláh.

> Indeed, He hath purposed no one other than Me. Unto this beareth witness every fair-minded and understanding soul.[26]
>
> Bahá'u'lláh

Once again Bahá'u'lláh invites Christians to investigate His Message and reminds them that He has suffered for their salvation:

> Though beset with countless afflictions, We summon the people unto God, the Lord of names. Say, strive ye to attain that which ye have been promised in the Books of God, and walk not in the way of the ignorant. My body hath endured imprisonment that ye may be released from the bondage of self. Set your faces then towards His countenance and follow not the footsteps of every hostile oppressor. ***Verily, He hath consented to be sorely abased that ye may attain unto glory***...[27]

Then Bahá'u'lláh reminds Christians that His claim is supported by proof:

> Lo! He is come in the sheltering shadow of Testimony, invested with ***conclusive proof and evidence***...[28]

The question of faith or belief should never be taken lightly. How can an individual protect himself from deception? ***Only by examining proofs***. This not only includes prophecies but also "the fruits" of divine revelation, which rank first among all proofs. That is the purpose of this six-volume series.

Bahá'u'lláh once again speaks of the blessings in store for the true seekers and the destiny of those who deny Him:

> Blessed is the man who turneth towards Him, and woe betide such as deny or doubt Him.[29]

Every question pales in comparison with this one: Who is Bahá'u'lláh, and how should we respond to His call? Ignore His call or investigate His call? What should be our verdict? "Yes" or "No"? Choosing the right word presents the most awesome challenge to every human being.

The verdict that we make is so critical, it should be made with the utmost care. That word—yes or no—is so powerful it can shape our eternal destiny. Astonishing as it may seem, one careless thought or word can prevent us from attaining the very purpose for which we came into the world. Jesus warns us against uttering our words, which express our thoughts and motives, carelessly, without adequate investigation:

> But I tell you that men will have to give account on the day of judgment for every ***careless word*** they have spoken.
> Christ (Matt. 12:36 NIV)

Bahá'u'lláh is not a philosopher, a saint, or simply a reformer. He speaks with divine authority and as the One whose advent is prophesied in all sacred Scriptures. He calls us to awaken to our spiritual responsibility and to be faithful to our covenant with God, so that when He sends a Redeemer, we embrace Him with all our hearts and souls and arise for the triumph of His cause.

> Be faithful, even to the point of death, and I will give you the crown of life. Christ (Rev. 2:10 NIV)

In this spiritual adventure, the only ***word*** we can choose is "***Yes***" or "***No***." Nothing else suffices:

> Simply let your 'Yes' be 'Yes,' and your 'No,' 'No'; anything beyond this comes from the evil one.
> Christ (Matt. 5:37 NIV)

Then Bahá'u'lláh declares His Message to all humankind in the most powerful and definitive terms:

> Proclaim then unto all mankind the glad-tidings of this mighty, this glorious Revelation. ***Verily, He Who is the Spirit of Truth is come to guide you unto all truth. He speaketh not as prompted by His own self, but as bidden by Him Who is the All-Knowing, the All-Wise.***
>
> Say, this is the One Who hath glorified the Son and hath exalted His Cause. Cast away, O peoples of the earth, that which ye have and take fast hold of that which ye are bidden by the All-Powerful, He Who is the Bearer of the Trust of God.[30]

Bahá'u'lláh then addresses His message to Christian leaders and teachers, such as pastors, priests, elders, bishops, and monks.

Bahá'u'lláh concludes His Epistle by showering His blessings on those who recognize Him. He repeats His message of blessings 21 times. Here are 7 of them:

> Say: Blessed the slumberer who is awakened...
>
> Blessed the wayfarer who directeth his steps toward the Tabernacle of my glory...
>
> Blessed the soul that hath been raised to life...and hath gained admittance into My heavenly Kingdom.
>
> Blessed the ear that hath heard and the tongue that hath borne witness and the eye that hath seen and recognized the Lord Himself, in His great glory...
>
> Blessed are they that have attained His presence.
>
> Blessed is he who hath remained faithful to My Covenant...
>
> Blessed is the man who hath detached himself from all else but Me...
>
> Upon him rest My mercy, My loving-kindness, My bounty and My glory.[31]

2

You Shall Be Called By a New Name

Isaiah 62:2 NEB

Part I

The Gift of a New Name

> By My Beauty! He Who is the Monarch of all names is come...[1]
> Bahá'u'lláh

Prophets have prayed, throughout history, that God's glory, beauty, and splendor may dawn:

> Let thy work appear unto thy servants, and ***thy glory*** unto their children. And let ***the beauty of the Lord*** our God be upon us...
> Psalms 90:16-17

> Praise be to ***his glorious name*** forever; may the whole earth be filled with ***his glory*** [glory of God].
>
> Psalms 72:19 NIV

Prophets have also asked us to rejoice at His glorious name and spread the news of its dawning to all nations:

> ***Shout with joy*** to God, all the earth! ***Sing*** to ***the glory of his name***; offer him glory and praise! Say to God, "How awesome are your deeds!" Psalms 66:1-3 NIV

> Sing to the Lord a new song; sing to the Lord, all the earth. Sing to the Lord, Praise his name; proclaim his salvation day after day. ***Declare his glory among the nations***, his marvelous deeds among all peoples. Psalms 96:1-3 NIV

Chapter 113 of Psalms is all in praise of the glorious name of the Lord. Here are a few verses:

> Let the name of the Lord be praised, both now and forevermore. From the rising of the sun to the place where it sets the name of the Lord is to be praised. ***The Lord*** is exalted over all the nations, ***his glory*** above the heavens.
>
> Psalms 113:2-4 NIV

What is the name or the title designated for the Redeemer of our age and His followers? Is He to be called Jesus Christ and are His followers to be called Christians? Or are they to receive a new name?

Contrary to what many expect, the prophecies point to a new name. When God renews His covenant, He calls it by a new name. As Jesus reminded the Jews:

> And no one pours new wine into old wineskins. If he does, the new wine will burst the skins, the wine will run out and the wineskins will be ruined. No, ***new wine must be poured into new wineskins***. Luke 5:37-38 NIV

We are living at the dawning of a new day, when all things are destined to be made new:

> ...the old order of things has passed away..."***I am making everything new***!" Revelation 21:4-5 NIV

> Behold, I will create ***new*** heavens and a ***new*** earth [a new heavenly and earthly civilization]. The former things will not be remembered, nor will they come to mind.
> Isaiah 65:17 NIV

> Then I saw a ***new*** heaven and a ***new*** earth, for the first heaven and the first earth had passed away...
> Revelation 21:1 NIV

> And they sang a ***new*** song... Revelation 5:9 NIV
> See also Revelation 14:3

Chapter 62 of Isaiah pertains entirely to our time. It starts by giving the tidings of a glorious day for Zion (the Holy Land), and then points to a new name:

> For Zion's sake I will not keep silent, for Jerusalem's sake I will not remain quiet, till her righteousness shine out like the dawn, her salvation like a blazing torch. ***The nations will see*** your righteousness, and the kings ***your glory; you will be called by a new name*** that the mouth of the Lord will bestow. You will be a crown of splendor [a glorious crown NEB] in the Lord's hand, a royal diadem in the hand of your God. Isaiah 62:1-3 NIV

Similarly, in Chapter 65, which points to our time, Isaiah predicts a new name for the followers of the new faith, whom he calls God's servants. The chapter raises the following points:

- People fail to search for the expected Messenger, the Lord of Hosts:

> ***I was there to be sought by a people who did not ask, to be found by men who did not seek me***. I said, 'Here am I, here am I,' to a nation that did not invoke me by name. I spread out my hands all day appealing to an unruly people who went their evil way...
> Isaiah 65:1-2 NEB

- The future of the Holy Land is glorious.
- Sharon and Achor (located in the northern half of Israel, where Bahá'u'lláh lived and passed away) will belong to those who seek the Lord. Many Bahá'ís traveled long distances on foot to attain the presence of Bahá'u'lláh:

> ...Sharon, and the Vale of Achor...shall belong to my people who seek me. Isaiah 65:10 NEB

- Divine punishment awaits those who refuse to respond to the new Call. Others—called God's servants—receive the gift of a new name:

> ...I called and you did not answer, I spoke and you did not listen; and you did what was wrong in my eyes and you chose what was against my will. Therefore these are the words of the Lord God: ***My servants*** shall eat [heavenly food] but you shall starve; ***my servants*** shall drink but you shall go thirsty; ***my servants*** shall rejoice but you shall be put to shame; ***my servants*** shall shout in triumph in the gladness of their hearts, but you shall cry from sorrow and wail from anguish of spirit; your name shall be used as an oath by my chosen, and the Lord God shall give you over to [spiritual] death; but ***his servants he shall call by another name*** [emphasis added throughout]. Isaiah 65:12-15 NEB

Bahá'u'lláh frequently uses the expression "My servants" or "My servant:"

> Know assuredly that My commandments are the lamps of My loving providence among ***My servants***, and the keys of My mercy for My creatures. Thus hath it been sent down from the heaven of the Will of your Lord, the Lord of Revelation.[2]

Here are three examples from *The Hidden Words of Bahá'u'lláh*:

> **O MY SERVANT!**
> Abandon not for that which perisheth an everlasting dominion, and cast not away celestial sovereignty for a worldly desire. This is the river of everlasting life that hath flowed from the well-spring of the pen of the merciful; well is it with them that drink![3]
>
> **O MY SERVANT!**
> Free thyself from the fetters of this world, and loose thy soul from the prison of self. Seize thy chance, for it will come to thee no more.[4]
>
> **O MY SERVANT!**
> Purge thy heart from malice and, innocent of envy, enter the divine court of holiness.[5]

- To emphasize God's novel creation, Isaiah points to new heavens and a new earth (a new world order), and then to the Holy Land—where Bahá'u'lláh lived for more than two decades—as a place of joy:

> ...the former troubles are forgotten and they are hidden from my sight. For behold, I create new heavens and a new earth. Former things shall no more be remembered nor shall they be called to mind. Rejoice and be filled with delight, you boundless realms which I create; for ***I create Jerusalem*** to be a delight and her people a joy... Isaiah 65:16-18 NEB

- Finally, the prophetic chapter ends with the tidings of a world in peace and unity:

> They shall not toil in vain or raise children for misfortune. For they are the offspring of the blessed of the Lord and their issue after them; before they call to me, I will answer, and while they are still speaking I will listen. The wolf and the lamb [antagonistic nations] shall feed together and the lion shall eat straw like cattle [domestication of warlike nations]. They shall not hurt or destroy in all my holy mountain, says the Lord.
> Isaiah 65:23-25 NEB

Christian Scriptures confirm the Jewish. The Book of Revelation indicates that those who overcome the many obstacles that stand in the path of the search for truth shall receive the gift of a new name, which is God's own name. Both Isaiah and Revelation refer to the new Jerusalem, the city of God, which symbolizes a new world order and a spiritual civilization for humankind:

> Him who overcomes I will make a pillar in the temple of my God. Never again will he leave it. ***I will write on him the name of my God*** [Bahá] ***and the name of the city of my God, the new Jerusalem*** [the divine Revelation, namely, Bahá'í] which is coming down out of heaven from my God; and I will also write on him my new name.
>
> Revelation 3:12 NIV

And again:

> To him who overcomes, I will give some of the hidden manna. I will also give him a white stone ***with a new name*** written on it, known only to him who receives it.
>
> Revelation 2:17 NIV

Robert Riggs in his book *The Apocalypse Unsealed* writes:

> The Báb presented His followers and Bahá'u'lláh with a scroll often called the ***White Stone*** on which He inscribed a pentacle (five pointed star) with 360 derivatives of the word ***Bahá***. This scroll represented a revelation of the name of the new Manifestation to follow him.[6]

The following prophecy from Revelation gives us not only the tidings of a new name, but several other clues as well:

> I saw heaven standing open and there before me was a white horse, whose rider is called Faithful and True. With justice he judges and makes war. His eyes are like blazing fire, and on his head are many crowns. ***He has a name written on him that no one but he himself knows.***

> He is dressed in a robe dipped in blood, and his name is the Word of God. The armies of heaven were following him, riding on white horses and dressed in fine linen, white and clean. Out of his mouth comes a sharp sword with which to strike down the nations. "He will rule them with an iron scepter." Revelation 19:11-15 NIV

The Book of Revelation is clothed with symbolism. For instance, ***heaven*** symbolizes the divine Revelation, from which descends the light of knowledge and truth. ***The rider*** is the divine Redeemer; ***the war*** he makes is spiritual:

> We have decreed that war shall be waged in the path of God with the armies of wisdom and utterance, and of a goodly character and praiseworthy deeds.[7] Bahá'u'lláh

Fire symbolizes many things, among them the power to burn the veils of man's separation from God, and to destroy evil. ***Many crowns*** symbolizes the vast expanse of the Redeemer's spiritual sovereignty. ***His vesture dipped in blood*** points to the great sufferings He and His followers endure. ***The armies of heaven*** symbolizes the heavenly blessings, or the Redeemer's devoted followers, who stand pure and refined as ***fine linen, white and clean***. ***Sharp sword*** stands for God's definitive and decisive Word, which separates the deniers and the believers, and ***iron scepter*** symbolizes authority and power (first spiritual and later earthly).

Here Bahá'u'lláh refers to His word as having the power to decide the destiny of all "created things:"

> I bear witness…that through a word from Thee Thou hast decided between all created things, causing them who are devoted to Thee to ascend unto the summit of glory, and the infidels to fall into the lowest abyss.[8]

The prophecy bestows several titles on the promised Messenger of our time but does not reveal His name.

The New Name Revealed

God has many names, such as the Creator, the Lord, and Jehovah; and many attributes, such as the All-Wise, the All-Powerful, and the All-Knowing. Prophecies indicate that God reveals a new Name for Himself, and bestows that Name on the Redeemer of our time. Although "Bahá" like "the Creator" is an attribute, it is called a Name. This Name has been prophesied but never divulged until the advent of the new revelation.

> He has a name written on him that no one but he himself knows. Revelation 19:12 NIV

> But on that day my people shall know my name...
> Isaiah 52:6 NEB

In His works, Bahá'u'lláh refers to this hidden name and hidden treasure:

> I testify that within thee [Tihrán] He who is ***the Hidden Name*** [Bahá'u'lláh] was revealed, and the ***Unseen Treasure*** uncovered.[9]

> I pray to Thee, O my Lord, by Thy ***hidden***, Thy ***treasured Name***...[10]

> By the righteousness of God! ***The Hidden Treasure***, ***the Impenetrable Mystery***, hath been uncovered to men's eyes...[11]

> Thou art He, by ***Whose name the Hidden Secret*** was divulged, and ***the Well-Guarded Name*** was revealed... shedding thereby its fragrance over all creation...[12]

Many passages glorify and praise ***the name*** of God. As we noted, God is beyond all praise. The only way we can praise Him is through His Messengers or Manifestations. Thus when we glorify them it is as if we have glorified God.

The following passages first and foremost seem to refer to the One who comes in the ***name*** of the Lord:

And blessed be His glorious ***name*** forever! And let the whole earth be filled with His glory. Psalms 72:19 NKJ

Praise the Lord! Praise, O servants of the Lord, praise the ***name*** of the Lord! Blessed be the ***name*** of the Lord from this time forth and forevermore! From the rising of the sun to its going down the Lord's ***name*** is to be praised.
Psalms 113:1-3 NKJ

I will take up the cup of salvation, and call upon the ***name*** of the Lord. I will offer to You the sacrifice of thanksgiving, and will call upon the ***name*** of the Lord.
Psalms 116:13, 17 NKJ

Not unto us, O Lord, not unto us, but to Your ***name*** give glory, because of Your mercy, because of Your truth.
Psalms 115:1 NKJ

Praise the Lord! Praise the ***name*** of the Lord.
Psalms 135:1

Blessed is He who comes in the ***name*** of the Lord!
Matthew 21:9

Knowing and acknowledging the Name of God brings spiritual blessings and honors:

Because he has set his love upon Me, therefore I will deliver him; ***I will set him on high, because he has known My name***. He shall call upon Me, and I will answer him; I will be with him in trouble; I will deliver him and honor him. With long life I will satisfy him, and show him My salvation. Psalms 91:14-16 NKJ

If the name of the new Redeemer were to be Jesus Christ, there would be no secrecy about it. Jesus Christ is perhaps known better than any other name.

Certain facts about the advent of the new Revelation have been kept secret:

- The day and the hour of the advent.

- The name of the Redeemer.
- The manner of His coming.

It was the Báb who first lifted the veil from the new name, from this long-kept secret. He prophesied the exact word with glaring clarity:

> Well it is with him, who fixeth his gaze upon the Order of ***Bahá'u'lláh***, and rendereth thanks unto his Lord! For He will assuredly be made manifest...[13]

This is how the new Name appears in Arabic and Persian:

بها Bahá

بهاءالله Bahá'u'lláh

In a conference held in a district called Badasht, Bahá'u'lláh adopted the title of Bahá for Himself. This took place before declaring His mission. At that conference, there were 81 guests[14]—9 units of 9. As stated, the numerical value of "Bahá" in Arabic is also equal to 9. Further, the 144,000 mentioned in Revelation is also a multiple of 9.

Seldom if ever does Bahá'u'lláh refer to Himself as Bahá'u'lláh. His favorite title for Himself is Bahá. He uses the same word to identify His followers: ***the people of Bahá*** (not of Bahá'u'lláh). The concordance from His Writings has 102 references to Bahá, but none to Bahá'u'lláh. Here are some examples:

> Oh, would that the world could believe Me! Were all the things that lie enshrined within the heart of ***Bahá***, and which the Lord, His God, the Lord of all names, hath taught Him, to be unveiled to mankind, every man on earth would be dumbfounded.[15]

> Who else but ***Bahá*** can speak forth before the face of men, and who else but He can have the power to pronounce that which He was bidden by God, the Lord of Hosts?[16]

> By the righteousness of God! It is not Our wish to lay hands on your kingdoms. Our mission is to seize and possess the hearts of men. Upon them the eyes of ***Bahá*** are fastened.[17]

> Say: Step out of Thy holy chamber, O Maid of Heaven, inmate of the Exalted Paradise! Drape thyself in whatever manner pleaseth Thee in the silken Vesture of Immortality, and put on, in the name of the All-Glorious, the broidered Robe of Light. Hear, then, the sweet, the wondrous accent of the Voice that cometh from the Throne of Thy Lord, the Inaccessible, the Most High...Cry out before the gaze of the dwellers of heaven and of earth: I am the Maid of Heaven, the Offspring begotten by ***the Spirit of Bahá***. My habitation is the Mansion of His Name, the All-Glorious.[18]

> Cling, O ye ***people of Bahá***, to the cord of servitude unto God, the True One, for thereby your stations shall be made manifest, your names written and preserved, your ranks raised and your memory exalted...[19]

Orthodox Jews consider the name of the Creator so sacred, they do not spell it fully. They write G-d, instead of God. Something like this has happened in relation to the name ***Bahá'u'lláh*** without anyone being aware.

The new name is so sacred and so secret, it seems a mysterious power has prevented people, since the dawn of history, from adopting it as a personal name. In the Persian and Arabic languages, parents use many attributes of God for their children. For instance, they pick names with such meanings or titles as:

spirit of God	friend of God
help of God	trustee of God
bounty of God	light of God
love of God	gift of God
might of God	grace of God
remembrance of God	

The one name I have never seen or heard adopted is Glory of God, Bahá'u'lláh. The name "Bahá'u'lláh" seems to have been off limits for no apparent reason. This is quite astonishing. The Qur'án is known to contain 99 names of God. The one name and attribute it does not contain is God's most glorious name—***Bahá***. Is this coincidence?

Besides "glory" and "glory of the Lord," Bahá'u'lláh has been identified by many titles. Shoghi Effendi has listed some of them in *God Passes By*.[20] Here is his list arranged in the following columns:

On His Head Are Many Crowns.
Revelation 9:12

God hath most excellent names.[21] Qur'án

He Who is the Lord of Names...[22] Bahá'u'lláh

The Monarch of all names.[23] Bahá'u'lláh

...the King of the names and attributes of God.[24]
Bahá'u'lláh

The Everlasting Father
The Lord of Hosts
The Most Great Name
The Ancient Beauty
The Pen of the Most High
The Hidden Name
He Whom God will make manifest
The Most Great Light
The Self-subsistent
The Speaker on Sinai
The Sifter of Men
The desire of the Nations

The Lord of the Covenant
The Glory of the Lord
The Prince of Peace
The Counselor
Lord of Lords
The Prince of this World
The Comforter
The Spirit of Truth
The Lord of the Vineyard
The Glory of God
Alpha and Omega
The First and the Last
The Judge

The Lawgiver
The Redeemer of all mankind
The Organizer of the entire planet
The Unifier of the Children of men
The Inaugurator of the Long-awaited Millennium
The Great Announcement
The Essence of Being
The Remnant of God
The Omnipotent Master
Lord of the visible and invisible
The Originator of a new "Universal Cycle"
The Establisher of the Most Great Peace
The Proclaimer of the coming of age of the entire human race
The Blessed Beauty
The Sun of Righteousness
The Creator of a new World Order
The Inspirer and Founder of a World Civilization
Christ returned in the glory of the Father
The Fountain of the Most Great Justice
Sháh Bahrám
The Spirit of God
The All Highest Horizon
The Most Great Ocean
The Supreme Heaven
The Pre-Existent Root
The Day Star of the Universe
The Wronged One of the World
The Wonderful
The Beginning and the End
The Tenth Avatar
The Most Great Spirit
The Immaculate Manifestation of Krishna
The Buddha of Universal Fellowship
The Fifth Buddha
The Buddha named Maitreye
The King of Glory
The Lord
The Son of Man Who shall come in the glory of His Father
The Tree beyond which there is no passing
The Rod come forth out of the stem of Jesse
The Branch grown out of His Roots
The Word of God
The preserved Treasure

Here are still a few other titles of Bahá'u'lláh:

Redeemer
The Holy One of Israel
Faithful and True.
The Throne
Before the Throne
Jehovah or Yahweh
The Lord God
The Spirit
David
The Most High
The King
King of Kings
The Ancient of Days
The Blessed
The Beauty
My Beauty
The Most Great Beauty
Our God
The God of gods
Ancient Root
Mighty Stock
The Holy Spirit
The Sun
Lord God Almighty
The Goodness of the Lord
The Lord Our Righteousness
A Teacher of Righteousness
The Root of Jesse
Youth
The Hidden Mystery
The Hidden Name
God
The Burning Bush
He who sits on the throne
The Father
Anointed King
The Bird of Heaven
Christ
Michael
The Great Prince
Bahrám
Súshíánt
Amitabha
The Ruler of the Kingdom of Names
The Revealer of the names of God
The Lord of Names
The Monarch of all names

The list of names and titles offered here is quite incomplete. Bahá'u'lláh's Writings contain many others. The following passage alone presents five titles:

> This, verily, is the Day wherewith Thy [God's] Scriptures ...have been adorned. And He Who now speaketh is, in

> truth, ***the Well-guarded Treasure***, and ***the Hidden Secret***, and ***the Preserved Tablet***, and ***the Impenetrable Mystery***, and ***the Sealed Book***. He, truly, is to be obeyed in whatsoever He commandeth, and decreeth, and revealeth, and is to be loved in everything He, through His sovereignty, enjoineth, and, through His power, ordaineth. Whoso will hesitate for less than the twinkling of an eye, hath, verily, denied Thy right, and repudiated all that Thou hast revealed in Thy Books, and in Thy Scriptures, and sent down with Thy chosen Ones, and Thy Prophets, and Thy Messengers, and the Trustees of Thy Revelation.[25]

Never before have so many titles been bestowed on or assumed by a divine Manifestation. Bahá'u'lláh is indeed "the Ruler of the Kingdom of Names."[26]

Although all these names or titles refer to the Redeemer of our age, the most specific name by which He is known is Glory of God or Glory of the Lord. The original form of this name in Arabic is ***Bahá'u'lláh***, consisting of two words: ***Bahá*** meaning glory and light, and ***Alláh*** meaning God. ***Bahá*** is a word with a unique combination of the most magnificent meanings.

According to Muhammad Muvahhid, a scholar well versed in Arabic, no other word in the vast vocabulary of the Arabic language can compare in grandeur and richness of meaning with ***bahá***. In addition to ***brightness***, ***radiance***, ***glory***, and ***splendor***, the dictionary lists the following meanings as well: ***beauty***, ***adornment***, ***goodness***, ***greatness***, and ***perfection***. (See *Mo'ín Persian Dictionary*.) One wonders if a word with such distinctions can be found in any other language. *The Random House Dictionary of the English Language* lists these meanings for glory:

- exalted praise, honor, or distinction.
- adoring praise or worshipful thanksgiving.
- a state of splendor, magnificence, or great prosperity.
- splendor and bliss of heaven; heaven.

- a state of absolute happiness; gratification, contentment, etc.
- something that makes one honored or illustrious; a distinguished ornament; an object of pride.
- resplendent beauty or magnificence.
- a ring circle, or surrounding radiance of light represented about the head or the whole figure of a sacred person, as Christ...[27]

According to some Christian authors, "***Glory of God*** expresses the sum total of the divine perfections."[28] It is "the manifestation of His divine attributes and perfections."[29] It is "the outward shining of God's inner being."[30]

According to Bahá'í Scriptures, all the divine names depend upon ***Bahá***. It has a unique power that influences all things both visible and invisible.[31] 'Abdu'l-Bahá describes it as "the name of comfort, protection, happiness, illumination, love and unity."[32]

These verses express the greatness of the glory of God:

> The moon shall grow pale and the sun hide its face in shame; for the Lord of Hosts has become king on Mount Zion and in Jerusalem, and ***shows his glory*** [the glory of God]... Isaiah 24:23 NEB

> ***Great is the glory of the Lord.*** Psalms 138:5

> The glory of Him Whom God shall make manifest [Bahá'u'lláh] is immeasurably above every other glory...[33]
> The Báb

Bahá'u'lláh repeatedly confirms the abundant outpourings of God's glory and the blessings destined for the receivers:

> The Ancient of Days is come in ***His great glory***!...[34]
> Bahá'u'lláh

> 'O ye peoples of the earth! Turn yourselves towards Him Who hath turned towards you. ***He, verily, is the Face of God amongst you***, and His Testimony and His Guide unto

> you. He hath come to you with signs which none can produce.' The voice of the Burning Bush is raised in the midmost heart of the world, and the Holy Spirit calleth aloud among the nations: 'Lo, the Desired One is come with manifest dominion!'[35]
> Bahá'u'lláh

> Set your faces towards Him (Bahá'u'lláh), on this Day which God hath exalted above all other days, and whereon the All-Merciful hath shed ***the splendor of His effulgent glory*** upon all who are in heaven and all who are on earth.[36]
> Bahá'u'lláh

The greatness of the name ***Bahá*** can be discerned not only from its meaning but from its numerical value (gematria) as well. For it carries a value of nine, which in the decimal system is the largest single number, and as such symbolizes both oneness and perfection.

The new name is eulogized in several Scriptures, especially the Judeo-Christian Scriptures. Few divine attributes, perhaps none, are repeated throughout the Bible as frequently and prophetically as ***glory***, the equivalent of the word ***Bahá***. The total number of biblical references to the word ***glory*** and its derivatives surpass five hundred—an average of about once every two pages.

One of the titles of Bahá'u'lláh that is used most frequently by His Son 'Abdu'l-Bahá, as well as by eastern Bahá'ís, is Blessed Beauty.

> ***The Blessed Beauty*** saith: 'Ye are all the fruits of one tree, the leaves of one branch.'[37]
> 'Abdu'l-Bahá

Bahá'u'lláh uses the title occasionally:

> We foresee that in every city people will arise to suppress ***the Blessed Beauty***...[38]

Bahá'u'lláh sometimes refers to His Name as "this ***blessed*** Name."[39] In the Bible we find a special reference made to this title:

> His name shall endure for ever: his name shall be continued as long as the sun: and men shall be blessed in him: ***all nations shall call him blessed***. Psalms 72:17

The title ***Blessed Beauty***❖ is often shortened as "***Blessed***." Bahá'u'lláh uses it occasionally to refer to Himself.[40] Among Persian Bahá'ís, the shortened form (Mubárak) is used quite frequently and has been gradually generalized to refer not only to Bahá'u'lláh but also to the Báb, 'Abdu'l-Bahá, and Shoghi Effendi. It is the only common title that identifies any or all of them. It is also used to refer to their words. For instance, instead of saying "the words of Bahá'u'lláh or 'Abdu'l-Bahá," they often say, "the words of ***the Blessed***."

Bahá'u'lláh refers repeatedly to the revelation of divine beauty in this age:

> All eyes are gladdened, for He Whom none hath beheld, Whose secret no one hath discovered, ***hath lifted the veil of glory***, and ***uncovered the countenance of Beauty***.[41]

In this prophecy David first prays for the return of the Promised One and then refers to His attributes of glory and beauty:

> Return, O Lord, how long?...Let thy work appear unto thy servants, and ***thy glory*** to their children...And let ***the beauty of the Lord our God*** [Bahá'u'lláh] be upon us...
> Psalms 90:13, 16, 17

❖ A dramatic and well-publicized case of near-death vision is that of Reinee Pasarow, a friend of this author, who has appeared on many television programs. She had one of the deepest known near-death experiences. To help her find her way in this confusing world, Reinee was given certain clues during her vision. One of them was the title "Blessed Beauty." At that time, she had no idea what the clue meant. Later, she found the Bahá'í Faith and subsequently learned that the Blessed Beauty is one of Bahá'u'lláh's titles. She is now a Bahá'í. Such experiences should never be used as proof, but rather as an inspiration to search for proofs that God Himself has established, such as prophecies.

David prays again to receive the honor of beholding the blessed Beauty of the Lord:

> One thing I have desired of the Lord, That will I seek: That I may dwell in the house of the Lord all the days of my life, to ***behold the beauty of the Lord***...
>
> Psalms 27:4 NKJ

These references further confirm the supreme expression of God's awesome beauty and glory in this age:

> Out of Zion, ***the perfection of beauty***, God will shine forth. Our God shall come, and shall not keep silent...
>
> Psalms 50:2-3 NKJ

> Give unto the Lord the glory due to His name; worship the Lord in ***the beauty of holiness***. Psalms 29:2 NKJ

> Oh, sing to the Lord a new song! Sing to the Lord, all the earth. Sing to the Lord, bless His name; proclaim the good news of His salvation from day to day. Declare His glory among the nations, His wonders among all peoples ...Honor and majesty are before Him; strength and ***beauty*** are in His sanctuary. Psalms 96:1-3, 6 NKJ

> Your eyes will see the King in His ***beauty***...
>
> Isaiah 33:17 NKJ

In addition to "Blessed Beauty," Bahá'u'lláh sometimes refers to Himself as "the Ancient Beauty," "the Beauty" "the Most Great Beauty," and "My Beauty" (God's Beauty):

> The Most Great Law is come, and ***the Ancient Beauty*** [Bahá'u'lláh] ruleth upon the throne of David.[42]

> ...He Who is ***the Ancient Beauty*** hath come in the Most Great Name [Bahá], that He may quicken the world and unite its peoples.[43]

> Verily this is that ***Most Great Beauty***, foretold in the Books of the Messengers, through Whom truth shall be distinguished from error and the wisdom of every command shall be tested...Be thou assured in thyself that verily, he

> who turns away from this ***Beauty*** hath also turned away from the Messengers of the past and showeth pride towards God from all eternity to all eternity.[44]

Most translations of the Bible attribute beauty to the ***followers*** of the new Revelation. *The American Revised Version* attributes the beauty to ***the Redeemer*** Himself:

> And Jehovah their God will save them in that day as the flock of his people; for they shall be as the stones of a crown, lifted on high over his land. For how great is his goodness, and how ***great is his beauty***!
>
> Zechariah 9:16-17 ARV

The following passage is from an Epistle by Bahá'u'lláh. It is recited by Bahá'ís around the world annually at the moment when He passed away. In this Epistle Bahá'u'lláh uses the word beauty again and again. Notice the authority with which Bahá'u'lláh speaks:

> The praise which hath dawned from Thy most august Self, and the glory which hath shone forth from ***Thy most effulgent Beauty***, rest upon Thee, O Thou Who art the Manifestation of Grandeur, and the King of Eternity, and the Lord of all who are in heaven and on earth! I testify that through Thee the sovereignty of God and His dominion, and the majesty of God and His grandeur, were revealed, and the Day-Stars of ancient splendor have shed their radiance in the heaven of Thine irrevocable decree, and ***the Beauty of the Unseen*** hath shone forth above the horizon of creation. I testify, moreover, that with but a movement of Thy Pen Thine injunction "Be Thou" hath been enforced, and ***God's hidden Secret hath been divulged***, and all created things have been called into being, and all the Revelations have been sent down.
>
> I bear witness, moreover, that ***through Thy beauty the beauty of the Adored One hath been unveiled***, and through Thy face the face of the Desired One hath shone forth...

I bear witness that he who hath known Thee hath known God, and he who hath attained unto Thy presence hath attained unto the presence of God. Great, therefore, is the blessedness of him who hath believed in Thee, and in Thy signs, and hath humbled himself before Thy sovereignty, and hath been honored with meeting Thee, and hath attained the good pleasure of Thy will, and circled around Thee, and stood before Thy throne. Woe betide him that hath transgressed against Thee, and hath denied Thee, and repudiated Thy signs, and gainsaid Thy sovereignty, and risen up against Thee, and waxed proud before Thy face, and hath disputed Thy testimonies, and fled from Thy rule and Thy dominion...[45]

The Two Well-Kept Secrets

According to prophecies, God has kept several secrets, but promised to reveal them in our time. One is the Beauty of His Countenance; the other is His greatest and most glorious Name. David prays for the revelation of His Countenance:

How long, O Lord…will You hide Your face from me?
Psalms 13:1 NKJ

O Lord...shine forth. Psalms 94:1 NIV

O Lord...show thyself. Psalms 94:1 NEB

And Ezekiel utters the promise of the disclosure of His countenance:

I will set ***My glory*** [glory of God] among the nations...***I will not hide My face*** from them anymore...
Ezekiel 39:21, 29 NKJ

Bahá'u'lláh confirms the fulfillment of the prayer and the promise and invites all true lovers and seekers of His Beauty to His presence:

He that was hidden from mortal eyes is come! His all-conquering sovereignty is manifest; ***His all-encompassing splendor is revealed***. Beware lest thou hesitate or halt.[46]

Here Bahá'u'lláh encourages the truth seekers to break through the clouds of concealment and behold the beauty of the Beloved:

> That hour is now come. The world is illumined with the effulgent glory of His countenance. And yet, behold how far its peoples have strayed from His path! None have believed in Him except them who, through the power of the Lord of Names, have shattered the idols of their vain imaginings and corrupt desires and entered the city of certitude. The seal of the choice Wine of His Revelation hath, in this Day and in His Name, the Self-Sufficing, been broken. Its grace is being poured out upon men. Fill thy cup, and drink in, in His Name, the Most Holy, the All-Praised.[47]

> It behoveth us, therefore, to make the utmost endeavor, that, by God's invisible assistance, these dark veils, these clouds of Heaven-sent trials, may not hinder us from beholding ***the beauty of His shining Countenance***, and that we may recognize Him only by His own Self.[48]

Bahá'u'lláh repeatedly refers to the revelation of divine countenance in this age:

> All eyes are gladdened, for He Whom none hath beheld, Whose secret no one hath discovered, hath lifted the veil of glory, and uncovered ***the countenance of Beauty***.[49]

Bahá'u'lláh declares that when the time came for the unveiling of the divine Countenance, He hid Himself "behind a thousand veils," so that those unworthy of His Beauty could not see Him:

> And when this process of progressive Revelation culminated in the stage at which His peerless, His most sacred, and exalted Countenance was to be unveiled to men's eyes, ***He chose to hide His own Self behind a thousand veils, lest profane and mortal eyes discover His glory***...He hath, verily, manifested a glory such as none in the whole creation hath witnessed...[50]

Even when God reveals the light of His Countenance with such intensity, it is astonishing that many still cannot see it. Bahá'u'lláh declares that God, in His Wisdom, conceals His glory from "mortal eyes"; from those who want to see His glory with their perishable and mortal, but not ***im***mortal, eyes; from those who care more for seeing His body come down in the clouds of vapor than witnessing His heavenly Soul shine in the clouds of glory.

In the following passage, Bahá'u'lláh addresses the people of our time, who are so fortunate to live in this glorious age, one that countless people have longed to witness. And yet they are so wrapt in worldly veils that they cannot behold the dazzling Beauty of their Beloved:

> **O SON OF DESIRE!**
> The learned and the wise have for long years striven and failed to attain the presence of the All-Glorious; they have spent their lives in search of Him, yet did not behold ***the beauty of His countenance***. Thou without the least effort didst attain thy goal, and without search hast obtained the object of thy quest. Yet, notwithstanding, thou didst remain so wrapt in the veil of self, that thine eyes beheld not ***the beauty of the Beloved***, nor did thy hand touch the hem of His robe. Ye that have eyes, behold and wonder.[51]

Christ predicted that only ***the faithful*** will see the glory of God:

> Did I not tell you that if you have ***faith*** you will see ***the glory of God***? John 11:40 NEB

He also predicted the faithful will be few:

> But when the son of man comes will he find ***faith*** on earth? Luke 18:8 NEB

Once again these verses indicate that certain veils will prevent Christians from seeing and recognizing the glory of God. This point is also confirmed in John:

> And I will ask the Father, and he will give you another Counselor to be with you forever—the Spirit of truth. The world cannot accept him, because it ***neither sees him nor knows him***.
> John 14:16-17 NIV

It is ironic that God's most glorious Name and the most awesome revelation of His Countenance have themselves become veils! It is like saying that the sun's glory and splendor prevent people from seeing it.

As you move forward, consider each chapter as a piece of a gigantic jigsaw puzzle. The coming of two supreme Messengers and Redeemers in the station of the Lord is unprecedented in all history. Yet that is the glorious honor God has bestowed on us. The next chapter presents prophecies, especially from the Book of Revelation, that proclaim and promise the twin comings.

The Symbol of the Greatest Name[52]

The Greatest Name carries such significance and enshrines such profound meanings, it has received a visible and symbolic image by 'Abdu'l-Bahá. Its image also appears on Bahá'í ringstone:

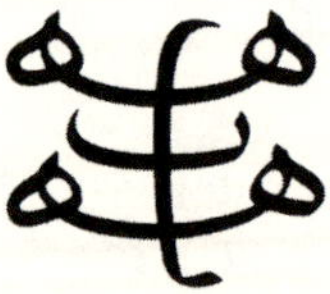

"For ***My name shall be great*** among the nations,"
says the Lord of hosts.
Malachi 1:11 NKJ

The symbol presents a perfect blending of the Arabic letters B and H:

ب = B

ه = H

The symbol for the Greatest Name contains three vertical levels, portraying the three levels of existence. The upper level symbolizes the world of God, the middle level the world of Revelation, Command, or Cause (the world of the great Messengers and Redeemers),* and the lower level the world of humanity or creation.

> ...the three planes represent the World of God, the World of Command, and the World of Creation...[53] 'Abdu'l-Bahá

Each plane stands on the separate level, yet is connected with every other. Each of the upper levels stands exalted far beyond the understanding of the level or levels below it. The great Messengers, who exist in the world of Command or Revelation, cannot comprehend the Essence of God; similarly we cannot comprehend the Essence of the great Messengers.

It is by the power of ***the world of Command***—the world in which all great Messengers and Redeemers function—that God created the universe and sent His Revelations. He said, "Be Thou!" and it was.

> I testify, moreover, that with but a movement of Thy [Bahá'u'lláh's] Pen Thine injunction "***Be Thou***" hath been enforced, and God's hidden Secret hath been divulged, and all created things have been called into being, and all the Revelations have been sent down.[54] Bahá'u'lláh

Here Bahá'u'lláh refers to three worlds: the world of God in which God's Essence remains concealed, the Greater Worlds, and the Lesser Worlds:

> Lauded be Thy name, O Lord my God! I testify that Thou wast ***a hidden Treasure*** wrapped within Thine immemorial

* The world of ***Command*** (also translated as the world, or kingdom, of ***Cause***) is known by several other titles such as: ***the Word, the Logos, the Primal Point***, and ***the Primal Will***.

> Being and an impenetrable Mystery enshrined in Thine own Essence. Wishing to reveal Thyself, Thou didst call into being ***the Greater*** and ***the Lesser Worlds***, and didst choose ***Man*** [any great Messenger] above all Thy creatures, and didst make Him a sign of both of these worlds, O Thou Who art our Lord, the Most Compassionate![55]

The twin stars, which appear on the Bahá'í ringstone, symbolize the Báb and Bahá'u'lláh. Literally, the Báb founded the Bábí Faith and Bahá'u'lláh the Bahá'í Faith. But spiritually, they are the twin founders of both the Bábí Faith and the Bahá'í Faith. Before declaring His Mission, Bahá'u'lláh was the most distinguished Follower and the supreme Supporter of the Báb. What Bahá'u'lláh endured in the Black Pit as a follower of the Báb surpasses human understanding. If Bahá'u'lláh had a thousand lives, He would have offered them, without hesitation, to His Beloved the Báb.

It is easy to underestimate the station of the Báb because of His title (the Gate), His position (the Herald), and His absolute humility before Bahá'u'lláh. Please remember the title that the Book of Revelation bestows on the Báb, ***Lord of Lords and King of Kings***, and the title it bestows on Bahá'u'lláh, ***King of Kings and Lord of Lords***. These titles point to perfect equality between the twin Redeemers. Similarly, in essence, all the titles that refer to Bahá'u'lláh also refer to the Báb. For instance, the title ***the Lord of Hosts*** is usually associated only with Bahá'u'lláh, but 'Abdu'l-Bahá declares that it points to both of them.[56] The Báb is as much the glory of the Lord as Bahá'u'lláh. They differ only in the ***expression*** of their glory.

Many laws of the Bahá'í Faith have their origin in the writings of the Báb. The twin Messengers only look different to us; in essence, they are one. The two suns on the cover of this book symbolize both their equality and oneness as well as the varying intensity of their revelation.

Bahá'u'lláh declares that no name, however exalted, can describe the greatness of God's Messengers and Redeemers:

> ...they have been at all times, and will through eternity continue to be, ***exalted above every praising name***, and sanctified from every descriptive attribute. The quintessence of every name can hope for no access unto their court of holiness, and the highest and purest of all attributes can never approach their kingdom of glory.[57]

The earthly titles bestowed on great Messengers are limited by human thinking and language. They are only symbols of their awesome greatness. No human being can fully comprehend the meaning of those symbols. Bahá'u'lláh states that in the next Kingdom He "beareth the most excellent titles."[58] Then He refers to one of the titles He has received in this world, the gift of the Name of God Himself:

> ...He Who, among the Concourse on high [the heavenly Kingdom], beareth the most excellent titles, and Who, in the kingdom of creation, is called by the name of God, the Effulgent, the All-Glorious.[59]

The Falsity of Claims Made in the Name of Christ

Jesus said:

> Watch out that no one deceives you. For many will come ***in my name***, claiming, 'I am the Christ,' and will deceive many. Matthew 24:4-5 NIV

Regarding the preceding prophecy, Elizabeth Cheney writes:

> Jesus warned His disciples to beware of those who claimed the name of Christ, for He knew that the Promised One of the latter days would not bear that holy name. It would be the same Word of God which Jesus brought, the same Divine Reality, but another human temple and another name. Ridpath's ***History of the World*** shows how Jesus' warning began to be fulfilled within a few years of His own passing, when in 70 A.D. one arose claiming the name of

> Christ and led the revolution of the Jewish nation. May not the warning be fulfilled today also by the hundreds of sects, each claiming the name of Christ, each asserting itself to be the true path to God, and each differing with the others concerning the divine Truth taught by His Holiness Jesus?[60]

A Christian writer, explaining the preceding words of Jesus, states:

> Notice carefully! These deceivers would come in Christ's name, saying Jesus is the Christ. They would be calling themselves "Christians."[61]

Bahá'u'lláh teaches that "return" is always spiritual not literal, that He is not the person of Jesus the Christ, but ***a new*** creation with divine attributes and powers similar to His. We find an example of this spiritual renewal in John the Baptist who was the "return" of Elijah (Matt. 11:14-15; 17:10-13).

The topic of the new name is so extensive that we will continue it into the next chapter.

3

You Shall Be Called By a New Name

Isaiah 62:2 NEB

Part II

The Coming of the Glory of God

Biblical prophecies apply the attribute of glory to the advent of the new day and its supreme Redeemer in various ways. In the following prophecy, Isaiah refers to both the darkness of our time and to the light and glory of the Lord. The word ***light*** in these verses stands for the ***Bahá'í Faith*** (***bahá*** means both ***light*** and ***glory***):

> Arise, shine, for your ***light*** has come, and ***the glory of the Lord*** rises upon you. See, darkness covers the earth and thick darkness is over the peoples, but the Lord rises upon you and ***his glory*** appears over you. Nations will come to your ***light***, and kings to the brightness of your dawn.
>
> Isaiah 60:1-3 NIV

Compare Isaiah's prophecy with this passage from Bahá'u'lláh:

> ***Arise*** thou to serve the Cause of thy Lord; then give the people the joyful tidings concerning this resplendent ***Light*** whose revelation hath been announced by God through His Prophets and Messengers.[1]

Let us compare the first verse of the previous passage with another like it:

> ***Arise***, ***shine***, for your ***light*** has come... Isaiah 60:1 NIV
>
> Come...let us walk in ***the light of the Lord***. Isaiah 2:5 NIV

Both passages encourage the seeker of truth to "walk in the light of the Lord" and to "shine" or be enlightened. To be a Bahá'í literally means to be enlightened. A person who becomes a Bahá'í literally walks in the light of God, for Bahá'u'lláh means ***the light of God***. A Bahá'í also allows the glory of the Lord to rise upon him and to glorify him:

> When Christ, who is your life, appears, then ***you also will appear with him in glory***. Colossians 3:4 NIV

This is how *Nelson's Pictorial Bible Dictionary* interprets the preceding verse: "Believers will be fully glorified at the end of time in God's heavenly prince."[2] Anyone who acknowledges Bahá'u'lláh, "will appear with Him in glory."

This prophecy from Micah declares that:

> ...we will ***walk in the name of*** Lord our ***God***.
>
> Micah 4:5 NKJ

Bahá'u'lláh invites us to walk in the name of God:

> ***Walk*** thou amongst men ***in the name of God***, and by the power of His might, that thou mayest show forth His signs amidst the peoples of the earth.[3]

Isaiah's well-known prophecy about peace contains the same critical expression:

> In the last days...Many peoples will come and say, "Come, let us go up to the mountain of the Lord, to the house of the God of Jacob. He will teach us his ways, so that we may ***walk in his paths***." The law will go out from Zion, the word of the Lord from Jerusalem. He will judge between the nations and will settle disputes for many peoples. They will beat their swords into plowshares and their spears into pruning hooks. Nation will not take up sword against nation, nor will they train for war anymore. Come, O house of Jacob, ***let us walk in the light of the Lord***.
>
> Isaiah 2:2-5 NIV

This prophecy also blesses those who walk in the light of the Redeemer's presence:

> Righteousness and justice are the foundation of your throne; love and faithfulness go before you. Blessed are those who have learned to acclaim you, who walk in ***the light*** of your presence... Psalms 89:14-15 NIV

Bahá'u'lláh declares the coming of the light and invites all lovers of the light to His presence:

> **O SON OF MAN!**
> ***The light hath shone on thee***...free thyself from the veils of idle fancies and enter into My court, that thou mayest be fit for everlasting life and worthy to meet Me. Thus may death not come upon thee, neither weariness nor trouble.[4]
>
> By the righteousness of God! The Dawn hath truly brightened and ***the light hath shone forth*** and the night hath receded. Happy are they that comprehend. Happy are they that have attained thereunto.[5]

> O My servants! Deprive not yourselves of ***the unfading and resplendent Light*** that shineth within the Lamp of Divine glory. Let the flame of the love of God burn brightly within your radiant hearts.[6]

In one prophecy, Haggai points to the coming of the One desired by all nations and then refers to His sublime and glorious Revelation. It declares that the glory of His "house" will be greater than that of former Revelations:

> This is what the Lord Almighty says: "...***the desired of all nations will come***, and I will fill this house [Revelation] with ***glory...The glory of this present house will be greater than the glory of the former house***."
>
> Haggai 2:6-8 NIV

Ezekiel predicts that in the last days God will unveil His face and His glory among the nations:

> ***I will set My glory among the nations***...I will not hide ***My face*** from them anymore; for I shall have poured out My Spirit on the house of Israel, says the Lord God.
>
> Ezekiel 39:21, 29 NKJ

> It shall be that I will gather all nations and tongues; and ***they shall come and see My glory*** [glory of God].
>
> Isaiah 66:18 NKJ

Like John the Revelator, Isaiah offers several clues concerning the new Name and the new Revelation:

> I am the Lord: that is my name: and ***my glory will I not give to another***...Behold the former things are come to pass, and new things do I declare...Sing unto the Lord a new song... Isaiah 42:8-10

Since Bahá'u'lláh came as ***the Lord***, only He is entitled to the promised glory, namely ***the glory of the Lord***. Moreover, Isaiah's prophecies, like those of the Book of Revelation and Haggai, quoted earlier, point to the passing of the old age and old order (end of the age) and the dawning of a new one.

Both sources refer to a new song (see Rev. 5:9), which would celebrate the arrival of a new cycle in human history.

The next prophecy also links the second advent with both glory and renewal:

> At the renewal of all things when the Son of Man sits on ***his glorious*** throne... Matthew 19:28 NIV

The following verse also links salvation to the glory of God:

> Will you not revive us again...?...Surely ***his salvation*** is near those who fear him, that ***his glory*** [the glory of God] may dwell in our land [Holy Land]. Psalms 85:5, 9 NIV

The Book of Revelation not only prophesies a new name, but specifies the name as well. Chapters 21 and 22 of this glorious book refer to the descending of the city of God (divine Revelation) from heaven, and then describe its distinct features.

To demonstrate and emphasize throughout this chapter the clarity and power of verses that specify the name of the Redeemer of our time, the prophecies that specify the title of "the glory of God" are repeated twice, once with ***the English*** translation of the title from the original language (Hebrew, Greek, or Aramaic), and again with ***the Arabic*** translation of the title:

> And he [an angel] carried me away in the Spirit to a mountain great and high, and showed me the Holy City, Jerusalem, coming down out of heaven from God. It shone with ***the glory of God***... Revelation 21:10-11 NIV

> And he [an angel] carried me away in the Spirit to a mountain great and high, and showed me the Holy City, Jerusalem, coming down out of heaven from God. It shone with ***Bahá'u'lláh***... Revelation 21:10-11

The prophecy continues:

> The city does not need ***the sun*** or ***the moon*** to shine on it, for ***the glory of God*** gives it light, and the Lamb is its

> lamp. The nations will walk by its light, and the kings of the earth will bring their splendor into it.
>
> Revelation 21:22-24 NIV

> The city does not need ***the sun*** or ***the moon*** to shine on it, for ***Bahá'u'lláh*** gives it light, and the Lamb is its lamp. The nations will walk by its light, and the kings of the earth will bring their splendor into it. Revelation 21:22-24

Bahá'u'lláh fulfills the preceding prophecy. In one of His Tablets (Epistles) He declares that anyone who enters the shadow of the divine Tree does not need the sun.[7]

Isaiah has a similar prophecy. It states that the sun and the moon, the two most splendid symbols and sources of light, will be ashamed before His glorious appearance:

> ***The moon*** will be abashed, ***the sun*** ashamed; for the Lord Almighty will reign...***gloriously***. Isaiah 24:23 NIV

When on the Mount of Olives (Mt. Olivet), Jesus prophesied saying:

> ...and they shall see the Son of man coming in the clouds of heaven with power and ***great glory***. Matthew 24:30

The phrase ***great glory*** is a subtle allusion to the name ***Glory of God***. For we may ask: What Glory is greater than the Glory of God? Further, as mentioned, the word ***Bahá*** means both greatness and glory.

Another prophecy points to the Glory of God as the divine Attribute under which Christ will return:

> ...when he comes ***in his glory*** and in ***the glory of the Father*** and ***of the holy angels*** [spiritual and heavenly disciples].
>
> Luke 9:26 NIV

> For the Son of Man is going to come in his ***Father's*** [God's] ***glory***...
>
> Matthew 16:27 NIV
>
> See also Mark 8:38

The "Glory of the Father" or the "Father's glory" is the same as "Glory of God."

A Christian author states that the glory predicted in the preceding prophecy is threefold, glory upon glory upon glory:

> His own, which He has of and for Himself as the exalted Messiah; the glory of God which accompanies him as coming down from God's throne, and the glory of the angels who surround Him with their brightness.[8]

A similar prophecy also appears in Matthew:

> When the Son of Man comes in ***his glory***, and all the angels with him, he will sit on his throne in ***heavenly glory***. Matthew 25:31 NIV

Note, it says ***heavenly***, not ***earthly*** glory.

Psalms also predicts the coming of the Glory of God:

> When the Lord...shall appear in ***his glory***. Psalms 102:16

> The Lord is come in ***his great glory***![9] Bahá'u'lláh

Here are two translations of a verse from Titus pointing to the glory of God:

> Looking for that blessed hope and ***the glorious appearing of the great God***... Titus 2:13

> Looking for the...appearing of ***the glory of the great God***... Titus 2:13 ARV

This frequently quoted verse not only has a literal but symbolic message as well:

> The heavens declare ***the glory of God***... Psalms 19:1 NIV

> The heavens declare ***Bahá'u'lláh***... Psalms 19:1

The word ***heaven*** symbolizes religion. All religions have predicted the coming of Bahá'u'lláh.

The Glory of God Fills the Earth

Many prophecies speak of the universal spread of glory to the farthest reaches of our planet—depicting ***Bahá*** as a sun that never sets.

> For the earth will be filled with the knowledge of ***the glory of the Lord***, as the waters cover the sea.
> Habakkuk 2:14 NIV

> For the earth will be filled with the knowledge of ***Bahá'u'lláh,*** as the waters cover the sea. Habakkuk 2:14

> And ***the glory of the Lord*** will be revealed, and all mankind together will see it. Isaiah 40:5 NIV

> And ***Bahá'u'lláh*** will be revealed, and all mankind together will see it. Isaiah 40:5

> ...as truly as I live, all the earth shall be filled with ***the glory of the Lord***. Numbers 14:21

> ...as truly as I live, all the earth shall be filled with ***Bahá'u'lláh***. Numbers 14:21

> The world is illumined with the effulgent ***glory*** of His countenance.[10] Bahá'u'lláh

> ...let ***your*** [God's] ***glory*** be over all the earth.
> Psalms 57:11 NKJ

> This is the Day in which ***the earth shineth with the effulgent light of thy Lord***, but the people are lost in error and have been shut out as by a veil.[11] Bahá'u'lláh

> I will display ***my glory*** [Glory of God] among the nations...
> Ezekiel 39:21 NIV

> ...I will fill this house [world, faith] with ***glory***...
> Haggai 2:7 NIV

> And after these things I saw another angel [Bahá'u'lláh] come down from heaven, having great power; and ***the earth was lightened with his glory***. Revelation 18:1

> But God...revealed this Light through His sovereign authority and protected it through the power of His might ***until earth and heaven were illumined by its radiance and brightness***.[12] Bahá'u'lláh

> Be thou exalted, O God, above the heavens; let ***thy glory*** be above ***all the earth***. Psalms 57:5

> And the earth will shine with the glory✤ of its Lord. Qur'án 39:69 Y

All the prophecies pointing to unity and universality find fulfillment in Bahá'u'lláh's New World Order and His supranational teachings proclaimed at a time when ***nationalism was the highest and most cherished goal of political leaders***. Unity and universality characterize all the teachings of the new Revelation:

> That one indeed is a man who, today, dedicateth himself to the service of the entire human race...It is not for him to pride himself who loveth his own country, but rather for him who loveth the whole world. The earth is but one country, and mankind its citizens.[13] Bahá'u'lláh

The time will come when everyone will acknowledge God and His great glory:

> "The time is coming," declares the Lord, "when I will make a new covenant...this is the covenant I will make with the house of Israel after that time," declares the Lord. "I will put my law in their minds and write it on their hearts. I will be their God, and they will be my people. No longer will a man teach his neighbor, or a man his brother, saying, 'Know the Lord,' because ***they will all know me***, from the least of them to the greatest," declares the Lord. Jeremiah 31:31-34 NIV

✤ The literal meaning of the Arabic word—Núr—translated here as "glory" is "light."

The Glory of God Personified

Some prophecies point to the Glory of God as a person, and not just as an attribute of God. This is quite unusual, for other attributes are seldom if ever personified. For instance, we never see ***the Love of God***, ***the Grace of God***, ***the Power of God***, ***the Knowledge of God***, ***the Justice of God***, or similar attributes used as if to signify a person. These examples show how the attribute of glory is personified.

> But Stephen, filled with the Holy Spirit, looked up to heaven and ***saw the glory of God***, and Jesus standing at the right hand of God. Acts 7:55 NIV

> But Stephen, filled with the Holy Spirit, looked up to heaven and ***saw Bahá'u'lláh,*** and Jesus standing at the right hand of God. Acts 7:55

> Did I not tell you that ***if you have faith you will see the glory of God***? John 11:40 NEB

> Did I not tell you that ***if you have faith you will see Bahá'u'lláh***? John 11:40

> And ***the glory of the Lord*** will be revealed, and all mankind together will see it. Isaiah 40:5 NIV

> And ***Bahá'u'lláh*** will be revealed, and all mankind together will see it. Isaiah 40:5

> And we rejoice in the hope of [seeing] ***the glory of God***. Romans 5:2 NIV

> And we rejoice in the hope of [seeing] ***Bahá'u'lláh***. Romans 5:2

> ...they will see ***the glory of the Lord***, the splendor of our God. Isaiah 35:2 NIV

> ...they will see ***Bahá'u'lláh,*** the splendor of our God. Isaiah 35:2

This frequently quoted verse also alludes to the glory of God primarily as a person:

> ...all have sinned and fall short of ***the glory of God***...
>
> Romans 3:23 NIV

> ...all have sinned and fall short of ***Bahá'u'lláh***...
>
> Romans 3:23

Why should we have this repeated use of ***the Glory of God***, and ***the Glory of the Lord*** pointing to a person? Only now can we recognize that this title represented an individual Soul who would walk in our midst, manifesting God's Glory and Splendor. Only now do we realize that the promise of seeing the Glory of God in the future refers to the realization of this attribute in a human being. Otherwise why would such a promise be needed, for the universe has always been an evidence of God's glory and greatness.

Some prophecies indicate that the glory of God entered ***the court*** or ***the temple***:

> Then the man brought me by way of the north gate to the front of the temple. I looked and saw ***the glory of the Lord*** filling the temple of the Lord, and I fell facedown.
>
> Ezekiel 44:4 NIV

> Then the man brought me by way of the north gate to the front of the temple. I looked and saw ***Bahá'u'lláh*** filling the temple of the Lord, and I fell facedown. Ezekiel 44:4

> ***The glory of the Lord*** entered the temple through the gate facing east. Then the Spirit lifted me up and brought me into the inner court, and ***the glory of the Lord*** filled the temple. Ezekiel 43:4-5 NIV

> ***Bahá'u'lláh*** entered the temple through the gate facing east. Then the Spirit lifted me up and brought me into the inner court, and ***Bahá'u'lláh*** filled the temple.
>
> Ezekiel 43:4-5

And the temple was filled with smoke* from ***the glory of God*** and from his power... Revelation 15:8 NIV

And ***the temple*** [tabernacle] was filled with smoke from ***Bahá'u'lláh*** and from his power... Revelation 15:8

O thou who art waiting, tarry no longer, for He is come. Behold His ***Tabernacle and His Glory dwelling therein***. It is the Ancient Glory, with a new Manifestation.[14]

Bahá'u'lláh

See also Ezekiel 3:12, 22-23; 8:3-4; 9:3; 10:4; 11:22-23; Exodus 16:10; Numbers 14:10; Leviticus 9:23; II Chronicles 7:3; Luke 2:9; I Kings 8:11-12.

The word ***temple***, in biblical terms, is synonymous with sanctuary, or tabernacle, and it consists of two parts: the inner court and the outer court. While in the Holy Land, Bahá'u'lláh had a tent, which He used during His visits to Mt. Carmel. He called this tent the Tabernacle of Glory:

It is here [on Mt. Carmel] that, by the grace of the Lord of Revelation, ***the Tabernacle of Glory*** hath been raised.[15]

One meaning of ***Bahá'u'lláh*** in Arabic is ***the Goodness of God***. A prophecy from Psalms clearly predicts the coming of this Goodness to the land of the living:

I am still confident of this: ***I will see the goodness of the Lord*** in the land of the living. Wait for the Lord; be strong and take heart and wait for the Lord. Psalms 27:13-14 NIV

I am still confident of this: ***I will see Bahá'u'lláh*** in the land of the living. Wait for the Lord; be strong and take heart and wait for the Lord. Psalms 27:13-14

* Smoke, like cloud, serves as a vehicle for the glory of God. It veils its intense splendor.

A Description of the Glory of God

In a vision, Ezekiel gets a glimpse of the awesome beauty and splendor of the Glory of the Lord:

> Above the expanse over their heads was what looked like a throne of sapphire, and high above on the throne was a figure like that of a man. I saw that from what appeared to be his waist up he looked like glowing metal, as if full of fire, and that from there down he looked like fire; and brilliant light surrounded him. Like the appearance of a rainbow in the clouds on a rainy day, so was the radiance around him. This was the appearance of the likeness of ***the glory of the Lord***. When I saw it, I fell facedown.
>
> Ezekiel 1:26-28 NIV

In his book *The Sign*, Christian scholar Robert Van Kampen offers this interpretation for the preceding prophecy:

> The "figure with the appearance of a man" clearly refers to Christ, who had "the likeness of the glory of the Lord." The prophet later sees the same figure, described in almost the exact same way: "The hand of the Lord fell on me there. Then I looked, and behold, a likeness as the appearance of a man; from His loins and downward there was the appearance of fire, and from His loins and upward the appearance of brightness, like the appearance of glowing metal" (8:2). Previously, like John in our Revelation account, the Lord gave Ezekiel a scroll to eat, which the prophet says "was sweet as honey in my mouth" (3:3).[16]

After quoting Hosea 11:10-11, the author concludes:

> Putting all these pieces together, it seems incontestable that "the figure with appearance of a man" depicted by Ezekiel corresponds to the angel described by John in Revelation 10, and that both passages correspond to ***the coming of the Lord***...When we take these passages together, then, there are at least four reasons why these passages from Ezekiel, Hosea, and Revelation refer to the literal

return of Christ to earth...First, the strong angel is shown "coming down out of heaven"...with His "open" little book or scroll. Second, Ezekiel's description of a "figure with the appearance of a man" who had "the likeness of the glory of the Lord" and John's description of the "strong angel" of Revelation are remarkably similar (Ezekiel 1:27, 28; 8:2; Revelation 10:1). Third, the heavenly persons give the two human witnesses of these events (the prophet Ezekiel and the Apostle John) small scrolls to eat that were sweet to the taste (Ezekiel 3:1-3; Revelation 10:9). And finally, the voices of the heavenly persons are compared to the roaring of lions (Hosea 11:10; Revelation 10:3; cf. 5:5), which, as we shall see, is directly associated with the salvation of the remnant of Israel.[17]

The New Name in Other Scriptures

Other sacred Scriptures also allude to the name ***Bahá***. According to the Islamic Scriptures, ***Bahá*** (glory) is God's greatest name. This knowledge was concealed in an Islamic dawn prayer. By comparing the names or attributes used in this and other prayers, a great mystic poet, who lived centuries before the advent of the Bahá'í Faith, discovered the mystery. The concealed name he found was ***Bahá***. Following this discovery, he adopted the name ***Bahá'í*** for himself. This famous mystic poet is known in the East as Shaykh Bahá'í. He may have been the first person to call himself ***Bahá'í***!

In one of his works Shaykh Bahá'í states:

> The Greatest Name is unknown to man, but in the list of all the Names of God it stands first.[18]

Another great mystic poet, Mawlaví, uses the word ***Bahá***:

> We have found ***Bahá*** and we hasten to offer our lives to Him. He is our ransom.[19]

Bahá'u'lláh often refers to His Name or to Himself as ***the Most Great Name***. In the following passage, He declares that

God reveals Himself in two ways: directly and indirectly. Every atom, every being expresses God's wisdom, knowledge, and glory. This influence is direct and universal. The other influence comes indirectly through God's Manifestations, and in this age it has come through ***His Most Great Name, Bahá'u'lláh***:

> Consider, for instance, the revelation of the light of the Name of God, the Educator. Behold, how in all things the evidences of such a revelation are manifest, how the betterment of all beings dependeth upon it. This education is of two kinds. The one is universal. Its influence pervadeth all things and sustaineth them. It is for this reason that God hath assumed the title, "Lord of all worlds." The other is confined to them that have come under the shadow of this Name, and sought the shelter of this most mighty Revelation. They, however, that have failed to seek this shelter, have deprived themselves of this privilege, and are powerless to benefit from the spiritual sustenance that hath been sent down through the heavenly grace of ***this Most Great Name***. How great the gulf fixed between the one and the other [the believer and the denier]! If the veil were lifted, and the full glory of the station of those that have turned wholly towards God, and have, in their love for Him, renounced the world, were made manifest, the entire creation would be dumbfounded.[20]

Here are two more quotations:

> It beseemeth all men, in this Day, to take firm hold on ***the Most Great Name***, and to establish the unity of all mankind. There is no place to flee to, no refuge that any one can seek, except Him.[21]

> ***The Most Great Name*** beareth Me witness! How sad if any man were, in this Day, to rest his heart on the transitory things of this world! Arise, and cling firmly to the Cause of God. Be most loving one to another. Burn away, wholly for the sake of the Well-Beloved, the veil of self with the

> flame of the undying Fire, and with faces joyous and beaming with light, associate with your neighbor.[22]

This passage from Psalms seems to point to the same great name:

> The Lord reigns, let the nations tremble; he sits enthroned between the cherubim, let the earth shake. Great is the Lord in Zion; he is exalted over all the nations. Let them praise ***your great and awesome name...*** Psalms 99:1-3 NIV

As the Islamic Scriptures refer to "Glory" as the ***Name*** of God, so do the Christian Scriptures:

> He who is victorious...I will write ***the name*** of my God upon him... Revelation 3:12 NEB

Consider the preceding prophecy in its context:

> Behold, I am coming quickly! Hold fast what you have, that no one may take your crown. He who overcomes, I will make him a pillar in the temple of ***My God*** [Bahá], and he shall go out no more. And I will write on him the name of My God and the name of the ***city of My God*** [Bahá'í], the New Jerusalem, which comes down out of heaven from My God. And I will write on him ***My new name*** [Bahá'u'lláh]. Revelation 3:11-13 NKJ

As the Islamic Scriptures refer to the secrecy surrounding the name, so do the Christian Scriptures:

> He has a name written on him that no one but he himself knows. Revelation 19:12 NIV

Anyone who overcomes the spiritual obstacles, anyone who conquers his self, receives the gift of the newly revealed ***Name*** of God: Glory. He becomes its follower. (The Bahá'í Faith means ***the Glorious and Enlightened Faith***.)

The word ***glory*** (an attribute) is granted the station of a ***Name*** of God—Names such as the Lord, God, or the Father:

> ...to the glory of God the Father. Philippians 2:11 NIV

Justice, love, and wisdom are referred to as attributes of God, but not as His Name.

Dedications are also made, as a rule, to persons, not to attributes:

> ...to ***the glory of God***. II Corinthians 1:20 NIV

> ...to ***Bahá'u'lláh***. II Corinthians 1:20

> Whatever you do, do it all for ***the glory of God***.
> I Corinthians 10:31 NIV

> Whatever you do, do it all for ***Bahá'u'lláh***.
> I Corinthians 10:31

William Miller, the leader of the Advent Movement in the West, might also have gained a glimpse of this mystery. He made this statement before the advent of the Báb:

> I believe the Scriptures reveal unto us, in plain language, that Jesus Christ will appear again on this earth...in ***the glory of God***.[23]

William Miller might have come to his discovery by pondering this prophecy:

> ...the Son of Man is going to come in His Father's glory...
> Matthew 16:27 NIV

If we substitute ***God*** for ***Father***, the verse reads:

> ...the Son of Man is going to come in God's glory [as the glory of God]...

The great Persian mystic, Mawlaví, refers to "Bahá" as the greatest name, one that stands above all other names.

Compare these prophecies from Ezekiel and the Qur'án:

> ...I saw the glory of the God of Israel...***the land was radiant with His glory***. Ezekiel 43:2 NIV

> And ***the earth will shine with the glory of its Lord***.
> Qur'án 39:69 Y

And ***the earth will shine with Bahá'u'lláh***. Qur'án 39:69

The following prophecies from Islamic Scriptures are very direct and clear; they point both to the name ***Bahá*** and ***'Akká***, where Bahá'u'lláh lived for many years as a prisoner and exile:

> Soon will God reveal a radiance from a most glorious face, whose name is ***Bahá***. He will appear in the day of ***Motlagh***✧ and enter the guest-house of 'Akká (Acre) and unify all humanity.[24]

> All the followers of the Promised Qá'im [the Báb] shall be put to death except One Whose face shall shine with ***Abhá*** [the All-Glorious] beauty in the plain of ***'Akká***.[25]

All the súrihs (chapters) of the Qur'án begin with the letter ***b***. There is a special significance to this: a prophecy states that the letter ***b*** stands for ***Bahá'u'lláh***. It indicates that whatever is in the Torah is in the Gospel, whatever is in the Gospel is in the Qur'án, whatever is in the Qur'án is in the first Súrih of the Qur'án, whatever is in the first Súrih is in the first verse of the Súrih,* whatever is in the first verse of the Súrih is in the letter ***b*** [which is the first letter of the first Súrih], and the letter ***b*** is [stands for] ***Bahá'u'lláh***.[26]

The above prophecy points to the oneness of the knowledge revealed by God's great Messengers and Redeemers. All the sacred Scriptures come from the same Source, the same generating Point, indicated by the letter "b," which stands for Bahá'u'lláh, the Glory of God. The essence of every sacred Scripture can be found in every other, and the essence of

---

✧ ***Motlagh*** means: 1. freed, liberated; 2. free; 3. not bound by limitations, unconditioned. It is also one of the attributes of God. Perhaps the third meaning is intended here. This day is so inconceivably great, no word can adequately describe it. It stands beyond the limitations of human understanding.

* The first verse of the first Súrih reads: "In the Name of God, the Compassionate, the Merciful."

all of them in Bahá'u'lláh. Thus the prophecy intimates that Bahá'u'lláh is the source and the essence of all knowledge.

The Writings of the Báb also refer to the next Manifestation or Messenger as ***the Glory of God***, naming Him by the exact titles ***Bahá*** and ***Bahá'u'lláh***. More often He uses the word ***Bahá***:

> Well is it with him who fixeth his gaze upon the Order of ***Bahá'u'lláh***, and rendereth thanks unto his Lord. For He will assuredly be made manifest.[27]

> When the Day-Star of ***Bahá*** will shine resplendent above the horizon of eternity it is incumbent upon you to present yourselves before His Throne...on that Day all the revelations of divine bounty shall circle around the Seat of His glory...[28]

The Buddhist Scriptures refer to their Promised One as Amitabha, meaning ***infinite Light***. The second part of this word (bha) is the exact name of Bahá'u'lláh as spelled in the original language. Whether it is by chance or by destiny, the spelling of the word ***bahá*** in Arabic is identical with the English spelling of ***bhá*** as used in Amitabha. For the name ***Bahá*** (which in Arabic means light and glory) contains the same letters in the same order: ***bha*** rather than ***baha***.*

It is even more astonishing that Amitabha's sacred syllables are ***ba*** and ***ah***. Similarly, the most sacred letters in the Bahá'í Faith are ***bá*** and ***há***.☆ The name of the Báb likewise contains ***bá*** in both directions.

---

* ***Bahá*** is the English version of the original form ***Bhá***. In Arabic some vowels, such as the short ***a*** and short ***o*** are not spelled out.

☆ In Arabic the letter ***b*** is pronounced ***bá***, the letter ***h*** is pronounced ***há***. Bahá'u'lláh refers to these two letters in *The Hidden Words*. (See the Persian section, No. 77, as well as the symbol of the Bahá'í ring stone.)

The letters B and H also seem to carry a special significance among the Jews:

> The Jewish mystics knew of the significance of the two letters "B" and "H" and attached much importance to them. Their spiritual leaders and philosophers wrote commentaries and drew the attention of seeking souls to these letters.[29]

A scholar in Buddhist Scriptures relates that he "had read the entire Gospel of Buddha in Sanskrit, every word of which he had understood with the exception of the meaning of a word composed of 'B,' 'H' and 'A,' which occasionally appears in Buddhist Scripture. When he learned of the Bahá'í Faith, the mystery was solved. The letters, joined together, formed the name of 'Bahá.'"[30]

The following prophecy from Buddha also contains a reference to the attribute of glory:

> I am not the first Buddha who came upon earth, nor shall I be the last. In due time another Buddha will arise...He shall reveal to you the same eternal truths which I have taught you. He will preach to you His religion, ***glorious*** in its origin, ***glorious*** at the climax and ***glorious*** at the goal...[31]

The Bhagavad-Gita, a Hindu Scripture, also uses a word like ***baha*** with a similar meaning and spelling: ***bhih***,* meaning effulgence or radiance. It describes the awesome majesty of Bahá'u'lláh in these words:

> Suppose a thousand suns should rise together...such ***is the glory of...God***.[32]

The Upanishads, another Hindu Scripture, declares:

---

* The only consonant letters found in both ***bha*** and ***bhih*** (as well as ***bahá***) are ***b*** and ***h***.

> Behold the universe in ***the glory of God***, and all that lives and moves on earth.[33] Upanishad 1:1-2

The word ***bahá*** has entered even the prophetic heritage of the Cuna Indians who live in the San Blas Islands, off the Atlantic coast of Panama.

> The Cuna's prophetic heritage includes a promise that God will send people to them from the outside world with a new Book, a new Message and a new Name. They believe that Message will teach them to live in harmony with all mankind. The Cuna word for God is ***Bahá***.[34]

The Native American prophecies also indicate that the second religion that comes to America will bring peace. Those who carry the message of this religion are called ***the Bahánís***, meaning ***the people of Bahá***. Some of the Native Americans in Washington who heard the word ***Bahá'í***, instantly recognized it as the promised religion for which they have been waiting.[35]

As we noted earlier, the title "Glory of God" is synonymous with the Most Great Spirit, the Primal Point, and the Word, through which God created the universe. The following prophecy from the *Avesta*, a Zoroastrian Scripture, confirms the creative power of this Spirit:

> We hail ***the glory***...that stands above all other beings...***the glory*** that is God's and from its effulgence ***He created the beings***—very good, beautiful, bright, and efficient...so that they may transform the world and make it new, a world that will neither die nor age nor rot, an eternal, proud, self-fulfilled world. That is a time when the dead will rise to immortal life, the time when Súshíánt will appear and transform the world as He pleases.[36]

Here is another prophecy from the *Avesta*:

> ***The glory that belongs to Súshíánt*** [Bahá'u'lláh] and His followers [Bahá'ís] at the time when they transform the world and build it anew...[37]

Súshíánt is the World-Savior and the last of the Redeemers promised in the Zoroastrian Scriptures. Bahá'u'lláh fulfills that promise. Sháh Bahrám (the Kingly Light) or Bahrám (the Light) is another title bestowed on Him in Zoroastrian Scriptures.

In one of the chapters of the *Avesta*, the two attributes of ***Light*** and ***Glory*** (Bahá) are glorified again and again—fourteen times within four pages.[38]

Even as in the Bible, no divine attribute is mentioned in the *Avesta* as frequently as glory. The Persian word used for this attribute is ***farr***, for which the dictionary offers these meanings: glory, radiance, beauty, and loftiness. This is how a Persian dictionary (Mo'ín) defines the meaning of ***farr*** as stated in the Zoroastrian Scriptures:

> It is a radiance from God. A heart that receives it transcends other hearts. It is by the power of this radiance that a person attains perfection and becomes a divine Redeemer.[39]

We also find references to God's greatest Name in Hindu Scriptures:

> The followers of Krishna also have many references to the name of Bahá'u'lláh. In the prayer, "the Mother of the Vedas," the Hindus stand with great reverence and beseech guidance from the "***Glory of God***" (Bahá'u'lláh). Also in Gita XI:30, it is said, "...Thine Blazing ***BHAH***, O Vishnu, (the Omnipresent God), doth glow intensely."[40]

The supreme potential of the word "Bahá" can also be found in its numerical value: 9. The number 9 symbolizes the principle of "unity in diversity" the ultimate fruit of Bahá'u'lláh's social teachings. It also symbolizes perfection: it contains all single digit numbers, which can, in spite of their fewness, produce an infinite array of numbers. The advent of the Bahá'í Faith corresponds to the dawning of the stage of the social and spiritual maturity of humankind. It represents the highest stage of unity or oneness in the social development of the citizens of our planet.

The Gift of Names

Belief in "exclusive salvation" stands contrary not only to the ways of reason, but to the words of the Scriptures as well. For we know by both reason and the testimony of the Bible that "God does not show favoritism" (Acts 10:34; Romans 2:11). How could He, the impartial Father who is Love itself (John 3:16; I John 4:8), ignore His children, leave them comfortless, keep them deprived, up to a certain point in history, and then—and not any sooner—decide to save them, to redeem them, to offer them the gift of eternal life? Can such an unjustified partiality be expected from the All-Knowing—the God of grace, compassion, love, and mercy? Could we accept or tolerate such treatment even from our own fallible parents?

> Is God the God of Jews only? Is he not the God of Gentiles too? Romans 3:29 NIV

Like parents who give their growing children new gifts, our Creator crowns each age and each of His Messengers and Redeemers with special blessings and bounties. But they are ***all*** invested with greatness, for they all come from the same Source and are tokens of love from the same great Spirit.

> ***There are varieties of gifts, but the same Spirit.***
> I Corinthians 12:4 NEB

God—The Great Spirit

God's Messengers or Manifestations	***The Gift of Names***
Abraham	The Friend of God
Moses	The Converser With God
Jesus	The Son of God The Son of Man
Muhammad	The Seal* of the Messengers
The Báb	The Gate of God Lord the Most High
Bahá'u'lláh	The Glory of God The Blessed Beauty

Should we adore the Name instead of the divine Spirit that bestows the Name? Should we say my way is the only way or my way is better than ***your*** way?

> Is not My way equal? Are not your ways unequal?
> Ezekiel 18:25

> This is ***the way***, walk ye in it.✧ Isaiah 30:21

> I am ***the way***—and the truth and the life. No one comes to the Father except through me. Christ (John 14:6 NIV)

> This is ***the right way***. Qur'án 19:37

> ...follow ye me: this is ***the right way***... Qur'án 43:61

* "Seal" implies both adornment and approval or acknowledgment of previous Messengers. It also implies the termination of the "Prophetic Cycle."

✧ This verse points to the Revelation destined for our time.

> Verily this is none other than the sovereign Truth; it is ***the Path*** which God hath laid out for all that are in heaven and on earth.[41] The Báb

God's way is always one way:

> This is ***the Way*** of God unto all who are in the heavens and who are on the earth.[42] Bahá'u'lláh

God is the only Savior:

> Truly You are God, who hide Yourself, God of Israel, ***the*** Savior. Isaiah 45:15 NKJ

> For I am the Lord your God, the Holy One of Israel, your Savior... Isaiah 43:3 NKJ

> I, even I, am the Lord, and ***besides Me there is no savior***... Isaiah 43:11 NKJ

Jesus was ***a*** Savior who spoke for God:

> ...God raised up for Israel ***a*** Savior—Jesus. Acts 13:23 NKJ

But God has many Saviors who speak for Him:

> Then ***Saviors*** shall come to Mount Zion [Israel]. Obadiah 21 NKJ

Bahá'u'lláh refers to the one divine Spirit that appears in many names:

> By God! This is He [Bahá'u'lláh] Who hath at one time appeared in the name of ***the Spirit*** [Jesus Christ], thereafter in the name of ***the Friend*** [Muhammad], then in the name of ***'Alí*** [the Báb], and afterwards in ***this blessed... Name*** [Bahá'u'lláh].[43]

These words are light to all those who search for truth:

> ***The letter killeth, but the spirit giveth life.*** II Corinthians 3:6

What is a ***name***? A word made of a few letters. What is the Spirit? The Creator and Possessor of names. In each age the

Spirit appears with a special name. For ***that age***, that name is ***the way*** to truth.

Although not generally recognized, the following verse also carries a prophetic message. It offers salvation to those who call or accept the One promised to come as the Lord:

> And everyone who calls on the name of his Lord [Bahá'u'lláh] will be saved... Joel 2:32 NIV

The Veils of Names

In the following statement, Bahá'u'lláh points to the unsealing of the new name and the unveiling of that which was hidden:

> The Best-Beloved is come. In His right hand is ***the sealed Wine of His name***. Happy is the man that turneth unto Him, and drinketh his fill, and exclaimeth: "Praise be to Thee, O Revealer of the signs of God!" By the righteousness of the Almighty! Every hidden thing hath been manifested through the power of truth. All the favors of God have been sent down, as a token of His grace. The waters of everlasting life have, in their fullness, been proffered unto men. Every single cup hath been borne round by the hand of the Well-Beloved. Draw near, and tarry not, though it be for one short moment.[44]

The Báb also alludes to the obstacle of names:

> Say, O peoples of the world! Do ye dispute with Me about God by virtue of ***the names*** which ye and your fathers have adopted for Him...?[45]

Some people cannot take even the first step; they stumble over the label. Many people decline to examine Bahá'u'lláh and His Revelation, because of the new name. They pass judgment without searching. Bahá'u'lláh reminds them not to be hindered by ***the veils of names***. Many cling to an old name without knowing the honors that are bestowed on those who accept ***the new*** name:

> Then you shall be called by ***a new name***...you will be ***a glorious crown*** in the Lord's hand... Isaiah 62:2 NEB

> And when the chief Shepherd appears, you will receive ***the crown of glory*** that will never fade away.
> I Peter 5:4 NIV

Never before has the name of God been "written" on people. Such an honor has been destined only for this dispensation:

> Him who overcomes [his attachment to a given name]...I will write on him ***the name of my God***...
> Revelation 3:12 NIV

Bahá is that name and ***Bahá'í*** is the one on whom God's own name is written.

What does the name Jesus mean? According to a Christian source:

> When the angel Gabriel told Joseph in a dream that Mary's child was of the Holy Spirit, the angel explained, "She will give birth to a son, and you are to give him the name Jesus, because he will save his people from their sins."

> The name Jesus is the Greek form of the Hebrew name Yehoshuah. The English rendition is usually Joshua. In Hebrew this name means "***God is salvation***" or "***God saves***."[46]

Saving humanity from sin and spiritual death did not begin with Jesus. God has always saved His people and will continue to save them. Any belief beyond this limits God. The sun does not withhold its light from the earth. The clouds do. The clouds arise out of our hearts and souls, not from God.

In every age, God focuses His light on a special mirror or mediator. For that age, that mirror is the only name or source of light from which we should seek enlightenment (Acts 4:12; John 14:6). When the age changes, so does the name. As Shakespeare said, "A rose by any other name is as sweet." If we pay close attention to the literal meaning of Jesus—God saves—we recognize that it is God the Creator who saves, not the ***word*** Jesus. It is the Spirit of God in the Son of Man that saves, not the name itself. That name may be different in different languages, but it has only one meaning: ***God saves***. That same God has always saved His beloved children and will continue to save them for all eternity. He loves them all equally.

Bahá'u'lláh refers to His new name repeatedly and asks us not to turn it into a veil:

> ***Beware lest any name debar you from Him Who is the Possessor of all names***...Turn unto God and seek His protection, O concourse of divines [religious leaders], and ***make not of yourselves a veil between Me and My creatures***. Thus doth your Lord admonish you, and command you to be just, lest your works should come to naught and ye yourselves be oblivious of your plight. Shall he who denieth this Cause be able to vindicate the truth of any cause throughout creation? Nay, by Him Who is the Fashioner of the universe!...***Tear the veils asunder*** in such wise that the inmates of the Kingdom will hear them being rent. This is the command of God, in days gone by and for those to come. Blessed the man that observeth that whereunto he was bidden, and woe betide the negligent.[47]

> Arise thou amongst men in the name of this all-compelling Cause, and summon, then, the nations unto God, the Mighty, the Great. ***Be thou not of them who called upon God by one of His names, but who, when He Who is the Object of all names appeared, denied Him and turned aside from Him***, and, in the end, pronounced sentence against Him with manifest injustice.[48]

The Muslims are as attached to names and labels as are the Christians. Here the Báb addresses them:

> Let not ***names*** shut you out as by a veil from ***Him Who is their Lord***, even the name Prophet, for such a name is but a creation of His utterance.[49]

The title "Son of God" has been emphasized so much by Christians, yet seldom did Jesus refer to Himself by that title. The following is a rare exception:

> He [Jesus] said to him, "Do you believe in the Son of God?" He answered and said, "Who is He, Lord, that I may believe in Him?" And Jesus said to him, "You have both seen Him and it is He who is talking with you."
>
> John 9:35-37 NKJ

A few times Jesus used "the Son" (Matthew 11:27; 28:19), but His favorite title was Son of Man, which He used over eighty times. In the following passage, the high priest calls Jesus Son of God. Jesus accepts that title, but as soon as ***He*** begins to speak on His own, He adopts "Son of Man:"

> "Tell us if you are the Christ, the Son of God." "Yes, it is as you say," Jesus replied. "But I say to all of you: In the future you will see ***the Son of Man*** sitting at the right hand of the Mighty One and coming on the clouds of heaven." Matthew 26:63-64 NIV

We find similar examples of humility in Bahá'u'lláh, who seldom called Himself by that most glorious title: the Glory of God. He often declares the exalted Station God has bestowed on Him, but He does not glorify His own self. He glorifies the Spirit of God in Him and the awesome Revelation of that Spirit in this great Day of the Lord.

The followers of every religion encounter special tests or stumbling blocks. What hinders Muslims from investigating the Message of Bahá'u'lláh is the strongly held belief that no Revelation or Prophet can come after Muhammad. What hinders Christians is the conviction that no Name can save but Jesus. When Bahá'u'lláh addresses Christians, He especially refers to His Name. He reminds them that He bears the greatest Name and is the Creator of all Names:

> O followers of the Son [Son of God, or Son of Man]! Have ye shut out yourselves from Me ***by reason of My name***?[50]

> ***Tear ye asunder the veils of names*** and cleave ye their kingdom. By My Beauty! ***He Who is the Monarch of all names is come***, He at Whose bidding every single name hath, from the beginning that hath no beginning, been created, He Who shall continue to create them as He pleaseth. He, verily, is the All-Powerful, the All-Wise.[51]

Jesus predicted that only the faithful will see the glory of God:

> Did I not tell you that ***if you have faith*** you will see ***the glory of God***? John 11:40 NEB

> Did I not tell you that ***if you have faith*** you will see ***Bahá'u'lláh***? John 11:40

Jesus also predicted that the faithful will be few:

> But when the Son of Man comes ***will he find faith on earth***? Luke 18:8 NEB

Once again these verses indicate that certain veils will prevent Christians from seeing and recognizing the glory of God. This point is also confirmed in John:

> And I will ask the Father, and he will give you another Counselor to be with you forever—the Spirit of truth. ***The world*** cannot accept him, because it ***neither sees him nor knows him***. John 14:16-17 NIV

It is ironic that God's most glorious Name—a Name so radiant, so resplendent—has itself become a veil! It is like saying that the sun's radiance, beauty, and splendor prevent people from seeing it.

The beauty in the universe is enhanced by diversity and contrast. The next two chapters offer an evidence of this. They portray the shadows that have followed and tried to extinguish the light in this great day of the Lord.

4

The Antichrist of Our Time

> The source of all evil is for man to turn away from his Lord and set his heart on things ungodly.[1] Bahá'u'lláh

> Christ was a divine Center of unity and love. Whenever discord prevails instead of unity, wherever hatred and antagonism take the place of love and spiritual fellowship, Antichrist reigns instead of Christ.[2] 'Abdu'l-Bahá

As part of the fulfillment of New Testament prophecies, many Christians expect the appearance of "the Antichrist," "the man of sin" who utters and spreads "the big lie." Few subjects stir people's imaginations as much as the coming of "the one" who dares to stand up to God.

Although many people love stories of sin and wickedness, it is with reluctance that I cover this theme, for it shows the vilest and most shameful in man, his lowest and meanest descent. My reason for covering it is not to present proofs, but to remove a stumbling block in the path of many Christians, to show that ***all*** predictions have been fulfilled. If you do not like to glimpse the worst in human beings, feel free to skip this chapter.

Psychologists tell us that most people like to learn about other people's sins. The knowledge helps them feel good about themselves; it gives them the sense of "I am glad I am not that bad." If this is true, then this chapter will be popular!

The Search for the Antichrist

The idea of an Antichrist is not unique in Christianity. The followers of some other faiths, such as Muslims and Zoroastrians, also expect such a being. Throughout the centuries, Christians have desperately searched for someone who would fit the description of the Antichrist. Among the candidates suggested are Stalin, Mussolini, Hitler, Napoleon, Atheism, Mormonism, and Christian Science. "The Reformers...looked upon the Pope as the Antichrist. The Pope in turn said the Antichrist was Luther...Some of the Reformers referred to Mohammed [Muhammad] as Antichrist."[3] Historically, the Popes have served as a common target, especially by Protestants. As Christian author Henry Feyerabend notes:

> Martin Luther…came reluctantly to believe that "the Papacy is in truth…very Antichrist." Even some Catholics came to the same conclusion. Arnulf, the bishop of Orleans, deplored the Roman Popes as "monsters of guilt" and declared in a council called by the king of France in 991, that the Pontiff, clad in purple and gold, was "antichrist, sitting in the temple of God and showing himself as God" …When the Western church was divided for about 40 years between two rival popes, one in Rome and the other in Avignon, France, each Pope called the other Pope the

> Antichrist. John Wycliffe is reputed to have regarded them both as being right: "two halves of Antichrist, making up the perfect Man of Sin between them."[4]

Because of the interest expressed by many political leaders of our time in a New World Order, as demonstrated in recent trends toward the unification of Europe, the idea of an Antichrist has once again emerged as the topic of the day among many religious leaders and scholars. Dr. Charles Taylor has recently published a book entitled, *The Antichrist King—Juan Carlos*, to show that the King of Spain is the true Antichrist. His views are supported by such Christian authors and scholars as Dr. Jack Van Impe and J. R. Church. They believe he is the chief and elusive figure behind the conspiracy to establish a world government and a New World Order. The advertisement for his book reads, "Dr. Charles Taylor is convinced that the world dictator who will soon take over all nations is none other than the King of Spain." Two other recent books on the topic are: *Prince of Darkness* and *Guardians of the Grail*. The latter source also points to the King of Spain as the expected one.

A common belief today is that the Antichrist is a political figure, a world dictator biding his time for the right moment to make his move to conquer the planet. This quotation by Vance Havner says it well:

> Our world is fast becoming a madhouse and the inmates are trying to run the asylum. It is a strange time when the patients are writing the prescriptions, the students are threatening to run the schools, the children to manage the homes, and church members—not the Holy Spirit—to direct the churches. Such lawlessness always brings a dictator and ***the last of the line will be the Antichrist, now in the offing awaiting his cue***.[5]

As a Christian author notes, "There are almost as many opinions about this as there are books and sermons on the subject! From the earliest times, there has been speculation and debate."[6] ***The reason for such a diversity of views is***

***that no one can be found to fulfill all the elements of the prophecies*.** This chapter introduces ***a figure, unknown to Christians, whose life perfectly fits all the pieces of the Antichrist puzzle*.**

The Forces of Light and Darkness

The world has always been characterized by contrasts: light and darkness. Even as in a painting, contrasts enrich and enhance the panorama of human life. The prophecies declare that the dawning of the great day of the Lord will be partly obstructed and obscured by murky clouds:

> That day is a day of wrath, a day of anguish and affliction ...a day of murk and gloom, a day of cloud and dense fog...
> Zephaniah 1:15 NEB

Ours is an age of extreme contrasts. For the coward it is a time of "vengeance," for the courageous a time of "recompense:"

> Say to those who are fearful-hearted, "Be strong, do not fear! Behold, your God will come with vengeance, with the recompense of God; He will come and save you."
> Isaiah 35:4 NKJ

Before examining the prophecies about the Antichrist, it is helpful to learn a little about an infamous and elusive figure named Azal, especially about the critical role he played in the divine drama.

Perhaps the murkiest and gloomiest cloud to appear in the heaven of the new Revelation was Bahá'u'lláh's half brother, known as Azal (Eternity). Azal envied with all his heart and soul the respect and the honor his elder brother Bahá'u'lláh received. It is hard to imagine a level of envy more intense than that experienced by Azal. We have similar examples in the story of Abel and Cain, and Joseph and his brothers.

Azal was nominated by the Báb as the leader of His followers, a sort of figurehead until the appointed time of Bahá'u'lláh.

Azal's thin but big ego was inflated to bursting by a special title he received from the Báb. The Báb bestowed the title of "Mirror" on some of His distinguished disciples, including Azal. The symbolism is this: When a mirror turns to the sun, it becomes a source of light, otherwise it turns into a dark stone. While the light of heavenly guidance shone on earth through the Báb, the Mirrors radiated with this light because they turned towards Him. But when that light began to shine forth from Bahá'u'lláh, those Mirrors who failed to accept Him and turn toward Him lost their light.

The Báb also compares the appointed "Mirrors" to the fish that, while immersed in water, fail to recognize the very source of their life. This passage shows how "fragile" those "Mirrors" were:

> O Sun-like Mirrors! Look ye upon the Sun of Truth [Bahá'u'lláh]. Ye, verily, depend upon it, were ye to perceive it. Ye are all as fishes, moving in the waters of the sea, veiling yourselves therefrom, and yet asking what it is on which ye depend.[7]

Every gift can be abused. The sun can help us see or blind our eyes. Similarly, the fish, by swimming to the depths of the sea can turn water, the very source of their life, into a veil of darkness. The preceding passage shows that the Báb knew how some of the appointed Mirrors would act. It seems to be a special warning to Azal to keep him humble.

When Azal heard that Bahá'u'lláh had declared Himself in Baghdad as the One promised by the Báb, he became extremely angry and "jealous fire consumed him."[8]

Suppose you put a crown on someone's head for a few minutes and then take it off, but the person continues to call himself king. This is what happened to Azal. After losing the crown, he kept on wearing it in the world of his dreams and delusions.

The Báb entrusted to a devoted disciple some of His Writings, including His seal. These Writings contained references to Bahá'u'lláh as the Promised One of the Báb.

> ...these precious things remained in the possession of Bahá'u'lláh until the days of Adrianople. When Azal asked to be permitted to see them, Bahá'u'lláh consented—but they were never returned. Azal kept them to support his claim to leadership, asserting that the Báb had given them to him![9]

Azal forged documents and used the Báb's seal to make them look authentic. He had much practice in imitating the Báb's handwriting. He used that skill to mix his own words with those of the Báb's "to produce texts in his own favor."[10]

Envy and pride even led Azal to murder. He issued a decree for the death of several distinguished disciples of the Báb. Among them was a man named Dayyán, who caused both rage and envy in Azal. Rage because he wrote an epistle to refute and undermine Azal's dreams of glory; envy because of the honors he had received from the Báb. Dayyán was given the glorious gift of true knowledge. The Báb referred to him as "the repository of the trust of the one true God," and "the treasury of the pearls of His knowledge:"

> O thou who art named Dayyán! This is a hidden and preserved Knowledge. We have entrusted it unto thee, and brought it to thee, as a mark of honor from God, inasmuch as the eye of thine heart is pure.[11] The Báb

Azal could not endure this supreme source of knowledge. Like a candle that loses its light before the sun, he felt pale and worthless. Instead of seeking enlightenment from Dayyán, Azal decided to get rid of him!

> Dayyán...was made by them to suffer so cruel a martyrdom that the Concourse on high [heavenly beings] wept and lamented.[12] Bahá'u'lláh

Azal's rage against Dayyán was so inflamed that he even ordered and accomplished the murder of an admirer of Dayyán, who was a close relative of the Báb.

> ...the deeds he [Azal] committed were such that Our Pen is ashamed to recount.[13]* Bahá'u'lláh

Azal accepted the Message of the Báb for selfish reasons. The Báb and Bahá'u'lláh knew the secrets of his heart, yet they treated him not according to what they knew, but what he professed. They concealed his true motives, and treated him with the utmost respect and love. They granted him important responsibilities and honors. These pampered his ego but hardly satisfied his unquenchable thirst for power.

Azal arose with all his might to extinguish the Glory of God and to replace it with his own delusions and dreams of glory. He knew he could not succeed in his dream by words and wisdom. He felt he could occupy Bahá'u'lláh's position only by removing Him from the scene. Since he had successfully accomplished the murder of several people, he felt confident he could repeat that success once again. In pursuit of his plot, he poisoned Bahá'u'lláh twice—which permanently affected His health—and once he asked a believer to assassinate Him. The enormity of Azal's evil intentions and the consequences of his delusions of glory can only be assessed when we realize that he was not attempting to assassinate an ordinary person, but the One sent by God to establish His Kingdom: King of Kings and Lord of Lords.

But By far the gravest agony that Bahá'u'lláh suffered from Azal was mental rather than physical. In Shoghi Effendi's words:

> It brought incalculable sorrow to Bahá'u'lláh, visibly aged Him, and inflicted, through its repercussions, the heaviest blow ever sustained by Him in His lifetime.[14]

But by hurting Bahá'u'lláh, Azal unknowingly helped Him. Azal provided an opportunity for Bahá'u'lláh to prove His

---

* For a brief review of his other vile acts, see *God Passes By*, pp. 112-113, 164-169.

nobility—by manifesting His boundless love, patience, and forgiveness. For some forty years Bahá'u'lláh treated him with the utmost compassion and kindness. Bahá'u'lláh did His best to teach him and protect him during all these years.[15] If we had no other evidence to judge Bahá'u'lláh, His treatment of His half-brother Azal would suffice to prove His divine distinction, His supreme love, patience, and forgiveness.

The pain and suffering that Azal alone inflicted on Bahá'u'lláh far outweigh what the rest of the world—including thousands of His enemies—inflicted on Him. God in His Wisdom puts everyone to the test, including His Messengers and Redeemers. Azal was the ultimate touchstone by which Bahá'u'lláh was tested. The purpose of such tests is ***to teach us a lesson***, not to measure the trust or patience of the Messengers, for they stand far beyond the range of temptations.

While in Baghdad, Bahá'u'lláh left His family, friends, and followers to spend about two years alone on the mountains of Kurdistán. Why did He leave? One reason was this: Azal believed that it was Bahá'u'lláh who prevented him from rising to leadership. He thought he could prove himself to all the skeptics if only Bahá'u'lláh somehow disappeared from the scene. Bahá'u'lláh, in His infinite wisdom and kindness, gave him that chance.

How could a man so timid, so shallow, so selfish prove himself? How could he command the respect of the believers? To gain an intimate view of Azal's character, let us hear from Bahá'u'lláh's daughter. As she grew up, she had ample opportunities to see her uncle Azal's behavior from day to day, from hour to hour. She especially had that chance during Bahá'u'lláh's absence. During that time Azal was a permanent and, from her perspective as a child, an unwelcomed guest in their house. During that time she got to know him quite well. Here are her words:

> At length my father decided to leave Baghdád for a time. During his absence, Azal could convince himself whether

or not the Bábís desired to turn their faces to him as their leader...

Before my father left for his retreat into the wilderness, he commanded the friends to treat Azal with consideration. He offered him and his family the shelter and hospitality of our house.

He asked Mírzá Músá [Bahá'u'lláh's faithful brother], my mother and me, to care for them and to do everything in our power to make them comfortable.

Our grief was intense when my father left us. He told none of us either where he was going or when he would return. He took no luggage, only a little rice, and some coarse bread.

So we, my mother, my brother 'Abbás ['Abdu'l-Bahá] and I, clung together in our sorrow and anxiety.

Azal rejoiced, hoping to gain his ends, now that the Blessed Beauty [Bahá'u'lláh] was no longer present.

Meanwhile, he was a guest in our house. He gave us much trouble, complaining of the food, though all the best and most dainty things were invariably given to him.

He became at this time more than ever terrified lest he should one day be arrested. He hid himself, keeping the door of our house locked, and stormed at anybody who opened it.

As for me, I led a very lonely life, and would have liked sometimes to make friends with other children. But Azal would not permit any little friends to come to the house, neither would he let me go out!

Two little girls about my own age lived in the next house. I used to peep at them; but our guest [Azal] always came and shouted at me for opening the door, which he promptly locked. He was always in fear of being arrested, and cared for nothing but his own safety.

> We led a very difficult life at this time as well as a lonely one. He would not even allow us to go to the Hammám [public bath] to take our baths. Nobody was permitted to come to the house to help us, and the work therefore was very hard.
>
> For hours every day I had to stand drawing water from a deep well in the house; the ropes were hard and rough, and the bucket was heavy. My dear mother used to help, but she was not very strong, and my arms were rather weak. Our guest never helped.
>
> My father having told us to respect and obey this tyrannical person, we tried to do so, but this respect was not easy, as our lives were made so unhappy by him.
>
> During this time the darling baby brother, born after our arrival in Baghdád, became seriously ill. Our guest would not allow a doctor, or even any neighbor to come to our help.
>
> My mother was heart-broken when the little one died; even then we were not allowed to have anybody to prepare him for burial.[16]

Bahá'u'lláh asked His jealous brother in kind but firm words to abandon his delusions of grandeur. In His *Most Holy Book*, He warned him of the consequences of persisting in his claims. Notice the blending of supreme power and mercy, of justice and love, of authority and grace in Bahá'u'lláh's words:

> O source of perversion! Abandon thy willful blindness, and speak forth the truth amidst the people. I swear by God that I have wept for thee to see thee following thy selfish passions and renouncing Him Who fashioned thee and brought thee into being. Call to mind the tender mercy of thy Lord, and remember how We nurtured thee by day and by night for service to the Cause. Fear God, and be thou of the truly repentant. Granted that the people were confused about thy station, is it conceivable that thou thyself art similarly confused? Tremble before thy Lord and recall

> the days when thou didst stand before Our throne, and didst write down the verses that We dictated unto thee—verses sent down by God, the Omnipotent Protector, the Lord of might and power. Beware lest the fire of thy presumptuousness debar thee from attaining to God's Holy Court. Turn unto Him, and fear not because of thy deeds. He, in truth, forgiveth whomsoever He desireth as a bounty on His part; no God is there but Him, the Ever-Forgiving, the All-Bounteous. We admonish thee solely for the sake of God. Shouldst thou accept this counsel, thou wilt have acted to thine own behoof; and shouldst thou reject it, thy Lord, verily, can well dispense with thee, and with all those who, in manifest delusion, have followed thee. Behold! God hath laid hold on him who led thee astray. Return unto God, humble, submissive and lowly; verily, He will put away from thee thy sins, for thy Lord, of a certainty, is the Forgiving, the Mighty, the All-Merciful.
>
> This is the Counsel of God; would that thou mightest heed it! This is the Bounty of God; would that thou mightest receive it! This is the Utterance of God; if only thou wouldst apprehend it! This is the Treasure of God; if only thou couldst understand![17]

Have you heard anyone speak in such kindly language to a brother who poisoned him twice, and tried to turn a faithful friend into an assassin to kill him? Have you known anyone who suffered so much mental anguish from his jealous brother as did Bahá'u'lláh, and yet out of compassion cried for him? Perhaps the clearest evidence of the divine grandeur and the exalted nobility of Jesus was His unshakable love for humanity, even for those who crucified Him. Instead of cursing them, He asked God to forgive them. We see the same exalted nobility and grandeur in Bahá'u'lláh. Notice how He offers hope to Azal by saying that, in spite of all his evil acts, he can still be forgiven. Please reread the passage again and again to get a glimpse of God's love even for the meanest, the most depraved, and sinful of all His creatures.

Once again Bahá'u'lláh invites Azal to come to his senses. The only evidence He presents is His Word. Notice both the power and distinction of divine utterance:

> Be fair, O My brother. Art thou able to express thyself when brought face to face with the billowing ocean of Mine utterance? Canst thou unloose thy tongue when confronted with the shrill voice of My Pen? Hast thou any power before the revelations of Mine omnipotence? Judge thou fairly, I adjure thee by God, and call to mind when thou didst stand in the presence of this Wronged One [Bahá'u'lláh] and We dictated to thee the verses of God, the Help in Peril, the Self-Subsisting. Beware lest the source of falsehood withhold thee from the manifest Truth.
>
> O thou who hast fixed thy gaze upon My countenance! Say: O ye heedless ones! By reason of a droplet ye have deprived yourselves of the ocean of heavenly verses and for the sake of an insignificant atom ye have shut yourselves out from the splendors of the Day-Star of Truth. Who else but Bahá hath the power to speak forth before the face of mankind? Judge ye fairly and be not of the unjust. Through Him the oceans have surged, the mysteries have been divulged and the trees have lifted up their voices exclaiming: The kingdoms of earth and heaven are God's...[18]

We should note that death, even with torture, does not always inflict the greatest pain. Mental anguish can be far more painful than physical. This passage from Bahá'u'lláh gives us only a glimpse of what He endured from a brother He nurtured for forty years:

> Alas, alas, for the things which have befallen Me! By God! There befell Me at the hands of him whom I have nurtured, by day and by night, what hath caused the Holy Spirit...to lament.[19]

The Most Great Separation

After many years of suffering, Bahá'u'lláh separated Himself from Azal. Eventually, His connection with His half brother was entirely severed.

For decades Bahá'u'lláh and His followers associated freely with Azal and his few supporters. As we noted earlier, Azal even lived in Bahá'u'lláh's house for some time. Eventually, the time of grace came to an end:

> He who works deceit shall not dwell within my house; he who tells lies shall not continue in my presence.
>
> Psalms 101:7 NKJ

To signal the arrival of a critical juncture in Bahá'í history, known as the time of "***The Most Great Separation***," Bahá'u'lláh secluded Himself. Believers now had to make a choice between the two half-brothers. The light shone, but the darkness did not understand it (John 1:5). ***For a while they were together, but from now on they would be separated.***

"The Most Great Separation" lasted about two months. During this period Bahá'u'lláh secluded Himself and His family. He did not allow any visits. His absence served a critical purpose: it allowed the budding desires and motives to bloom into action. It emboldened a man known as Siyyid Muhammad, Azal's intimate instigator and co-conspirator, to openly oppose Bahá'u'lláh and support Azal. When the sun is shining, the birds of darkness hide in their nest; they only come out during the night. Bahá'u'lláh's brief departure created a vacuum, a state of spiritual darkness. The forces of envy and lust for power in the two intimate dreamers and schemers turned into action, blossomed into an aggressive campaign of lies, distortions, and accusations against Bahá'u'lláh.

The False Morning

Azal in Prophecies of Hebrew Scriptures

Azal's rise and role in the new Revelation are predicted not only in the New Testament but the Old as well. Let us begin with a reference from a Hebrew prophet. To decode it, one point needs to be explained. Among the titles bestowed on Azal by his followers is Subh-i-Azal, meaning ***Morning of Eternity***. They adopted that title from an Islamic dawn (morning) prayer that glorifies Bahá'u'lláh and refers specifically to the promised Redeemer of our time as Bahá. Here is a brief passage from that prayer:

> Behold, a light hath shone forth out of the Morn of eternity, and lo! its waves have penetrated the inmost reality of all men.[20]

To exalt him and validate his claim, Azal's followers simply extended his authorized title Azal (Eternity) to Subh-i-Azal (Morning of Eternity).

But as the prophecies predict and Bahá'u'lláh confirms, Azal was an eternity not of light but of darkness, not of morning but of night. He cherished the grand illusion that as an eternal night he could prevent the sun from rising and shining. But he served only as a backdrop that made the sun appear even brighter, if that is possible.

As a dark Night of Eternity, Azal offered a perfect contrast to Bahá'u'lláh—the ever-glowing Light and Glory of God, the most awesome and splendid Morning of Eternity to dawn upon the earth.

> ...endeavor...that perchance thou mayest, through the power of God and the light of divine guidance, distinguish the Morn of everlasting splendor from the darksome night of error.[21]
>
> Bahá'u'lláh

> O My servants! There shineth nothing else in Mine heart except the unfading light of the Morn of Divine guidance, and out of My mouth proceedeth naught but the essence of truth, which the Lord your God hath revealed.[22]
>
> Bahá'u'lláh

The following verse predicts how the God of hosts who walks on the high places of the earth turns "morning" into darkness:

> For, lo, he that formeth the mountains, and createth the wind, and declareth unto man what is his thought, ***that maketh the morning darkness***, and ***treadeth upon the high places of the earth***, the Lord, the God of hosts, is his name. Amos 4:13

In one of His Writings, Bahá'u'lláh quotes the preceding prophecy, and indicates by allusion its fulfillment in Azal. He states that at the time of the dawning of the divine Manifestation, if:

> ...anyone were to regard himself as the true morn, he will, through the might and power of God, be turned into darkness. He truly is the false dawn, though believing himself to be the true one. Woe unto him, and woe unto such as follow him without a clear token from God, the Lord of the worlds.[23]

This is exactly what happened to Azal, who, out of envy, pride, and vanity, opposed Bahá'u'lláh and declared himself to be the true Morn of divine guidance. The Lord of hosts (Bahá'u'lláh) turned "the Morning" into "Darkness" exactly as Amos predicted.

Azal glowed for a moment with the light of the Báb and Bahá'u'lláh, but suddenly dark clouds rose from his heart and obscured the light.

> **O YE THAT ARE FOOLISH,**
> **YET HAVE A NAME TO BE WISE!**
> Wherefore do ye wear the guise of shepherds, when inwardly ye have become wolves, intent upon My flock? Ye

> are even as ***the star, which riseth ere the dawn***, and which, though it seem radiant and luminous, leadeth the wayfarers of My city astray into the paths of perdition.[24] Bahá'u'lláh

A true morning is always bright and beautiful, without clouds:

> The Spirit of the Lord spoke by me, and His word was on my tongue. The God of Israel said, the Rock of Israel spoke to me: "***He who rules over men must be just, ruling in the fear of God. And he shall be like the light of the morning when the sun rises, a morning without clouds***, like the tender grass springing out of the earth, by clear shining after rain." II Samuel 23:2-4 NKJ

The prophecy from Amos identifies Bahá'u'lláh by several titles among them "***he that…treadeth upon the high places of the earth***" (Amos 4:13). Bahá'u'lláh spent nearly two years of His Ministry upon the mountains of Kurdistán. Later He walked upon Mt. Carmel. (As we noted earlier, the Báb is also identified by the same title.) Bahá'u'lláh left His followers and went to Kurdistán to live alone on mountains mostly because of Azal's and his co-conspirator's consuming jealousy. They could not bear to see the respect and the honor He received. Note that the prophecy from Amos speaks of "mountains" and "high places of the earth." It also refers to the Lord of Hosts who turns the morning into darkness. This is exactly what happened. When Bahá'u'lláh left for the mountains of Kurdistán, Azal's true nature—the darkness of his soul—became more evident than ever before. He lost the glorious light that Bahá'u'lláh shed on all people, especially on Azal who was close to Him.

In the following passages Bahá'u'lláh explains His reasons for leaving:

> The one object of Our retirement was to avoid becoming a subject of discord among the faithful, a source of disturbance unto Our companions, the means of injury to any soul, or the cause of sorrow to any heart.[25]

> I shunned all else but God, and closed Mine eyes to all except Him, that haply the fire of hatred may die down and the heat of jealousy abate.[26]

Here Bahá'u'lláh briefly describes His sufferings during His stay on those mountains:

> "The birds of the air were My companions and the beasts of the field My associates."[27] "From Our eyes there rained tears of anguish, and in Our bleeding heart there surged an ocean of agonizing pain. Many a night We had no food for sustenance, and many a day Our body found no rest... Alone, We communed with Our spirit, oblivious of the world and all that is therein."[28]

The story of Lucifer symbolizes the same sense of pride and arrogance displayed by Azal. As a Christian author notes:

> Lucifer challenged God's right to rule the universe He had created. He was literally demanding equality with God: "I will be like the most High." It was an insolent assault upon God's throne.[29]

Lucifer symbolizes a fallen angel:

> How you have fallen from heaven, ***O morning star, son of the dawn***! You have been cast down to the earth...You said in your heart... "I will raise my throne above the stars of God; I will sit enthroned on the mount of assembly, on the utmost heights of the sacred mountain. I will ascend above the tops of the clouds; I will make myself like the Most High." But you are brought down to the grave, to the depths of the pit. Isaiah 14:12-15 NIV

Notice Bahá'u'lláh's words:

> ...if, at the time of the Manifestation of Him Who conversed on Sinai [Bahá'u'lláh] anyone were to regard himself as the true ***morn***, he will, through the might and power of God, be turned into darkness. He truly is the false ***dawn***...[30]

Some Christian scholars link Lucifer to the Antichrist of our time.[31] Azal and Lucifer have a lot in common. They both swelled with pride and rebelled against God; they both started with light and ended in darkness; they both appeared in the high heavens with exalted titles and fell down "to the lowest depths of the Pit" (Isaiah 14:15). In some of His Writings Bahá'u'lláh refers to Azal as Satan and compares him to a fallen angel.[32]

Harper's Bible Dictionary offers these meanings for Lucifer: "light bringer," "shining one," and "morning (or day) star."[33] Lucifer, like Azal, was a false star that misled the light-seekers. Bahá'u'lláh uses the same metaphor:

> **O YE THAT ARE FOOLISH,**
> **YET HAVE A NAME TO BE WISE!**
> Wherefore do ye wear the guise of shepherds, when inwardly ye have become wolves, intent upon My flock? Ye are even as the star, which riseth ere the dawn, and which, though it seem radiant and luminous, leadeth the wayfarers of My city astray into the paths of perdition.[34]

Chapter 36 of Psalms perfectly fits Azal's sinful life and the abundance of God's forgiveness. Note the similarity between the Psalms' prophecy and Bahá'u'lláh's statement about Azal's sinfulness and God's mercy and forgiveness, quoted earlier:

> An oracle is within my heart concerning ***the sinfulness of the wicked***: There is no fear of God before his eyes. ***For in his own eyes he flatters himself too much to detect or hate his sin***. The words of his mouth are wicked and deceitful; he has ceased to be wise and to do good. Even on his bed ***he plots evil***; he commits himself to a sinful course and does not reject what is wrong.
>
> Your love, O Lord, reaches to the heavens, your faithfulness to the skies. Your righteousness is like the mighty mountains, your justice like the great deep. O Lord, you preserve both man and beast. How priceless is your unfailing love! Both high and low among men find refuge in the shadow

> of your wings. They feast on the abundance of your house; you give them drink from your river of delights. For with you is the fountain of life; in your light we see light. Continue your love to those who know you, your righteousness to the upright in heart. May the foot of the proud not come against me, nor the hand of the wicked drive me away. ***See how the evildoers lie fallen—thrown down, not able to rise***! Psalms 36:1-12 NIV

Note this passage from the above prophecy: "in your [Lord's] light we see light." The word "Bahá'u'lláh" has several meanings, among them "God's light." In effect the prophecy says, "In Bahá'u'lláh we see the light."

The next prophecy from Nahum offers several clues concerning the advent of both the Antichrist and Christ. Here are some of its basic points:

- God has patience, but in time punishes His enemies.
- He will not "acquit ***the wicked***."
- Those who conspire against the Lord will meet their end.
- "A wicked counselor" emerges from people "who plots evil against the Lord."
- There appears another figure who walks "on the mountains." He brings "good tidings" and "proclaims peace." (As we noted earlier, Bahá'u'lláh links "the One who brings good tidings" to the Báb, who was imprisoned on mountains.)
- Be happy and celebrate, for "the wicked one" shall be "utterly cut off."

Here is the prophecy:

> The Lord will take vengeance on His adversaries, and He reserves wrath for His enemies; the Lord is slow to anger and great in power, and ***will not at all acquit the wicked*** …What do you conspire against the Lord? He will make an utter end of it. Affliction will not rise up a second

> time. For while tangled like thorns, and while drunken like drunkards, they shall be devoured like stubble fully dried. From you comes forth ***one who plots evil against the Lord, a wicked counselor***...Behold, on the mountains the feet of him who brings good tidings, who proclaims peace! O Judah, keep your appointed feasts, perform your vows. For ***the wicked one*** shall no more pass through you; he is utterly cut off. Nahum 1:2-3, 9-11, 15 NKJ

Once again the Psalms refer to "the wicked," who faces the consequences of his own evil deeds:

> God is a just judge, and God is angry with ***the wicked*** every day. If he does not turn back, He will sharpen His sword; He bends His bow and makes it ready. He also prepares for Himself instruments of death; He makes His arrows into fiery shafts. Behold, ***the wicked*** brings forth iniquity; yes, he conceives trouble and brings forth falsehood. He made a pit and dug it out, and has fallen into the ditch which he made. His trouble shall return upon his own head, and his violent dealing shall come down on his own crown. Psalms 7:11-16 NKJ

The Man of Sin

Azal in Prophecies of the New Testament

Let us begin with a Gospel prophecy frequently quoted and believed by the masses of Christians to refer to the coming of "the Antichrist:"

> Let no one deceive you by any means; for that Day will not come unless the falling away comes first, and ***the man of sin*** is revealed, ***the son of perdition***, who opposes and exalts himself above all that is called God or that is worshipped, so that he sits as God in the temple of God, showing himself that he is God. II Thessalonians 2:3-4 NKJ

It may help to see *The Amplified* translation of the same verses:

> Let no one deceive ***or*** beguile you in any way, for that day will not come except the apostasy comes first—that is, unless the [predicted] great falling away of those who have professed to be Christians has come—and the man of lawlessness (sin) is revealed, who is the son of doom (of perdition)...Who opposes and exalts himself so proudly ***and*** insolently against ***and*** over all that is called God or that is worshipped, taking his seat in the temple of God, proclaiming that he himself is God.

Shoghi Effendi, the Guardian of the Bahá'í Faith, confirms the relevance of the preceding prophecy to Azal, and the fulfillment of its message, by him.[35] The prophecy describes his character, his claims, and his relationship with the Bahá'í Revelation. The verses quoted point out that the man of sin exalts himself above that which is called God and shows himself to ***be*** God. Azal did both of these. First, he exalted himself above Bahá'u'lláh, whose advent is regarded in the Scriptures as the coming of God; and second, he claimed to ***be*** God.

In one of His Epistles Bahá'u'lláh states that the idolaters—those who join partners with God—have taken him as the Lord.[36] He refers to Azal as the first one to turn against God. Like Annas and Caiaphas, the two leaders who condemned Jesus to death, he and his instigator, Siyyid Muhammad, will be remembered for all eternity as symbols of sin and denial.

Let us now look at the titles by which the Antichrist is described. In reference to him, different translations of the Bible use different, but similar, titles: ***Man of Sin, Son of Perdition, that Wicked*** (KJ); ***the man of lawlessness, the lawless one*** (NIV); ***the Enemy, that wicked man*** (NEB). All these titles accurately describe Azal. Let us take "the lawless one," and "the man of sin." Azal's life was a perfect demonstration of sin and lawlessness. It is hard to find a law he did not break, a crime he did not commit, a sin he did not cherish. If we had to choose a perfect model of sin, he would be an ideal choice. He would need to do nothing more to make himself qualified for the title.

The following verse gives further details about Azal's deceptive schemes:

> The coming of ***the lawless one*** will be in accordance with the work of Satan displayed in all kinds of ***counterfeit*** miracles, signs and wonders, and in every sort of evil that deceives those who are perishing. II Thessalonians 2:9 NIV

Azal produced, displayed, and distributed ***counterfeits*** from the Writings of the Báb and Bahá'u'lláh, and sometimes claimed their Works as his own. He spread rumors that he wrote *The Book of Certitude*, a book written by Bahá'u'lláh. He altered the Writings of the Báb in such ways as to make himself appear as the Redeemer heralded and promised by Him. To make the altered material look authentic, he would use the Báb's seal which, as mentioned earlier, he had secured from Bahá'u'lláh as a trust but failed to return to Him. Azal was such a prolific and accomplished master of lies and deceit, that, as Bahá'u'lláh declares, even Azal's pen pleaded with God for deliverance from his hands!

Further, in an attempt to compete with Bahá'u'lláh, Azal claimed "counterfeit miracles, signs and wonders." In one case he invited Bahá'u'lláh to a "Public Challenge" or "Public Confrontation." It has been customary among Muslims that when disagreements cannot be settled by words, one of the parties challenges the other to settle the issue and prove his case by attempting a dangerous act, such as jumping from a minaret or holding burning charcoal in hands. Whoever declines the challenge is considered by the public as the loser. The principle behind a "Public Challenge" or "Public Confrontation" is the performance of miracles. The message is this: "If we cannot come to a decisive conclusion, we will show our faith in God by risking our lives or safety, and let Him intervene through His supernatural powers." Azal, of course, wanted to prove, in words and by sheer claim, his supremacy over Bahá'u'lláh. He did not believe Bahá'u'lláh would welcome or accept the challenge, because he knew Bahá'u'lláh was adamantly against the display of His divine powers. Bahá'u'lláh accepted the invitation much to Azal's surprise, and appeared not once but on two separate occasions at the appointed time and place, only to meet with Azal's absence.

Azal believed Bahá'u'lláh would not come; Bahá'u'lláh knew Azal would not come. By not showing up, Azal lost his case, and Bahá'u'lláh did not have to perform any miracles against His will.

A Qur'ánic verse states that people plot against God, but God is the best plotter. Imagine the consequences if Bahá'u'lláh did not respond to Azal's invitation to confront him. What a weapon that would have given Azal to promote his delusions of glory!

The following prophecy may refer to this confrontation, because, as we noted, the Scriptures call Azal ***that wicked man***. Further, the prophecy from Zechariah asks that a ***sword*** be used against the shepherd:

> Arise, O Lord [Bahá'u'lláh], ***confront*** him, cast him down; deliver my life from ***the wicked*** [Azal] with Your sword [Word]...
>
> Zechariah 17:13 NKJ

Compare the preceding prophecy with these prophecies, quoted earlier. They point to the destruction of "the wicked one" with the sword of the mouth:

> And then shall ***that Wicked*** be revealed, ***whom the Lord shall consume with the spirit of his mouth***, and shall destroy with the brightness of his coming.
>
> II Thessalonians 2:8

The book of Isaiah also contains a similar prophecy:

> A shoot will come up from the stump of Jesse [Bahá'u'lláh] ...he will strike the earth with the rod [command, authority]

> of his mouth, ***with the breath of his lips*** [words] ***he will slay the wicked.*** Isaiah 11:1, 4 NIV

> For the wicked one shall no more pass through you; He is utterly cut off. Nahum 1:15 NKJ

The false ***Morn*** was finally dimmed and destroyed by the brightness of the Glory of God; it was turned into the eternal night of extinction. For although at the beginning Azal attracted some followers, at the end he was abandoned by even his close disciples. All his hopes of glory and dreams of grandeur crumbled.

Bahá'u'lláh states that no one in all the world can compare with him ***in sin***. He compares Azal with Judas Iscariot, because both of them seemingly at first believed, but later turned against their Masters. Both of them lusted for power, and had death wishes for their Lord. One succeeded, the other tried but failed. And both of them qualify for the same titles. Bahá'u'lláh called Azal ***Satan***; Jesus called Judas ***a devil*** (John 6:70-71). Christian author, Dr. Ray Stedman also finds the two figures comparable:

> ...the long-expected Antichrist, the false Messiah, the "hopelessly lost one, the son of perdition." Only one other person in the New Testament is called by that name: Judas, the betrayer of our Lord.[37]

Both of them also had "tempters." Azal was tempted by the Satan within himself and the Satan without (Siyyid Muhammad); Judas was also tempted by those negative forces:

> …the devil had already prompted Judas Iscariot, son of Simon, to betray Jesus. John 13:2 NIV

Besides these similarities, we also find profound differences between the two figures. First, after betraying Jesus, Judas became remorseful, and eventually took his own life. But Azal had no regrets for his vile acts. In fact to the end of his life he continued to live with his dreams of glory, of replacing Bahá'u'lláh. Second, in terms of upbringing, Judas was far less privileged. During his growing years, Azal had Bahá'u'lláh as a perfect Model to emulate. Bahá'u'lláh had cared for, educated, and protected him as the most loving father would for twenty years. He had the privilege of observing for many years his distinguished brother, Bahá'u'lláh, exemplify the noblest deeds and the profoundest wisdom and knowledge. Third, instead of taking his own life, Azal ordered the murder of others—some of the noblest, wisest, and most learned people. He loved and thrived on sinful living, and lived many years to pursue his delusions. It is impossible to imagine an individual more privileged spiritually and yet more decadent, to find a person with ampler opportunities for enlightenment and more ignorant, to think of a human being given more love and compassion and yet be found so ungrateful.

The twin Satanic symbols of falsehood, denial and deception, along with their followers, had their short day:

> Woe to you, ***O destroyer***, you who have not been destroyed! Woe to you, ***O traitor***, you who have not been betrayed!
> Isaiah 33:1 NIV

The seeds of falsehood may sprout and spread, but they cannot grow deep roots. The destruction of the "destroyer" and "traitor" was clearly predicted:

> ***Destroyed they shall be***, because they did not open their minds to love of the truth, so as to find salvation. Therefore God puts them under a delusion, which works upon them to believe ***the lie***, so that they may all be brought to judgment, all who do not believe the truth but make sinfulness their deliberate choice. II Thessalonians 2:10-12 NEB

Azal always feared for his life, and used secrecy as his chief guard. He often hid himself and used elaborate means to escape detection. He was indeed a master of disguise, deceit, and counterfeit. When Bahá'u'lláh was arrested and put in the Black Pit (Tihrán's most horrible dungeon), Azal was terribly frightened. He "concealed himself, a bewildered fugitive, in the guise of a dervish, with kashkúl [alms box] in hand,

wandered in mountains and plains..."[38] He traveled with extreme caution in disguise and used frequent changes of costumes to escape detection.[39] Secrecy was the main method of survival used not only by Azal but by his small band of followers. Until recently, some of them took politically prestigious positions in Persia but pretended to be Muslims. 'Abdu'l-Bahá states that they always hide themselves in holes.[40] Just the opposite has been true for Bahá'ís. They are asked to acknowledge their faith even in the face of torture and death. Many of them have paid with their lives for their openness.

As for ***the lie*** (II Thess. 2:10-12), in which they believed and spread, it is inconceivable that anyone could come up with a lie bigger than this: that Azal was the Christ and Bahá'u'lláh the Antichrist. This is, of course, the message Azal and his small band of followers believed and spread. It is impossible to think of two human beings who could differ more, who could be farther apart in character, greatness, and glory, who could more closely personify utter light and utter darkness, who could more vividly exemplify the station of ***the Son of God*** and ***the son of Perdition***.

The prophecy from Thessalonians speaks also of a "restraining hand:"

> ...you must now be aware of ***the restraining hand*** which ensures that he [the man of sin] shall be revealed only at the proper time. II Thessalonians 2:6 NEB

The preceding prophecy has baffled Christian commentators for centuries. Bible scholars Winkie and Chant acknowledge this:

> There is one puzzling part of all that Paul says about this man of iniquity. This 'secret power of lawlessness' is already at work, he writes, but it is also being restrained until the one who holds it back is removed and then it will be revealed...Fifteen hundred years ago, the learned Augustine wrote, 'I frankly confess I do not know what he

means' (*City of God,* 20, 19). More recently, the renowned Australian scholar, Leon Morris, said exactly the same thing![41]

In general, every prophecy has a time-table. The restraining power of God does not allow it to unfold sooner or later than ordained. More specifically, this prophecy pinpoints an event in the life of ***the man of sin***.

The supreme honors bestowed on Azal ***restrained him*** from revealing his true motives. They protected him for many years from bold and open opposition to the Báb and Bahá'u'lláh. But, according to God's Wisdom, at an appointed hour, the armor of protection was withdrawn. At that hour, what had been simmering secretly in his heart suddenly burst open. From then on ***the restraining power of God did not control him any more***. He was let loose to participate in the divine drama with full freedom and with all his evil powers.

> ***For whatever is hidden is meant to be disclosed...***
>
> Christ (Mark 4:22 NIV)

> ...wait till the Lord comes. ***He*** will bring to light what is hidden in darkness and ***will expose the motives of men's hearts***. I Corinthians 4:5 NIV

> The time is at hand when whatsoever lieth hid in the souls and hearts of men will be disclosed.[42] Bahá'u'lláh

> Verily, God will bring everything to light, though it were but the weight of a grain of mustard-seed, and hidden in a rock or in the heavens or in the earth... Qur'án 31:16

In the following statement, Shoghi Effendi refers to these restraining forces:

> It [the supreme crises caused by Azal] had been brewing ever since the early days of Bahá'u'lláh's sojourn in Baghdád, ***was temporarily suppressed by the creative forces...and finally broke out, in all its violence***, in the years immediately preceding the proclamation of His Message.[43]

Christian scholar J. R. Church believes that Psalms 109 "concentrates on the antichrist."[44] Consider these verses from that chapter about two figures who symbolize spiritual death and darkness:

> Do not keep silent, O God of my praise! For the mouth of ***the wicked*** [Azal] and the mouth of ***the deceitful*** [Siyyid Muhammad, Azal's companion and co-conspirator] have opened against me; they have spoken against me with a lying tongue. They have also surrounded me with words of hatred, and fought against me without a cause. In return for my love they are my accusers, but I give myself to prayer. Thus they have rewarded me evil for good, and hatred for my love. Psalms 109:1-5 NKJ

Chapter 109 also contains certain pleas and prayers such as:

> Let his children continually be vagabonds, and beg; let them seek their bread also from their desolate places. Let the creditor seize all that he has, and let strangers plunder his labor. Let there be none to extend mercy to him, nor let there be any to favor his fatherless children. Let his posterity be cut off, and in the generation following let their name be blotted out. Psalms 109:10-13 NKJ

The preceding verses accurately describe the final destiny of Azal and his posterity, who abandoned him. He died alone without the comfort of his children or any of his followers. Today, no trace of Azal remains except a few followers, who still carefully conceal their identity. Some of Azal's children expressed a sense of shame for having such a father.

The Sword Against the Shepherd

A prophecy from Zechariah may have double fulfillments. At the time of the betrayal of Judas, Jesus quoted part of it (Matthew 26:31). To decode its message, we should see it in its context in two translations:

> Sword, awake [arise] against ***my shepherd, against him who works with me***. Strike the shepherd, and the sheep will be scattered, and I shall turn my hand against the lambs. This also is the word of the Lord: It will happen throughout the land that two thirds of the people will be struck down and die, while one third of them will be left there. Then I shall pass this third through the fire; I shall refine them as silver is refined and assay them as gold is assayed. They will invoke me by my name, and I myself shall answer them; I shall say, "These are my people"; they will say, "The Lord is my God." Zechariah 13:7-9 REB

> Awake, sword, against my shepherd and ***against the man who is my companion—it is Yahweh Sabaoth who speaks***. ***I*** [Yahweh] ***am going to strike the shepherd so that the sheep may be scattered***, and I will turn my hand against the weak [in faith]. And it will happen throughout this territory—it is Yahweh who speaks—that two thirds in it will be cut off ("will be killed.") I will lead that third into the fire [of tests], and refine them as silver is refined, test them as gold is tested. They will call on my name and I shall listen; and I shall say: These are my people; and each will say, "Yahweh is my God!" Zechariah 13:7-9 JB

Some Christian scholars believe that Zechariah's prophecy refers to Jesus, because He was a shepherd struck by His enemy. But a careful study shows that the prophecy as a whole points to ***God's judgment against the masses of disobedient people, among them a shepherd***, who is struck with a celestial sword, a symbol of God's wrath. Consider these examples about ***the sword***:

> But ***as for you who forsake the Lord*** and forget my holy mountain…***I will destine you for the sword***, and you will all bend down for the slaughter; for I called but you did not answer, I spoke but you did not listen.
> Isaiah 65:11-12 NIV

> Repent therefore! Otherwise, I will soon come to you and will fight against them with ***the sword of my mouth***.
>
> Revelation 2:16 NIV

> ...out of his [the Redeemer of our Age] mouth came a sharp double-edged ***sword***. Revelation 1:16 NIV

> These are the words of him who has the sharp, double-edged ***sword***. Revelation 2:12 NIV

> ...the indignation of the Lord is against all nations...***My sword shall be bathed in heaven***; indeed it shall come down on Edom, and on the people of My curse, for judgment. Isaiah 34:2, 5 NKJ

Prophecies sometimes have multiple meanings and fulfillments. The preceding prophecy from Zechariah may be one of them. Let us see how it may refer to both Judas and Azal:

- In what way were Judas and Azal "shepherds"? Judas received the honor of being selected as one of "the Twelve." The title of "Apostle" raised him to become a source of enlightenment or a shepherd for others. Azal received a similar honor. He was called a Mirror.
- Judas was a companion to Jesus; RSV reads, "the man who stands next to me." As Azal stood next to Bahá'u'lláh and ate food with Him so did Judas with Jesus. He "dipped his hand into the bowl with" Jesus (Matthew 26:23).
- After they betrayed their Lord, both Judas and Azal were stricken with the sword of God's judgment. They were called "Satan" and "Devil" (John 6:70-71) by their Masters.
- The fall of each false shepherd was followed by the fall of others. After Judas betrayed Jesus, the remaining Eleven fell, for a short while, from grace; they abandoned their Lord. Similarly, after Azal betrayed Bahá'u'lláh, some of the believers abandoned their Lord.

Zechariah's prophecy also declares a warning to humankind:

> "In the whole land," declares the Lord, "two-thirds will be struck down and perish; yet one-third will be left in it."
>
> Zechariah 13:8 NIV

Some interpreters believe that the perishing of two-thirds of the earth's population is literal. They think because of natural or human-caused disasters, a large segment of humankind will perish. Major disasters have occurred in the past, and scientists believe they can occur again in the future. In His Writings, Bahá'u'lláh predicts great sufferings and calamities for humankind, but His warnings are crowned with hope. He declares that we can prevent the calamities by turning to God:

> We have a fixed time for you, O peoples. If ye fail, at the appointed hour, to turn towards God, He, verily, will lay violent hold on you, and will cause grievous afflictions to assail you from every direction. How severe, indeed, is the chastisement with which your Lord will then chastise you![45]

Such warnings place an awesome responsibility on every one of us. They show that by recognizing the Redeemer of the Age and promoting His message of love, unity, peace, and harmony we can save countless millions from a punishment that is caused by our own rejection of truth. But as has been the trend throughout history, humanity's response to the divine call so far has been limited. After 150 years, only a thousandth of the earth's population has accepted Bahá'u'lláh.

The prophecies about the Antichrist have not been exhausted. The next chapter brings the topic to its final conclusion.

5

Satan, the Devil

Prophecies point not only to two divine Redeemers but also to two demonic deceivers. One of them was Azal. The other was Azal's instigator and most intimate friend and supporter, Siyyid Muhammad.

The prophecy that refers to ***that wicked man*** or ***the man of sin*** refers also to another figure—identified as ***Satan***—who directs ***that wicked man***:

> But the coming of ***that wicked man*** is the work of ***Satan***.
>
> II Thessalonians 2:9 NEB

If what people call Satan ever existed and needed a perfect medium to manipulate, it could find no readier or abler instrument than ***Siyyid Muhammad***, a native of Isfahán. Even as Satan is recognized as the tempter, Siyyid Muhammad constantly tempted and enticed Azal's vile intentions and perilous delusions of glory. Bahá'u'lláh describes him as the "source of envy and the quintessence of mischief,"[1] and Shoghi Effendi characterizes him as the one "notorious for his inordinate ambition, his blind obstinacy and uncontrollable jealousy."[2]

Let us see the preceding biblical passage in *The Amplified Version*, for the wording is more clear. Further, the translators consider "the lawless one" to be "the Antichrist"; they insert the title between brackets:

> The coming [of the lawless one, the Antichrist] is through the activity ***and*** working of Satan...

Although Azal was armed with all the evil intentions, he suffered from several weaknesses that could stifle his dreams of grandeur: he was both fearful and feeble-minded. He needed a shrewd collaborator who would tempt him, prod him, comfort him, manipulate him, and mastermind his schemes for him. He could not have asked for an abler and more qualified assistant than Siyyid Muhammad, who was not only bold but extremely cunning and crafty as well. He kept Azal's delusions of glory brewing by constantly feeding the fire of his envious heart, and fanning the flame of his passion for power. The Scriptures could not have selected and predicted more fitting titles for these two intimate schemers.

Siyyid Muhammad would tell Azal that the stature of the new Revelation has risen high throughout the world, that people honored and trusted the new believers, that he should make a name for himself, that he should come out of hiding and have no fear, for the danger had passed. "Cease, then, to follow," he would admonish Azal, "that thou may be followed by the world..."[3] As a result of his influence, Azal "began to sow the seeds of doubt in the minds of those who had become Bahá'u'lláh's ardent admirers and were attracted to His person."[4]

Azal's vanity and jealousy pushed him to the edge, beyond heavenly rescue. He was led to temptation by his ego and could not be delivered from the Evil One, Siyyid Muhammad. The two schemers were a perfect match; they met each other's needs to the fullest. 'Abdu'l-Bahá compares Azal to a "sucking child" and Siyyid Muhammad to "the much-prized breast."[5] They had much in common; in an Epistle Bahá'u'lláh states that Azal has found someone like himself.[6] In *The Book of Certitude* Bahá'u'lláh identifies Siyyid Muhammad as "a one-eyed man" who arose "with the utmost malevolence" against Him.[7]

Here Bahá'u'lláh refers to both betrayers, and then prays for them:

> My Pen, verily, lamenteth over Mine own Self, and My Tablet weepeth sore over what hath befallen Me at the hands of one [Azal] over whom We watched for successive years, and who, day and night, served in My presence, until he was made to err by one of My servants, named Siyyid Muhammad…And there befell Me at the hands of both of them that which made every man of understanding to cry out, and he who is endued with insight to groan aloud, and the tears of the fair-minded to flow.
>
> We pray to God to graciously assist them that have been led astray to be just and fair-minded, and to make them aware of that whereof they have been heedless. He, in truth, is the All-Bounteous, the Most Generous. Debar not Thy servants, O my Lord, from the door of Thy grace, and drive them not away from the court of Thy presence. Assist them to dispel the mists of idle fancy, and to tear away the veils of vain imaginings and hopes. Thou art, verily, the All-Possessing, the Most High. No God is there but Thee, the Almighty, the Gracious.[8]

The Book of Revelation, the most astonishing book of prophecy, a book that covers many events over the last two thousand years and a few in the next thousand, also refers to Azal and his supporter Siyyid Muhammad. It calls them "the beast" and "the false prophet:"

> Then I saw ***the beast*** [Siyyid Muhammad] and ***the kings of the earth*** [several kings opposed Bahá'u'lláh] and their armies gathered together to make war against ***the rider on the horse*** [Bahá'u'lláh] and his army [followers]. But the beast was captured, and with him ***the false prophet*** [Azal] who had performed the miraculous signs on his behalf. With these signs he had deluded those who had received the mark of the beast and worshipped his image [beastlike or evil-minded people]. The two of them were thrown alive into the fiery lake of burning sulfur. The rest of them were killed with the sword that came out of the mouth of the rider on the horse, and all the birds gorged themselves on their flesh. Revelation 19:19-21 NIV

As we noted earlier, other prophecies also point to the opposition of the kings of the earth to the Báb and Bahá'u'lláh:

> The kings of the earth take their stand and the rulers gather together against ***the Lord*** [Bahá'u'lláh] and against ***his Anointed One*** [the Báb]. Psalms 2:2 NIV

The title "false prophet" perfectly describes Azal. The beast also accurately characterizes Siyyid Muhammad; he indeed acted like a cruel and cunning beast toward many, especially Bahá'u'lláh and His followers. The prophecies of Paul and Revelation both refer to the one (Azal) who uses miracles to deceive people. Both of them declare that in doing his work he gets help from, or does his work on behalf of, another figure (the Satan, or the beast), and both of them point to the destruction of the deceivers and their followers. In one prophecy, the power that destroys these negative forces is "the Lord's brightness" and "the spirit of His mouth," and in the other "the fiery lake" and "the sword that comes out of the mouth of the rider." ***Fire*** here symbolizes God's wrath, and ***the sword*** His Word.

Azal and Siyyid Muhammad personify the spirit of the Antichrist, but the title applies to anyone who denies the truth. Other figures who qualified for the title of "the Antichrist," also appeared during the time of the Báb and 'Abdu'l-Bahá. See *God Passes By,* by Shoghi Effendi.

> Who is the liar? Who but he that denies that Jesus is the Christ? He is Antichrist... I John 2:22 NEB

> You were told that Antichrist was to come, and now many antichrists have appeared... I John 2:18 NEB

Pratney and Chant make this comment about the preceding passage:

> Two things are clear in this passage. First of all, there was an expectation of one particular anti-Christian figure—'the antichrist.' But there were also many lesser antichrists in existence.[9]

Biederwolf states:

> These antichrists in John's time were the heretical teachers who had gone out from the Church...and were the forerunners of the coming personal Antichrist.[10]

A Christian author describes the Antichrist as anyone who "will try to pass himself off as the Christ."[11] Here is one more biblical quotation about the Antichrist:

> But do not trust any and every spirit, my friends; test the spirits, to see whether they are from God, for among those who have gone out into the world there are many prophets falsely inspired. This is how we may recognize the Spirit of God: every spirit which acknowledges that Jesus Christ has come in the flesh is from God, and every spirit which does not thus acknowledge Jesus is not from God. This is what is meant by 'Antichrist'; you have been told that he was to come, and here he is, in the world already!
>
> I John 4:1-3 NEB
> See also II John

The preceding passage carries several messages. These are a few:

- Do not be complacent. Test those who claim to speak for God.

- One way to identify a true Spirit is to see if He acknowledges the identity and validity of Jesus Christ.
- Antichrist is the title applied to a person who claims to be a Messenger or a Spirit from God, yet he denies Jesus Christ.

The last message applies to Azal. By denying Bahá'u'lláh (the return of Christ), he also denied Jesus Christ. To summarize, the term ***Antichrist*** may convey any of these meanings:

- Anyone who denies Jesus Christ.
- Any impostor who makes false claims.
- Anyone who denies or opposes God's Messengers and Redeemers.
- Anyone who tempts people with falsehood and tries to keep them from the truth.

Both Azal and Siyyid Muhammad fulfilled all these conditions; the title applies to both of them.

> Christ was a divine Center of unity and love. Whenever discord prevails instead of unity, wherever hatred and antagonism take the place of love and spiritual fellowship, Antichrist reigns instead of Christ.[12] 'Abdu'l-Bahá

The Book of Revelation predicts that after a thousand years, "Satan will be released from his prison" (Rev. 2:7). This indicates that after that span of time the spiritual state of the world will again decline. This timing matches Bahá'u'lláh's prediction that His Revelation will last at least a thousand years. The Book of Revelation then goes on to predict that the devil or Satan will again be thrown "into the lake of burning sulfur, where ***the beast*** and ***the false prophet*** had been thrown" (Rev. 20:10 NIV). Here again the two demonic figures, the beast (Siyyid Muhammad) and the false prophet (Azal) are mentioned together.

As we noted, Chapter 19 of Revelation speaks of two forces waging war against "the rider on the horse" (Bahá'u'lláh).

The two forces mentioned are the kings who waged war against Bahá'u'lláh ***from without*** and the beast who waged war ***from within***. Let us consider that prophecy once again:

> Then I saw the beast [Siyyid Muhammad] and the kings of the earth [four kings have been involved] and their armies gathered together to make war against the rider on the horse [Bahá'u'lláh] and his army [His followers]. But the beast was captured, and with him ***the false prophet*** [Azal] ***who had performed the miraculous signs on his behalf***. With these signs he had deluded those who had received the mark of the beast and worshipped his image. The two of them were thrown alive into the fiery lake of burning sulfur. The rest of them were killed with the sword [Word of God] that came out of the mouth of the rider on the horse... Revelation 19:19-21 NIV

One lesson we can learn from this prophecy is this: truth is not proven by miracles. The false prophet deluded people with his false claims of miracles. Prophecies continue:

> In that day the Lord will punish with his sword [Word]... the gliding ***serpent***...the coiling ***serpent***; he will slay ***the monster of the sea***. Isaiah 27:1-2 NIV

The "serpent" and the "monster of the sea" may symbolize Siyyid Muhammad and Azal. The symbols are quite suitable. Siyyid Muhammad was as deceptive and clever as "a gliding serpent." "The sea" symbolizes many meanings, among them ***idle fancies*** or ***illusions***.

In one of His Epistles, after referring to Azal, Bahá'u'lláh reveals this prayer:

> O God, my God! Debar not Thy servants from turning their faces towards the light of certitude...Take Thou, O my God, the hands of such as have been drowned in ***the sea of idle fancies***, and deliver them by Thy power and Thy sovereignty. Save them, then, with the arms of Thy might. Powerful art Thou to do what Thou willest, and in

> Thy right hand are the reins of all that is in the heavens and all that is on earth.[13]

In this passage, Bahá'u'lláh uses both the metaphors of "the ocean" and "the sea:"

> Most of the people in Persia are steeped in deception and idle fancy. How great the difference between the condition of these people and the station of such valiant souls as have passed beyond ***the sea of names*** and pitched their tents upon the shores of the ***ocean of detachment***... "Few of My servants are truly thankful." People for the most part delight in superstitions. They regard a single drop of ***the sea of delusion*** as preferable to an ***ocean of certitude***. By holding fast unto names they deprive themselves of the inner reality and by clinging to vain imaginings they are kept back from the Dayspring of heavenly signs.[14]

As we previously noted, ***the Most Great Ocean*** symbolizes Bahá'u'lláh's Revelation. At some time, Azal and Siyyid Muhammad were believers who lived in that ocean. Can such a vast Ocean be without a "monster"?

We can find similar uses for "sea" in the Book of Revelation:

> Then I saw a new heaven and a new earth, for the first heaven and the first earth had passed away, and there was no longer any ***sea*** [of delusions]. Revelation 21:1 NIV

> The sea [of delusions] gave up the [spiritually] dead that were in it... Revelation 20:13 NIV

Sometimes prophecies partly decode a metaphor:

> ***The waters*** you saw, where the prostitute [disloyal leaders or leader] sits [rules], ***are*** [deluded] ***peoples***, multitudes, nations and languages. Revelation 17:15 NIV

In the following passage from the Olivet Discourse, "the sea" may symbolize the masses of unstable, disturbed, and deluded people, or the flood of illusions that are sweeping the human race:

> On the earth, nations will be in anguish and perplexity at the roaring and tossing of ***the sea***. Luke 21:25 NIV

The next prophecy also points to two figures: "the foe" and "the avenger:"

> O Lord, our Lord, how majestic is your name in all the earth! You have set your glory above the heavens. From the lips of children and infants you have ordained praise because of your enemies, to silence ***the foe*** and ***the avenger***.
> Psalms 8:1-2 NIV

The Revised English Bible of verse 2 reads:

> You have established a bulwark against your adversaries ***to restrain*** the ***enemy*** and the ***avenger***.

As we noted, the word "restrain" was also used in Paul's prophecy:

> ...you must now be aware of ***the restraining hand*** which ensures that he [the man of sin] shall be revealed only at the proper time. II Thessalonians 2:6 NEB

The following prophecy also seems to point to two figures. Christian scholar J. R. Church believes that Chapter 109 of Psalms points mostly to the Antichrist:

> Do not keep silent, O God of my praise! For the mouth of ***the wicked*** [Azal] and the mouth of ***the deceitful*** [Siyyid Muhammad] have opened against me; they have spoken against me with a lying tongue. They have also surrounded me with words of hatred, and fought against me without a cause. In return for my love they are my accusers, but ***I give myself to prayer***. Thus they have rewarded me evil for good, and hatred for my love. Psalms 109:1-5 NKJ

As we just noted, after referring to Azal, Bahá'u'lláh prayed for all those "drowned in the sea of idle fancies."

The following prophecy points to two divine Figures and two impostors:

> He who dwells in the secret place of ***the Most High*** [the Báb] shall abide under the shadow of the ***Almighty*** [Bahá'u'lláh]. I will say of the Lord, "He is my refuge and my fortress; my God, in Him I will trust." Surely He shall deliver you from the snare of the ***fowler*** [Siyyid Muhammad] and from the perilous ***pestilence*** [Azal]...Because you have made ***the Lord*** [Bahá'u'lláh], who is my refuge, even ***the Most High*** [the Báb], your dwelling place.
>
> Psalms 91:1-3, 9 NKJ

Some Christian scholars believe that the following prophecy refers to Satan, because it points to a being who stands against God. *The Amplified Bible* is more clear:

> Set the trumpet to your lips. [The enemy] comes as a [great] vulture against the house of the Lord because they have broken My covenant, and transgressed against My law. [Brackets belong to original.] Hosea 8:1

The prophecy seems to contain the main ingredients of the Antichrist. It refers to a vulture that stands against God's house or sanctuary (symbolic of divine Revelation). The vulture is both a ***lawbreaker*** and a ***covenant-breaker***. The word "they" may refer to the covenant-breakers in all ages or to specific figures.

The Death of the Devil

Chapter 12 of Revelation speaks about Islam and specifies the period of its dispensation by the figure 1260 days. (See *I Shall Come Again.*) That chapter also offers a graphic description of the last war between positive and negative forces:

> And there was war in heaven [religion]. Michael and his angels fought against the dragon, and the dragon and his angels fought back. But he was not strong enough, and ***they lost their place in heaven***. The great dragon was hurled down—that ancient serpent called the devil, or Satan, who

> leads the whole world astray. ***He was hurled to the earth, and his angels with him.*** Revelation 12:7-9 NIV

The war between positive and negative powers has endured for thousands of years, and is now coming to a close. We are witnessing the dawning of peace. After giving us the good news of the destruction of the Satanic forces, the prophecy becomes more specific. It refers to two divine Figures who stand on one side of the struggle, and a demonic or destructive figure who stands on the other:

> Then I heard a loud voice in heaven say: "Now have come the salvation and the power and the kingdom of ***our God*** [Bahá'u'lláh], and the authority of ***his Christ*** [the Báb]. For ***the accuser*** [Azal] of our brothers [followers of Bahá'u'lláh], who accuses them before our God day and night, has been hurled down. They overcame him by the blood of the ***Lamb*** [the Báb] and by the word of their testimony; they did not love their lives so much as to shrink from death. Revelation 12:10-11 NIV

The prophecy once again declares bad news for evil forces:

> Therefore rejoice, you heavens and you who dwell in them! But woe to the earth and the sea, because the devil has gone down to you! He is filled with fury, because he knows that ***his time is short***. Revelation 12:12 NIV

The "devil" is dying before our very eyes. It has just a little time to live:

> Soon will the present-day order be rolled up, and a new one spread out in its stead.[15] Bahá'u'lláh

The "devil" symbolizes all the negative forces of the world, but it may also symbolize Azal and Siyyid Muhammad. Bahá'u'lláh called both of them Satan. The murder of Siyyid Muhammad may also symbolize the death of "the devil," or destruction of the forces of darkness upon the earth.

Astonishing as it may seem, during the last period of his life, Azal was exiled to Cyprus (also known as Qibris), which the

Turks call "the Island of Satan."[16] *The Covenant of Bahá'u'lláh* quotes these prophecies, attributed to Islamic traditions:

> Soon will the Satan appear in the Isle of Q [Qibris, i.e. Cypress] and will prevent people from attaining the presence of the Lord. When that time comes turn ye towards the Holy Land wherefrom the sweet savors of God will be wafting.[17]

> The Satan will appear in the island related to him...When he should come, turn toward Carmel, the holy vale, the gathering place of mankind, this snow-white spot.[18]

Christian scholars believe that the following verses from Genesis describe the divine plan and is the first prophecy about Jesus. Many authors start their books of proofs and prophecies about Jesus with these verses. They believe the phrase "he shall bruise your head" refers to Jesus:

> So the Lord God said to the serpent [Satan]: "Because you have done this, you are cursed...And I will put enmity between you and the woman [Eve], and between your seed and her seed; ***he*** [Jesus] ***shall bruise your head***, and you shall bruise his heel." Genesis 3:14-15 NKJ

Here is how a Christian author interprets the preceding verses:

> God, however, made it known to Satan that his rule over mankind was temporary and that Satan's reign would, in God's sovereign time, be destroyed...God made clear to Satan how his defeat would come, saying, "I will put enmity between you and the woman..." In other words, a male descendant of the woman would bring the ultimate downfall and destruction of Satan. That descendant would come from the line of Abraham (Gal. 3:16).[19]

Whether the preceding interpretation is accurate or not, one point is clear: The serpent's head, which may symbolize the negative forces, is not yet crushed, but its dominance will soon come to an end.

Warning Against Secrecy

In His Olivet Discourse, Jesus gave this critical warning:

> So if anyone tells you, 'There he is, ***out in the desert***,' do not go out; or, 'Here he is, ***in the inner rooms***,' do not believe it. For as the lightning comes from the east and flashes to the west, so will be the coming of the Son of Man. Wherever there is a ***carcass***, there the vultures will gather. Matthew 24:26-28 NIV

Failure to understand the purpose of the preceding warning has prevented many Christians from investigating Bahá'u'lláh's advent. It has strengthened both their excessive fear of being deceived and their intense desire to remain in their familiar comfort zone. Christian scholar Biederwolf makes this comment about the preceding prophecy:

> ***The coming of the false Christs shall be more or less concealed in the wilderness or in the secret chamber, the quiet of the desert*** and the secrecy of the chamber being convenient places for the fomenting of new movements or of rebellion, ***but the Coming of Christ shall be open and discernible like an all-illuminating flash of light*** which no one can mistake, its presence to be announced everywhere from east to west over the whole world.[20]

Jesus' prophecy about openness and secrecy may indeed refer to how Bahá'u'lláh and Azal appeared in public. As stated before, Azal was the master of disguise. He was good at the art. He was so good that sometimes even the people close to him, such as his brother, could not recognize him.[21] Of course, he hid himself for self-protection. He was terrified of being hurt. Living in disguise was his best skill: "he could be relied upon to hide himself very effectively, till it should be overpast!"[22] He was so proud of his ability to conceal his identity that he called himself: The Concealed Face.

At the other extreme was Bahá'u'lláh, who never hid Himself. Once there was an attempt on the life of Násiri'd-Dín Sháh by two mentally incompetent followers of the Báb. This act was so serious, no one would have dreamed that Bahá'u'lláh could escape death, because He was the most prominent follower of the Báb. Although He had an excellent opportunity to escape to Russia, He refused to go, or even hide anywhere in the land. On the contrary, He openly walked among the people. People were utterly astonished, even confused by His courage and audacity. He followed the same course of action during His entire ministry. Bahá'u'lláh often speaks of never hiding Himself:

> The One true God beareth Me witness, and His creatures will testify, that not for a moment did I allow Myself to be hidden from the eyes of men, nor did I consent to shield My person from their injury. Before the face of all men I have arisen, and bidden them fulfill My pleasure. My object is none other than the betterment of the world and the tranquillity of its peoples.[23]

> God knows that at no time did We attempt to conceal Ourself or hide the Cause which We have been bidden to proclaim.[24]

From Bahá'u'lláh's prayers and meditations:

> So highly didst Thou exalt Him [Bahá'u'lláh] that He openly delivered unto the kings Thy messages and commandments, and hath never for one moment sought His own protection, but striven to protect Thy servants from whatever might withhold them from approaching the kingdom of Thy nearness, and from setting their faces towards the horizon of Thy good-pleasure.[25]

The prophecy in Matthew also states that "wherever there is a carcass, there the vultures will gather." ***The carcass*** symbolizes decayed beliefs and ideologies espoused by corrupt leaders. We see how true this is today. Simple-minded people (the birds) are gorging themselves with false beliefs and doctrines proclaimed by deceptive leaders and false prophets everywhere on our planet. One of those carcasses who found a few followers was Azal.

The prophecy from Jesus first refers to the coming of the Son of Man openly like "the lightning," then it points to "a carcass" that attracts some vultures. It is hard to imagine a sharper contrast between the two metaphors. The lightning shines in heaven with power and brilliance. It is a majestic sight that every sighted person can see. Compare that with a carcass on the ground in a remote forest or field, surrounded by a few beasts and vultures. The carcass may symbolize Azal. As we noted, Revelation 19:19 refers to Siyyid Muhammad as "the beast." To protect the leftovers, some animals hide their kill. That is, of course, what Azal's few followers would do: they would help him hide from other predators!

Bahá'u'lláh was spiritually a perfect contrast to Azal. Azal's intense desire to hide himself is one example of this contrast. Jesus warns us not to look for Him "***out in the desert***" or "***in the inner rooms.***" ***Those were the very places Azal chose to hide himself. He was either running in secrecy to remote outer areas—mountains and deserts—or hiding in inner rooms.***

Let us once again see Jesus' prophecy about secrecy:

> So if anyone tells you, "There he is, out in ***the desert,***" do not go out; or, "Here he is, in ***the inner rooms,***" do not believe it. Matthew 24:26 NIV

Now consider the following quotes to see how clearly Azal fulfilled Jesus' prophecy. How did Azal behave when an attempt was made on the life of Násiri'd-Dín Sháh?

> [He] concealed himself, a bewildered fugitive, in the guise of a dervish, with kashkúl [alms box] in hand, ***wandered in mountains and plains…***"[26]

> …he was so frightened for his own life that he disguised himself in the garb of a dervish and, leaving his wife and

> child behind, ***fled into the mountains*** of Mázindarán... Thus ***he roamed the countryside*** in fear and trepidation.[27]

When Azal was hiding in Baghdad, a famous follower of Bahá'u'lláh wanted to meet him. Azal would not give his consent. "After much pleading...[he] agreed to meet him ***outside the city on a hilltop***."[28] As we noted, during his stay in Bahá'u'lláh's house, Azal lived with such fear that:

> ***He hid himself, keeping the door of our house locked, and stormed at anybody who opened it***.[29]

Notice how clearly and closely the preceding descriptions correspond to Jesus' warning that ***we should not look for Him in the desert*** or ***in the inner rooms***! Azal's concern for his safety was very great. He would not take any chances even when everything looked safe:

> And although throughout this journey [from Baghdad to Constantinople] the governors and officials observed the utmost consideration and respectfulness [toward Bahá'u'lláh] ...nevertheless was he [Azal] always concealed in change of raiment, and acted cautiously, on the idea that some act of aggression was likely to occur.[30]

A common deception used by Azal was to attribute his own guilt to Bahá'u'lláh. He was the source of many false rumors. Consider this statement from Bahá'u'lláh:

> It is reported in the press that this Servant [Bahá'u'lláh] hath fled from the land of Tá (Tihrán) and gone to Iráq. Gracious God! ***Not even for a single moment hath this Wronged One [Bahá'u'lláh] ever concealed Himself***. Rather hath He at all times remained steadfast and conspicuous before the eyes of all men. Never have We retreated, nor shall We ever seek flight. In truth it is the foolish people who flee from Our presence. We left Our home country accompanied by two mounted escorts, representing the two honored governments of Persia and Russia until We arrived in Iráq ***in the plenitude of glory and power***. Praise be to

> God! The Cause whereof this Wronged One is the Bearer standeth as high as heaven and ***shineth resplendent as the sun. Concealment hath no access unto this station, nor is there any occasion for fear or silence***.[31]

Many people need a miracle before they can believe something. It is hard to imagine a miracle more astonishing than this: ***A Man with thousands of fanatical enemies walks among them without fear. He has no bodyguards, yet lives for forty years (1852-1892) to accomplish His miraculous mission!***

Notice God's standards. Bahá'u'lláh was a captive and a prisoner, yet He appeared "***in the plenitude of glory and power***." He stood "***as high as heaven***" and shined as brilliantly as "***the sun***." Jesus used the metaphor of "***the lightning***" for His second Advent. In the preceding passage, Bahá'u'lláh uses the metaphor of "the sun." Jesus declared He was the light of the world (John 8:12), yet He had only a few followers.

In the following statement, Bahá'u'lláh first speaks about the brilliance of His Light, and then refers to some followers of the Báb who had turned to Azal:

> ...despite ***the brightness of this Light***, the like of which none of them hath ever beheld, witness how the people of the Bayán [followers of the Báb] have denied and contended with Me...Among them is he [Azal]...who condemned Me as one that deserved to be put to death, and who imputed to Me the very offenses of which he himself was guilty.[32]

As Bahá'u'lláh states, after Azal failed in his attempt to take Bahá'u'lláh's life, he accused Bahá'u'lláh "of the very offenses of which he himself was guilty."[33] The sun shines brightly on the horizon, but a "fallen star" attributes its darkness to the sun. After being poisoned, Bahá'u'lláh asked His followers not to spread the news. How did Azal react? He spread the rumors that Bahá'u'lláh tried to poison ***him***. Thus the Bahá'ís were forced to tell their side of the story.

We should recognize that there was also a positive side to Azal's supreme talents for secrecy: On the surface, his concealment contributed to Bahá'u'lláh's safety. Only a guilty person has a reason to be fearful and to hide himself. "If Bahá'u'lláh was the central Figure behind the new Faith," people thought, "why would He not hide Himself?" Thus most of their attention was drawn to Azal, the shadowy and the ever-elusive figure. "If he was not the guilty one, why would he hide himself?" they wondered.

If Násiri'd-Dín Sháh and the religious leaders of the time had realized who Bahá'u'lláh truly was, they would not have allowed Him to leave Iran for Iraq. They would have instantly killed Him. We should give Azal full credit and even be grateful to him for this significant contribution. He served:

> ...as a screen in attracting the attention of the people to himself, thus preventing the premature recognition of "Him Whom God should make Manifest" [Bahá'u'lláh] until His Own appointed time.[34]

By the time Bahá'u'lláh reached Baghdád, the well-kept secret—who was the true Leader?—was divulged.[35] By then it was too late for the Sháh to execute Bahá'u'lláh.

We should also note that God uses "instruments" to achieve His purpose:

> He Who is the Eternal Truth—exalted by His glory—hath made the fulfillment of every undertaking on earth dependent on material means.[36]
>
> Bahá'u'lláh

Sometimes even "***the Enemy***" unknowingly serves as an essential instrument or actor in the ever-unfolding divine drama of "***the Friend***."

"The Idol" and "the Evil One"

A prophecy from Isaiah uses a metaphor similar to the one used by Jesus—carcass or carrion—to refer to Azal:

> For behold, the Lord will come with fire and with His chariots, like a whirlwind, to render His anger with fury, and His rebuke with flames of fire. For by fire and by His sword the Lord will judge all flesh; and ***the slain of the Lord shall be many***. "Those who sanctify themselves and purify themselves, to go to the gardens ***after an idol in the midst, eating swine's flesh and the abomination and the mouse***, shall be consumed together," says the Lord.
>
> Isaiah 66:15-17 NKJ

The prophecy declares that the Lord will come with the fire of His judgment and the sword of His Word. He is angry because His servants deny His Message. What consequence do they face? Spiritual death. The spiritually "slain of the Lord" will lie all over the planet. Among those who face death, there will be some who will try to purify and sanctify themselves by following ***an idol in their midst***. An idol is a substitute for God. The word describes Azal perfectly. The idol worshippers will not hesitate to eat that which is filthy and forbidden, such as flesh or carcass of swine and mouse. These people also will not escape God's wrath. Both prophecies of Jesus and Isaiah refer to eating the flesh of undesirable animals.

Bahá'u'lláh refers to Azal as "***the Idol***,"[37] and Shoghi Effendi refers to him as "***the Most Great Idol***,"[38] which was cast out of the new Revelation. He declares that Azal was powerless to divide the Bahá'í community despite all his efforts:

> The Covenant of the Báb…with its immutable truths, incontrovertible prophecies, and repeated warnings, stood guard over that Faith, insuring its integrity, demonstrating its incorruptibility, and perpetuating its influence.[39]

The flesh of dead and undesirable animals symbolizes illusions, and false and decaying doctrines offered by some religious leaders to the masses of people who gorge themselves with whatever they are fed. The next prophecy predicts that in this age people will crave to hear false and distorted doctrines:

> For the time will come when men will not put up with sound doctrine. Instead, to suit their own desires, ***they will gather around them a great number of teachers to say what their itching ears want to hear***. II Timothy 4:3 NIV

In the following passage, Bahá'u'lláh mourns the lack of spiritual capacity in people. He uses a similar symbol—that of ***carcass*** or ***carrion*** (dead and decaying flesh)—to portray corrupt beliefs and doctrines:

> Even as the people of Israel, in the time of Moses, bartered away the bread of heaven for the sordid things of the earth, these people, likewise, sought to exchange the divinely-revealed verses for their foul, their vile, and idle desires. In like manner, thou beholdest in this day that although spiritual sustenance hath descended from the heaven of divine mercy, and been showered from the clouds of His loving kindness, and although the seas of life, at the behest of the Lord of all being, are surging...yet these people, ravenous as the dogs, ***have gathered around carrion***, and contented themselves with the stagnant waters of a briny lake. Gracious God! how strange the way of this people! They clamor for guidance, although the standards of Him Who guideth all things are already hoisted. They cleave to the obscure intricacies of knowledge, when He, Who is the Object of all knowledge, shineth as the sun. They see the sun with their own eyes, and yet question that brilliant Orb as to the proof of its light. They behold the vernal showers descending upon them, and yet seek an evidence of that bounty. The proof of the sun is the light thereof, which shineth and envelopeth all things. The evidence of the shower is the bounty thereof, which reneweth and investeth the world with the mantle of life.[40]

Elsewhere Bahá'u'lláh uses the same symbol to portray the corrupt souls of people who are devoured by "voracious beasts," a metaphor for religious leaders who rob their followers in the name of God:

> ...***voracious beasts*** have gathered and preyed upon the ***carrion of the souls of men***.[41]

The preceding verse from Isaiah declares that "the slain of the Lord shall be many." Prophecies of this kind are as a rule symbolic. They point to spiritual death, but Isaiah's prophecy may also have a literal meaning. The history of the Bahá'í Faith shows that thousands of those who persecuted the Bahá'ís faced death and disaster on a scale far beyond what chance would allow. Consider this one example among others: all the 750 Muslim soldiers who participated in the martyrdom of the Báb were killed, some of them by a wall that crashed on them while resting, the others because of mutiny against the government. All the kings and rulers who totally ignored Bahá'u'lláh's call to them faced death or defeat and humiliation. Siyyid Muhammad, perhaps the closest person to Azal, faced a similar fate: he too was killed.

Who killed him and why? Because of his superb cunning, Siyyid Muhammad enjoyed enormous success in his schemes against Bahá'u'lláh and devoted followers of the new Revelation. His schemes were especially effective against those followers who walked from Persia to Palestine to get a glimpse of their Lord. His favorite hobby was to report these pilgrims to authorities, who would arrest them and send them back to Persia. The pilgrims returned without attaining their most cherished and precious purpose. Siyyid Muhammad's numerous crimes, especially his persistent and extreme cruelty to these pilgrims, pushed some devoted Bahá'ís to the edge; they could not take it any longer. These few zealous believers ignored Bahá'u'lláh's admonition that Bahá'ís must avoid all acts of violence, that they should not take revenge, and that it is better to be killed than to kill. Secretly they plotted and murdered Siyyid Muhammad.

We should note that only society has the authority to punish. No human being has the right to take the law into his own hands. Bahá'u'lláh condemned and deplored violent acts of revenge. Statements such as the following are abundant in Bahá'í Scriptures:

> Beware lest ye harm any soul, or make any heart to sorrow; lest ye wound any man with your words, be he known to you or a stranger, be he friend or foe. Pray ye for all; ask ye that all be blessed, all be forgiven. Beware, beware, lest any of you seek vengeance, even against one who is thirsting for your blood. Beware, beware, lest ye offend the feelings of another, even though he be an evil-doer, and he wish you ill. Look ye not upon the creatures, turn ye to their Creator. See ye not the never-yielding people, see but the Lord of Hosts. Gaze ye not down upon the dust, gaze upward at the shining sun, which hath caused every patch of darksome earth to glow with light.[42]
>
> 'Abdu'l-Bahá

We must condemn every evil act, yet we must refuse to judge people. Consider this extreme example: how many of us would approve of Hitler being murdered before he had risen to power? Ours is not to judge, but to witness, in this exceptional case, the literal fulfillment of an unusual prophecy.

As evil as this violent act of revenge appears to us, it is prudent for us to assume that it was part of the Divine Drama. God knew this would happen, and He simply predicted it. But He did not choose the actors. The power to act is given to us by God, but we always choose our roles.

> "Do you refuse to speak to me?" Pilate said. "Don't you realize I have power either to free you or to crucify you?" Jesus answered, "***You would have no power over me if it were not given to you from above.***" John 19:10-11 NIV

> The Son of Man will go just as it is written [prophesied] about him. ***But woe to that man who betrays the Son of Man***! It would be better for him if he had not been born.
>
> Christ (Mark 14:21 NIV)

God is Merciful, All-Knowing, and All-Powerful. He can always forgive those who have committed evil and compensate anyone who has been wronged. He can certainly lessen the sufferings of Siyyid Muhammad in the life to come because he lost his life at the hands of a few believers who knew they were violating a fundamental law of God. Imagine that he had lived for many more decades and committed more atrocities. His burden of sin would be much heavier. From an eternal perspective, death for him was definitely preferable to life.

The backbone of all religions is this: God is the perfect judge and ultimately perfect justice will be done to every human being. Whatever comes from God is to our advantage, even if His verdict is death! Without this conviction, faith has no meaning. If God took Siyyid Muhammad, this was in his best interest.

The following prophecy may also refer to the two demonic figures:

> The field is the world, the good seeds are the sons [followers] of the kingdom, but the tares are the sons of ***the wicked one*** [Azal]. ***The enemy*** [Siyyid Muhammad] who sowed them is the devil… Matthew 13:38-39 NKJ

Bahá'u'lláh in one of His Epistles refers to Siyyid Muhammad as Satan,[43] which is the equivalent of the devil.

What will happen to the weeds and those who grow them?

> The Son of Man will send out his angels [ambassadors of love and harmony], and ***they will weed out of his kingdom everything that causes sin and all who do evil***. They will throw them into the fiery furnace [of remoteness from God], where there will be weeping and gnashing of teeth.
> Matthew 13:41-42 NIV

"The weeding out" happened not only spiritually but literally as well, because those who entered "the new garden" with evil intentions were cast out of the new Revelation. In the

Bahá'í Faith such people are called "covenant breakers." They make a commitment to protect the garden, but after entering it, they begin to destroy it from within. The prophecy declares that in this Revelation the weeds will be cast out. The prophecy ends with this verse:

> Then the righteous will shine like the sun in the kingdom of their Father. He who has ears, let him hear.
>
> Matthew 13:43

The following prophecy points to the fall of Satan. It may refer either to Azal or Siyyid Muhammad. They both fell from heaven:

> I saw ***Satan*** fall like lightning from heaven.
>
> Luke 10:18 NIV

The next prophecy refers to a figure called "the wicked" who is slayed by Bahá'u'lláh. It may refer to either of the two demonic figures:

> A shoot [Bahá'u'lláh] will come up from the stump of Jesse...He will strike the earth with the rod of his mouth; with the breath of his lips ***he will slay the wicked***.
>
> Isaiah 11:1, 4 NIV

Christian scholar Dr. Jack Van Impe states that among those "who are damned for all eternity [are]...covenant breakers." He then adds: "The Antichrist is the supreme example of this type of person."[44] In the Bahá'í Writings, Azal is called "***the arch Covenant Breaker of Bahá'u'lláh's Revelation***."

This prophecy also predicts the destruction of the leader of the wicked:

> In wrath you strode through the earth and in anger you threshed the nations. You came out to deliver your people, to save your anointed one. You crushed ***the leader of the land of wickedness***, you stripped him from head to foot.
>
> Habakkuk 3.12-13 NIV

Christian scholar Robert Van Kampen confirms the relevance of the preceding prophecy to the coming of Christ and the Antichrist.[45]

The following verses portray a contrast between the Lord and His positive power, and the one who "has broken the covenant" and has no regard for "man," a symbol of God's Messengers and Redeemers. It also refers to the mourning of Israel and its shame for harboring this covenant breaker on its land:

> O Lord, be gracious to us; we have waited for You. Be their arm every morning, our salvation also in the time of trouble...The Lord is exalted, for He dwells on high; He has filled Zion with justice and righteousness. Wisdom and knowledge will be the stability of your times, and the strength of salvation; the fear of the Lord is His treasure... The highways lie waste, the traveling man ceases. ***He has broken the covenant***, he has despised the cities, ***he regards no man***. The earth mourns and languishes, Lebanon is shamed and shriveled; Sharon is like a wilderness, and Bashan and Carmel shake off their fruits. Isaiah 33:2-9 NKJ

Another translation of verse 8:

> ...***the enemy hath broken the covenant***...he regardeth not man [the Promised One]. Isaiah 33:8 ARV

The following verse states that the Antichrist is a person who denies Jesus Christ (the Son) and God (the Father):

> Who is the liar? It is the man who denies that Jesus is the Christ. Such a man is the antichrist—he denies the Father and the Son. I John 2:22 NIV

In the preceding statement we can see a second meaning. As stated earlier, the Scriptures refer to Bahá'u'lláh as the Father, and to the Báb as the Son. Thus the statement can also mean that the Antichrist is the person who "denies the Father [Bahá'u'lláh] and the Son [the Báb]." Both Azal and Siyyid Muhammad qualify for the title. By denying Bahá'u'lláh, they also denied the Báb.

Jesus used the expression "the evil one" to refer to anyone dominated by the negative forces of his heart and temptations of others. His words may also contain a prophetic message:

> Our Father in heaven, hallowed be your name...deliver us from ***the evil one***. Matthew 6:9 NIV

The Báb and Bahá'u'lláh often use the expression "the Evil One" to refer to anyone who appears in the guise of sincerity but tempts people into the trap of degradation and denial:

> Watch over yourselves, for ***the Evil One*** is lying in wait, ready to entrap you...The Evil One is he that hindereth the rise and obstructeth the spiritual progress of the children of men.[46] Bahá'u'lláh

> The essence of abasement is to pass out from under the shadow of the Merciful and seek the shelter of ***the Evil One***.[47] Bahá'u'lláh

The following passages from Muhammad and the Báb may refer to Azal who made people disbelieve in the One who had come as the Lord, and to believe in himself as an equal with God:

> Yet there are men who take (for worship) others besides God, as equal (with God). Qur'án 2:165 Y

> O peoples of the earth! Bear ye allegiance unto this resplendent light wherewith God hath graciously invested Me through the power of infallible Truth, and walk not in the footsteps of ***the Evil One***, inasmuch as he prompteth you to disbelieve in God, your Lord...[48] The Báb

Here Bahá'u'lláh seems to refer to two beings, "the Idol" and "the Evil One:"

> Empower us, then, O my God, to forsake ourselves and cleave steadfastly to Him Who is the Manifestation of Thy Self, the Most Exalted, the Most High. Supply us also with that which is best for us, and write us down with such of Thy servants as have repudiated ***the Idol*** (Mírzá

> Yahyá) [Azal], and firmly believed in Thee, and been so established on the throne of certitude that the whisperings of ***the Evil One*** have been powerless to hinder them from turning their faces towards Thy name, the All-Merciful.[49]

As we noted previously, the Scriptures call "the man of sin" "the Enemy" (NEB). Here both Muhammad and the Báb call "the Evil One" "an enemy:"

> O ye servants of the Merciful One! Enter ye, one and all, through this Gate [the Báb] and follow not the steps of ***the Evil One***, for he prompteth you to walk in the ways of impiety and wickedness; he is, in truth, ***your declared enemy***.[50] The Báb

> And do not follow the footsteps of ***the Evil One***, for he is to you ***an avowed enemy***. Qur'án 2:168 Y

The Psalms refer to two figures "the enemy" and "the avenger."

> O Lord, our Lord, how excellent is Your name in all the earth, who have set Your glory [Glory of God] above the heavens! Out of the mouth of ***babes and nursing infants*** [pure-hearted and humble people] You have ordained strength, because of Your enemies, that You may silence ***the enemy*** and ***the avenger***. Psalms 8:1-2 NKJ

In His Wisdom, God uses "little" people to silence the proud and the pompous. This is how God manifests His power to His enemies. This is how Jesus and His humble disciples gained victory over their powerful opponents.

"The Humans" and "the Jinns"

It seems everything exists in pairs. The Qur'án classifies people into two groups: "humans" and "jinns." What seems to separate the two groups more than anything else is the quality of their faith—firmness and openness versus vacillation and secrecy. In this context, "humans" tend toward openness and firmness; "jinns" tend toward secrecy and vacillation. Each group contains a wide range of people. Some of the jinns keep moving from denial to faith and from faith to denial. Others are sheer pretenders and hypocrites (Qur'án 46:29; 34:41). Those called "humans" can also be deceptive, but they work from without. As enemies, they do not wear the garb of a friend. "Jinns" may confess their faith in God's covenant without having any intention of honoring it. Covenant breaking is often their way of life.

The word "jinn" offers a perfect description of Azal (called "the arch covenant breaker of the Báb's Revelation") and his followers, who wavered constantly and pretended to be faithful supporters of the Báb, while acting as His enemies.

Several verses in the Qur'án seem to refer to Azal, Siyyid Muhammad, and their followers. Consider the following passages as parts of a jigsaw puzzle:

> And they regard the jinn [Azal and Siyyid Muhammad]✦ to be partners with God, though He created them...
>
> Qur'án 6:100 Y

The word "jinn," used in the preceding verse and many others, has puzzled Muslim commentators for centuries. The most common and accepted feature of "jinn" is his ability to hide himself. Literally the word means "to be covered or hidden."[51] (Genie has the same root.)

As we noted, the most distinct characteristic of Azal and his followers was secrecy. They developed and practiced this skill to perfection. They were superb actors of deception in the divine drama. The verse refers both to a claim to equality with God and to secrecy—the dreams and thoughts that dominated Azal's life.

Consider also this verse:

✦ Azal and Siyyid Muhammad were two beings, yet acted as if they were one.

> Relate to them the story of the man to whom We sent Our signs. But he passed them by. So Satan followed him up, and he went astray. Qur'án 7:175 Y

Who was the man who received the signs of God, who witnessed the Glory of God in Bahá'u'lláh? Who was the man who rejected those signs? Who was the man with a follower titled "Satan"? And who was the man who went astray mostly after the Satan followed him? Azal and Siyyid Muhammad fulfilled all four conditions.

The Qur'án continues:

> If it had been Our Will, We should have elevated him with Our signs. But he inclined to the earth, and followed his own vain desires…Many are the jinns [Azal and his followers] and men [other deniers of truth] that We have made for hell. They have hearts wherewith they understand not, eyes wherewith they see not, and ears wherewith they hear not. They are like cattle—nay more misguided, for they are heedless (of warning). Qur'án 7:175-176, 179 Y

Consider also this verse:

> Behold! We said to the angels, "Bow down to Adam [the Spirit of God in Bahá'u'lláh and all great Messengers]." They bowed down except Iblís [the fallen angel]. He was one of the Jinns, and he broke the Command of his Lord. Will ye then take him and his progeny as protectors rather than Me? And they are enemies to you! Evil would be the exchange for the wrongdoers! Qur'án 18:50 Y

"Iblis" is the title of the fallen angel who, like Lucifer, showed pride before God:

> Then We bade the angels bow down to Adam, and they bowed down; not so Iblis. He refused to be of those who bow down. Qur'án 7:11 Y

As we just noted, the Qur'án 18:50 clearly links the fallen angel, Iblis, to "the jinns." Azal was given a supreme station by the Báb, that of an angel, but he refused to bow down before his Lord, Bahá'u'lláh, the Glory of God.

The Qur'án declares that "the jinns" are made of "fire," but "the humans" are made of "clay" (55:14-15). What meanings lie behind those metaphors? Clay is a neutral and inactive substance. Fire is an active force with the potential to destroy. The quality of deception—the chief weapon used by jinns—combined with blind zeal, is as destructive as a raging fire. Unchecked, it can destroy even the Faith of God, if that is possible. All religious wars have been waged with that fire—deception and hypocrisy fueled by selfish desires.

In one of His Tablets, Bahá'u'lláh declares that it is better to be an infidel or a drunkard than to be a deceiver. That is how dangerous deception is. No wonder, Jesus warned us against false prophets who are in essence wolves (outsiders), but appear in the church as sheep (insiders). Every religion has been destroyed not by outsiders, but by insiders, by believers who claimed to be doing everything for the Lord. That is how they gained people's trust. And that is the strategy the twin deceivers—Azal and Siyyid Muhammad—adopted and applied.

The last Surah or Chapter of the Qur'án consists only of six verses. It seems to prophesy the dawning of the light and the darkness that seeks to extinguish that light. As we noted, the Qur'án, like the Bible, refers repeatedly to the coming of Bahá'u'lláh as the advent of the Lord or God. The last chapter of the Qur'án bestows three titles on Bahá'u'lláh. It calls Him ***the Lord, the King,*** and ***the God of humankind.*** It refers to Azal as "the Whisperer"—a word that carries the connotation of secrecy:

> In the name of God, the Most Gracious, the Most Powerful. Say: I seek refuge in ***the Lord of mankind***, ***the King of mankind***, and ***the God of mankind***, from the mischief of the Whisperer [Azal] who withdraws (after his whisper), the one who whispers into the hearts of mankind—among

> ***jinns*** [Azal's followers] and among ***men*** [Bahá'u'lláh's followers].
>
> Qur'án 114:1-6 Y

Resist the Devil

When a new Redeemer comes, many pure-hearted and humble people feel a desire to investigate. But they find themselves surrounded by friends, family members, or "authority figures" who discourage them by making ***seemingly innocent*** statements such as "Are you not afraid of being deceived? What is wrong with ***your own*** faith?" "Deceivers are everywhere! How can you be sure?" "Ask your pastor, priest, or rabbi!" These people discourage others without any reason other than simply assuming that their inherited illusions and interpretations are the truth. ***They confess God's command "Seek and ye shall find," but violate it in deeds with a clear conscience! This is sheer hypocrisy, among the gravest of sins, condemned by Jesus in the harshest of words***.

How can we protect our spiritual life from such tempters who discourage independent investigation of truth? By following the instructions of the apostle James:

> ***Resist the devil*** [the tempter] and he will flee from you.
>
> James 4:7 NKJ

Rejecting the Redeemer of the Age is the grievest of misdeeds or sins we can commit. And among the most evil people are those who discourage or prevent others from exercising their freedom of choice to investigate the truth for themselves. How does God view them?

> It would be better for him to be thrown into the sea with a millstone tied around his neck than for him to cause one of these ***little ones*** [humble and innocent believers] to sin.
>
> Christ (Luke 17:2 NIV)

Failing to exercise the gift of spiritual freedom reduces a human being from his exalted station—the image of his

Creator—to a level lower than that of insects. It is our freedom to choose good instead of evil that sets us above animals. What does "the snake" in the story of Adam and Eve symbolize? And what did it accomplish? "The snake" symbolizes anyone who tempts others away from paradise. The consequences of having an opportunity to enter the heaven of faith, but failing because of timidity or temptation are enormous. Titles such as "the Evil One" "the Satan" or "the Devil" are not inappropriate or too strong to describe deceivers and tempters. Imagine having a chance to enter the highest paradise, but failing because of ***seemingly innocent*** illusions such as "The tried and true is better." or "Why are you unfaithful to your faith?" "What's wrong with being a Jew?" "What's wrong with being a Buddhist?" "What's wrong with being an atheist?" These simple, innocent statements only ***appear*** simple and innocent. If heeded blindly, they will lead to everlasting consequences. No wonder Jesus said that ***we are accountable for every careless word we speak*** (Matthew 12:36).

The symbolic story of creation demonstrates how easy it is to disobey God and how a "little" disobedience can cause inconceivable consequences. As a seemingly innocent risk by a driver can lead to his death, so does a little risk in the spiritual journey. This is among the most fundamental and yet least recognized principles in human life. It is known as "the law of the weakest critical link" discussed in detail by this author in *One God, Many Faiths; One Garden, Many Flowers*.

When we deal with evil people or evil forces, it is good to look at the big picture. Here are a few pieces of the puzzle:

- Like a piece of a painting, life is enriched by contrasts. Joy always feels better after pain. The spring always shines more brightly after a harsh winter.

- God never makes us engage in misbehavior, but He does allow us to do so.

- Sometimes God prevents evil persons from carrying out their plans. We cannot always know where He draws the line. If God had left us entirely to ourselves, we would have already destroyed the planet and its people.

It seems that as the intensity of good increases, so does the intensity of evil. The intense expression of heavenly light in this age led to a similar expression from the forces of darkness. This supreme contrast gains special significance when it appears from two half-brothers—Bahá'u'lláh and Azal—who grew up and lived together for more than half a century. Imagine the honor of being Bahá'u'lláh's brother and the shame of trying to kill Him! Two brothers having so much in common, yet differing so much! Human language has no word to describe their differences. In the Bahá'í Revelation, the same contrast appears a second time between 'Abdu'l-Bahá and His half-brother, who like Azal, was also honored with a special title. How can such a contrast appear between two brothers raised by the supreme Manifestation of God?

For someone who lacks a conscience, the ends always justify the means. No lie was too big or out of Azal's reach, if it would feed his starving ego. Only some of what he said or did is recorded. From the pieces of the puzzle we have, we can see a clear match between the prophecies and the lives of the two demonic figures: the Man of Sin (Azal), and Satan (Siyyid Muhammad).

Most people prefer to have a single source of focus, to concentrate on only one person who stands for a title. That way most or all the blame for the prevailing evils can be placed on him. The idea of Satan follows this principle and fulfills this need. As stated, we have had hundreds, or even thousands, who qualify for the title of the Antichrist. But if we had to narrow down our choice, Azal and Siyyid Muhammad would definitely emerge as the champions. Since they were intimately united in their thoughts and acts against Bahá'u'lláh, any title that applies to one of them, must necessarily apply to the other. They worked like one soul in two bodies. Together, they more than qualify for the appearance of the Antichrist that the Christians have expected and are still expecting.

Azal was a balloon filled with honors and set afloat by the winds of divine destiny. While floating, he was caught by a violent storm of pride and vanity. When the storm raised him beyond his limits, he lost the outer protection, and continued to climb and expand until it burst open and he fell from glory to infamy and abasement. We should despise his evil ***acts***, but not the ***actor himself***. May we pray that he too, like all God's children, will receive abundant blessings from his Master, and will bask in the glory and forgiveness of his Lord, Bahá'u'lláh, who suffered so much.

> ...We have never gloried in any thing, nor did We seek preference over any soul. To everyone We have been a most kindly companion, a most forbearing and affectionate friend. In the company of the poor We have sought their fellowship, and amidst the exalted and learned We have been submissive and resigned. I swear by God, the one true God! grievous as have been the woes and sufferings which the hand of the enemy and the people of the Book inflicted upon Us, yet all these fade into utter nothingness when compared with that which hath befallen Us at the hand of those who profess to be Our friends.[52] Bahá'u'lláh

False Prophets

Prophecies about false prophets refer mainly to figures ***within*** the Christian Faith, not without. Consider how easy it has been to divide the one house of God, Christianity, into thousands of denominations and sects. According to *Christianity Today*, every year over 200 new denominations are formed! Now look ***outside*** Christianity. Try to find even one independent religion, totally outside Christianity, that is founded on the second advent of Christ. I do not know even a single case, except the Bahá'í Faith. A few who dared to make any claims started as pastors and preachers, gained people's confidence, and then made some vague references to their station. One of them was arrested and imprisoned for tax evasion!

God has always allowed denominations to be formed, but He has promised to prevent false ***independent*** religions to be established in His name:

> Every plant which My heavenly Father has not planted will be uprooted. Christ (Matt. 15:13 NKJ)

Besides God's promise, we can find other reasons. The difference between the true Christ and a false one is like the difference between day and night, provided people use ***God's standards***, such as His Word, and not their own, such as miracles. If all false prophets, who will ever live, put all their deceptive geniuses together, they will be unable to come up even with a small fraction of the evidence the Báb and Bahá'u'lláh present.

False prophets are those who cast fear in the hearts of people to prevent them from looking anywhere except at their denomination and the beliefs that ***they*** hold to be true. These leaders violate the most emphatic commands of Jesus to all Christians, that they should search for Him with courage and confidence, and trust in His guidance and protection.

Fear is among the most powerful emotions. Every Christian remembers this warning:

> …many false prophets will appear and deceive many people. Matthew 24:11 NIV

> For false Christs and false prophets will appear…
> Matthew 24:24 NIV

As we previously noted, the forces of light and darkness have always been at work. Being deceived is not unique or new. But what was Jesus' purpose in giving us this warning? Was it to cast fear, avoidance, and complacency in our hearts or to teach us prudence and caution? Most people have turned Jesus' warning into a phobia and built with it an iron-cast cubicle of self-protection, avoidance, escape, and unawareness.

Consider this example. In this age of high crime rates, we are all concerned about our safety. Imagine if this concern reached a point where we always stayed in our houses and refused to open them to anyone who knocked, including our loved ones. This is exactly the way many Christians are responding to Bahá'u'lláh's invitation to open their hearts and souls just to get a glimpse of His glory. They completely ignore the supreme honor of responding:

> I stand at the door and knock. If anyone hears My voice and opens the door, I will come in to him and dine with him, and he with Me. Revelation 3:20 NKJ

> ...be like men who wait for their master, when he will return from the wedding, that when he comes and knocks they may open to him immediately. Blessed are those servants whom the master, when he comes, will find watching. Assuredly, I say to you that he will gird himself and have them sit down to eat, and will come and serve them. Luke 12:36-37 NKJ

Since fear and complacency dominate so many lives, let us examine Jesus' warning to be cautious ***in its context***:

> At that time if anyone says to you, "Look, here is the Christ!" or, "There he is!" do not believe it. For ***false Christs*** and false prophets will appear and perform great ***signs and miracles*** to deceive even the elect—if that were possible. See, I have told you ahead of time.
> Matthew 24:23-25 NIV

In these verses ***Jesus clearly links false prophets with miracles***. In fact, His warning is primarily aimed against miracles. He shows that a ***miracle can be a deceptive device***. After referring to miracles as the first sign of deception, Jesus mentions ***the second sign: secrecy***.

> So if anyone tells you, "***There he is, out in the desert***," do not go out; or, "Here he is, ***in the inner rooms***," do not believe it. For as lightning that comes from the east

> is visible even in the west, so will be the coming of the Son of Man. Wherever there is a carcass [such as Azal], there the vultures will gather. Matthew 24:26-28 NIV

We noted how clearly Azal fulfilled both of the preceding signs and many more. In one of His Writings, quoted earlier, Bahá'u'lláh first speaks of "the brightness of His Light" and then refers to Azal as the hidden star, who accused Bahá'u'lláh of "the very offenses he himself was guilty" of, including escape and concealment from danger. Later in the same discourse, Jesus makes this statement:

> Therefore keep watch, because you do not know on what day your Lord will come. But understand this: If the owner of the house had known at what time of night the thief was coming, he would have kept watch and would not have let his house be broken into. So you also must be ready, because the Son of Man will come at an hour when you do not expect him. Matthew 24:42-44 NIV

Jesus raises the flag of caution by giving the two signs of falsehood—***miracles*** and ***secrecy***. He then instills courage in the sincere seekers of truth by asking them ***to search, and to be spiritually ready*** because the hour comes and goes undetected, just as a thief comes and goes undetected. Then Jesus asks this question, and offers this encouragement:

> Who then is the faithful and wise servant [leader], whom the master has put in charge of the servants in his household ***to give them their food at the proper time***? It will be good for that servant whose master finds him doing so when he returns. I tell you the truth, he will put him in charge of all his possessions. Matthew 24:45-47 NIV

In the preceding verses, Jesus encourages the wise and faithful religious leaders to prepare Christians for His advent, to give them the spiritual food or the true knowledge they need to recognize their Master. After instilling courage to investigate, Jesus gives this warning to those leaders who fail "to offer the food at the proper time" to their followers:

> But suppose that servant [leader] is wicked and says to himself, "***My master is staying away a long time***," and he then begins to beat [spiritually abuse] his fellow servants [followers] and to ***eat and drink with*** [spiritually] ***drunkards***. The master of that servant will come on a day when he does not expect him and at an hour he is not aware of. He will cut him to pieces and assign him a place with the hypocrites, where there will be weeping and gnashing of teeth. Matthew 24:48-51 NIV

The warning is addressed to unwise and unfaithful religious leaders, who do not do their job of preparing Christians for their Lord. It is directed at negligent, worldly, and self-righteous leaders who keep telling people that the time for the coming of the Master is in the future. The implication of Jesus' prophecy is clear: The advent takes place, but it remains undetected by many religious leaders. They lack the wisdom to search and recognize the time and are not faithful in obeying their Master's instructions for finding Him. They keep telling people that the Master has not yet come, they keep pointing to the future, saying "He is staying away a long time." These leaders by their very teachings—discouraging search, instilling unjustified fear of false prophets, and always predicting that Christ will come in the future—themselves become false prophets! Statements like the following are found in virtually every book of biblical prophecy:

> His [Jesus'] return will be very, very soon![53]

Today's books of prophecy are filled with countless speculations about the future coming of Christ. Prophesying in the name of the Lord is a popular topic and subject of debate and disagreement, especially among evangelical Christians. Unlike evangelicals, the Catholic church avoids the issue. Catholics seldom talk about the second Advent. Countless books of prophecy are being published and promoted. The authors and promoters of these predictions think they are doing a great service to their Lord. Notice how clearly, in the following statement, Jesus predicted their illusion that they should be rewarded for making predictions in His name. Notice the phrase "***in Your name***." It indicates that ***these false prophets are Christians***:

> Not everyone who says to Me, 'Lord, Lord,' shall enter the kingdom of heaven, but ***he who does the will of My Father*** in heaven. Many will say to Me in that day, 'Lord, Lord, ***have we not prophesied IN YOUR NAME***?...And then I will declare to them, 'I never knew you; depart from Me, you who practice lawlessness!' Matthew 7:21-23 NKJ

What is "***the will of the Father***"? It is to acknowledge our shortcomings and ignorance before ***the Glory of God*** and to listen to ***His*** interpretation:

> ...all have sinned and ***fall short of the glory of God***...
> Romans 3:23 NIV

> ...judge nothing before the appointed time; wait till the Lord comes. ***He will bring to light what is hidden in darkness***... I Corinthians 4:5 NIV

As we just noted, the negligent leaders, who are supposed to give people spiritual food or true knowledge about the return of the Master, remain preoccupied with their physical and selfish needs, such as eating and drinking, and associating with people like themselves, who are "drunkards" or unaware of what has happened or is happening. They are so deeply asleep, so unaware, so self-righteous that they even prevent other Christians from paying attention to or watching for the news of the advent of their Master, Bahá'u'lláh. What is their punishment? Where will they go? According to Jesus, their final destiny is hell, "the place of weeping and gnashing of teeth." Why are they sent to hell? Because of their hypocrisy. They pay lip service to the Master, but do not accomplish their task of preparing Christians for Him. They fail to encourage them to watch, to inquire and to investigate. That is exactly what is happening today. Instead of helping Christians to search, many leaders keep telling them just the opposite: to wait and wish, and to keep their churches and their hearts closed to all outsiders. They themselves refuse to investigate. Notice how clearly Jesus predicted the response of the people of our age, especially the religious leaders, to Bahá'u'lláh's invitation.

We have no right to judge people. ***We must love and respect every human being***. If we break this rule, we fall from grace. Instead of judging we should learn about ***God's judgment***. The purpose of knowing is to protect our soul from denying our Master. If there were no need to know the severe consequences of our denial, why would God give us that knowledge? ***There is a clear difference between knowing and judging***.

You should have noticed that God is extremely angry at those who occupy positions of authority, but use those positions for selfish ends. Jesus' words are aimed at those leaders who neglect their duty to stay awake and watchful, who encourage complacency rather than courage and a need for an urgent search for the Master. Their action may not appear too serious to us, but how does God view it? He calls those who engage in this violation ***wicked*** and ***hypocritical***. Notice the harsh metaphors Jesus uses to describe their punishment:

- They will be cut to pieces.
- They will be assigned a place with the hypocrites.
- They will be sent to hell, a place of sadness and weeping for lost opportunities, and of anger (grinding of teeth) at their negligence to accomplish their divine duty.

Why does God condemn them so harshly? Because they are hypocrites: they say they believe but they don't. How would you feel if your fiancé or your husband told you that he loved you, but in his heart he loved someone else?

God's anger grows intense, especially against the privileged, who have ample opportunities, but fail to act. He calls them hypocrites and wicked. Why? The backbone of all virtues is honesty and sincerity. Such people lack those prized virtues.

Daniel uses the same two words—***wise*** and ***wicked***—to describe either the leaders who accomplish their task or those who fail to do so.

> Many shall purify themselves and be refined, making themselves shining white, but ***the wicked*** shall continue in wickedness and none of them shall understand; only ***the wise leaders*** shall understand [the meaning of prophecies].
>
> Daniel 12:10 NEB

Daniel offered the preceding statement along with a time prophecy that specifies the year of the advent of Bahá'u'lláh. (See *I Shall Come Again.*)

In the parable of the talents, Jesus used one additional word to describe the servant, or the leader, who fails to invest his talents to search for the Master. He called him not only ***wicked*** but ***lazy*** as well:

- The fearful leader says: "So I was afraid and went out and hid your talent in the ground..." (Matthew 25:25 NIV)
- The Master responds: "You ***wicked***, ***lazy*** servant!" (Matthew 25:26 NIV)

The question is this: ***Why are so many Christians afraid of being deceived, but not afraid of denying the very Lord and Master they love and worship?***

True Christians—Christ lovers—need not fear Bahá'u'lláh, the Glory of God, whose magnificent rainbow has circled the world. They do not need to run away from the glorious "lightning" that flashed forth from the East to the West. They need fear only "***the Evil One***" and "***the Idol***" who stood high for a moment, and dared to challenge the awesome powers of heaven, but "***the lightning***" struck them dead and turned them into an abandoned "***corpse and carcass***" in the dark of disbelief and remoteness from God and His glorious angels.

> For as ***the lightning*** comes from the east and flashes as far as the west, so will be the coming of the Son of Man.

Wherever ***the corpse*** is, there the vultures will gather.
Matthew 24:27-28 NRSV

In the Holy Books it is recorded that when the Sun of Truth dawns, it will appear in the East, and its light will be reflected in the West. Already its dawning has taken place in the East, and its signs are appearing in the West. Its illumination shall spread rapidly and widely in the Occident. The Sun of Truth has risen in Persia, and its effulgence is now manifest here in America. This is the greatest proof of its appearance in the horizon of the world, as recorded in the heavenly Books. Praise be to God! That which is prophesied in the Holy Books has been fulfilled.[54] 'Abdu'l-Bahá

Say: In the East the light of His Revelation hath broken; in the West have appeared the signs of His dominion. Ponder this in your hearts, O people, and be not of those who have turned a deaf ear to the admonitions of Him Who is the Almighty, the All-Praised. Let the Breeze of God awaken you. Verily, it hath wafted over the world. Well is it with him that hath discovered the fragrance thereof and been accounted among the well-assured.[55]
Bahá'u'lláh

Jesus shone as brightly as the sun. He was the light of the world (John 8:12), but He went unnoticed by most people. The historians of His time barely mentioned Him. To the majority of humankind, that light still is invisible. Some scholars have even come to the conclusion that Jesus did not exist because of scarcity of evidence about Him! They assume that He was simply a fictitious figure created by early Christians!

Human beings have always cast their vote for a victorious Redeemer. It is hard to imagine a divine Being who is gentle and defenseless. It is hard to follow and believe in someone who accepts ridicule, humiliation, suffering, and death at the hand of his enemies as if they are gifts from heaven. The next few chapters shatter this entrenched illusion.

6

I Was Sick and in Prison and You Did Not Look After Me

The prophecies and parables pointing to rejection are found throughout the Bible. It is hard to believe so many have failed to notice them. Often our attitudes and expectations, rather than reality, determine our perceptions. Just as the color of the glasses we wear affects every object we see, so do our attitudes and expectations, especially if they are ingrained upon us from childhood by parents and culture.

One reason prophecies of rejection have remained unnoticed is a deep desire in all human beings for rewards without delay and effort. It is far more pleasant to see the City of God descend upon us with heavenly splendor than to arise and build that City brick by brick.

But God always has work for us to do. He has a master plan that unfolds progressively, "little by little day by day." Many Jewish and Christian scholars acknowledge God's ***progressive*** plan, but make an exception for the Advent of their own Redeemer. Consider this statement from a Jewish scholar, rabbi Avrohom Chaim, who believes that:

> It is both unreasonable and unwise to pass judgment on a work of art before it has been completed; even a masterpiece may look like a grotesque mass of strokes and colors, prior to its completion. Human history is God's masterpiece. Physical creation was completed at the end of the sixth day, but the spiritual development of mankind will continue...When the panorama of human history is completed, the seventh millennium will be ushered in as the day of everlasting Sabbath. At that time all Adam's descendants will look back and admire God's ***completed*** masterpiece.[1]

To appreciate God's progressive plan, consider this analogy. To build a house, we must go through three stages:

- Prepare the ground. (The birth of the global village.)
- Obtain the materials—the bricks, the blocks, the doors, the windows, and the lights. (The experiences, insights, and appreciations the human race has gained), and then
- Begin to build.

Human history has passed through the first two stages. We are now at the beginning of the third stage. Only now are we given the blueprint for building God's Kingdom on earth as it is in heaven. Even after the House of God is built, the work will not end. It will need constant care and repair.

Recently two famous theologians representing Judaism and Christianity conducted a debate on national television about certain Christian beliefs. Among the ideas they exchanged was the validity of Jesus' claim as the Messiah of the Jews.

The Jewish theologian said that according to the prophecies of the Hebrew Scriptures the Messiah must bring peace. About 2,000 years have passed since the advent of Jesus and still peace has not prevailed upon our planet. The Christian theologian responded that according to the same prophecies the Messiah must also suffer; He cannot do both. (Bringing peace requires a great deal of power. A person with power does not fall prey to people's cruelty.) The Christian theologian concluded that the fulfillment of one part of the prophecy meant we can be certain that the other part too will be fulfilled. Then the Jewish theologian wondered how long the Jews should wait for the second part. (They have already suffered; what they now need is glory.)

Most Christians of today cherish a dream similar to that cherished by the people of Israel since ancient times. They cannot believe that their Redeemer comes to suffer again. (He has already suffered enough; now He needs glory.) Like the people of Israel, they can quote prophecies to prove their point.

Christian authors often indicate that the Jews somehow missed the prophecies about a suffering Messiah. Examples like this are found abundantly in their works:

> It is most unlikely that the Jews would have rejected an earthly kingdom. What they rejected, was a Messiah who disappointed them by not carrying out their expectations. Had they studied the prophecies, they would have known that He would come as "a man of sorrows, and acquainted with grief," (Isaiah 53:3) who was "wounded for our transgressions," and "was bruised for our iniquities: the chastisement of our peace was upon him; and with his stripes we are healed" (Isaiah 53:5).[2]

Christian authors and scholars look objectively at the prophecies of the ***first*** Advent, but when they see the prophecies of the ***second*** Advent, their vision and standards suddenly change. Consider this statement from Dr. Ray Stedman:

> The last time it [the world] saw him [Jesus] was on a bloody cross, writhing in the agonies of death, apparently a shameful failure with no glory, no power and no success. But when it sees him again it will see him coming triumphant in power and glory.[3]

This chapter is written to awaken Christians to many prophecies that point to suffering, to tests and trials—the ones they somehow miss! It presents prophecies that seldom if ever receive due attention: those that do not conform to the prevailing expectations.

> How numerous the verses which have been revealed concerning the grievous tests ye shall experience on the Day of Judgment, yet it appeareth that ye have never perused them; and how vast the number of revealed traditions regarding the trials which will overtake you on the Day of Our Return, and yet ye seem never to have set your eyes upon them.[4]
>
> The Báb

Why do the great Messengers and Redeemers suffer? Why does God offer the deepest and bitterest cup of pain to the Ones He loves the most? Why does He allow some cruel people to oppose and persecute those who respond to His call?

- Pain and suffering add diversity and contrast to life's portrait. Without them the world would lose much of its luster and drama. Compare the birth of each religion to the birth of a baby. The joy and honor of raising children comes partly from the pains, the hazards, and the challenges of raising them!

- Every achievement requires a sacrifice. The celestial Seed must sacrifice itself to bear heavenly fruits. Creating a new civilization requires the supreme sacrifice.

- God's Messengers and Redeemers always serve as models of perfection for humankind. They excel us in every imaginable way. Their resignation to their sufferings shows their patience, trust, endurance, and detachment from worldly pleasures and desires.

- Their willingness to subject themselves to every conceivable loss and humiliation serves as the first and most obvious evidence of their dedication to the divine. Such supreme self-sacrifice, detachment, and devotion rule out any ulterior motives, any selfish desires in advancing their claim.

Consider these critical questions from Bahá'u'lláh:

> Do ye imagine that He seeketh His own interests, when He hath, at all times, been threatened by the swords of the enemies; or that He seeketh the vanities of the world, after He hath been imprisoned in the most desolate of cities? Be fair in your judgment and follow not the footsteps of the unjust.[5]

The purpose of suffering becomes evident in the light of all other proofs and signs of distinction. We can appreciate the wisdom of pain and adversity only when we discern the light behind the clouds, when we recognize its higher purpose. Its wonders become manifest when we see the wisest and the most spiritually advanced individuals the world has ever known endure it and even accept it as a glorious gift from God.

The State of the World

> How long, O you sons of men, will you turn my glory to shame?
> Psalms 4:2 NKJ

Prophecies portray a negative picture of the people of our time. This picture gives us our first clue about the way the expected Redeemer will be treated.

> But when the son of man comes, will he find faith on earth?
> Luke 18:8 NEB

If people are not faithful to the one they know and worship, how can they be faithful to the new Redeemer, to the One they do not know? What can be expected from those who have lost their faith, spiritual strength, and sincerity? No prophecy could better describe the state of religion in our time than this:

> For the time will come when men will not put up with sound doctrine. Instead, to suit their own desires, they will gather around them a great number of teachers to say what their itching ears want to hear. ***They will turn their ears away from the truth and turn aside to myths.***
>
> II Timothy 4:3-4 NIV

Consider also these well-known prophecies:

> But know this, that in the last days perilous times will come: for men will be lovers of themselves, lovers of money, boasters, proud, blasphemers, disobedient to parents, unthankful, unholy, unloving, unforgiving, slanderers, without self-control, brutal, despisers of good, traitors, headstrong, haughty, lovers of pleasure rather than lovers of God, having a form of godliness but denying its power. And from such people turn away! For of this sort are those who creep into households and make captives of gullible women loaded down with sins, led away by various lusts, always learning and never able to come to the knowledge of the truth. Now as Jannes and Jambres resisted Moses, so do these also resist the truth: men of corrupt minds, disapproved concerning the faith; but they will progress no further, for their folly will be manifest to all, as theirs also was.
>
> II Timothy 3:1-9 NKJ

Do not such prophecies apply to followers of all religions, including Christians? Can the followers of any religion claim an exemption? Christian author Van Impe states that all the 19 signs prophesied in the preceding prophecy have come to pass.[6]

Several prophecies indicate that the people of our time will be drunk. Drunkenness can be both physical and spiritual. It can come from alcohol, drugs, and being surrounded by worldly comforts and wonders. It can also come from a false sense of security, self-satisfaction, and self-righteousness.

Such states of the mind create unawareness. They prevent people from recognizing spiritual blessings surrounding them. Today a state of spiritual drunkenness pervades all the peoples of the earth:

> We see men drunken in this Day, the Day in which men and angels have been gathered together.[7] Bahá'u'lláh

> Thou hast made thy people drunk with a bitter draught, thou hast given us wine that makes us stagger.✣
>
> Psalms 60:3 NEB

Our age is not unique. Whenever God sends a Redeemer, He faces people who are at the lowest point of spiritual development.

> For whatsoever the people of a former Dispensation have manifested, the same hath been shown by the people of this latter generation.[8] Bahá'u'lláh

Micah portrays a rather detailed description of human life on our planet in this "terrible day of the Lord:"

> Woe is me! For I am as when the summer fruits have been gathered, as when the vintage grapes have been gleaned, and there is no cluster to eat, no first-ripe fig for which my appetite craves. The godly man has perished from the earth, and there is none upright among men; they all lie in wait for blood; each hunts his brother with a net. Both their hands are put forth and are upon what is evil to do it diligently; the prince and the judge ask for a bribe, and the great man utters his evil desire. Thus they twist between them (the course of justice). The best of them is like a brier; the most upright or the straightest is as a thorn hedge. The day of your watchmen, even of God's judgment and your punishment is come; now shall be their perplexity and confusion. Trust not in a neighbor, put not

✣ God does not give us "wine." He simply gives us ***the ability*** to create it and drink it. Without this power, we would have no freedom.

confidence in a friend; keep the doors of your mouth from her who lies in your bosom. For the son dishonors the father, the daughter rises up against her mother, the daughter-in-law against her mother-in-law; a man's enemies are the men of his own house. But as for me, I will look to the Lord and (confident) in Him I will keep watch; I will wait with hope and expectancy for the God of my salvation; my God will hear me. Micah 7:1-7 AB

Bahá'u'lláh confirms Micah's and Paul's description of the people of our time. He portrays the same picture of our generation as did Jesus of His:

What an unbelieving and perverse ***generation***!
Christ (Matt. 17:17)

All this ***generation*** could offer Us were wounds from its darts, and the only cup it proffered to Our lips was the cup of its venom. On our neck We still bear the scar of chains, and upon Our body are imprinted the evidences of an unyielding cruelty.[9] Bahá'u'lláh

Reflect upon the villainous behavior of this ***generation***, and witness their astounding ingratitude. Observe how they have closed their eyes to all this glory...[10] Bahá'u'lláh

Had it been in my power, I would have, under no circumstances, consented to distinguish myself amongst men, for the Name I bear utterly disdaineth to associate itself with this ***generation*** whose tongues are sullied and whose hearts are false.[11] Bahá'u'lláh

Denial of the Bahá'í Faith is even more puzzling: The evidence pointing to its divine origin is far stronger than the evidence pointing to any other Faith. Apparently the abundance of proofs and prophecies seem to make no difference to the sleeping masses. A person whose eyes are covered cannot tell the difference between the sunlight and candlelight.

Though the clearest proofs attest the truth of His Cause ...yet, behold how this ***generation*** hath rejected His authority, and rebelled against Him![12] Bahá'u'lláh

> Say: "The True One is come evident as the shining sun; O pity that He should have come into the city of the blind!"[13]
>
> Bahá'u'lláh

> Their eyes are drunken; they are indeed a blind people.[14]
>
> Bahá'u'lláh

What about the leaders of our time?

> In that day...O My people, your leaders cause you to err, and confuse (destroy and swallow up) the course of your paths. Isaiah 3:7, 12 AB

If people are worldly, if the leaders cause them to err, confuse them, and destroy their paths, then what can we expect except apathy, ignorance, and denial? The role of the leaders has never changed:

> Is there a single one of our rulers who has believed in him...? John 7:48 NEB

Bahá'u'lláh confirms:

> Leaders of religion, in every age, have hindered their people from attaining the shores of eternal salvation, inasmuch as they held the reins of authority in their mighty grasp. Some for the lust of leadership, others through want of knowledge and understanding, have been the cause of the deprivation of the people. By their sanction and authority, every Prophet of God hath drunk from the chalice of sacrifice…Content with a transitory dominion, they have deprived themselves of an everlasting sovereignty. Thus, their eyes beheld not the light of the countenance of the Well-Beloved…For this reason, in all sacred books mention hath been made of the divines of every age.[15]

And again:

> …the reins of every community have fallen into the grasp of foolish leaders, who lead after their own whims and desire. On their tongue the mention of God hath become an empty name; in their midst His holy Word a dead letter.

> Such is the sway of their desires, that the lamp of conscience and reason hath been quenched in their hearts…[16]
>
> The denials and protestations of these leaders of religion have, in the main, been due to their lack of knowledge and understanding.[17]

The main problem is this: ***no one is willing to admit that the prophecies that portray a negative picture of the people of our time may point to himself***. Everyone believes that they point to someone else! Christians believe that they refer to peoples of other faiths and no faith and to non-churchgoers, especially those who are not "born again." Non-churchgoers believe that they refer to the established church, which is dominated by division, worldliness, inertia, apathy, hypocrisy, a sense of pride, and self-righteousness. It may be hard to find even one person on our planet who would admit the relevance of these prophecies to himself!

Here is one more prophecy that describes the spiritual state of the people of our time. It specifically asks ***the Christian churches*** to hear its message:

> I know your deeds; ***you have a reputation of being alive, but you are dead. Wake up!*** Strengthen what remains and is about to die, for I have not found your deeds complete in the sight of my God...But if you do not wake up, I will come like a thief, and you will not know at what time I will come to you. ***He who has an ear, let him hear what the Spirit says to the churches***. Revelation 3:1-6 NIV

It may be helpful to see the reasons why people always deny their Redeemers:

- Conformity to social groups or peers.
- Unreasonable expectations from the Redeemer due to literal-mindedness.
- Fear of rejection by relatives and friends.
- Fear of being deceived.

- Conditioning of behavior and attitudes; the emotional aspect of religion grows too deep to allow thought processes to work.
- Lack of faith.
- Lack of self-confidence in one's ability to find the truth.
- Unawareness, lack of knowledge of the new Revelation, or having preconceived notions about it.
- The example and influence of religious leaders.
- Attachment to one's beliefs.
- Worldliness, selfishness.
- Apathy, negligence.
- Impurity of the heart, lack of sincerity.
- Shortcoming of the new believers; their inability to gain knowledge and teach their Faith with tact and wisdom.

Christian author Dr. David Reagan gives four reasons for lack of interest in the Second Coming: unbelief, ignorance, fear, and carnality.[18]

For 2,000 years Christians have been converting people from all religions to their faith. Now they see themselves in the same position they have put others. The roles are reversed. They feel this way, "We have always converted others. Now you have come to convert us! No way!" We should sympathize with anyone in this position.

The way Christians can become impartial and objective is to put themselves in the position of those they have converted. They should ask, "What attitude would I expect from a Jew or a Buddhist to become Christian?" They should adopt that attitude.

If people believe someone has come to deceive them, they take a defensive position. This is the position many Christians are assuming, yet they expect an opposite position from others!

Reasons for denial are extremely complex, interrelated, and circular. For instance, people deny because of ignorance. But what causes ignorance? Perhaps laziness. What causes laziness? Perhaps lack of purpose. What causes lack of purpose? Perhaps ignorance.

Can we find deeper reasons for ignorance? Yes, ignorance can be purposeful. Why? Perhaps because of fear. Why? Because the believer fears the loss of his spiritual possessions. Why? Because he lacks faith. Why? Because he keeps himself intentionally ignorant.

The same rule applies to the ***strategies*** people use to remain ignorant. Instead of investigating, a person may depend on religious leaders. Why? Perhaps he does not want to take the time to investigate. Why? Because he is worldly. Why? Because he lacks faith. Why? Because he is ignorant. Why? Because he depends on religious leaders.

Why do religious leaders deny? Because they are security conscious. Why? Because they lack faith...What strategies do religious leaders use to deny? By far the most common strategy is literal-mindedness. Why? Because they have been influenced by their theology professors. Why are the theology professors literal minded? Because of tradition. Why? Because it is easy to stay on the track. Why? Because they keep themselves ignorant Why? Because they lack faith...

> "But when the Son of Man comes, will he find faith on earth?" (Luke 18:8 NEB). "At that time many will turn away from the faith" (Matthew 24:10 NIV). "the love of most [for truth] will grow cold" (Matthew 24:12 NIV).

Matthew 24:10 is also translated as, "And then shall many stumble." Christian scholar William Biederwolf interprets the verse by saying that many Christians will "stumble...because of new phases of truth presented [to them], or because of the delayed coming of the Lord."[19] This indeed has happened. Many Christians reject Bahá'u'lláh because He reveals "new phases of truth" that require them to leave their traditions and comfort zones. Many have also stumbled because they think the Lord has delayed His return.

Isaiah predicts that the Lord, the Redeemer of our time, shall ***rebuke many people***:

> He shall judge between the nations, and ***rebuke many people***... Isaiah 2:4 NKJ

Why would the Lord rebuke many people if they welcomed Him? Both the Báb and Bahá'u'lláh have fulfilled Isaiah's prophecy. Consider these words of rebuke from *The Hidden Words of Bahá'u'lláh*. Notice the divine authority with which He speaks:

> **O MOVING FORM OF DUST!**
> I desire communion with thee, but thou wouldst put no trust in Me. The sword of thy rebellion hath felled the tree of thy hope. At all times I am near unto thee, but thou art ever far from Me. ***Imperishable glory I have chosen for thee, yet boundless shame thou hast chosen for thyself. While there is yet time, return, and lose not thy chance***.[20]
>
> **O YE THAT ARE LYING AS DEAD ON THE COUCH OF HEEDLESSNESS!**
> Ages have passed and your precious lives are well-nigh ended, yet not a single breath of purity hath reached Our court of holiness from you. ***Though immersed in the ocean of misbelief, yet with your lips ye profess the one true faith of God***. Him whom I abhor ye have loved, and of My foe ye have made a friend. Notwithstanding, ***ye walk on My earth complacent and self-satisfied, heedless that My earth is weary of you and everything within it shunneth you. Were ye but to open your eyes, ye would, in truth, prefer a myriad griefs unto this joy, and would count death itself better than this life***.[21]
>
> **O SON OF DESIRE!**
> The learned and the wise have for long years striven and failed to attain the presence of the All-Glorious; they have spent their lives in search of Him, yet did not behold the beauty of His countenance. Thou without the least effort

didst attain thy goal, and without search hast obtained the object of thy quest. Yet, notwithstanding, ***thou didst remain so wrapt in the veil of self, that thine eyes beheld not the beauty of the Beloved***, nor did thy hand touch the hem of His robe. Ye that have eyes, behold and wonder.[22]

O YE THAT ARE FOOLISH,
YET HAVE A NAME TO BE WISE!
Wherefore do ye wear the guise of shepherds, when inwardly ye have become wolves, intent upon My flock? Ye are even as the star, which riseth ere the dawn, and which, though it seem radiant and luminous, leadeth the wayfarers of My city astray into the paths of perdition.[23]

O YE SEEMING FAIR YET INWARDLY FOUL!
Ye are like clear but bitter water, which to outward seeming is crystal pure but of which, when tested by the divine Assayer, not a drop is accepted. Yea, the sun beam falls alike upon the dust and the mirror, yet differ they in reflection even as doth the star from the earth: nay, immeasurable is the difference![24]

O LOVERS OF WORLDLY DESIRE!
Even as the swiftness of lightning ye have passed by the Beloved One, and have set your hearts on satanic fancies. Ye bow the knee before your vain imagining, and call it truth. Ye turn your eyes towards the thorn, and name it a flower. Not a pure breath have ye breathed, nor hath the breeze of detachment been wafted from the meadows of your hearts. Ye have cast to the winds the loving counsels of the Beloved and have effaced them utterly from the tablet of your hearts, and even as the beasts of the field, ye move and have your being within the pastures of desire and passion.[25]

Consider also these words of rebuke from the Báb:

What hath befallen you, O people of the Book? Will ye not fear the One true God, He Who is your Lord, the Ancient of Days?...Hath your learning deluded you by

> ***reason of your impiety?*** Take ye heed then, for verily your God, the Lord of Eternal Truth, is with you and in very truth is watchful over you...[26]

In the Book of Revelation Jesus uttered perhaps the harshest example of rebuke found in all sacred Scriptures. It is directed at apathetic and lukewarm Christians who say they believe in Him, yet ignore the news of His return:

> I know your deeds, that you are neither cold nor hot. I wish you were either one or the other! So, because you are lukewarm—neither hot nor cold—I am about to spit you out of my mouth. You say, 'I am rich; I have acquired wealth and do not need a thing.' But you do not realize that ***you are wretched, pitiful, poor, blind and naked***. I counsel you to buy from me gold refined in the fire, so you can become rich; and white clothes to wear, so you can cover your shameful nakedness; and salve to put on your eyes, so you can see. ***Those whom I love I rebuke...***
> Christ (Rev. 3:15-19)

Notice God's infinite love for the people He calls ***wretched, pitiful, poor, blind and naked***. He rebukes them in such harsh words, and then He says He loves them!

Epistles to the Kings

Micah predicts that the Lord will rebuke "strong" or powerful nations:

> Now it shall come to pass in the latter days that the mountain of the Lord's house shall be established on the top of the mountains, and shall be exalted above the hills; and peoples shall flow to it. Many nations shall come and say, "Come, and let us go up to the mountain of the Lord, to the house of the God of Jacob; He will teach us His ways, and we shall walk in His paths." For out of Zion the law shall go forth, and the word of the Lord from Jerusalem. ***He shall judge between many peoples, and rebuke strong nations afar off.***
> Micah 4:1-3 NKJ

Bahá'u'lláh sent Epistles to the most powerful nations of His time. (See *The Proclamation of Bahá'u'lláh.*) He both counseled them and rebuked them for their injustices. To Napoleon III He wrote:

> For what thou hast done, thy kingdom shall be thrown into confusion, and thine empire shall pass from thine hands, as a punishment for that which thou hast wrought. Then wilt thou know how thou hast plainly erred. Commotions shall seize all the people in that land, unless thou arisest to help this Cause, and followest Him Who is the Spirit of God (Jesus Christ) in this, the Straight Path. Hath thy pomp made thee proud? By My Life! It shall not endure; nay, it shall soon pass away, unless thou holdest fast by this firm Cord. We see abasement hastening after thee, whilst thou art of the heedless. It behoveth thee when thou hearest His Voice calling from the seat of glory to cast away all that thou possessest, and cry out: "Here am I, O Lord of all that is in heaven and all that is on earth!"[27]

> Exultest thou over the treasures thou dost possess, knowing they shall perish? Rejoicest thou in that thou rulest a span of earth, when the whole world, in the estimation of the people of Bahá, is worth as much as the black in the eye of a dead ant? Abandon it unto such as have set their affections upon it, and turn thou unto Him Who is the Desire of the world. Whither are gone the proud and their palaces? Gaze thou into their tombs, that thou mayest profit by this example, inasmuch as We made it a lesson unto every beholder. Were the breezes of Revelation to seize thee, thou wouldst flee the world, and turn unto the Kingdom, and wouldst expend all thou possessest, that thou mayest draw nigh unto this sublime Vision.[28]

Chapter 110 of Psalms is devoted entirely to the Lord's victory over His enemies:

> The Lord says to my Lord: "Sit at my right hand until I make your enemies ***a footstool for your feet***."...***you will***

> ***rule in the midst of your enemies***...The Lord is at your right hand; ***he will crush kings*** on the day of his wrath. He will judge the nations, heaping up the [spiritually] dead and crushing the rulers of the whole earth.
>
> Psalms 110:1-6 NIV

All the kings who were addressed by Bahá'u'lláh were literally "crushed." They were either assassinated, deposed, or humiliated in defeat. They were indeed made a "footstool" of divine power. Even their names are forgotten; they are only symbols of history. But Bahá'u'lláh's Kingdom continues to extend until it will encompass the whole world. Both Bahá'u'lláh and the country that was later born (Israel) have been ruling in the midst of their enemies.

Bahá'u'lláh showed His supreme glory and power even during His exile and imprisonment. 'Abdu'l-Bahá testifies to Bahá'u'lláh's literal sovereignty, especially during the final years of His earthly life:

> He [Bahá'u'lláh] proclaimed His Cause in prison and hoisted His standard under the menace of the sword. He was a person against whom two reigning monarchs arose in enmity and were bent upon His extermination. These two sovereigns gave orders that the Blessed Beauty [Bahá'u'lláh] should be imprisoned in one room.[29]
>
> Although the policy of Sultán 'Abdu'l-Hamíd was harsher than ever; although he constantly insisted on his Captive's strict confinement—still, the Blessed Beauty now lived, as everyone knows, with all power and glory...occasionally His tent would be pitched on the heights of Mount Carmel. Friends from everywhere presented themselves and gained an audience. The people and the government authorities witnessed it all, yet no one so much as breathed a word. And this is one of Bahá'u'lláh's greatest miracles:...The prison changed into a palace, the jail itself became a Garden of Eden. Such a thing has not occurred in history before; no former age has seen its like: that a man confined to a prison should move about with authority and

> might; that one in chains should carry the fame of the Cause of God to the high heavens, should win splendid victories in both East and West, and should, by His almighty pen, subdue the world.[30]

Consider the following example and try to see if anything like it has ever happened. Once an order came from the capital that two individuals must visit Bahá'u'lláh. One of them was "the governor of the city" who was Turkish, the other was a European who also had a significant position in the government. The governor asked for permission to visit Bahá'u'lláh. Permission was granted. When the two visitors attained the presence of Bahá'u'lláh, they felt so transformed and humbled they sat on their knees near the door on the ground. Out of courtesy, they refused to use the water-pipe that was brought for them. Their humility astonished all those who were present.[31] Has anything like this ever happened? This is a total reversal of roles: the Prisoner acts as the ruler, and the ruler as the prisoner!

Which Comes First, Suffering or Glory?

The Book of Revelation shows the order in which suffering and glory come:

> And I saw a Lamb [the Báb] standing as though it had been slain...worthy is the Lamb that hath been ***slain to receive the power and glory***... Revelation 5:6, 12

The prophecy shows clearly that "power and glory" come as a result of being slain. The statement made by Jesus in His Olivet discourse about His return clearly shows which comes first, suffering or glory. Chapters 24 and 25 of Matthew are parts of the same discourse. The two chapters contain the most significant instructions Jesus gave about His return, delivered just before His crucifixion. That discourse may indeed be considered His Will and Testament to His faithful followers. As we noted in Volume I, at the beginning of His discourse Jesus twice referred to His suffering and rejection by the people:

- But ***first*** he must suffer and be rejected... (Luke 17:25 NIV)[✣]
- Just as it was in the days of Noah... (Luke 17:26 NIV)

At the end of His discourse, Jesus predicted again suffering and pain for His new followers and Himself:

> Then he [the Son of Man] will say to those on his left, 'Depart from me, you who are cursed, into the eternal fire prepared for the devil and his angels. For I was hungry and you gave me nothing to eat, I was thirsty and you gave me nothing to drink, I was a stranger and you did not invite me in, I needed clothes and you did not clothe me, I was sick and in prison and you did not look after me.' They also will answer, 'Lord, when did we see you hungry or thirsty or a stranger or needing clothes or sick or in prison, and did not help you?' He will reply, 'I tell you the truth, whatever you did not do for one of the least of these [lowliest], you did not do for me.' Then they will go away to eternal punishment, but the righteous to eternal life.
> Matthew 25:41-46 NIV

Bahá'u'lláh spent the whole span of His ministry, about 40 years, a prisoner and an exile, a stranger in different countries and cities. Only a few of those who wanted to help could reach Him. But many of His suffering servants, who had not lost their freedom, were reachable, and could be helped. Those who extended a helping hand to these suffering servants, indeed extended it to the Master Himself.

We should note that the above prophecy refers not only to the sufferings of the Redeemer's followers as stated earlier, but also to the sufferings of the Redeemer Himself. It seems

[✣] We should note that Jesus used both the pronouns "I" and "He" to refer to Himself.

quite unlikely that the Redeemer's followers would suffer, while He would remain in safety and comfort.

All the pains and anguish included in the above prophecy (being hungry, thirsty, a stranger, without clothes, sick, and homeless) came true in Bahá'u'lláh's life. For instance, when He was imprisoned in a horrible dungeon known as Síyáh-Chál (the Black Pit), He endured every physical pain and discomfort imaginable. Imagine a person accustomed to comfort experiencing all these 12 tortures, pains, and annoyances simultaneously:

- ***Total darkness***. The underground prison had neither lights nor windows.
- ***A terrible stench***. About 150 of the worst criminals were thrown in that dark, deep, damp dungeon with no air circulation or sanitary facilities.
- ***Mud***. The ground was covered with several inches of filthy mud and mire.
- ***Heavy chain on His neck***. To hold the weight of the chain, Bahá'u'lláh had to press His hand against the ground covered with slime up to His wrist.
- ***Stocks on His feet***.
- ***Fleas***. The closed environment was infested with fleas.
- ***Hunger and thirst***. For the first three days and nights Bahá'u'lláh received neither food nor water.
- ***Severe pain and lack of mobility***. Bahá'u'lláh's feet were put in stocks and on His neck was placed a chain so heavy that He could not hold Himself straight. From the weight of the harsh metal, His neck became inflamed and injured.
- ***Little if any sleep***. Under those terrible conditions Bahá'u'lláh could hardly sleep.
- ***Lack of clothes***. His outer garments were stripped away on His way to prison.

- ***Illness***. Because of the unsanitary conditions, and poison put in His food, Bahá'u'lláh suffered grave illness.
- ***Homelessness***. All His property was confiscated.

Bahá'u'lláh also suffered mental anguish:

- Being surrounded by the worst criminals who had little if any hope of survival or freedom.
- Anxiety about His family. Bahá'u'lláh's family, which included young children ('Abdu'l-Bahá was then nine years old), were at the mercy of fanatical mobs filled with rage and incited to vengeance.
- Deep grief and concern for His devoted and distinguished followers who were being hunted, tortured, and killed by enraged mobs outside the prison.
- Concern about the future. From that prison Bahá'u'lláh was banished to strange lands. He became a stranger (an exile) as the prophecy states. Never again did He see His homeland.
- Loneliness. "During this time none of His friends were able to get access to Him."[32] Only His nine-year-old Son was once allowed to see Him.
- Deep sorrow for people who were rejecting God's choicest blessings and bounties.

Isaiah utters a similar prophecy:

> I looked, but there was no one to help, I was appalled that no one gave support; so my own arms worked salvation for me...
> Isaiah 63:5 NIV

Bahá'u'lláh's arrest and imprisonment in that dungeon gives us only a glimpse of the sufferings that He endured for almost forty years. How could anyone survive the scourge of such unrelenting pressures? How much pain can a human being endure? Why would God allow the One He loved the most to go through so much suffering? Did not Jesus go through similar ordeals?

It is helpful to see in their context all the events that occurred in the Síyáh-Chál (the Black Pit) as portrayed by Shoghi Effendi's masterly pen. This account includes the testimony of Bahá'u'lláh Himself, and the recollections of 'Abdu'l-Bahá as well:

> From Níyávarán [a resort town near Tihrán] He was conducted "on foot and in chains, with bared head and bare feet," exposed to the fierce rays of the midsummer sun, to the Síyáh-Chál of Tihrán. On the way He several times was stripped of His outer garments, was overwhelmed with ridicule, and pelted with stones. As to the subterranean dungeon into which He was thrown, and which originally had served as a reservoir of water for one of the public baths of the capital, let His own words, recorded in His "Epistle to the Son of the Wolf," bear testimony to the ordeal which He endured in that pestilential hole.[33]

This is how Bahá'u'lláh describes the Black Pit:

> We were consigned for four months to a place foul beyond comparison...Upon Our arrival We were first conducted along a pitch-black corridor, from whence We descended three steep flights of stairs to the place of confinement assigned to Us. The dungeon was wrapped in thick darkness, and Our fellow-prisoners numbered nearly one hundred and fifty souls: thieves, assassins and highwaymen. Though crowded, it had no other outlet than the passage by which We entered. No pen can depict that place, nor any tongue describe its loathsome smell. Most of these men had neither clothes nor bedding to lie on. God alone knoweth what befell Us in that most foul-smelling and gloomy place![34]

Shoghi Effendi continues:

> Bahá'u'lláh's feet were placed in stocks, and around His neck were fastened...chains of such galling weight that their mark remained imprinted upon His body all the days of His life. "A heavy chain," 'Abdu'l-Bahá Himself has

> testified, "was placed about His neck by which He was chained to five other Bábís [followers of the Báb]; these fetters were locked together by strong, very heavy, bolts and screws. His clothes were torn to pieces, also His head-dress. In this terrible condition He was kept for four months."
>
> For three days and three nights, He was denied all manner of food and drink. Sleep was impossible to Him. The place was chill and damp, filthy, fever-stricken, infested with vermin, and filled with a noisome stench. Animated by a relentless hatred His enemies went even so far as to intercept and poison His food, in the hope of obtaining the favor of the mother of their sovereign, His most implacable foe—an attempt which, though it impaired His health for years to come, failed to achieve its purpose. "'Abdu'l-Bahá," Dr. J. E. Esslemont records in his book, "tells how, one day, He was allowed to enter the prison yard to see His beloved Father, where He came out for His daily exercise. Bahá'u'lláh was terribly altered, so ill He could hardly walk, His hair and beard unkempt, His neck galled and swollen from the pressure of a heavy steel collar, His body bent by the weight of His chains."[35]

It was under such conditions that the "Most Great Spirit" (represented as "Dove" in the Gospel) "descended upon the agonized soul of Bahá'u'lláh." This is how He describes the workings of that "Most Great Spirit" on His own Spirit:

> One night, in a dream, these exalted words were heard on every side: 'Verily, We shall render Thee victorious by Thyself and by Thy pen. Grieve Thou not for that which hath befallen Thee, neither be Thou afraid, for Thou art in safety. Ere-long will God raise up the treasures of the earth—men who will aid Thee through Thyself and through Thy Name, wherewith God hath revived the hearts of such as have recognized Him.'[36]

The Black Pit of Tihrán was an underground public bath reservoir, which was used as a prison. ***Its ground was covered***

with mud and slime several inches deep. The information comes from an Austrian physician who served the shah and had the honor of visiting Bahá'u'lláh briefly in the Black Pit. He states that he found Bahá'u'lláh's hand in mud up to His wrist. (Bahá'u'lláh had to put His hand on the ground to support the heavy weight of the chain on His neck.) Several prophecies in Psalms speak of pain and suffering. Some verses, especially in Psalms 31, 38, and 40 seem to relate to Bahá'u'lláh's life. For instance:

> ***I*** waited patiently for the Lord; he turned to me and heard my cry. ***He lifted me out of the slimy pit, out of the mud and mire***; he set my feet on a rock and gave me a firm place to stand. He put a new song in my mouth.
>
> Psalms 40:1-3 NIV

Who is the "I" in the preceding prophecy? It is David who speaks, but it seems he speaks not only for himself but also for another Being. David's prayers and meditations may be a blending of his own destiny and feelings as well as those of the Redeemer of our time. Thus David sometimes speaks for himself and sometimes on behalf of Jehovah to Jehovah!

After Bahá'u'lláh was released from the Black Pit, ***He had many wounds*** and needed constant care. But who would have the courage to provide a shelter for Him and serve Him? People were terrified to associate with Him for fear of retribution. ***Most of His many friends and relatives abandoned Him***. Two young ladies of exceptional courage—close relatives of Bahá'u'lláh—took upon themselves the honor of taking Him to their home and providing the care He needed. The abandonment of Bahá'u'lláh after His release from the Black Pit may also have been predicted:

> ***My friends and companions avoid me because of my wounds; my neighbors stay far away***. Those who seek my life set their traps [poisoning], those who would harm me talk of my ruin; all day long they plot deception. I am like a deaf man, who cannot hear, like a mute, who cannot open his mouth; I have become like a man who does not

> hear, whose mouth can offer no reply. I wait for you, O Lord; you will answer, O Lord my God.
>
> Psalms 38:11-15 NIV

Many conspired to assassinate Bahá'u'lláh. The following prophecy seems to describe not only the abandonment of Bahá'u'lláh by His friends but also the plotting of His enemies to take His life:

> Because of all my enemies, I am the utter contempt of my neighbors; ***I am a dread to my friends—those who see me on the street flee from me***. I am forgotten by them as though I were dead; I have become like broken pottery. For I hear the slander of many; there is terror on every side; ***they conspire against me and plot to take my life***.
>
> Psalms 31:11-13 NIV

Consider Bahá'u'lláh's favorite title as a clue to His sufferings. In all of His works translated into English, there is only one case where "Bahá'u'lláh" is used. Even in that case, the original title He used is ***Bahá***. We may wonder why. What was Jesus' favorite title for Himself? ***Son of Man***. Why did He not choose ***Son of God***? Perhaps to express His humility. Bahá'u'lláh's preference for ***Bahá*** instead of ***Bahá'u'lláh*** may indicate the same purpose.

What is Bahá'u'lláh's ***favorite*** title for Himself? ***The Wronged One***. *A Concordance to the Writings of Bahá'u'lláh* lists 219 uses of "the Wronged One," but only 29 uses of "Bahá." Bahá'u'lláh's favorite title, "the Wronged One," gives us a clue to His burden of suffering.

Plots Against Bahá'u'lláh

The previous prophecies from Psalms refer to plots against Bahá'u'lláh:

> …all day long they ***plot*** deception. Psalms 38:12 NIV

> …they conspire against me and ***plot*** to take my life.
>
> Psalms 31:13 NIV

Another prophecy from Psalms also refers to rejection and hostility of nations and rulers and their plots against the twin Redeemers of our time:

> Why do the nations rage and the peoples ***plot*** in vain? The kings of the earth take their stand and the rulers gather together against the Lord [Bahá'u'lláh] and against his Anointed One [the Báb]. "Let us break their chains [of authority]," they say, "and throw off their fetters." The One enthroned in heaven laughs; the Lord scoffs at them. Then he rebukes them in his anger and terrifies them in his wrath, saying, "I have installed my King on Zion, my holy hill." I will proclaim the decree of the Lord...
>
> Psalms 2:1-7 NIV

Scofield, a Christian scholar, states that the preceding verses give the order of the establishment of God's kingdom upon the earth. He states that the first stage is "the rage of the Gentiles [non-Jews], the vain imaginings of the 'people' (the Jews), and the antagonism of the rulers against Jehovah's Anointed."[37]

J. R. Church, a Christian author, says this about the quoted verses from Psalms (2:1-7): "This is no ordinary mockery but rather it is the last laugh. Nowhere does Scripture record God laughing except on this day."[38]

In the history of the Bahá'í Faith there are many records of plots to destroy Bahá'u'lláh and His influence. Here are a few examples, including three plots to take His life:

> Whilst at Constantinople, the fame of the wisdom of Bahá'u'lláh had gone abroad, and many noble-minded people were anxious to come into His presence. Such a profound impression was made on these visitors, that they spoke of the majesty of His person, and the holiness of His teaching to their friends. This made His enemies again uneasy, and ***they plotted*** on some pretext or another to get Him removed from Constantinople. This plan was successful, and our Beloved One was sent to Adrianople.[39]

On one occasion, when Bahá'u'lláh's half brother Azal read one of His Epistles about His station, he became intensely angry and "jealous fire consumed him."

> He invited Bahá'u'lláh to a feast and shared a dish with Him, one half of which he had mixed with poison. For twenty-one days Bahá'u'lláh was seriously ill from the effects of this attempt.
>
> Incensed at this failure, Azal tried another plan. He asked the bath attendant (for a bribe) to assassinate Bahá'u'lláh whilst he should be taking His bath, suggesting how easily it could be done without fear of detection.[40]

Next to Azal's plots, perhaps the most vicious and persistent conspiracy against Bahá'u'lláh ensued from a collaboration between a powerful religious leader and a political figure while He lived in Baghdad. It is hard to imagine a person more evil than this religious leader. He was so troublesome that even the Shah of Iran could not stand him in his country. He banished him to Baghdad. Bahá'u'lláh describes this religious leader (Shaykh 'Abdu'l-Husayn) as the "'scoundrel,' the 'schemer,' the 'wicked one,' who 'drew the sword of his self against the face of God,' 'in whose soul Satan hath whispered,' and 'from whose impiety Satan flies,' the 'depraved one,' 'from whom originated and to whom will return all infidelity, cruelty and crime.'"[41] Here is just one example of several plots planned by these two collaborators:

> The consul-general had even gone so far as to hire a ruffian, a Turk, named Ridá, for the sum of one hundred tumáns, and to provide him with a horse and with two pistols, and to order him to seek out and kill Bahá'u'lláh, promising him that his own protection would be fully assured. Ridá, learning one day that his would-be-victim was attending the public bath, eluded the vigilance of the Bábís in attendance, entered the bath with a pistol concealed in his cloak, and confronted Bahá'u'lláh in the inner chamber, only to discover that he lacked the courage to

accomplish his task. He himself, years later, related that on another occasion he was lying in wait for Bahá'u'lláh, pistol in hand, when, on Bahá'u'lláh's approach, he was so overcome with fear that the pistol dropped from his hand; whereupon Bahá'u'lláh bade Áqáy-i-Kalím [Bahá'u'lláh's brother], who accompanied Him, to hand it back to him, and show him the way to his home.[42]

...they conspire against me and plot to take my life.

Psalms 31:13 NIV

The Most Great Prison

Bahá'u'lláh met horrible conditions again when He entered the 'Akká prison (known as the Most Great Prison). This time He had His family and quite a few of His devoted disciples with Him. Bahá'u'lláh's sufferings in this prison even surpassed those He had endured in the Black Pit. These are some of the conditions—13 of them—Bahá'u'lláh and His loved ones encountered when they entered that infamous prison in a desolate city He called "the metropolis of the owl:"[43]

- Overcrowded prison cells.
- Unbearable filth.
- Excessive heat.
- Terrible stench.
- Lack of sanitary facilities.
- Uncontrolled fleas.
- Widespread disease (malaria, Dysentery, etc.) among Bahá'u'lláh's family and disciples.
- Hunger and thirst.
- Foul water and terrible food.
- Sudden death of three of Bahá'u'lláh's disciples.
- No friends to help them.
- Insult and enmity from the residents of the city. (Bahá'u'lláh called the people of 'Akká "the generation of vipers.")

- Strict control and harsh treatment of the new prisoners by the soldiers.

'Abdu'l-Bahá, who as a child had been accustomed to comfort and luxury, was placed in an extremely damp room previously used as a slaughter house. Yet He was one of the two, among 70 inmates, who remained healthy and able to serve others. Bahá'u'lláh often describes the horrible conditions that He and His disciples had to endure in that prison:

> None knoweth what befell Us, except God, the Almighty, the All-Knowing...[44]

> He [Bahá'u'lláh] hath, during the greater part of His life been sore-tried in the clutches of His enemies. His sufferings have now reached their culmination in this afflictive Prison, into which His oppressors have so unjustly thrown Him.[45]

In 1911, in an interview with a newspaper editor in Great Britain, 'Abdu'l-Bahá gave a brief description of the 'Akká prison:

> We had no communication whatever with the outside world. Each loaf of bread was cut open by the guard to see that it contained no message...There were one-hundred and fifty of us together in two rooms and no one was allowed to leave the place with the exception of four persons, who went to the bazaar or market each morning, under guard. The first summer was dreadful. 'Akká is a fever-ridden town. It was said that a bird attempting to fly over it would drop dead. The food was poor and insufficient, the water was drawn from a fever-infected well...During the intense heat, malaria, typhoid and dysentery attacked the prisoners, so that all, men, women, and children, were sick at one time. There were no doctors, no medicines, no proper food, and no treatment of any kind.[46]

'Abdu'l-Bahá's sister offers a few other details:

> All the townspeople had assembled to see the arrival of the prisoners. Having been told that we were infidels, criminals, and sowers of sedition, the attitude of the crowd was threatening. Their yelling of curse and execrations filled us with fresh misery. We were terrified of the unknown! We knew not what the fate of our party, the friends and ourselves would be.
>
> We were taken to the old fortress of 'Akká, where we were crowded together. There was no air; a small quantity of very bad coarse bread was provided; we were unable to get fresh water to drink; our sufferings were not diminished. Then an epidemic of typhoid broke out. Nearly all became ill.[47]

Bahá'u'lláh described 'Akká as:

> ...the most desolate of the cities of the world, the most unsightly of them in appearance, the most detestable in climate, and the foulest in water. It is as though it were the metropolis of the owl...[48]

Bahá'u'lláh repeatedly refers to His sufferings:

> By the righteousness of God! Every morning I arose from My bed, I discovered the hosts of countless afflictions massed behind My door; and every night when I lay down, lo! My heart was torn with agony at what it had suffered from the fiendish cruelty of its foes. With every piece of bread the Ancient Beauty breaketh is coupled the assault of a fresh affliction, and with every drop He drinketh is mixed the bitterness of the most woeful of trials. He is preceded in every step He taketh by an army of unforeseen calamities, while in His rear follow legions of agonizing sorrows.[49]

Once Bahá'u'lláh had this dream:

> I saw...the Prophets and the Messengers gather and seat themselves around Me, moaning, weeping and loudly lamenting. Amazed, I inquired of them the reason, whereupon

> their lamentation and weeping waxed greater, and they said unto me: "We weep for Thee, O Most Great Mystery, O Tabernacle of Immortality!" They wept with such a weeping that I too wept with them. Thereupon the Concourse on high addressed Me saying: "...Erelong shalt Thou behold with Thine own eyes what no Prophet hath beheld....Be patient, be patient...." They continued addressing Me the whole night until the approach of dawn.[50]

The Book of Revelation confirms the message of the Olivet discourse and other prophecies. It predicts suffering for the Báb, Bahá'u'lláh, and their followers:

> He was clothed with a robe dipped in blood, and His name is called The Word of God. Revelation 19:13 NKJ

> Then one of the elders asked me, "These are in white robes—who are they, and where did they come from?" I answered, "Sir, you know." And he said, "These are they who have come out of great tribulation [the great massacre of the Báb's followers]; they have washed their robes and made them white [purified their souls] in the blood of the Lamb [martyrdom of the Báb]. Revelation 13:14 NIV

> All inhabitants of the earth will worship the beast [they will side with the negative forces]—all whose names have not been recorded in the book of life belonging to the Lamb [the Báb]. Revelation 13:8 NIV

> They will make war against the Lamb [the Báb], but the Lamb will overcome them... Revelation 17:13 NIV

Did the world recognize Christ in His first advent?

> He was in the world...***the world did not recognize him.*** John 1:10 NIV

Jesus once again predicts rejection:

> And I will ask the Father, and he will give you another Counselor to be with you forever—***the Spirit of truth.***

> ***The world*** cannot accept him, because it ***neither sees him nor knows him.*** John 14:16-17 NIV

The preceding prophecy confirms the prophecies of "the thief in the night." In the preceding prophecy Jesus explains that the reason people will reject the other Counselor, or the Spirit of truth that God will send, is that the world will not "***see***" him. The thief comes and leaves unnoticed and unknown.

"The Spirit" is a title bestowed in both Islamic and Bahá'í Scriptures on Jesus. Jesus refers to Bahá'u'lláh as the Spirit of truth. Bahá'u'lláh also calls Himself the Spirit and the Spirit of truth. The following is not recognized as a prophecy but may indeed contain a prophetic message:

> Do not quench [extinguish] the Spirit [Bahá'u'lláh]. Do not despise prophecies. Test all things; hold fast what is good. I Thessalonians 5:19-21 NKJ

It seems there is no end to prophecies of denial. We will continue this topic in the next chapter and beyond.

7

The Parables and Prophecies

The Parable of the Wedding

In one of His parables of a wedding scene, Jesus clearly points to the rejection and persecution that He and His humble servants must again endure:

> The kingdom of heaven is like a king who prepared a wedding banquet for his son. He sent his servants [the new believers] to those who had been invited to the banquet to tell them to come, but they refused to come. Then he sent some more servants and said, 'Tell those who have been invited that I have prepared my dinner...Come to the wedding banquet.' But they paid no attention and went off—one to his field, another to his business. The rest [the

> fanatic non-believers] seized his servants, mistreated them and killed them. Christ (Matt. 22:2-6 NIV)

The "king" may refer to all great Messengers and Redeemers; they all manifest the glory of God's Kingdom, and "servants" may point to their followers, for they were, in all ages, mistreated. But in the preceding passage, the "king" may specifically symbolize Bahá'u'lláh, and the "son" may symbolize the Báb. (See *Lord of Lords* for other biblical references to the Báb as the Son.)

As the prophecy foretells, Bahá'u'lláh asked His servants or supporters to invite people to the Báb's glorious Banquet. Most of them paid no attention and continued with their own lives. But "the rest," namely the Muslim fanatics, seized the Báb's servants, mistreated them, and killed them.

During its brief but turbulent history, the Bahá'í Faith has encountered countless obstacles. Thousands of its followers have been put to death with the utmost cruelty. At this writing, 300,000 Bahá'ís are being persecuted by fanatic Muslims in Iran. Some are in prison; others have faced firing squads, or been hanged. They have chosen the dignity of death over the humiliation of denying their Master. These are among the noblest people on our planet. Their exemplary courage will inspire countless generations to come. They indeed are the "salt of the world:"

> How blest you are, when you suffer...for my sake. Accept it with gladness and exultation, for you have a rich reward in heaven; in the same way they persecuted the prophets before you. You are salt of the world.
>
> Christ (Matt. 5:11-13 NEB)

The parable of the wedding contains a few more messages:

- After people refused to come to the banquet, the king was enraged. He sent His "heavenly army" to punish the wrongdoers who murdered His followers. The history of the Bahá'í Faith shows that those who persecuted the Bahá'ís did not escape the consequences of their cruelties.

Time and again they met with disaster. (See *The Dawn-Breakers* for examples.)

- After thc King was disappointed with those who were self-righteous, who considered themselves the saved and faithful, He asked His new followers to invite ***other*** people, anyone they could find, both good and bad, including non-Christians; and many accepted the invitation and came. But among those who came some were found unfit for the banquet. They had come for the wrong reason; they called themselves by the new name but were not living up to the required standards. In the Bahá'í Faith, there have been a few calling themselves "Bahá'ís" who have tried to confuse the believers, and divide the banquet. They are called "covenant breakers."
- The king ordered the disloyal believers out of His banquet, where they would experience only grief and anger.
- The final message of the parable is this:

> For many are invited, but ***few are chosen***.
>
> Christ (Matt. 22:14 NIV)

The Parable of the Wise and Foolish Maidens

As we noted in Volume I, the Olivet discourse contains a most marvelous and touching parable (Matt. 25:1-13) about the fate of ten young girls who wished to go to the wedding banquet of the kingdom. They fell asleep while waiting for the bridegroom. Then at midnight a cry was heard: "Here is the bridegroom! Come out to meet him" (Matt. 25:6). Those who were wise had taken along not only their lamps but some extra oil as well. The foolish ones had taken ***only*** their lamps. Since the bridegroom was late, their oil was burnt up, and they had no light to guide them. And when they asked the others for some oil, they were told there was not enough to go around.

The foolish ones went to buy some oil. While they were away, the bridegroom arrived. Those who had lighted lamps entered the banquet. But by the time the others returned, the door to the wedding banquet was shut. They asked if anyone would open the door for them. They were told they were strangers, and did not belong to the banquet.

This parable clearly implies that anyone who wishes to enter the heavenly banquet must carry ***his own*** lighted lamp, without depending on others. It is one of God's laws that every soul must carry its own spiritual burden:

> ...no soul laden bears the load of another. Qur'án 17:15 A

Wisdom, the inner light or insight (oil), is not something the wise girls could simply give to the foolish. Each individual must acquire it through ***his or her own*** endeavors. Those who fail to do so, cause their own deprivation of the divine bounties.

> Every man shall bear his own burden... Galatians 6:5

It is God's wish that everyone enter the banquet of His kingdom. It is also His wish to honor the freedom of choice He has granted to every human being. All great religions declare that without spiritual guidance and preparation, a soul cannot enter the heavenly banquet. Why should the Master reward equally those who honor His words by "dressing" for the banquet, and those who disregard His words?

Those active in the Advent Awakening of the mid-19th century believed that they played a part in the fulfillment of this parable, and that their voice was indeed ***the midnight cry*** raised in the darkness of complacency, indifference, and worldliness. Because of their "cry" people were buying and reading the Bible more than ever before.[1] Miller, the pioneer preacher, declared:

> It is to me almost a demonstration, that God's hand is seen in this thing. Many thousands, to all human appearance,

> have been made to study the Scriptures by the preaching of the time.[2]

In 1831 William Thorp wrote about the sleeping church:

> The...slumber of the church; and the midnight cry that has recently been raised, and that is now ringing in the ears of an infidel world, and a sleeping church; all indicate that the 1260 years have nearly, at least, run out their course. And when ye see these things, know that the kingdom of heaven is at hand. Of that day and that hour knoweth no man; but we may know with certainty, by these signs and these prophecies, that it is fast approaching.[3]

> The midnight cry is now heard: is not his coming, therefore, near, very near; even at the door?[4] ...the midnight cry is now heard, from a thousand voices; behold the bridegroom cometh; he comes in clouds of flaming fire.[5]

The parable of the coming of Christ—the Bridegroom—at midnight, the darkest hour, when many are asleep, clarifies and supports the prophecies that point to the coming of the Redeemer in a way a thief would come: quietly and in the midst of darkness, on a day and at an hour people do not expect. The Báb—the Bridegroom—fulfilled the prophecies not only symbolically, but literally as well; symbolically, because the masses of people were spiritually asleep and unconscious, without an inner light to guide them; literally, because He declared His Mission in the dark hours of the evening, and declared it not to a waiting crowd, but to ***one*** seeker, a total stranger who had been led to His presence for no ***apparent*** reason. The Báb's conversation with the stranger continued through the evening, past midnight, and until the dawn broke.

The Parable of the Vineyard

Jesus also used the parable of the vineyard to refer to people's denial of the divine message in all ages. The parable starts in the past and extends into the future. He used the following passage to refer not only to the Jews who rejected Him but to the followers of all religions who would reject Him at His Second Coming:

> Therefore I tell you that the kingdom of God will be taken away from you [deniers] and given to the people who will produce the fruit. Matthew 21:44 NIV

Again:

> Therefore, when the owner of the vineyard comes...he will rent the vineyard to ***other tenants***, who will give him his share of the crop at harvest time. Matthew 21:40-41 NIV

Sacred Scriptures have promised that the kingdom of God will be established in this age. Therefore, the privilege of building God's kingdom is taken away from those who reject Christ at His Second Coming. "The harvest" time also stands for "the end of the age," which is our time. Jesus quoted the following passage from the Hebrew Scriptures to clarify His point:

> The stone the builders rejected has become the capstone; the Lord has done this, and it is marvelous in our eyes.
> Matthew 21:42 NIV

The rejected "stone" primarily symbolizes disadvantaged people; those who are looked down upon by the established segment of society. In all ages, the disadvantaged are the first to recognize their Redeemer. Mary Magdalene, a peasant with a bad reputation, and Peter, a very simple fisherman, recognized their Lord, but the great theologians, the self-righteous Pharisees, and the powerful leaders all rejected Him. It is fascinating to note that that is how God prefers it. He says, "It is marvelous in our eyes." The Olivet Discourse pertains to the second Advent and is addressed to Christians. In that discourse Jesus predicted:

> And then many will bc ***offended and repelled*** and begin to distrust and desert [Him Whom they ought to trust and obey] and will stumble and fall away [brackets belong to original]...
> Matthew 24:10 AB

The hearts of some self-righteous Christians are so closed, that after hearing the news of the Second Coming of Christ, instead of welcoming the news and looking into it, they feel "offended and repelled," exactly as the prophecy has predicted.

In interpreting the previous prophecy, Christian scholar Biederwolf states that many Christians stumble "because of new phases of truth presented, or because of the delayed coming of the Lord."[6]

Numerous prophecies (II Tim 3:1-8; 4:3-4) predict that at the end of the age people will descend to the lowest level of morality and spiritual development. What can we expect from such people? Acceptance or rejection?

Jesus compared the events surrounding His Second Coming with those that surrounded Noah. His prophecy is as clear, as literal, and as definitive as any prophecy can be, yet it is widely ignored. It does not fit the paradigm of a powerful Redeemer who comes from heaven with angels and fire:

> The coming of the Son of Man will repeat what happened in Noah's time.
> Matthew 24:37 NAB

If we judge with fairness, the preceding verse alone will give us the insight to awaken from the never-ending illusions of waiting and wishing that somehow the sky will disclose its glorious Gift, that someday the clouds will deliver their celestial Rider.

Isaiah's Prophecies

Earlier we reviewed some verses from Chapter 65 of Isaiah's prophecy about the gift of the new name. But most of the chapter points to the response of the people to the divine call. It seems fitting to see some of those prophecies again.

Chapter 65 of Isaiah offers numerous clues about the people's response to God's message. First it states that people ignore the divine call:

> I revealed myself to those who did not ask for me; I was found by those who did not seek me. To a nation that did not call on my name, I said, '***Here am I, here am I.***' All day long I have held out my hands to an obstinate people, who walk in ways not good, ***pursuing their own imaginations***—a people who continually provoke me to my very face... Isaiah 65:1-3 NIV

Isaiah's prophecy is similar to the verse from the Olivet discourse where Jesus declared that people would ignore Him: "I was hungry and you gave me nothing to eat" (Matt. 25:34-46).

As our Creator offers His hand, saying "Here am I," we should also extend our hand and say, "Here am I:"

> It behoveth whosoever hath hearkened to the Call of God, as voiced by Him Who is the Day Spring of Glory [Bahá'u'lláh], to arise and cry out: "***Here am I, here am I***, O Lord of all Names; ***here am I, here am I***, O Maker of the heavens! I testify that, through Thy Revelation, the things hidden in the Books of God have been revealed, and that whatsoever hath been recorded by Thy Messengers in the sacred Scriptures hath been fulfilled."[7] Bahá'u'lláh

Isaiah then describes those who ignore the divine call. He says they are infected with pride and a sense of superiority. To other people, who are outside their circle, they say:

> Keep away; don't come near me, for I am too sacred for you! Isaiah 65:5 NIV

Isaiah then points to the glory of Sharon and Achor as a place of rest for those who hear the divine call and seek their Redeemer:

> Sharon will become a pasture for flocks, and the Valley of Achor a resting place for herds, for my people who seek me. Isaiah 65:10 NIV

Isaiah refers again to those who ignore the divine call:

> But as for you who forsake the Lord and forget my holy mountain...I will destine you for the sword [a means of separation], and you will all bend down for the slaughter [spiritual death]; for I called but you did not answer, I spoke but you did not listen. You did evil in my sight and chose what displeases me. Isaiah 65:112 NIV

Then Isaiah declares that the rewards of the believers (referred to as "My servants") is spiritual nourishment and joy, and the punishment of disbelievers is anguish, thirst, hunger, and death. At the end of the prophecy he declares that to the new believers (His servants), He will give them a new name.

> Therefore this is what the Sovereign Lord says: "***My servants*** will eat, but you will go hungry; ***my servants*** will drink, but you will go thirsty; ***my servants*** will rejoice, but you will be put to shame. ***My servants*** will sing out of the joy of their hearts, but you will cry out from anguish of heart and wail in brokenness of spirit. You will leave your name to my chosen ones as a curse; the Sovereign Lord will put you to death, but ***to his servants he will give another name***." Isaiah 65:13-15 NIV

Bahá'u'lláh calls His followers "***My servants***" quite frequently. In one of His Epistles addressed to a "banished and faithful friend" He refers to His followers as "O My servants!" nine times. Consider these few passages from that Epistle. In these verses, He invites all seekers and lovers of truth to His Kingdom with supreme kindness and authority:

> ***O My servants!*** Were ye to discover the hidden, the shoreless oceans of My incorruptible wealth, ye would, of a certainty, esteem as nothing the world, nay, the entire creation…
>
> ***O My servants!*** My holy, My divinely ordained Revelation may be likened unto an ocean in whose depths are concealed innumerable pearls of great price, of surpassing luster. It is the duty of every seeker to bestir himself and strive to attain the shores of this ocean, so that he may, in proportion to the eagerness of his search and the efforts he hath exerted, partake of such benefits as have been pre-ordained in God's irrevocable and hidden Tablets…
>
> ***O My servants!*** The one true God is My witness! This most great, this fathomless and surging Ocean is near, astonishingly near, unto you. Behold it is closer to you than your life-vein! Swift as the twinkling of an eye ye can, if ye but wish it, reach and partake of this imperishable favor, this God-given grace, this incorruptible gift, this most potent and unspeakably glorious bounty…
>
> ***O My servants!*** Could ye apprehend with what wonders of My munificence and bounty I have willed to entrust your souls, ye would, of a truth, rid yourselves of attachment to all created things, and would gain a true knowledge of your own selves—a knowledge which is the same as the comprehension of Mine own Being. Ye would find yourselves independent of all else but Me, and would perceive, with your inner and outer eye, and as manifest as the revelation of My effulgent Name.[8]

Isaiah finally gives the tidings of a new heavenly (spiritual) and earthly (material) civilization:

> Behold, I will create new heavens and a new earth. The former things will not be remembered... Isaiah 65:17 NIV

Chapter 63 of Isaiah also confirms Bahá'u'lláh's sufferings and God's anger at the deniers:

> Who is this coming from Edom, from Bozrah, ***with his garments stained crimson***? Who is this, ***robed in splendor***,

> striding forward in the greatness of his strength? "It is I, speaking in righteousness, mighty to save." Why are your garments red, like those of one treading the winepress? "I have trodden the winepress alone; from the nations no one was with me. I trampled them in my anger and trod them down in my wrath; their blood spattered my garments, and I stained all my clothing. For the day of ***vengeance*** [justice] was in my heart, and the year of my ***redemption*** has come. ***I looked, but there was no one to help***, I was appalled that no one gave support; so my own arm worked salvation for me, and my own wrath sustained me. I trampled the nations in my anger; in my wrath I made them drunk and poured their blood on the ground." Isaiah 63:1-6 NIV

Edom symbolizes the land of rebellion. In this age, Persia, the birthplace of Bahá'u'lláh is that land. Bozrah was the main city of Edom and the home of an Edomite king. In this age, that city is Tihrán, the place of residence for Persian kings at the time of Bahá'u'lláh. Edomites were constantly in conflict and at war with the Israelites and their kings, including Saul, David, and Solomon. According to *Unger's Bible Dictionary*:

> When Nebuchadnezzar besieged Jerusalem the Edomites joined him, and took an active part in the plunder of the city and slaughter of the Jews. Their cruelty at that time seems to be especially referred to in the 137th Psalm. It was on account of these acts of cruelty committed upon the Jews in the day of their calamity that the Edomites were so fearfully denounced by the later prophets (Isaiah. 34:5-8; 63:1-4; Jeremiah 49:17; Lam. 4:21; Ezekiel 25:13-14; Amos 1:11-12; Obadiah 8, 10).[9]

> "The prophets foretold judgment on Edom for her bitter hatred" (Joel 3:19). "Like Sodom and Gomorrah, Edom is a despised city" (Isaiah 49:18). "Concerning Edom...Has their wisdom decayed? Edom will become an object of horror..." (Jeremiah 49:7, 17 NIV). "It is under God's vengeance" (Ezekiel 25:14).

Crimson or red symbolizes both suffering and God's wrath. The one who wears garments "stained crimson" may symbolize any suffering soul, but specifically Bahá'u'lláh, because the verse speaks of the ***One robed in splendor***. Bahá'u'lláh means the glory and splendor of God. ***The verses clearly point to a divine Being who can both punish and offer redemption***. The verses also point to the lack of support for the Redeemer from the nations as did Chapter 65 of Isaiah. The idea of rebellion is also found in Chapter 65:

> I have stretched out My hands all day long to a rebellious people... Isaiah 65:2 NKJ

"Crimson garments" may give us a further clue. It is well known that Bahá'u'lláh owned a red garment made of many pieces of cloth. His garment may symbolize both the spiritual wars He encountered, and His triumph in unifying the warlike and diverse segments of the world. Here is the story of the red garment as told by Bahá'u'lláh's granddaughter:

> I was told how my grandmother and Khánum made a wonderful coat for Bahá'u'lláh, to be ready for Him when He should return from the retreat in the wilderness of Sulaymáníyyih. They worked at this labor of love, using small pieces of ***red*** tirmih, very precious stuff, which had survived, in some way, the loss of nearly all her extensive and rare wedding treasures. For six months they sewed and fitted these pieces together, and a beautiful coat was the result. Very acceptable indeed, for He came back in the coarse, rough coat of a dervish. And they had no money for buying coats at that time in Baghdád.[10]

The Book of Revelation refers not only to a red robe, but also to one of Bahá'u'lláh's titles, ***the Word of God***:

> He is dressed in a ***robe dipped in blood***, and his name is ***the Word of God***. Revelation 19:13 NIV

Many people have had the honor of seeing Bahá'u'lláh in their dreams and visions, including this author. Consider the following dream dreamt by Roma Freeman, when she had not even heard the name of Bahá'u'lláh. The reason I am quoting the dream is because of "the red robe:"

> We were expecting our third child...It had been an extremely difficult pregnancy from beginning to end. At the same time, I was suffering from a broken rib and pneumonia, and every cough racked my body with pain...almost two months early, severe labor pains began to develop. I thrashed about the bed, whipping from side to side, turning, twisting, thinking and verbalizing many thoughts that were far, far from lofty or noble.
>
> All of a sudden to the right of the bed, approximately five feet away, there appeared a male figure clad in a floor-length ***deep red robe***. His beautiful hands were opened and extended towards me. He had a black, neatly groomed beard and black shoulder-length hair that produced red highlights in the sunlight streaming through the bedroom window. His eyes were gentle, filled with love and compassion, yet those same eyes seemed to register such disappointment and sorrow, as he witnessed the behavior I was exhibiting.
>
> At that moment, I felt such shame and yet such fright! Who was he? What was he doing here! He reminded me of the statues and paintings I had seen of Jesus Christ, but I knew he wasn't Jesus...I quickly turned my head away from those eyes and those beautiful hands. When I turned back to look again, he was gone. I began to cry uncontrollably. 'Oh God, what did all this mean?'
>
> There was no one I could ask. What would they think? Perhaps they would believe that I was losing touch with reality, or hallucinating because of the many months of pain and difficulty. But I knew in my heart that it was real! It was true. Yet I had never, never believed such things. I had always scoffed at those who mentioned such experiences, which I viewed as figments of the imagination.[11]

Several years later, after much spiritual struggle, Roma became a Bahá'í and went on pilgrimage to the Bahá'í World Centre in Haifa, Israel. Her vision of the unknown figure reached its climax and conclusion after she entered the building in which the Bahá'í sacred relics are treasured:

> In the Archives Building on Mount Carmel, I saw for the first time the precious photograph of Bahá'u'lláh. I was devastated and completely overwhelmed! ***It was He whom I had seen in my bedroom fifteen years before—one year prior to hearing the word Bahá'í.*** Another long search had ended.[12]

Chapter 52 of Isaiah also refers to the Second Coming. First it points to the Lord's great glory:

> How beautiful on the mountains are the feet of those who bring good news, who proclaim peace, who bring good tidings, who proclaim salvation, who say to Zion, "Your God reigns!" Listen! Your watchmen lift up their voices; together they shout for joy. When the Lord returns to Zion, they will see it with their own eyes. Burst into songs of joy together, you ruins of Jerusalem, for the Lord has comforted his people, he has redeemed Jerusalem. The Lord will lay bare his holy arm in the sight of all the nations, and all the ends of the earth will see the salvation of our God. Isaiah 52:7-10 NIV

After referring to glory, the chapter ends with a brief description of both glory and suffering. *The New International Version* divides the chapter into two parts. It adds this subheading to the second part (verses 13 to 15): *The Suffering and Glory of the Servant.* These verses are presented under part II:

> See, my servant will act wisely; he will be raised and lifted up and highly exalted. Just as there were many who were appalled at him—his appearance was so disfigured beyond that of any man and his form marred beyond human likeness. Isaiah 52:13-14 NIV

The previous verses about suffering perfectly describe Bahá'u'lláh's appearance during His imprisonment in the Black Pit. He was so disfigured that His friends and relatives could hardly recognize Him. They were literally appalled by what they saw.

The next chapter of Isaiah points to the first Advent, to both the sufferings and glory of Jesus. As a Christian scholar notes, "In Isaiah 53, the Messiah is portrayed as both the suffering Servant and the conquering King."[13] Just as the Jews failed to see the relevance of Chapter 53 to Jesus, so have many Christians failed to see the relevance of Chapter 52 to Bahá'u'lláh. The parallels between the first advent and the second are astonishing.

In both Chapters 52 and 53 of Isaiah we are given two opposite portraits of the promised Redeemer. Which portrait is easy to miss? The suffering portrait, of course. Who wants a suffering Savior? But God's way and the human way are often in conflict:

> ...how can My way accord with thine?[14] Bahá'u'lláh

The Kingdom of Heaven does not start with a great tree; it always starts with a little seed that must be nourished and helped by every human being to grow:

> To what shall we liken the kingdom of God? Or with what parable shall we picture it? It is like a mustard seed which, when it is sown on the ground, is smaller than all the seeds on earth; but when it is sown, it grows up and becomes greater than all herbs, and shoots out large branches, so that the birds of the air may nest under its shade. Mark 4:30-32 NKJ

Daniel's Prophecy

To those who understand the meaning of prophecies of the last days, Daniel refers as "the wise:"

> Go your way, Daniel, because the words are closed up and sealed until the time of the end. Many will be purified, made spotless and refined, but the wicked will continue to be wicked. None of the wicked will understand, but ***those who are wise will understand***. Daniel 12:9-10 NIV

As we noted earlier, ***wisdom*** was the attribute that empowered the five young women to enter the heavenly banquet. In another prophecy, Daniel refers to the sufferings of "the wise," the ones who have recognized the Redeemer and are teaching the good news of His coming to others:

> Those who are wise will instruct many [teach the Good News], ***though for a time they will fall by the sword or be burned or captured or plundered***. Daniel 11:33 NIV

After referring to the sufferings of these teachers of the Word of God, Daniel predicts two more events:

- Some people who are not sincere will join "the wise."
- Some of "the wise" will face grave tests that will make them pure.

Here is the whole prophecy:

> Those who are wise will instruct many, though for a time they will fall by the sword or be burned or captured or plundered. When they fall, they will receive a little help, and many who are not sincere will join them. Some of the wise will stumble, so that they may be refined, purified and made spotless until the time of the end, for it will still come at the appointed time. Daniel 11:33-35 NIV

As we noted in the Parable of the Wedding, when the King asked His followers to invite ***other*** people, many came, among them some who were unfit for the banquet. This point of the prophecy has also been fulfilled. Sometimes people who are spiritually unfit enter the Bahá'í Faith. Once again we see harmony between Jesus' and Daniel's prophecies.

The believers in Bahá'u'lláh have faced, and are still facing, countless tests and trials. Purity requires tests and trials. Storms uproot the shallow plants, but strengthen the well grounded.

> Blessed is the man who perseveres under trial, because when he has stood the test, he will receive the crown of life… James 1:12 NIV

Joel's Prophecy

Chapter 1 of the Book of Joel is devoted entirely to the terrible conditions of our time. It portrays in a poetic and moving language the low state to which religion has fallen in these terrible times:

> The word of the Lord that came to Joel the son of Pethuel. Hear this, you elders, and give ear, all you inhabitants of the land! Has anything like this happened in your days, or even in the days of your fathers? Tell your children about it, let your children tell their children, and their children another generation.
>
> What the chewing locust [destroyers of religion] left, the swarming locust has eaten; what the swarming locust left, the crawling locust has eaten; and what the crawling locust left, the consuming locust has eaten.
>
> Awake, you [spiritually] drunkards, and weep; and wail, all you drinkers of wine [of unawareness], because of [being deprived of] the new wine [new Revelation], for it has been cut off from your mouth. For a nation [of faithless people] has come up against My land [spiritual dominion], strong, and without number; his teeth are the teeth of a lion, and he has the fangs of a fierce lion. He has laid waste My vine [God's garden], and ruined My fig tree; he has stripped it bare and thrown it away; its branches are made white.

> ***Lament*** like a virgin girded with sackcloth for the husband of her youth. The grain offering and the drink offering have been cut off from the house of the Lord; the priests ***mourn***, who minister to the Lord. The field is wasted, ***the land mourns***; for the grain [spiritual food] is ruined, the new wine is dried up, the oil [of wisdom] fails.
>
> Be ashamed, you farmers, ***wail***, you vinedressers, for the wheat and the barley; because the harvest of the field has perished. The vine has dried up, and the fig tree has withered; the pomegranate tree, the palm tree also, and the apple tree; all the trees of the field are withered; surely joy has withered away from the sons of men.
>
> Gird yourselves and ***lament***, you priests; ***wail***, you who minister before the altar; come, lie all night in sackcloth, you who minister to my God; for the grain offering and the drink offering are withheld from the house of your God. Consecrate a fast, call a sacred assembly; gather the elders and all the inhabitants of the land into the house of the Lord your God, and cry out to the Lord.
>
> Alas for the day! For the day of the Lord is at hand; it shall come as destruction from the Almighty. Is not the [spiritual] food cut off before our eyes, joy and gladness from the house of our God? The seed shrivels under the clods, storehouses are in shambles; barns are broken down, for the grain has withered. How the animals groan! The herds of cattle are restless, because they have no pasture; even the flocks of sheep suffer punishment.
>
> O Lord, to You I cry out; for fire has devoured the open pastures, and a flame has burned all the trees of the field. The beasts of the field also cry out to You, for the water brooks are dried up, and fire has devoured the open pastures. Joel 1:19-20 NKJ

Let us review the main points of the prophecy:

- Insects (who rob religion of its nourishment) have destroyed the heavenly harvest.
- You who are spiritually drunk, wake up and weep, because you have lost the ***new*** wine (the new Revelation).
- People, strong and of great number, have occupied God's land and turned His vineyard into a wasteland.
- Lament, because all the nourishing food has been cut off from the house of the Lord.
- Be ashamed, you farmers (teachers and promoters of the Word of God) because God's harvest has perished; "joy has withered away" from the heart of humankind.
- Wail, you priests and pastors because the water of life and the celestial grain are withheld from the house of the Lord.
- Gather together, in a sacred assembly, all you leaders and peoples of the world in the house of your Lord, and cry out to Him for His help and blessings.
- The day of the Lord is at hand, but it is a day of destruction (spiritual death).
- All joy and gladness are gone. Storehouses (religious centers) are in shambles, their grain is gone.
- People are restless and without food.
- The fire of remoteness from God has burned the pasture.
- Because of lack of faith, people have destroyed the earth, even the "beasts of the field" cry out for help. Their forests have burned, and their sources of water made dry.

Light always follows darkness. In Chapter 2, Joel gives us the good news: that the heavenly harvest will finally be restored:

> Fear not, O land; be glad and rejoice, for the Lord has done marvelous things! Do not be afraid, you beasts of the field; for the open pastures are springing up, and the tree

> bears its fruit; the fig tree and the vine yield their strength. Be glad then, you children of Zion, and rejoice in the Lord your God; for He has given you the former rain faithfully, and He will cause the rain to come down for you; the former rain, and the latter rain [the two Revelations] in the first month. The threshing floors shall be full of wheat, and the vats shall overflow with new wine and oil. So I will restore to you the years that the swarming locust has eaten, the crawling locust, the consuming locust, and the chewing locust, My great army which I sent among you. You shall eat in plenty and be satisfied, and praise the name of the Lord your God, who has dealt wondrously with you; and My people shall never be put to shame. Then you shall know that I am in the midst of Israel: I am the Lord your God and there is no other. My people shall never be put to shame. Joel 2:21-27 NKJ

Contrary to what many people believe, ***rejection or repudiation in itself validates Bahá'u'lláh's claim***. Concerning the firmness and dedication of His heroic followers in spite of the grave sufferings they endured, Bahá'u'lláh wrote:

> The one God is My witness!...the repudiation, cursing, and execration, pronounced by the people of the earth, are in themselves the mightiest proof and the surest testimony of the truth of these heroes of the field of resignation and detachment.[15]

It is God's way to exalt the humble and humiliate the proud. He chooses a "rejected stone" and builds a magnificent edifice upon it.

> The stone which the builders rejected has become the chief cornerstone. This was the Lord's doing, and it is marvelous in our eyes? Matthew 21:42 NKJ

Beauty comes from contrast. We see Jesus rejected and ridiculed upon the cross and then witness with wonder and awe His glory and power not only on earth but in heaven, indeed in all creation. The same contrast, the same story is once again repeated in our time.

God has always been powerful, yet He has never used His power to make us believers. Why would He suddenly change His ways now? Notice the authority with which God speaks through the Báb:

> Had it been Our [God's] wish, We would have brought all men into one fold round Our Remembrance [the Báb]…[16]

Prophecies that point to rejection should make everyone vigilant. What do all the negative messages imply? Do they indicate that the majority will respond to the divine call or reject that call? If they indicate that the majority will reject, then following the majority means being on the wrong path. No wonder Jesus said:

> Enter by the narrow gate; for wide is the gate and broad is the way that leads to destruction, and there are many who go in by it. Mark 7:13 NKJ

> …many are called, but few chosen. Matthew 20:16

Lessons of History

The Jews of the time of Jesus faced the same puzzle we do. They had two opposite profiles of their Messiah: the suffering one, and the supreme one. They ignored the first and insisted on the second. Consider the following statement from a Christian author, written under the topic of "The Puzzle of the Two Portraits of Messiah:"

> In one sense, it's easy to see how they [the Jews] were confused about Jesus and his claim to be Messiah. The Old Testament seemed to predict two very contradictory pictures of Messiah. One showed him as coming from the family of King David, rising from obscurity into national prominence, destroying all the enemies of Israel and setting up a kingdom of universal peace, both politically and

> spiritually. The Jewish people were to be appointed as political and spiritual leaders in the kingdom. Such a picture fit in well with the nationalistic hopes of the Jews suffering under the iron-fisted oppression of the Roman Empire.
>
> The other picture of the Messiah, which emerged from the prophecies in the Old Testament, was that of a humble, gentle servant who would teach patiently, but would suffer and die for the sins of his people. He would be rejected by his own countrymen as well as hated by other peoples. This picture of Messiah is sometimes called 'The Suffering Messiah' and Isaiah speaks much about him.
>
> Before Jesus lived on this earth, the two pictures were confusing to students of prophecy. They grasped the two roles of Messiah clearly but the connection between them escaped the most brilliant of interpreters. How could one man have such contradictory aspects? Most Jewish scholars just left the problem of how to harmonize these two roles to be solved by any future prophets who might come.
>
> Other commentators invented a theory that perhaps two Messiahs were meant to come. The conquering King would be the Son of David and the suffering, lowly one would be in the tradition of Joseph, the Jewish lad who had suffered so badly at the hands of his brothers by being sold into slavery in Egypt and then had risen to prominence there. This Messiah began to be referred to as Messiah ben Joseph.
>
> What all these learned men failed to see was that ***all*** the predictions of the Messiah, both concepts of him, were to be fulfilled in one man, but not at one time.[17]

History is once again repeating itself. The parallels between the two Advents are astonishing. Once again we face two seemingly opposite portraits of our Redeemer. The two portraits are so puzzling that some Christian scholars have come up with the same solutions the Jewish scholars considered some 2,000 years ago. Notice the following from Christian scholar Dr. Ray Stedman, who believes Jesus comes twice, once as a thief, and again as a King:

> Some friends of mine live in a two-story house, with bedrooms upstairs. One morning they came downstairs to find that while they had slept peacefully in their beds upstairs a thief had been very busy downstairs. Their silverware and many other costly items and furnishings had been stolen. They had heard nothing, because a thief never knocks, never rings the doorbell, never announces his presence. He enters silently, takes what he wants, then disappears again.
>
> The Lord says that is what His coming again will be like—not His visible coming when He appears to establish His kingdom, when every eye will see Him, as described in Revelation 1:7.[18]

Some of the most brilliant Rabbis have failed to understand the true meaning of Hebrew prophecies about their Messiah. The only solution to their failure is a little humility. The only remedy is to say, "We do not understand all the mysteries, we are not infallible." Christian theologians are facing the puzzle that Jewish theologians have been facing for 2,000 years. All they need to do is express a little humility, all they need to say is, "We too, like the Jewish scholars and leaders, may be unable to resolve the paradox of ***the suffering Redeemer*** and ***the powerful Conqueror***. To be true to our faith, to be obedient to our Scriptures, we must act exactly as we are told, ***to let the Lord*** bring to light what is hidden in darkness:

> Therefore judge nothing before the appointed time; ***wait till the Lord comes. He will bring to light what is hidden in darkness***. I Corinthians 4:5 NIV
>
> ...no prophecy of Scripture is of any private interpretation. II Peter 1:20
>
> He who has an ear, let him hear what the Spirit says to ***the churches***. Christ (Rev. 2:7 NKJ)

Do the churches have the ear to hear this most clear and categorical command: that they should ***let the Lord*** bring to light what is hidden in darkness?

The Good News

After many centuries, the good news is that the tragedies will turn into triumphs, the sufferings into celebrations, and lamentations into joy and laughter:

> Then I saw a new heaven and a new earth, for the first heaven and the first earth had passed away, and there was no longer any sea. I saw the Holy City, the new Jerusalem, coming down out of heaven from God, prepared as a bride beautifully dressed for her husband. And I heard a loud voice from the throne saying, "Now the dwelling of God is with men, and he will live with them. They will be his people, and God himself will be with them and be their God. ***He will wipe every tear from their eyes. There will be no more death or mourning or crying or pain, for the old order of things has passed away.***" Revelation 21:1-4 NIV

> ...all nations and kindreds will be gathered together under the shadow of this Divine Banner, which is no other than the Lordly Branch itself, and will become a single nation. Religious and sectarian antagonism, the hostility of races and peoples, and differences among nations, will be eliminated. All men will adhere to one religion, will have one common faith, will be blended into one race, and become a single people. All will dwell in one common fatherland, which is the planet itself.[19] 'Abdu'l-Bahá

> National rivalries, hatreds, and intrigues will cease, and racial animosity and prejudice will be replaced by racial amity, understanding and cooperation. The causes of religious strife will be permanently removed, economic barriers and restrictions will be completely abolished, and the inordinate distinction between classes will be obliterated.[20]
>
> Shoghi Effendi

Whatsoever is latent in the innermost of this holy cycle shall gradually appear and be made manifest, for now is but the beginning of its growth, and the dayspring of the revelation of its signs. Ere the close of this century and of this age, it shall be made clear and evident how wondrous was that spring-tide, and how heavenly was that gift![21]

'Abdu'l-Bahá

The Lord their God will save them on that day as the flock of his people. They will sparkle in his land like jewels in a crown. How attractive and beautiful they will be! Grain [heavenly food] will make the young men thrive, and new wine [teachings] the young women.

Zechariah 9:16-17 NIV

8

The Day of Mourning

Some prophecies declare that "on that day" the peoples of the earth will ***mourn***. These prophecies point to several kinds of mourning. The first comes from the stresses, the pains, and pressures of being remote from God:

> ...all the nations of the earth will ***mourn***.
>
> Christ (Matt. 24:30 NIV)

Bahá'u'lláh interprets the previous prophecy, and declares its fulfillment:

> These words signify that in those days men will lament ***the loss of*** the Sun of the divine ***beauty***, of the Moon of ***knowledge***, and of the Stars of divine ***wisdom***.[1]

> Verily, the Inevitable is come...and mankind is sore vexed [disturbed] and fearful...and the tribes have ***lamented***, for fear of God...[2] Bahá'u'lláh

> ...all the tribes of the earth have ***mourned***...[3] Bahá'u'lláh

Everywhere we look we see spiritual starvation and death, we find people who hunger for the Light of truth, who thirst for celestial beauty, heavenly knowledge, and divine wisdom. The famine and the thirst are so intense, many have lost the will to live. People instinctively know something is seriously wrong but cannot pinpoint the disease. Only God knows the inner pain and hears the mourning of humankind. The spiritual state of the world is so grave, so desperate that even the earth mourns:

> ***The earth mourns*** and fades away, the world languishes and fades away; the haughty people of the earth languish. The earth is also defiled under its inhabitants, because they have transgressed the laws, changed the ordinance, broken the everlasting covenant. Therefore the curse has devoured the earth, and those who dwell in it are desolate. Therefore the inhabitants of the earth are burned [with the fire of remoteness from God], and few men are left. The new wine fails, the vine languishes, all the merry-hearted sigh. The mirth of the tambourine ceases, the noise of the jubilant ends, the joy of the harp ceases. They shall not drink wine with a song; strong drink is bitter to those who drink it. The city of confusion is broken down; every house is shut up, so that none may go in. There is a cry for [heavenly] wine in the streets, all joy is darkened, the mirth of the land is gone. In the city desolation is left, and the gate is stricken with destruction. When it shall be thus in the midst of the land among the people, it shall be like the shaking of an olive tree, like the gleaning of grapes when the vintage is done. Isaiah 24:4-13 NKJ

This kind of "mourning" is not an outward crying, but a subconscious longing of the souls for God. The "mourning" of the souls becomes especially intense at the dawn of the advent of great Messengers and Redeemers. The advent of spring stirs a new life into the world. Plants begin to wake up and flourish. Now assume plants had a soul like us. How would the flowers feel if they sensed that the spring has sprung, but they are unable to awaken, to smile, to embrace the sun, and dance with the winds. That is the inner state of the souls who are out of touch with the Spring of divine Revelation, with this supreme outpouring of the light and glory of God. Jesus quoted part of this prophecy from Isaiah to show the purpose of His coming:

> The Spirit of the Sovereign Lord is on me, because the Lord has anointed me to preach good news to the poor. He has sent me to bind up the brokenhearted, to proclaim freedom for the captives and release from darkness for the prisoners, to proclaim the year of the Lord's favor and the day of vengeance of our God, ***to comfort all who mourn***, and provide for those who grieve in Zion—to bestow on them a crown of beauty instead of ashes, the oil of gladness instead of mourning, and a garment of praise instead of a spirit of despair. They will be called oaks of righteousness, a planting of the Lord for ***the display of his splendor***.
>
> Isaiah 61:1-3 NIV

Most Christian scholars believe that Jesus did not quote several verses of the prophecy because He did not intend to fulfill them in His first advent. He stopped with "to proclaim the year of the Lord's favor." They believe He intended to accomplish the following goals at His second advent:

- To proclaim the day of vengeance of our God, and
- To comfort all who mourn

The purpose for which Jesus came is now accomplished. Bahá'u'lláh, the supreme Comforter, has come to comfort all who mourn for His splendor and glory. This kind of mourning is wonderful; it is a sign of spiritual health, like a hungry baby who cries. No wonder we are told:

> Blessed are those who ***mourn***, for they shall be comforted.
> Matthew 5:4 NKJ

> ***Wail***, for the day of the Lord is near... Isaiah 13:6 NIV

The souls who do ***not*** mourn are the sickest: they have lost the will to live. They are the complacent people who are satisfied with hibernating in a cold and dark winter, who feel secure and not in need of the new Spring:

> This is what the Lord Almighty says: "I am very ***angry with the nations that feel secure***..." Zechariah 1:14-15 NIV

In the Book of Revelation, Jesus chastised two groups of Christians most severely: ***the complacent, and the fearful***. He threatened the fearful with hell-fire (Revelation 21:8). Concerning the complacent or apathetic, He said:

> ...because you are lukewarm—neither hot nor cold—I am about to spit you out of my mouth. You say, 'I am rich; I have acquired wealth and do not need a thing.' ***But you do not realize that you are wretched, pitiful, poor, blind and naked***. Revelation 3:16-17 NIV

The reason Jesus condemned fear and complacency so harshly is this: He knew these two qualities more than any other would prevent Christians from seeking Him and finding Him at His second coming. Fear makes a person run away from the truth, while apathy causes him to ignore it. Can you teach bats to love light? Can you instill excitement in the hard-headed turtles?

Christ addressed the following parable, which ***contains the most severe warning, specifically to the masses of complacent Christians*** who glorify themselves as Jesus' chosen or intimate friends. He addressed it to the self-righteous ones, who believe they are their Lord's intimate neighbors, who assume they walk, drink, and eat with Jesus, the ones who think they are the inspired teachers of the Gospel, the ones who regard themselves as truly saved, and ***the first*** among Christians:

> Make every effort to enter through the narrow door, because many, I tell you, will try to enter and will not be able to. Once the owner of the house [the Redeemer] gets up and closes the door, you will stand outside knocking and pleading, 'Sir, open the door for us.' "But he will answer, 'I don't know you or where you come from.' Then you will say, 'We ate and drank with you, and you taught in our streets.' But he will reply, 'I don't know you or where you come from. Away from me, all you evildoers!' There will be weeping there, and gnashing of teeth, when you see Abraham, Isaac and Jacob and all the prophets in the kingdom of God, but you yourselves thrown out. People will come from east and west and north and south, and will take their places at the feast in the kingdom of God. ***Indeed there are those who are last who will be first, and first who will be last.***" Luke 13:24-30 NIV

It is clear, "the first" are not the ones who are the first in God's sight; they are the first only in the darkness of their own illusions and imaginations. These people are so sure of owning the truth that they become totally careless and deaf to all invitations. Because of their pride they fall from the first position to the last. The higher a person positions himself, the harsher the crash.

God's judgment against such people is extremely harsh. In the preceding prophecy, Jesus calls them "evildoers." In the parable of the talents, He refers to them as "wicked and lazy." Daniel uses the same word: "wicked:"

> …none of ***the wicked*** shall understand, but ***the wise*** shall understand. Daniel 12:10 NKJ

Why use such harsh words? Because such people are hypocrites. In God's sight, hypocrisy ranks among the most grievous sins. Why did Jesus condemn the Pharisees so severely? Because of their hypocrisy. To show His anger and indignation for such people, He told them "***WOE TO YOU***" ***eight times*** (Matthew 23:13-29). The Pharisees also considered themselves the first, while in God's sight they were the last. They also felt self-satisfied and complacent. Complacency, self-righteousness, and hypocrisy are perfect partners. They always support one another.

The Báb made a similar prediction about the way some of His followers—who considered themselves "God-fearing witnesses"—would respond to Bahá'u'lláh:

> On that Day ye will continue to rove distraught, even as camels, seeking a drop of the water of life. God will cause oceans of living water to stream forth from the presence of Him Whom God shall make manifest [Bahá'u'lláh], while ye will refuse to quench your thirst therefrom, notwithstanding that ***ye regard yourselves as the God-fearing witnesses of your Faith***...yet when He cometh ye will tarry and will fail to be of those who are well-assured in His Faith.[4]

Bahá'u'lláh states that His advent has upset the prevailing balance in people's lives. The loss of balance creates a subconscious awareness in the soul that a new dawn has broken. The awareness leads to a longing to arise and witness the wonders of the new Day.

> The world's equilibrium hath been upset through the vibrating influence of this most great, this new World Order. Mankind's ordered life hath been revolutionized through the agency of this unique, this wondrous System—the like of which mortal eyes have never witnessed.[5] Bahá'u'lláh

Here are two more excerpts from Bahá'u'lláh describing how the power released by His Revelation has caused a revolution in the planet and its people, how it has disturbed the established balance to create a new and dramatic growth, how it has awakened the souls to wail and mourn for their Beloved:

> Thus have the mighty verses of Thy Lord been again sent down unto thee, that thou mayest arise to remember God, the Creator of earth and heaven, in these days ***when all the tribes of the earth have mourned, and the foundations of***

> ***the cities have trembled***, and the dust of irreligion hath enwrapped all men, except such as God, the All-Knowing, the All-Wise, was pleased to spare. Say: He Who is the Unconditioned is come, in the clouds of light, that He may quicken all created things with the breezes of His Name, the Most Merciful, and unify the world, and gather all men around this Table which hath been sent down from heaven.[6]
>
> Wash from your hearts all earthly defilements, and hasten to enter the Kingdom of your Lord, the Creator of earth and heaven, ***Who caused the world to tremble and all its peoples to wail***, except them that have renounced all things...[7]

The Qur'án confirms the same message:

> One Day everything that can be in commotion ***will be in violent commotion***, followed by oft-repeated (commotions). Hearts that Day will be in agitation... Qur'án 79:6-8 Y
>
> One day, the disturbing trumpet-blast [the advent of the Báb] shall disturb it [the world order], which the second blast shall follow [the advent of Bahá'u'lláh]. Men's hearts on that day shall quake. Qur'án 79:6-8 R

The severe and universal ***distress*** prophesied by Jesus in the Olivet Discourse has occurred because of the loss of spiritual strength, the disturbance of old values, norms, and systems, and the soul's subconscious awareness of being deprived of all the joys and blessings of the glorious advent of the divine springtime:

> For then ***there will be great distress***, unequaled from the beginning of the world until now—and never to be equaled again. If those days had not been cut short, no one would survive, but for the sake of the elect those days will be shortened. Christ (Matt. 24:21-22 NIV)

The evidences of distress and disturbance are everywhere. The rising waves of violence, crime, mental disease, depression, loneliness, stress, suicide, divorce, child abuse, rape, racism, fraud, and relentless destruction of the environment are all symptoms of souls who are out of touch with God, who are withering and shaking in the cold of winter, who are mourning the loss of hope and joy.

There is yet another kind of "mourning." It comes from the anger of the deniers, who witness the triumph of the Redeemer of the age, but are unable to stop Him. This prophecy is similar to the one in Matthew, but with the additional phrase "because of Him:"

> ...all the peoples of the earth will mourn ***because of him***.
> Revelation 1:7 NIV

In this case, people's mourning is connected to the Redeemer. In their book, *The Return*, Christian scholars Dr. Barry Chant and Winkie Pratney have recognized such a "mourning:"

> We can see once again why the nations of the world will mourn when they see Him come! The dismay, the confusion, the disbelief will be plain to see. How can it be, they will ask. How can it be that this carpenter from Nazareth Whom we dismissed so easily from our thinking as an irrelevant, impotent figure is now towering over us in indisputable and irresistible glory?
>
> All those who thought that they were so strong, so influential, so dominating, so self-sufficient, so independent of God or man, will find themselves cringing in terror at the fierce gaze of the Son of God.[8]

The Book of Psalms asks, "***Why do the nations rage?***" (Psalms 2:1). They rage because they see the triumph of the One they have rejected; they see the spread of a new social Order they do not like. They rage and mourn because they see their security threatened, because they see someone else is receiving attention, gaining influence, and becoming popular. Fear and envy make them burn, fume and fret. Raging is an act of seething and protesting in anger.

> The great day of the Lord is near—near and coming quickly. Listen! ***The cry on the day of the Lord will be bitter***...
> Zephaniah 1:14 NIV

> ...***fear and trembling*** seized the people of ***envy*** and ***wickedness***...[9]
> Bahá'u'lláh

People cannot stand the triumph of truth over their cherished traditions, but their efforts to withstand the mighty forces released by the new Revelation are in vain:

> For the great day of His wrath has come, and ***who is able to stand***?
> Revelation 6:17 NKJ

This kind of bitter mourning and raging have already occurred. The continuous advancement of the Bahá'í Faith has astonished, angered, and made envious the fanatical believers of past religions. Many years ago I met a young zealous Muslim who had just come from Iran to the United States. Soon after his arrival he encountered some American Bahá'ís. He could not believe educated Americans would accept a man from Iran as their Redeemer. His astonishment turned into jealousy, disappointment, and anger, when he found an active Bahá'í community in Saginaw, Michigan, but no society of active Muslims there! We can hardly imagine the bitter feelings of prejudiced people who dismiss the Bahá'í Faith as a small passing wave, and suddenly discover that the wave is encircling the globe!

Some years ago I spoke with a university student about the Bahá'í Faith and lent him a part of the *I Shall Come Again* manuscript. He spent many hours in the library trying to find a flaw in my reasoning. The flaw he found was this: "Daniel did not say, 'after 2,400 days.' The Greek word He used meant, 'After 2,400 ***evenings and mornings***.' You cannot count those as days." Then in a state of consuming rage, he added, "You use the university library and other state facilities to prove and spread your Faith!" On his face I saw all the negative feelings I have known: anger, envy, bitterness, and frustration. He would do anything to prevent me from spreading the Bahá'í message, but he felt totally powerless.

At the university in which I now teach, the Bahá'í community has faced continuous harassment from a small group of zealous Christians. Before they had fully recognized our beliefs, we enjoyed a period of total freedom. But when they learned that we believe Christ has come again, they tried to prevent us from spreading our message. They have repeatedly removed our fliers from bulletin boards over a course of some 30 years. Such a response has not been sporadic. It has been persistent and relentless. We have also received many anonymous telephone calls. Early on, the callers would talk and ask questions to measure our strength. When they realized that some of us may know the Bible better than they do, they began to call without saying a word. To stop the ringing, we would disconnect our phone for several hours. Once a few zealous believers blocked the Bahá'í display in a university fair, so that people could not see it. A pastor came forward and said, "Not all Christians are like them." He apologized for the unseemly behavior of his fellow-believers.

'Abdu'l-Bahá predicts that a time will come when the "mourning" and "crying" of all nations will be raised. He mentions even the name of the countries, such as China and India.[10] A Bahá'í friend of mine recently had a dream in which 'Abdu'l-Bahá confirmed this prediction by saying, "Yes, even the 'mourning' of China and India will be raised."

Many prophecies predict widespread rage and anger from both political and religious figures and institutions:

> The Lord roars from Zion, and utters His voice from Jerusalem; the pastures [religious institutions] of the shepherds ***mourn***, and the top of Carmel [those in high positions of power] withers. Amos 1:2 NKJ

> ***The noise*** of a multitude in the mountains [institutional powers], like that of many people! A tumultuous noise of

> the kingdoms of nations gathered together!...***Wail***, for the day of the Lord is at hand! Isaiah 13:4, 6 NKJ

> God is our refuge and strength, a very present help in trouble. Therefore we will not fear, even though the earth [the old systems] be removed, and though the mountains [institutions] be carried into the midst of the sea; though its waters [masses of people] roar and be troubled, though the mountains shake with its swelling. There is a river [of knowledge and wisdom] whose streams shall make glad the city of God [the city of Bahá'u'lláh, the Bahá'í Faith], the holy place of the tabernacle of ***the Most High*** [the Báb]. ***God*** [Bahá'u'lláh] is in the midst of her [the river], she shall not be moved; God shall help her, just at the break of dawn. The nations ***raged***, the kingdoms were moved; He uttered His voice [proclaimed His message], the earth melted [the old order vanished].✤
> Psalms 46:1-6 NKJ

The preceding prophecy from Psalms asks us not to fear, "even though ***the earth be removed, and though the mountains be carried into the midst of the sea***." Here Bahá'u'lláh refers to the state of the earth and the mountains:

> ***The earth hath been shaken, and the mountains have passed away***, and the angels have appeared, rank on rank, before Us. Most of the people are bewildered in their drunkenness and wear on their faces the evidences of anger.[11] Bahá'u'lláh

The preceding prophecy from Psalms offers a perfect example of the metaphoric language God speaks. That language differs radically from our language. Let us take one word: river. What is the ***river*** that will bring joy to the two Revelations, that "shall make glad the city of ***God***" as well as "the holy place

---

✤ As we noted earlier, verses 4 and 5 also have a literal fulfillment. A pilgrim in the presence of Bahá'u'lláh saw a scene described in this prophecy and suddenly remembered the verses.

of ***the Most High***"? ***River*** symbolizes all the blessings of God. Consider these examples from the Writings of Bahá'u'lláh:

> This is the Day whereon the true servants of God partake of the life-giving waters of reunion, the Day whereon those that are nigh unto Him are able to drink of the soft-flowing ***river of immortality***, and they who believe in His unity, the wine of His Presence...[12]

> O MY SERVANT!
> Abandon not for that which perisheth an everlasting dominion, and cast not away celestial sovereignty for a worldly desire. This is ***the river of everlasting life*** that hath flowed from the well-spring of the pen of the merciful; well is it with them that drink![13]

> ***The River of Mercy*** floweth, and the Ocean of Utterance surgeth, and the Sun of Revelation shineth forth resplendent.[14]

> Make haste...that while there is yet time our lips may taste of the immortal draught, for the breeze of life, now blowing from the city of the Well-Beloved, cannot last, and ***the streaming river of holy utterance*** must needs be stilled...[15]

Here are a few other metaphoric uses of 'river' in Bahá'u'lláh's Writings:

> the river of divine knowledge[16]
> the sacred river of wealth[17]
> the River of God, and His favor[18]
> the River that is life[19]
> Whose heavenly River is Thy love[20]
> the river of glory[21]
> the heavenly river of My loving providence[22]
> the river of divine wisdom[23]

Bahá'u'lláh often uses the word "mourn" in reference to those who protest His coming, because they cannot stand

His triumphs. Concerning the Muslim clergy who raised their voices against the spread of the Bahá'í Faith in Iran, Bahá'u'lláh wrote:

> ***The lamentations of the pulpits***, in that country, are being raised continually...pulpits, erected for the purpose of remembering the True One—exalted be His glory—have now, in Persia, become places wherefrom blasphemies are uttered against Him Who is the Desire of the worlds.[24]

The Hebrew Scriptures have stated the reasons why the lamentation of religious leaders will be raised:

> At that time...Hear the ***cry*** of the shepherds, the ***wailing*** of the leaders of the flock, ***for the Lord is destroying their pasture.*** Jeremiah 25:33, 36 NIV

Leaders who weep and wail against the Lord can never win:

> ***Weep and wail***, you shepherds; roll in the dust, you leaders of the flock. For your time to be slaughtered has come; you will fall and be shattered like fine pottery. ***The shepherds will have nowhere to flee, the leaders of the flock no place to escape.*** Jeremiah 25:34-35 NIV

Can anyone escape from God's plan and purpose? In an Epistle to a powerful religious leader, Bahá'u'lláh used the same expression found in the preceding prophecy:

> By My life! There is ***no place for you to flee*** to in this day.[25]

The wailing, raging, and mourning will find their fullest expression in countless speeches that will be delivered and books written against Bahá'u'lláh. The wailers and mourners will look for loopholes in His Writings to discredit Him, exactly as the Pharisees did some 2,000 years ago. The lamentation is absolutely essential for the triumph of truth. It will awaken many sincere seekers who would not learn about Bahá'u'lláh in any other way. This will set in motion the process of "sifting" the peoples of the earth, bringing out what lies hidden in the hearts and souls of humankind. God never imposes

Himself on His people; He always leaves a way out for those who do not like His banquet.

When Bahá'u'lláh's House in Baghdád was desecrated, He predicted that the abasement and desecration will continue until "the day of lamentation." That is the time when the supreme honors bestowed on His House will cause His enemies to mourn:

> This is not the first humiliation inflicted upon My House. In days gone by the hand of the oppressor hath heaped indignities upon it. Verily, it shall be so abased in the days to come as to cause tears to flow from every discerning eye. Thus have We unfolded to thee things hidden beyond the veil, inscrutable to all save God, the Almighty, the All-Praised. In the fullness of time, the Lord shall, by the power of truth, exalt it in the eyes of all men. He shall cause it to become the Standard of His Kingdom, the Shrine round which will circle the concourse of the faithful. Thus hath spoken the Lord, thy God, ere ***the day of lamentation*** arriveth.[26] Bahá'u'lláh

This prophecy shows a clear contrast between the followers of the new Redeemer and the deniers:

> My servants [new believers] will sing out of the joy of their hearts, but you [deniers] will ***cry out*** from anguish of heart and ***wail***... Isaiah 65:14 NIV

Bahá'u'lláh confirms such a contrast between God's chosen ones, who have recognized and glorified "the Most Great Name" (Bahá'u'lláh), and those who have lamented because of the new Name:

> Glory be to Thee, O Thou the Best-Beloved, for that Thou hast uncovered Thy Beauty, and written down for ***Thy chosen ones*** what will cause them to attain unto the seat of the revelation of Thy Most Great Name [Bahá'u'lláh], through which ***all the peoples have lamented*** except such as have detached themselves from all else except Thee...[27]

As we noted, Jesus predicted that "all the peoples of the earth will mourn ***because of Him***." A prophecy from Amos declares that people will mourn because the Lord passes through them, because ***God passes by***. If people recognized their Redeemer and their Lord, they would celebrate rather than lament His presence and His walking among them:

> Therefore this is what the Lord, the Lord God Almighty, says: "There will be wailing in all the streets and cries of anguish in every public square. The farmers will be summoned to weep and the mourners to wail. ***There will be wailing in all the vineyards, for I will pass through your midst***," says the Lord. Amos 5:16-17 NIV

The mourning does not stop with human beings; it can permeate the whole creation. This happened at the crucifixion of Jesus:

> Know thou that when the Son of Man yielded up His breath to God, the whole creation wept with a great weeping.[28]
>
> Bahá'u'lláh

Because of His deep love, when we reject God's immortal blessings, Our Creator also mourns our pitiful plight:

> **O BOND SLAVE OF THE WORLD!**
> Many a dawn hath the breeze of My loving-kindness wafted over thee and found thee upon the bed of heedlessness fast asleep. ***Bewailing then thy plight*** it returned whence it came.[29]
>
> Bahá'u'lláh

People can lament for many reasons. Another reason is this: hearing the news of the coming of King of Kings and Lord of Lords not only makes them angry but casts fear in their hearts. They might fear this possibility: "I know I am too attached to my beliefs to investigate or accept the new message. What if it is true? What will I lose?"

> Hath the Hour come? Nay, more; it hath passed, by Him Who is the Revealer of clear tokens! Verily, the Inevitable is come, and He, the True One, hath appeared with proof

> and testimony...and ***the tribes have lamented, for fear of God***, the Lord of Strength, the All-Compelling.[30]
>
> Wash from your hearts all earthly defilements, and hasten to enter the Kingdom of your Lord, the Creator of earth and heaven, ***Who caused the world to tremble and all its peoples to wail***, except them that have renounced all things...[31]

Another kind of wailing and mourning comes from the citizens of the next Kingdom because of the pain they feel for the rejected and reviled Redeemer:

> The dwellers in the pavilion of glory and the celestial concourse [heavenly beings] ***bewail and lament***, while ye repose in the realm of negligence, and esteem yourselves as of the true friends. How vain are your imaginings![32]
>
> Bahá'u'lláh
>
> I implore Thee, by the eternity of Thy Self, to enable me [Bahá'u'lláh] to be patient in these tribulations which have caused the concourse on high [heavenly beings] ***to wail*** and the denizens of the everlasting Paradise ***to weep***...[33]

There is yet another kind of mourning: that of the followers for the sufferings of ***their Redeemer***. The following prophecy is attributed to Jesus, but it also applies to the Báb, as He was also "pierced." The phrase "on that day" pertains especially to our time:

> It shall be ***in that day*** that I will seek to destroy all the nations that come against Jerusalem. And I will pour on the house of David and on the inhabitants of Jerusalem the Spirit of grace and supplication; then they will look on Me ***whom they pierced***. Yes, ***they will mourn for Him*** as one mourns for his only son, and grieve for Him as one grieves for a firstborn. Zechariah 12:9-10 NKJ

As mentioned before, suffering comes not only to the Lamb of God but also to His followers:

> These are they who have come out of the great tribulation; they have washed their robes and made them white in the blood of the Lamb. Revelation 7:14 NIV

After referring to the martyrdom of the Báb—"the Lamb that was slain from the creation of the world" (Revelation 7:14)—the Book of Revelation speaks again of the sufferings of His followers:

> If anyone is [destined] to go into captivity, into captivity he will go. If anyone is [destined] to be killed with the sword, with the sword he will be killed. This calls for patient endurance and faithfulness on the part of the saints [the suffering followers]. Revelation 13:10 NIV

Christian authors often see an irony in the rejection of Jesus:

> How ironic that in rejecting Jesus the Jews fulfilled prophecies that identified Him as the Messiah![34]

It seems that history always repeats itself. Once again we need to say "how ironic" that those who say "how ironic" about the Jews' denial of Jesus do not see the irony that by denying Bahá'u'lláh, they too fulfill the prophecies!

The Thunderous Lord

Some prophecies point to the supreme power displayed by the promised Lord:

> Then the Lord will appear over them; his arrow will flash like lightning. The Sovereign Lord will sound the trumpet… Zechariah 9:14 NIV

> They will follow the Lord; he will roar like a lion.
> Hosea 11:10 NIV

These prophecies find their fulfillment in Bahá'u'lláh's supreme utterance. He proclaims His advent in thunderous words. Have you ever heard anyone speak with such power and authority?

> This is the Day whereon the All-Merciful hath come down in the clouds of knowledge, clothed with manifest sovereignty. He well knoweth the actions of men. He it is Whose glory none can mistake, could ye but comprehend it. The heaven of every religion hath been rent, and the earth of human understanding been cleft asunder, and the angels of God are seen descending. Say:✣ This is the Day of mutual deceit; whither do ye flee? The mountains have passed away, and the heavens have been folded together, and the whole earth is held within His grasp, could ye but understand it. Who is it that can protect you? None, by Him Who is the All-Merciful! None, except God, the Almighty, the All-Glorious, the Beneficent...
>
> Say: Is there any doubt concerning God? Behold how He hath come down from the heaven of His grace, girded with power and invested with sovereignty. Is there any doubt concerning His signs? Open ye your eyes, and consider His clear evidence. Paradise is on your right hand, and hath been brought nigh unto you, while Hell hath been made to blaze. Witness its devouring flame. Haste ye to enter into Paradise, as a token of Our mercy unto you, and drink ye from the hands of the All-Merciful the Wine that is life indeed.[35] Bahá'u'lláh

Some people who hear Bahá'u'lláh's mighty "voice" flee in fear. They cannot endure the message:

> At the thunder of your [the Lord's] voice, ***the people flee***; when you rise up, ***the nations scatter***. Isaiah 33:3 NIV

Why do people flee? For many reasons. What happens when there is a thunderstorm? As Christian scholar Biederwolf observes:

✣ The word "Say" in the form of a command, appears frequently in the Writings of Bahá'u'lláh. It indicates that the speaker is the Spirit of God. It is equivalent to the biblical expression, "Thus says the Lord."

> The approach of Jehovah is likened to an advancing thunder storm, which is His voice, causing the peoples… to flee.[36]

Bahá'u'lláh's "Voice" is indeed like a thunderstorm. Have you ever seen or heard anyone speak with such power and authority?

> He Who is the Lord of Lords is come overshadowed with clouds, and the decree hath been fulfilled by God, the Almighty, the Unrestrained.[37]

Many prophecies point to fear, terror, and trembling.

> Enter into the rock, and hide in the dust, from ***the terror of the Lord*** and the glory of His majesty. The lofty looks of man shall be humbled, the haughtiness of men shall be bowed down, and the Lord alone shall be exalted in that day. Isaiah 2:10-11 NKJ

Bahá'u'lláh confirms their fulfillment:

> The All-Merciful is come invested with undoubted sovereignty. The Balance hath been appointed, and all them that dwell on earth have been gathered together. The Trumpet hath been blown, and lo, ***all eyes have stared up with terror***, and the hearts of all who are in the heavens and on the earth have trembled, except them whom the breath of the verses of God hath quickened, and who have detached themselves from all things.[38] Bahá'u'lláh

> Cry and weep! The day is coming when the mighty Lord will bring destruction. All people will be terrified. Hands will grow limp; courage will melt away. Everyone will tremble with pain like a woman giving birth; ***they will stare at each other with horror*** on their faces.
> Isaiah 13:6-8 CEV

> This is the Day on which ***all eyes shall stare up with terror***, the Day in which the hearts of them that dwell on earth shall tremble, save them whom thy Lord, the All-Knowing, the All-Wise, pleaseth to deliver…Drunken are

> the eyes of those men that have openly refused to behold the face of God, the All-Glorious, the All-Praised.[39]
>
> Bahá'u'lláh

To a believer not overcome by "terror," Bahá'u'lláh wrote:

> The manifold bounties of God have ever been and will continue to be vouchsafed unto thee. Praised be God! Thou hast been shielded from ***the most great terror*** and hast succeeded in drawing nigh unto the Most Great Bounty at a time when all men were prevented from recognizing the eternal King by the interposition of the veils of outward glory, namely the divines [religious leaders] of this day.[40]

In a prayer, Bahá'u'lláh refers to the various responses displayed by people to "the Great Terror:"

> No sooner had He [Bahá'u'lláh] proclaimed Thy [God's] Cause, and risen up to carry out the things prescribed unto Him in the Tablets of Thy decree, than ***the Great Terror fell upon Thy creatures***. Some turned towards Thee, and detached themselves from all except Thee, and sanctified their souls from the world and all that is therein, and were so enravished by the sweetness of Thy voice that they forsook all Thou hadst created in the kingdom of Thy creation. Others recognized Thee and then hesitated, others allowed the world to come in between them and Thee and to withhold them from recognizing Thee. Others disdained Thee, and turned back from Thee, and wished to prevent Thee from achieving Thy purpose.[41]

What do people do when they cannot stand something? They run away in fear. The various names of Bahá'u'lláh such as ***Jehovah***, ***Lord Almighty***, ***King of Kings and Lord of Lords*** are so awesome, that they cause the fearful to tremble, they even make the earth move:

> The Lord reigns; let the peoples tremble! He dwells between the cherubim; ***let the earth be moved***! The Lord is great in Zion, and He is high above all the peoples. Let them praise your great and ***awesome name***; He is holy...

> Exalt the Lord our God, and worship at His footstool; He is holy.
> Psalms 99:1-5 NKJ

Bahá'u'lláh speaks frequently about those who try to avoid, ignore, or flee from encountering the news of His coming:

> The thing that must come hath come suddenly; behold how they ***flee*** from it! The inevitable hath come to pass; witness how they have cast it behind their backs![42]

> We, verily, have come for your sakes, and have borne the misfortunes of the world for your salvation. ***Flee*** ye the One Who hath sacrificed His life that ye may be quickened?[43]

> O high priests! The Hand of Omnipotence is stretched forth from behind the clouds; behold ye it with new eyes. The tokens of His majesty and greatness are unveiled; gaze ye on them with pure eyes...Say, O high priests! Ye are held in reverence because of My Name, and yet ye ***flee*** Me![44]

> There is no place to ***flee*** to, no refuge that any one can seek, except Him.[45]

When a new order, a new way of thinking appears, the established order feels threatened. As futurist Alvin Toffler, in his classic book *The Third Wave*, declares:

> A new civilization is emerging in our lives, and blind men everywhere are trying to suppress it...Pieces of this new civilization exist today. Millions are already attuning their lives to the rhythms of tomorrow. ***Others, terrified of the future, are engaged in a desperate, futile flight into the past and are trying to restore the dying world that gave them birth***. The dawn of this new civilization is the single most explosive fact of our lifetimes.[46]

Some prophecies declare that the promised Redeemer will be as powerful and majestic as a lion (Rev. 5:5), and that people who encounter His message will be gripped with fear. Many will be unable to bear His news or stand the greatness and the wrath of His day (Rev. 6:17).

> ...all hands will go limp, every man's heart will melt. ***Terror will seize them***... Isaiah 13:7-8 NIV

Bahá'u'lláh confirms:

> Verily, the Inevitable is come...and mankind is sore vexed [disturbed] and ***fearful***...and the tribes have lamented, for fear of God...[47]

> ...the blast of the trumpet [proclamation of Bahá'u'lláh's Message] must needs spread confusion throughout the world, and ***fear and trembling*** amongst all men. Well is it with him who hath been illumined with the light of trust and detachment. The tribulations of that Day will not hinder or alarm him.[48]

In the following passage, "the Ark of God" symbolizes the Bahá'í Faith, which like Noah's Ark is the ship of safety and salvation, and "the Mariner" symbolizes Bahá'u'lláh, who guides the ship:

> Waves have encompassed the Ark of God, the Help in Peril, the Self-Subsisting. Fear not the tempestuous gales, O Mariner! He Who causeth the dawn to appear is, verily, with Thee in ***this darkness that hath struck terror into the hearts of all men***, except such as God, the Almighty, the Unconstrained, hath been pleased to spare.[49]

Bahá'u'lláh links the spread of fear to the greatness of His Revelation:

> In the Book of Isaiah it is written: "Enter into the rock, and hide thee in the dust, for fear of the Lord, and for the glory of His majesty." No man that meditateth upon this verse can fail to recognize the greatness of this Cause, or doubt the exalted character of this Day—the Day of God Himself.[50]

What does fear lead to? To fight or flight. Some people try to suppress the news; others run away from it or ignore it. What is it that people cannot stand? More than anything else,

Bahá'u'lláh intimates, it is ***His station as the Father***. Imagine the consequences if Jesus had called Himself the Father. In this age people have the ***potential*** to bear this awesome message: the coming of Lord of Lord and King of Kings. No wonder Jesus said:

> I still have many things to say to you, but ***you cannot bear them now***. However, when He, the Spirit of truth, has come, He will guide you into all truth; for ***He will not speak on His own authority***, but whatever He hears He will speak; and He will tell you things to come. John 16:12-13 NKJ

Bahá'u'lláh confirms the fulfillment of Jesus' prophecy:

> Proclaim then unto all mankind the glad-tidings of this mighty, this glorious Revelation. Verily, ***He Who is the Spirit of Truth is come to guide you unto all truth. He speaketh not as prompted by His own self***, but as bidden by Him Who is the All-Knowing, the All-Wise.[51]

Prophecies that point to "fleeing" or "escaping" have already been fulfilled. Many Muslims are told by their religious leaders to shun the Bahá'ís. The same is gradually happening in the West. I have already encountered many fearful Christians who shun the Bahá'ís for fear of being deceived. They also fear the rejection of their loved ones, the ridicule of the world, and the loss of power and possessions.

This indeed is a bitter day for all those who cling to old and archaic beliefs and institutions:

> I will turn your feasts into mourning, and all your songs into lamentation; I will bring sackcloth on every waist, and baldness on every head; I will make it like mourning for an only son, and its end like a bitter day.
> Amos 8:10 NKJ

The punishment is extremely grave for those who flee their responsibility and refute reality through their fear of the truth, for whatever reason—whether it is being ridiculed by others for recognizing the new Redeemer, stepping out of their comfort zone, or witnessing the awesome power and glory of the Lord:

"But ***the cowardly***" declares Jesus, "***their place will be in the fiery lake of burning sulfur***" (Rev. 21:8 NIV). To ***the fearful*** servant who concealed his "talents" Jesus said: "***You wicked and lazy servant***" (Matt. 25:26).

Prophecies declare that the people of our time will be fearful, faithless, confused, asleep, blind, and drunk! If we truly believe in the Word of God, what can we expect other than denial? The problem is this: a drunk does not know he is drunk until he is sober, and a sleeper does not know he is asleep until he wakes up. No wonder people who live in the darkness of denial fail to see the state of their soul. How can an unconscious person know he is unconscious?

We should recognize God's supreme love for all human beings. In the following passage, Bahá'u'lláh declares that people are "in a state of stupor" like someone sleeping. He asks us to be forbearing with such sleepers, and not to shake them up, but gently wake them up:

> Being overcome by the drunkenness of corrupt inclinations, the people of the earth find themselves in a state of stupor. They are, therefore, debarred from the wondrous signs of God, are prevented from attaining the ultimate goal and are deprived of the liberal effusions of divine grace.
>
> It behoveth the people of God ***to be forbearing***. They should ***impart the Word of God according to the hearer's particular measure of understanding and capacity***, that perchance the children of men may be roused from heedlessness and set their faces towards this Horizon which is immeasurably exalted above every horizon.[52]

Here Am I

An expression used in several Scriptures to identify Bahá'u'lláh or the Bahá'í Faith is the expression "Here am I," or "Here I am." What does the expression imply? It indicates a willingness to give or receive without any reservations. It points to a state of readiness, an absolute desire to be the bestower or the receiver of truth and knowledge. When our Creator declares, "Here am I," it means, "I am ready to give you My blessings and the knowledge of immortal life. I am your Lover and Beloved. Come and embrace Me." Our response should be, "Here am I ready to receive your glorious gifts. I am infinitely honored to receive such a wholehearted invitation from my Creator!"

Here is a prophecy from Isaiah with this expression:

> Then your light [Bahá] shall break forth like the morning, your healing shall spring forth speedily, and your righteousness shall go before you; the glory of the Lord [Bahá'u'lláh] shall be your rear guard. Then you shall call, and the Lord will answer; you shall cry, and He will say, "***Here I am***."
>
> Isaiah 58:8-9 NKJ

Another expression with a similar meaning is "It is I."

> Therefore My people shall know My name; therefore they shall know in that day that I am He who speaks: "***Behold, it is I***." How beautiful upon the mountains are the feet of him who brings good news, who proclaims peace, who brings glad tidings of good things, who proclaims salvation, who says to Zion, "Your God reigns!" Isaiah 52:6-7 NKJ

In an Epistle addressed to a religious leader who rejected His invitation, the Báb wrote:

> For hadst thou uttered "***Here am I***" at the time We sent thee the Book, We would have admitted thee to the company of such of Our servants as truly believe, and would have graciously praised thee in Our Book, until the Day when all men shall appear before Us for judgment. This

> is in truth far more advantageous unto thee than all the acts of worship thou hast performed for thy Lord during all thy life, nay, from the beginning that hath no beginning. Assuredly this is what would have served and will ever serve thy best interests. Verily We are cognizant of all things.[53]

God's great Messengers and Redeemers express utter love and infinite humility toward each other. Bahá'u'lláh confers the most glorious titles upon Jesus, such as the Spirit of God and the Lord of the visible and invisible. Jesus bestows similar titles on the twin Redeemers of our time. In His Epistle to Christians, Bahá'u'lláh points to Jesus' supreme love for Him. The implication is clear: if the one you worship expresses such love for Me, why are you failing to follow His example? Here is a passage from the Epistle containing the expression "Here am I."

> Say: We, in truth, have opened unto you the gates of the Kingdom. Will ye bar the doors of your houses in My face? This indeed is naught but a grievous error. He, verily, hath again come down from heaven, even as He came down from it the first time. Beware lest ye dispute that which He proclaimeth, even as the people before you disputed His utterances. Thus instructeth you the True One, could ye but perceive it.
>
> ...the Son [Jesus], in the holy vale, crieth out: "***Here am I, here am I O Lord, my God!***", whilst Sinai circleth round the House, and the Burning Bush calleth aloud: "He Who is the Desired One is come in His transcendent majesty." Say, Lo! The Father is come, and that which ye were promised in the Kingdom is fulfilled![54]

Today a state of spiritual apathy prevails throughout the world. People are far more attached to gold than to God. In the following passage Isaiah refers both to God's invitation and the people's refusal or failure to respond:

> I revealed myself to those who did not ask for me; I was found by those who did not seek me. To a nation that did

> not call on my name, I said, "***Here am I, here am I***." All day long I have held out my hands to an obstinate people, who walk in ways not good, pursuing their own imaginations... Isaiah 65:1-2 NIV

This Revelation is so great that all past Messengers have uttered the words "Here am I, Here am I," yet the people who were created by these Messengers refuse to do so! They studied their Scriptures, prayed for His coming, recited the words "Here am I," but when they saw Him, they rose against Him:

> Behold, how the divers peoples and kindreds of the earth have been waiting for the coming of the Promised One. No sooner had He, Who is the Sun of Truth, been made manifest, than, lo, all turned away from Him, except them whom God was pleased to guide.[55] Bahá'u'lláh

> Whenever His [the Báb's] blessed name was mentioned, all would say: "May God hasten the joy His coming will bring!" On the day of the Revelation of that Sun of Truth, however, all, as hath been observed, have exclaimed, saying: "May God hasten His chastisement!" He Who was the Essence of being and Lord of the seen and unseen [the Báb] they suspended,[✦] and committed what made...the Pen to groan, and the cries of the sincere to break forth, and the tears of the favored ones to flow.[56] Bahá'u'lláh

Selections from the Writings of Bahá'u'lláh

The Purpose of Suffering

> The Ancient Beauty [Bahá'u'lláh] hath consented to be bound with chains that mankind may be released from its bondage, and hath accepted to be made a prisoner within this most mighty Stronghold that the whole world may

[✦] The Báb was suspended above the ground and shot.

attain unto true liberty. He hath drained to its dregs the cup of sorrow, that all the peoples of the earth may attain unto abiding joy, and be filled with gladness. This is of the mercy of your Lord, the Compassionate, the Most Merciful. We have accepted to be abased, O believers in the Unity of God, that ye may be exalted, and have suffered manifold afflictions, that ye might prosper and flourish.[57]

Say: We have accepted to be tried by ills and troubles, that ye may sanctify yourselves from all earthly defilements. Why, then, refuse ye to ponder Our purpose in your hearts? By the righteousness of God! Whoso will reflect upon the tribulations We have suffered, his soul will assuredly melt away with sorrow. Thy Lord Himself beareth witness to the truth of My words. We have sustained the weight of all calamities to sanctify you from all earthly corruption, and ye are yet indifferent.[58]

Suffering, the Destiny of all Great Messengers or Manifestations of God

...as far back as the First Manifestation, all have at the time of Their appearance suffered grievously. Some were held to be possessed, others were called impostors, and were treated in a manner that the pen is ashamed to describe. By God! There befell Them what hath made all created things to sigh, and yet the people are, for the most part, sunk in manifest ignorance! We pray God to assist them to return unto Him, and to repent before the door of His mercy. Potent is He over all things.[59]

Suffering as an Evidence

Consider, therefore, how the generality of mankind, whatever their beliefs or theories, have recognized the excellence, and admitted the superiority, of these Prophets of God. These Gems of Detachment are acclaimed by some as the embodiments of wisdom, while others believe them to be the mouthpiece of God Himself. How could such

Souls have consented to surrender themselves unto their enemies if they believed all the worlds of God to have been reduced to this earthly life? Would they have willingly suffered such afflictions and torments as no man hath ever experienced or witnessed?[60]

The Abundance of Suffering

So great have been Our sufferings that even the eyes of Our enemies have wept over Us, and beyond them those of every discerning person.[61]

Thankful Despite Suffering

He [Bahá'u'lláh] summoned men unto the most sublime Paradise, and yet they seized Him and paraded Him through cities and countries. How many the nights during which slumber fled from the eyes of My loved ones, because of their love for Me; and how numerous the days whereon I had to face the assaults of the peoples against Me! At one time I found Myself on the heights of mountains; at another in the depths of the prison of Tá (Tihrán), in chains and fetters. By the righteousness of God! I was at all times thankful unto Him, uttering His praise, engaged in remembering Him, directed towards Him, satisfied with His pleasure, and lowly and submissive before Him. So passed My days, until they ended in this Prison ('Akká)...[62]

An Expression of Both Supreme Power and Resignation

O Jews! If ye be intent on crucifying once again Jesus, the Spirit of God, put Me to death, for He hath once more, in My person, been made manifest unto you. Deal with Me as ye wish, for I have vowed to lay down My life in the path of God. I will fear no one, though the powers of earth and heaven be leagued against Me...I have come in the shadows of the clouds of glory, and am invested by God with invincible sovereignty. He, verily, is the Truth, the Knower of things unseen. I, verily, anticipate from you the treatment ye have accorded unto Him that came before Me [the Báb].[63]

A Prayer for the Suffering Believers

Thy glory is my witness! At each daybreak they who love Thee wake to find the cup of woe set before their faces, because they have believed in Thee and acknowledged Thy signs. Though I firmly believe that Thou hast a greater compassion on them than they have on their own selves, though I recognize that Thou hast afflicted them for no other purpose except to proclaim Thy Cause, and to enable them to ascend into the heaven of Thine eternity and the precincts of Thy court, yet Thou knowest full well the frailty of some of them, and art aware of their impatience in their sufferings.

Help them through Thy strengthening grace, I beseech Thee, O my God, to suffer patiently in their love for Thee, and unveil to their eyes what Thou hast decreed for them behind the Tabernacle of Thine unfailing protection, so that they may rush forward to meet what is preordained for them in Thy path, and may vie in hasting after tribulation in their love towards Thee.[64]

A Prayer About Suffering

Glory to Thee, O my God! But for the tribulations which are sustained in Thy path, how could Thy true lovers be recognized; and were it not for the trials which are borne for love of Thee, how could the station of such as yearn for Thee be revealed? Thy might beareth Me witness! The companions of all who adore Thee are the tears they shed, and the comforters of such as seek Thee are the groans they utter, and the food of them who haste to meet Thee is the fragments of their broken hearts. How sweet to my taste is the bitterness of death suffered in Thy path, and how precious in my estimation are the shafts of Thine enemies when encountered for the sake of the exaltation of Thy Word! Let me quaff in Thy Cause, O my God and my Master, whatsoever Thou didst desire, and send down upon me in Thy love all Thou didst ordain. By Thy glory! I wish only what Thou wishest, and cherish what Thou cherishest. In Thee have I, at all times, placed My whole trust and confidence. Thou art verily the All-Possessing, the Most High. Raise up, I implore Thee, O my God, as helpers to this Revelation such as shall be counted worthy of Thy Name and of Thy sovereignty, that they may remember Thee among Thy creatures, and hoist the ensigns of Thy victory in Thy land, and adorn them with Thy virtues and Thy commandments. No God is there but Thee, the Help in Peril, the Self-Subsisting.[65]

The Tablet of Visitation

The following is part of a Tablet or Epistle by Bahá'u'lláh that enumerates some of His sufferings. Bahá'ís read this prayer when they visit His final resting place. They also recite it throughout the Bahá'í world, at the moment of Bahá'u'lláh's passing:

I bear witness that he who hath known Thee [Bahá'u'lláh] hath known God, and he who hath attained unto Thy presence hath attained unto the presence of God. Great, therefore, is the blessedness of him who hath believed in Thee, and in Thy signs, and hath humbled himself before Thy sovereignty, and hath been honored with meeting Thee, and hath attained the good pleasure of Thy will, and circled around Thee, and stood before Thy throne. Woe betide him that hath transgressed against Thee, and hath denied Thee, and repudiated Thy signs, and gainsaid Thy sovereignty, and risen up against Thee, and waxed proud before Thy face, and hath disputed Thy testimonies, and fled from Thy rule and Thy dominion...

...I bear witness that the eye of creation hath never gazed upon one wronged like Thee [Bahá'u'lláh]. Thou wast immersed all the days of Thy life beneath an ocean of tribulations. At one time Thou wast in chains and fetters; at another Thou wast threatened by the sword of Thine enemies. Yet, despite all this, Thou didst enjoin upon all men to observe what had been prescribed unto Thee by Him Who is the All-Knowing, the All-Wise.

May my spirit be a sacrifice to the wrongs Thou didst suffer, and my soul be a ransom for the adversities Thou didst sustain. I beseech God, by Thee and by them whose faces have been illumined with the splendors of the light of Thy countenance, and who, for love of Thee, have observed all whereunto they were bidden, to remove the veils that have come in between Thee and Thy creatures, and to supply me with the good of this world and the world to come. Thou art, in truth, the Almighty, the Most Exalted, the All-Glorious, the Ever-Forgiving, the Most Compassionate.[66]

9

War Against God

And war broke out in heaven... Revelation 12:7 NKJ

...in righteousness He judges and makes war...
Revelation 19:11

People have always waged war against God:

O children of Israel, do not fight against the Lord God of your fathers, for you shall not prosper!
II Chronicles 13:12 NKJ

And now I say to you, keep away from these men [early Christians] and let them alone; for if this plan [of Jesus] or this work is of men, it will come to nothing; but if it is of God, you cannot overthrow it; ***lest you even be found to fight against God***. Acts 5:38-39 NKJ

An awesome war, the like of which the world has never known, is predicted to be waged in this age. Prophecies pointing to war are numerous. They indicate that the earth will turn into a battleground between God and His enemies—those whose security or power is threatened. The following prophecies present us with more evidence of the universal rejection of the Redeemer of our time:

> Then the Lord will be seen over them, and His arrow will go forth like lightning. The Lord God will blow the trumpet...
> Zechariah 14:14 NKJ

> The great day of the Lord is near...a day of trumpet and alarm against the fortified cities [strong institutions] and against the high towers [people of high status].
> Zephaniah 1:14, 16 NKJ

Notice the phrase "weapons of his indignation" in the *American Revised Version*:

> The noise of a multitude in the mountains [established institutions]...Jehovah of hosts is mustering the host for the battle...and ***the weapons of his indignation***, to destroy the whole land.
> Isaiah 13:4-5

Are these wars promised to be waged with bullets, bombs, missiles, and arrows, or with God's "weapons of indignation"? Are they declared with trumpets or with potent thoughts and words? Are these wars physical, for the mass killing of non-believers, or are they spiritual, for conquering the hearts and minds of humankind? Today, most Christians take the predicted wars literally. Some of them actually believe that Jesus will use nuclear weapons to destroy His enemies. Some interpreters even give detailed accounts of the war between God and the earthly residents:

> Jesus speaks the Word which releases a plague to smite the vast armies of the Antichrist and the 200 million strong Oriental army. They are immediately blinded; their eyes are consumed away in their sockets. They are immediately dumb; their tongues are consumed away in their mouths.

> In fright, they reach out and grab one another for security. That only frightens them more, so they turn to fight among themselves. Their flesh begins to consume away from their bones. Their blood gushes to the earth, creating the pool of blood described in Revelation 14. It stretches over an area of about 185 miles in the valley of Megiddo and the Plains of Jezreel.[1]

The idea of God fighting with bombs, bullets, and battalions against His own creatures is the most awesome, amazing, strange, irrational, unlikely, and incredible thought. Yet it is extremely popular. Why? Perhaps for the same reasons that science fiction is popular. Human imagination craves the miraculous, the sensational, the spectacular. There is one more reason: human beings love the fulfillment of their "I told you so!" predictions. They like this kind of scenario, "Jim tells Joe again and again to accept Jesus Christ as his Lord and Savior." But Joe continues to brush aside Jim's invitation. Then suddenly the Lord comes and lifts Jim to heaven, but leaves Joe to face pain and utter destruction. Jim looks at Joe for the last time and says, "Buddy, it is too late. You deserve what you get." Today's books of prophecy are filled with sensational descriptions of wars between the forces of Jesus Christ and non-Christians. Let us consider a few descriptions from some popular authors:

> ...the weapons will be made out of wood. We know this from verse 9, which tells us that it will take seven years for them to burn all of the weapons. If Russia were to invade the nation of Israel today, they certainly would not be using wooden weapons. However, during the millennium, without any foundries and factories (which pollute), there will not be a source of metal available and so any weapons would, of necessity, have to be made of wood. We also see in this passage that it will take seven months to bury the dead. Some of them will be consumed by the fire and some of them will be eaten by predatory birds and beasts, but the remainder will require seven months to bury.[2] *The Coming Climax of History*

The Russian and Muslim armies initially launch a co-ordinated two-pronged attack from the north and south of Israel. The Russian commander sweeps through the strategic land bridge that begins at Istanbul and continues southward to the Suez canal...This battle plan seems to indicate that the Russian commander double-crosses many of the Muslim nations, including Egypt. Perhaps they are nations that will not go along with Iran's fanatical brand of Islamic Fundamentalism...Even demonic power helps facilitate this largest-of-all-time army's rapid advance into the Middle East. The mighty Euphrates River, the recognized boundary-barrier between East and West for ages past, will be supernaturally dried up to facilitate the rapid march of this Oriental juggernaut...[3] *Apocalypse Code*

He [Jesus] will come powerfully...accompanied by myriads of angels...At this point, we must recognize our need to dispense with the traditional, rather effeminate concepts of angels, that many people have. Angels are not just inoffensive, mild creatures, who spend all their time playing gentle harps on heavenly clouds, their golden wings glowing in the sunlight. They are powerful servants of God, ministering spirits whose role is to serve His people (Hebrews 1:7, 14). Just one angel was able to destroy a whole army in one night (2 Kings 19:35). Angels are awesome beings.[4]
The Return

Armageddon is the closing scene of three and one-half years of skirmish in the Middle East. It begins with Russia's invasion of Israel...Armageddon itself climaxes the campaign as the Lord and His armies appear from heaven...hundreds of millions of men (Revelation 9:16) will engage in this Middle East military confrontation...So great and complete will be the destruction resulting from this battle that the blood of those killed will form a river 200 miles long, rising even unto the horse bridles (Revelation 14:20). Seven months will be required to bury the dead (Ezekiel 39:12).[5] *Everything You Always Wanted to Know About Prophecy but Didn't Know Who to Ask!*

Bahá'ís believe that it is infinitely below the dignity and kindness of heavenly Redeemers and Teachers to use bombs and bullets to purify the earth. But ***spiritual*** wars have always been waged between the forces of light and darkness.

> And war broke out in heaven [of divine Revelation]...
>
> Revelation 12:7 NKJ

> Aid ye your Lord with ***the sword of wisdom and of utterance. This indeed well becometh the station of man. To depart from it would be unworthy of God***, the Sovereign Lord of all, the Glorified. [Emphasis added throughout.][6]
>
> Bahá'u'lláh

> The eternal God is your refuge, and underneath are ***the everlasting arms***. He will drive out your enemy before you...***He is*** your shield and helper and ***your glorious sword***. Your enemies will cower before you, and you will trample down their high places. Deuteronomy 33:27, 29 NIV

Who are God's soldiers? Who are His "heavenly hosts"? They are the servants who obey Him.

> Praise the Lord, you his angels, you mighty ones who do his bidding, who obey his word. Praise the Lord, all his ***heavenly hosts***, you his ***servants who do his will***.
>
> Psalms 103:20-21 NIV

God has always taught us to win our "wars" through the power of reason, not rockets; proofs and prophecies, not supersonic planes; gentle persuasion, not soldiers and generals; open minds, not military officers; sincere hearts, not hatred and savagery. I felt honored when someone once told me that she dreamed she had gone to war with *I Shall Come Again* as her sole weapon!

The Bahá'í Faith is a religion of peace, love, joy, and gentleness, yet its Scriptures contain many metaphors of war. The Ten Year Crusade (1953-1963) is the best-known Bahá'í plan devised by Shoghi Effendi, the Guardian of the Bahá'í Faith, for the spiritual conquest of the planet. (See the prophecy of

1335 in *Lord of Lords*.) The abundant use of metaphors of war in Bahá'í Writings point to the ***spiritual*** purpose and fulfillment of prophecies. Consider these examples:

> The stage is set. The hour is propitious. The signal is sounded. ***Bahá'u'lláh's spiritual battalions*** are moving into position. The initial clash between the forces of darkness and ***the army of light***, as unnoticed as the landing, two millenniums ago, of the apostles of Christ on the southern shores of the European continent, is being registered by the denizens of the Abhá Kingdom [Heavenly Kingdom]. The Author of the Plan that has set so titanic an enterprise in motion is Himself mounted at the head of these battalions, and leads them on ***to capture the cities of men's hearts***.[7] Shoghi Effendi

> He Who leadeth to true ***victory*** is come. By the righteousness of God! He is fully capable of revolutionizing the world through the power of a single Word. Having enjoined upon all men to observe wisdom, He Himself hath adhered to the cord of patience and resignation.[8] Bahá'u'lláh

> Who is it that can dismay you? A touch of moisture sufficeth to dissolve the hardened clay out of which this perverse generation is molded. The mere act of your gathering together is enough to ***scatter the forces*** of these vain and worthless people.[9] Bahá'u'lláh

> Verily God rendereth His Cause ***victorious*** at one time through the aid of His enemies and at another by virtue of the assistance of His chosen ones.[10] Bahá'u'lláh

Fire and Sword

Many prophecies contain the words "fire and sword:"

> For behold, ***the Lord will come with fire*** and with His chariots, like a whirlwind, to render His anger with fury, and His ***rebuke with flames of fire***. For by fire and by

His sword the Lord will judge all flesh; and the slain of the Lord shall be many. Isaiah 66:15-16 NKJ

From Zion, perfect in beauty, God shines forth. Our God comes and will not be silent; ***a fire devours before him***, and around him a tempest rages. Psalms 50:2-3 NIV

I watched till thrones were put in place, and the Ancient of Days was seated; His garment was white as snow, and the hair of His head was like pure wool. ***His throne was a fiery flame, its wheels a burning fire; a fiery stream issued and came forth from before Him.*** A thousand thousands ministered to Him; ten thousand times ten thousand stood before Him. Daniel 7:9-10 NKJ

The Lord Jesus is revealed from heaven with His mighty angels, ***in flaming fire*** taking vengeance on those who do not know God, and on those who do not obey the gospel...

II Thessalonians 1:7-8 NKJ

See also Matthew 13:41-42

...for the day shall declare it, because it shall be revealed by ***fire***; and the ***fire*** shall try every man's work...

I Corinthians 3:13

...every one shall be salted with ***fire***... Christ (Mark 9:49)

Come and see the works of the Lord...He makes wars cease to the ends of the earth; he ***breaks the bow*** and ***shatters the spear***, he ***burns the shields with fire***.

Psalms 46:8-9 NIV

See, the Name of the Lord comes from afar, with burning anger and ***dense clouds and smoke***; his lips are full of wrath, and his tongue is a consuming ***fire***...

Isaiah 30:27 NIV

The Lord shall appear above them, and his ***arrow*** shall flash like lightning; the Lord God shall blow a blast on ***the horn*** and march with the storm-winds of the south.

Zechariah 9:14 NEB

Are the words ***fire***, ***smoke***, ***sword***, ***horn***, ***spears***, ***arrow***, ***tempest***, ***breaking***, ***burning***, and ***shattering*** literal or symbolic? Bahá'u'lláh has written an Epistle called ***The Fire Tablet***. In it we can find both "the fire," and "the sword." Here is a brief quotation:

> Coldness hath gripped all mankind: Where is the warmth of Thy [God's] love, O ***Fire*** of the worlds? Calamity hath reached its height: Where are the signs of Thy succor, O Salvation of the worlds? Darkness hath enveloped most of the peoples: Where is the brightness of Thy splendor, O Radiance of the worlds? The necks of men are stretched out in malice: Where are ***the swords*** of Thy vengeance, O Destroyer of the worlds? Abasement hath reached its lowest depth: Where are the emblems of Thy glory, O Glory of the worlds? Sorrows have afflicted the Revealer of Thy Name, the All-Merciful: Where is the joy of the Dayspring of Thy Revelation, O Delight of the worlds? Anguish hath befallen all the peoples of the earth: Where are the ensigns of Thy gladness, O Joy of the worlds?[11]

What does "the fire" stand for? Tests and trials:

> This third [of people] I will bring into the fire; I will ***refine them*** like silver and ***test them*** like gold. Zechariah 13:9 NIV

Fire also symbolizes God's wrath for those who deny His Redeemers:

> ***These verses…are*** a light unto those who believe in them and ***a fire*** of afflictive torment for those who turn away and reject them.[12] The Báb

What type of sword does God use? Consider this prophecy about the Redeemer of our time:

> Now I saw heaven opened, and behold, a white horse. And He who sat on him was called Faithful and True, and ***in righteousness He judges and makes war***. His eyes were like a flame of fire, and on His head were many

> crowns. He had a name written that no one knew except Himself. He was clothed with a robe dipped in blood, and His name is called The Word of God. And the armies in heaven, clothed in fine linen, white and clean, followed Him on white horses. ***Now out of His mouth goes a sharp sword, that with it He should strike the nations***. And He Himself will rule them with a rod of iron. He Himself treads the winepress of the fierceness and wrath of Almighty God. Revelation 19:11-15 NKJ

What type of weapon does the heavenly Warrior carry? A sword. Where does He carry it? In His hand? No, in His mouth. What does His army wear? Suits of armor and helmets? No, they wear "fine linen, white and clean." What does "white linen" symbolize? Purity, gentleness, and an impeccable character. These warriors have stainless hearts rather than hearts of steel. What does ***the sword*** symbolize? The Word of God. Bahá'u'lláh has declared war for winning the hearts and minds of humankind. He commands His followers to arise for the "battle" with ready "swords:"

> Beware lest ye shed the blood of any one. ***Unsheathe the sword of your tongue*** from the scabbard of utterance, for therewith ye can conquer the citadels of men's hearts.[13]

> O people of Bahá! Subdue the citadels of men's hearts with ***the swords of wisdom and of utterance***.[14]

What kinds of ***swords*** can conquer the heart of humanity? What can produce the sharpest blade?

> By the righteousness of God! ***The sword of a virtuous character*** and upright conduct is sharper than blades of steel.[15] Bahá'u'lláh

> ***The sword of wisdom*** is hotter than summer heat, and sharper than blades of steel, if ye do but understand. Draw it forth in My name and through the power of My might, and conquer, then, with it the cities of the hearts of them that have secluded themselves in the stronghold of their

corrupt desires. Thus biddeth you the Pen of the All-Glorious, whilst seated beneath the swords of the wayward.[16]

Bahá'u'lláh

What kind of sword do God's enemies use?

In these days there are some who, far from being just and fair-minded, have assaulted Me with ***the sword of hatred and the spear of enmity***...[17] Bahá'u'lláh

At present no day passeth without the fire of a fresh tyranny blazing fiercely, or ***the sword of a new aggression*** being unsheathed.[18] Bahá'u'lláh

When those who had for years been hiding behind the veils perceived that the horizon of the Cause was resplendent and that the Word of God was all-pervasive, they rushed forth and with ***swords of malice*** inflicted such harm as no pen can portray nor any tongue describe.[19]

Bahá'u'lláh

In one city, the governor accused the Bahá'ís "that they had been laying up arms." To that accusation, Bahá'u'lláh offered this response:

This people need no weapons of destruction, inasmuch as they have girded themselves to reconstruct the world. ***Their hosts are the hosts of goodly deeds, and their arms the arms of upright conduct, and their commander the fear of God.*** Blessed that one that judgeth with fairness. By the righteousness of God! Such hath been the patience, the calm, the resignation and contentment of this people that they have become the exponents of justice, and so great hath been their forbearance, that they have ***suffered themselves to be killed rather than kill***...What could have caused such resignation and serenity?[20]

The predicted war against God has been waged in several Muslim countries with both literal and symbolic swords. In Iran, the birthplace of the Bahá'í Faith, Bahá'u'lláh's opponents have spread every conceivable lie and accusation to uproot the Bahá'í Faith. Such a war has not started in Christian countries, but it is bound to happen, especially when the established churches are threatened.

Once again consider the following prophecy about the greatest of all wars, known as the Armageddon:

> ***The armies of heaven*** were following him [the Promised One], riding on white horses and dressed in fine linen, white and clean. Out of his mouth comes a sharp ***sword*** with which to strike down the nations...The rest of them were killed with the ***sword*** that came out of the mouth of the rider on the horse... Revelation 19:14-15, 21 NIV

Are ***the armies of heaven*** heavenly or earthly? Is ***the sword*** of the Lord made of iron or of the divine power? This verse alone should convince every seeker of truth that God's battle is spiritual, that the war is waged by "the sword" of the tongue, for the Word of God cuts like a sword, separating truth from falsehood. Isaiah 13:5 declares that the Lord will wage war with "His weapons of indignation." Again we see the symbolism involved. Yet most Christians consider Armageddon a literal war that will be by far the bloodiest of all wars.

Hal Lindsey, a very popular Christian author, believes that Armageddon "will be so dreadful that blood will stand to the horses' bridles for a total distance of 200 miles northward and southward of Jerusalem." The depth of blood is calculated to be over one meter.[21]

Ezekiel 39:12 predicts a war so horrible that "for seven months the house of Israel will be burying them [the people of Cog] in order to cleanse the land." A Christian writer has estimated "that this would involve 360 million corpses."[22]

Zechariah states that "all the nations of the earth" will be gathered in Jerusalem to fight the Lord. A literal interpretation would mean that Christians and Muslims will put their armies together to fight a common enemy: Christ. It would mean that Buddhists, Hindus, Atheists, Agnostics, Russians,

Chinese, Japanese, Swedish, Islanders and people of over 200 other countries and dependencies will form a united front against the heavenly angels!

Armageddon is a Greek word for part of the mountain range (Mt. Carmel) on which Bahá'í International Institutions are located. According to *Nelson's Bible Dictionary*:

> Armageddon...(mountain of Megiddo)—is the site of the final battle of this age in which God intervenes to destroy the armies of Satan and to cast Satan into the bottomless pit (Rev. 16:16; 20:1-3, 7-10). Scholars disagree about the exact location of this place, but the most likely possibility is the valley between Mount Carmel and the city of Jezreel...
>
> Because of this history, Megiddo became a symbol of the final conflict between God and the forces of evil. According to the Book of Revelation, at Armageddon "the cup of the wine of the fierceness of His [God's] wrath" (Rev. 16:19) will be poured out, and the forces of evil will be overthrown and destroyed.[23]

Thus on one side stands ***the Bahá'í World Centre*** on Mt. Carmel, the Mountain of the Lord, and on the other, countless millions of fanatical warriors, from every region, nation, and culture, who wish and even try to eradicate that ***Centre of Divine Guidance***. This is the metaphoric meaning of Armageddon.

The metaphors of "***sword***" and "***fire***" appear abundantly in Bahá'u'lláh's Writings with both positive and negative meanings. Here are some examples of metaphoric uses of "the fire:"

the fire of hatred[24]
the fire of rebelliousness[25]
the fire of tyranny[26]
veiled in fire[27]
the fire of separation from God[28]
the flames of the nethermost fire[29]
the fire of bereavement[30]
the fire of Hell[31]
the fire of the tongue[32]
the fire of self[33]

fire of unbelief[34]
fire of blindness[35]
the fire of your desires[36]
the fire of oppression[37]
the lowest abyss of the fire[38]
the fire of Thy wrath[39]
the fire of animosity[40]
the fire of a fresh tyranny[41]
the fire of the impious[42]
the fire of strife and disorder[43]
the fire of wisdom[44]
the fire of yearning[45]
the fire of Thy Cause[46]
the fire of Thy glorification[47]
the fire of their hearts[48]
the fire of my remembrance of Thee[49]
the fire of being[50]
the fire of hope[51]
the fire of the lover's heart[52]
the fire of Thy Sacred Tree[53]
the fire that blazed in the Burning Bush[54]
the fire of God[55]
the fire of love[56]
the flame of this undying Fire[57]

A few more examples:

> Religious fanaticism and hatred are a world-devouring fire…[58]
>
> The most burning fire is to question the signs of God…[59]
>
> …hell hath been made to blaze with the fire of the impious.[60]
>
> …the fire of the love of Jesus consumed the veils of Jewish limitations…[61]
>
> …with fire We test the gold, and with gold We test Our servants.[62]
>
> I know not, O my God, what the Fire is which Thou didst kindle in Thy land.[63]
>
> …O Thou my God who settest my soul on fire…[64]

Although "war" is far more often used as a metaphor for spiritual warfare, we cannot deny that the metaphor may also have a literal meaning. For instance, more people have been killed in the 20th century than during all past centuries. Each of the two world wars of that century may demonstrate a literal fulfillment of the prophecies of the Armageddon.

The followers of the Báb were attacked several times by the Persian army. But instead of submitting, they took defensive positions. The story of their incredible courage and sacrifice against a well-prepared and powerful army is a book in itself. (See *The Dawn Breakers.*) Although the Báb's followers were not trained as soldiers, they withstood the Persian army for months. Never before in the history of warfare has such a small group of untrained people attained the astonishing victories gained by the Báb's followers. Chapter 2 of Joel seems to describe their valor and mighty powers. In the course of these wars and other tribulations, thousands of those saintly souls were killed. The Book of Revelation confirms such wars against the Lamb and His followers:

> Then one of the elders asked me, "These in white robes—who are they, and where did they come from?" I answered: "Sir, you know." And he said, "***These are they who have come out of the great tribulation***; they have washed their robes and made them white in the blood of the Lamb [the Báb]. Revelation 7:13-14 NIV

> When he opened the fifth seal, ***I saw under the altar the souls of those who had been slain because of the word of God and the testimony they had maintained***. They called out in a loud voice, "How long, Sovereign Lord, holy and true, until you judge the inhabitants of the earth and avenge our blood?" Then each of them was given a white robe, and they were told to wait a little longer, ***until the number of their fellow servants and brothers who were to be killed as they had been was completed***.
> Revelation 6:9-11 NIV

> ***These will make war with the Lamb***, and the Lamb will overcome them, for He is Lord of lords and King of kings; and those who are with Him are called, chosen, and faithful. Revelation 17:14 NKJ

The Book of Revelation even points to the way many of the followers of the Báb and Bahá'u'lláh were killed. Beheading, at that time, was the most common means of execution:

> Then I saw the souls of those who had been beheaded for their witness to Jesus [the Báb] and for the word of God [Bahá'u'lláh]. Revelation 2:6 NKJ

It is commonly accepted that Jesus' sacrifice was a price that had to be paid for the salvation of Christians. Prophecies of the Book of Revelation indicate that the drama of sacrifice and suffering will be repeated again.

> Now has come the salvation and the power and the kingdom of our God [Bahá'u'lláh], and the authority of his Christ [the Báb]. For the accuser of our brothers [new believers], who accuses them before our God day and night, has been hurled down. ***They overcame him by the blood of the Lamb*** [the Báb] and by the word of their testimony; ***they did not love their lives so much as to shrink from death***. Therefore rejoice, you heavens and you who dwell in them! Revelation 12:10-12 NIV

"The accuser of our brothers" symbolizes the negative forces of our planet, the enemies of truth and justice. It may also symbolize a specific person, an antichrist, such as Azal or Siyyid Muhammad. The prophecy declares that those forces were defeated. The victory was achieved "by the blood of the Lamb [the Báb]," and the testimony of His followers, who testified to the truth of His Word and without fear offered their lives just as their Master had done.

Daniel also predicts suffering for the followers of the new Faith:

> Those who are wise will instruct many [about the second advent], though ***for a time they will fall by the sword or be burned or captured or plundered***. Daniel 11:33 NIV

War Against Jerusalem

Some prophecies declare that all nations will gather together to fight against Jerusalem:

> I am going to make Jerusalem a cup that sends all the surrounding peoples reeling. Judah will be besieged as well as Jerusalem. On that day, when all the nations of the earth are gathered against her, I will make Jerusalem an immovable rock for all the nations. All who try to move it will injure themselves. Zechariah 12:2-3 NIV

Jerusalem is selected symbolically as the center of spiritual conflict for several reasons. First, it symbolizes the heart of religion; and second, the Book of Revelation refers to the Bahá'í Faith as "the new Jerusalem coming down out of heaven from God" (21:2). Jerusalem even has a close literal connection with the Bahá'í Faith. It stands in the same country in which the Bahá'í international institutions have been established.

> On that day I will set out to destroy all the nations that attack Jerusalem. Zechariah 12:9 NIV

The prophecy was partially fulfilled when a few Muslim countries fought against Israel. But how is it possible for ***all*** nations, including the western powers, to fight or stand against Israel? It is possible if we look at the inner meaning of the prophecy. "Jerusalem" symbolizes the City of God, or God's Blueprint for a new civilization. As we noted earlier, a time will come when all nations will wage spiritual warfare against the spread of the Bahá'í Faith—a Faith that brings a New World Order, a New Jerusalem, from heaven.

The Book of Revelation points to an army of 200 million who will be gathered in Jerusalem. In a recent war in the Middle East, it took the United States with all its might several weeks to gather half a million soldiers. Imagine gathering and transporting 200 million soldiers—four times the population of

France—to one city to fight against Jesus Christ and His angels!

This prophecy points to both the humiliation and the final victory of the residents of the City of God:

> I will gather all the nations to battle against Jerusalem; the city shall be taken, the houses rifled, and the women ravished. Half of the city shall go into captivity, but the remnant of the people shall not be cut off from the city. Then the Lord will go forth and fight against those nations, as He fights in the day of battle. Zechariah 14:2-3 NKJ

In the next passage, Bahá'u'lláh uses the metaphor of war. He portrays the futility of wars waged against Him. Can 10,000 soldiers stop the sun from shining?

> The Sun of Truth shineth resplendently, at the bidding of the Lord of the kingdom of utterance, and the King of the heaven of knowledge, above the horizon of the prison-city of 'Akká [in the Holy Land]...and ten thousand hosts arrayed against it were powerless to withhold it from shining.[65]

> The Lord foils the plans of the nations; he thwarts the purposes of the peoples. But the plans of the Lord stand firm forever, the purposes of his heart through all generations. Psalms 33:10-11 NIV

> Verily, We shall render Thee victorious by Thyself and by Thy Pen.[66] Bahá'u'lláh

> The day is approaching when God will have exalted His Cause and magnified His testimony in the eyes of all who are in the heavens and all who are on the earth.[67]
> Bahá'u'lláh

> Know ye of a certainty that He will render you victorious, will exalt you among the peoples of the world and will demonstrate your high rank before the gaze of all nations.[68]
> Bahá'u'lláh

The Day of Vengeance

Our age is called "the day of vengeance:"

Isaiah 61:1-2	The Spirit of the Lord God is upon Me ...To proclaim...the day of ***vengeance*** of our God.
Isaiah 63:4	For the day of ***vengeance*** is in My heart.

The following is a prayer and a pleading for the coming of Bahá'u'lláh:

> O Lord God, to whom ***vengeance*** belongs; O God, to whom vengeance belongs, shine forth! Rise up, O Judge of the earth; render punishment to the proud. Lord, how long will the wicked, how long will the wicked triumph?
> Psalms 94:1-3 NKJ

The word ***vengeance*** appears also in this prophecy:

> ...when the Lord Jesus is revealed from heaven with His mighty angels, in flaming fire taking ***vengeance*** on those who do not know God, and on those who do not obey the gospel of our Lord Jesus Christ. II Thessalonians 1:7-8 NKJ

What does "vengeance" mean? It means treating others the way we are treated. All sacred Scriptures promise that God will treat us the way we treat Him. For instance, if we ignore Him, He will ignore us; if we deny His new Redeemer, He will deny us:

> ...with the measure you use, it will be measured to you.
> Christ (Matt. 7:2 NIV)

> God will verily do unto them that which they themselves are doing, and will forget them even as they have ignored His Presence in His day.[69] Bahá'u'lláh

> ...he who disowns me...will be disowned.
> Christ (Luke 12:9 NIV)

Thus vengeance in the preceding prophecies indicates mutual denial both by people and by God on a wide scale. Disobedience always leads to "vengeance," which we always impose on ourselves; it is always a consequence of our choices.

> I will take ***vengeance*** in anger and wrath upon the nations that have not obeyed me. Micah 5:15 NIV

People may say, "I am a good Christian, a good Muslim, or a good Jew. I am honest, sincere, loving, and faithful. I am not the kind who would deny his Lord. Only evil people would do such a thing." This deadly attitude of self-protection, self-righteousness, and self-comfort has always prevailed. It is like having fun in a room and feeling totally safe, while the house is on fire. Only a sense of absolute humility can save a person from denying his Lord:

> He guides ***the humble*** in what is right and teaches them his way. Psalms 25:9 NIV

> I was brought ***low*** and he saved me. Psalms 116:6 NEB

> ...seek ***humility***; perhaps you will be sheltered on the day of ***the Lord's anger***. Zephaniah 2:3 NIV

The virtue of humility, as a prerequisite for recognizing the Lord, is confirmed in all sacred Scriptures. Are people humble enough to see the relevance of the message of humility to their souls?

Why would God save humble people? Because they do not start with the assumption of "I am safe and saved!" They step out of their room to check their surroundings and to see what is going on in the rest of the house.

The Scriptures clearly indicate that our perception of our righteousness and God's perception are often radically different. What we think of ourselves has absolutely no significance. Only what God thinks is valid. According to God's judgment, anyone who denies His new Redeemer falls from the highest pinnacles of grace and glory to the lowest depths of dishonor and disgrace. Bahá'u'lláh calls anyone who denies Him an infidel, and as we noted, both Jesus and Daniel refer to such a person as wicked.

The invisible trap of self-satisfaction captured many Pharisees, some of them as noble in character as we find in the best Christians and Jews of our time. They had no idea of their spiritual state. They lived with a clear conscience, and died with the hope of eternal life with their Lord. Yet Jesus condemned them in the harshest words. The lesson of the Pharisees speaks so clearly and so loudly, it is hard to imagine any sincere Christian failing to hear it.

A Heavenly War Against Edom

Hebrew Scriptures speak of a heavenly war against Edom—a metaphor for rebellious people. Where does the metaphor come from? From the story of Isaac's twin sons: Jacob and Esau. Esau was Isaac's favored son, but because of an unseemly behavior he fell from grace (Gen. 25:29-34).[70] "Most of the biblical narratives about Esau draw a great contrast between him and his [twin] brother, Jacob."[71]

Genesis 36:8-9 refers to Esau as "the father of the Edomites." Who were the Edomites? They were an idolatrous (II Chronicles 25:14) and warlike people, who continually plagued the Jews. They refused to let Moses pass through their land. Herod, who mocked Jesus, was an Edomite and is considered by some Christian scholars a type of antichrist. Biederwolf considers Edom to be "representative of all heathen nations."[72] According to *The Amplified Bible*, "Moab and Edom represented symbolically the enemies of Christ."[73]

Before examining several prophecies about the Edom of our time, we should note that since 1844 thousands of the followers of the Báb and Bahá'u'lláh in the Middle East and North Africa have been killed and persecuted by fanatical Muslims in their own country. The persecutions have been most severe in Iran, the birth-place of the Bahá'í Faith. When a Muslim recognizes the Báb and Bahá'u'lláh, often family members turn against him:

> How many fathers have turned away from their sons; how many lovers have shunned their beloved! So mercilessly trenchant was this wondrous sword of God that it cleft asunder every relationship![74] Bahá'u'lláh

The Bahá'ís, and the cruel Muslims who persecuted them, were, just like Jacob and Esau, of one nation; they were brothers and sisters. A prophecy from Obadiah likens the Muslims and Bahá'ís of our time to Esau and Jacob:

> Thus says the Lord God concerning Edom [an Islamic power]: "Behold, I will make you small among the nations; you shall be greatly despised. The pride of your heart has deceived you, you who dwell in the clefts of the rock, whose habitation is high; you who say in your heart, 'Who will bring me down to the ground?' Though you ascend as high as the eagle, and though you set your nest among the stars, from there I will bring you down," says the Lord…"the men at peace with you shall deceive you and prevail against you. Those who eat your bread shall lay a trap for you. No one is aware of it.
>
> Will I not in that day," says the Lord, "Even destroy the wise men from Edom, and understanding from the mountains of Esau [Islamic institutions]?…For violence against your brother Jacob [the Báb and His followers], shame shall cover you, and you shall be cut off forever…For the day of the Lord upon all the nations is near; as you have done, it shall be done to you; your reprisal shall return upon your own head…But on Mount Zion [Israel] there shall be deliverance, and there shall be holiness; the house of Jacob shall possess their possessions. The house of Jacob [the Báb's Revelation] shall be a fire, and the house of Joseph [Bahá'u'lláh's Revelation] a flame; but the house of

> Esau [the dead body of Islam] shall be stubble; they [the fire and the flame] shall kindle them [the dead residents] and devour them, and no survivor shall remain of the house of Esau," for the Lord has spoken. Obadiah 1-18 NKJ

Similar prophecies are also found in Jeremiah and Isaiah. In these prophecies, several ancient cities in Edom—such as Bozrah, Teman, and Dedan in a neighboring district—are used symbolically to refer to their counterparts in our age. Only the names have changed, not the people or the system that govern them. ***The names refer first and foremost not to places but the kind of people who appear in every age and the unjust system they establish to serve their self-interests***. Prophecies about the Edom of our time are being fulfilled at this very moment. As events unroll, their meanings will become progressively clearer.

> Concerning Edom: This is what the Lord Almighty says: "Is there no longer wisdom in Teman? Has counsel perished from the prudent? Has their wisdom decayed? Turn and flee, hide in deep caves, you who live in Dedan, for I will bring disaster on Esau at the time I punish him. If grape pickers came to you, would they not leave a few grapes? If thieves came during the night, would they not steal only as much as they wanted? But I will strip Esau bare; I will uncover his hiding places, so that he cannot conceal himself. His children, relatives and neighbors will perish, and he will be no more. Leave your orphans; I will protect their lives. Your widows too can trust in me."
>
> This is what the Lord says: "If those who do not deserve to drink the cup must drink it, why should you go unpunished? You will not go unpunished, but must drink it. I swear by myself," declares the Lord, "that Bozrah will become a ruin and an object of horror, of reproach and of cursing; and all its towns will be in ruins forever."
>
> I have heard a message from the Lord: An envoy was sent to the nations to say, "Assemble yourselves to attack it!

> Rise up for battle! Now I will make you small among the nations, despised among men. The terror you inspire and the pride of your heart have deceived you, you who live in the clefts of the rocks, who occupy the heights of the hill. Though you build your nest as high as the eagle's, from there I will bring you down," declares the Lord. "Edom will become an object of horror; all who pass by will be appalled and will scoff because of all its wounds.
>
> As Sodom and Gomorrah were overthrown, along with their neighboring towns," says the Lord, "so no one will live there; no man will dwell in it. Like a lion coming up from Jordan's thickets to a rich pastureland, I will chase Edom from its land in an instant. Who is the chosen one I will appoint for this? ***Who is like me and who can challenge me? And what shepherd*** [religious leader] ***can stand against me?*** " Therefore, hear what the Lord has planned against Edom, what he has purposed against those who live in Teman: The young of the flock will be dragged away; he will completely destroy their pasture [religious institutions] because of them. At the sound of their fall the earth will tremble; their cry will resound to the Red Sea. Look! An eagle [of victory] will soar and swoop down, spreading its wings over Bozrah. In that day the hearts of Edom's warriors will be like the heart of a woman in labor.
>
> Jeremiah 49:7-22 NIV

> ***O ye leaders of religion! Who is the man amongst you that can rival Me in vision or insight? Where is he to be found that dareth to claim to be My equal in utterance or wisdom?*** No, by My Lord, the All-Merciful! All on the earth shall pass away; and this is the face of your Lord, the Almighty, the Well-Beloved.[75] Bahá'u'lláh

A prophecy from Isaiah refers to the coming of Bahá'u'lláh from Bozrah, which may symbolize Tihrán. Bozrah was the capital or the main city of Edom:

> Who is this who comes from Edom, with dyed garments from Bozrah, this One who is glorious in His apparel, traveling in the greatness of His strength?; "I who speak in righteousness, mighty to save." Why is Your apparel red [a symbol of suffering], and Your garments like one who treads in the winepress? "I have trodden the winepress alone, and from the peoples no one was with Me. For I have trodden them in My anger, and trampled them in My fury; their blood is sprinkled upon My garments, and I have stained all My robes. For the day of vengeance is in My heart, and the year of My redeemed has come. I looked, but there was no one to help, and I wondered that there was no one to uphold; therefore My own arm brought salvation for Me; and My own fury, it sustained Me. I have trodden down the peoples in My anger, made them drunk in My fury, and brought down their strength to the earth."
>
> Isaiah 63:1-6 NKJ

God's Way of Attaining Victory

The emphasis in Bahá'u'lláh's works is always on noble deeds. That weapon more than anything else assures God's victory:

> O God, my God! Adorn the heads of Thy loved ones with the crown of detachment and attire their temples with the raiment of righteousness.
>
> It behoveth the people of Bahá ***to render the Lord victorious through the power of their utterance and to admonish the people by their goodly deeds and character***, inasmuch as deeds exert greater influence than words.[76]
>
> Bahá'u'lláh

> This Wronged One hath forbidden the people of God to engage in contention or conflict and hath exhorted them to righteous deeds and praiseworthy character. ***In this day the hosts that can ensure the victory of the Cause are those of goodly conduct and saintly character***. Blessed

> are they who firmly adhere unto them and woe betide such as turn away therefrom.[77] Bahá'u'lláh

The armies of victory need a commander. That commander is fear of God:

> Verily I say, ***fear of God*** is the greatest commander that can render the Cause of God victorious, and the hosts which best befit this commander have ever been and are an upright character and pure and goodly deeds.[78] Bahá'u'lláh

What does "fear" mean? It means an awareness of divine justice. It is a reminder that denying God's great Messengers and Redeemers has grave consequences. The consequences are not torture and pain inflicted by angels of wrath, but a state of ***spiritual poverty***, as 'Abdu'l-Bahá describes it. Punishment is not inflicted on us; we inflict it on ourselves. We are not dragged into darkness; we decide to stay in darkness. When we deny the truth, in effect we say, "I have no need for the Sun. I ***choose*** to live in the dark of my own illusions and selfish desires."

Heaven is reaching out for God's blessings and bounties; hell is refusing to reach out. Heaven is running toward God; hell is fleeing away from God.

People need to be reminded, in the kindest and gentlest way, that denying or ignoring Bahá'u'lláh—the most awesome expression of God's glory and grandeur—is a grave injury they inflict on their everlasting essence—their souls. This ***seemingly*** and ***deceptively*** minor injury has unimagined, unparalleled, and ever-enduring consequences. From God's perspective, we remain spiritually dead until we reach out for His remedy.

Instead of forcing people to believe, instead of firing missiles, God unsheathes "the sword" of His utterance: His creative and supreme Word. He untaps the power of persuasion as a means of transforming the hearts and souls of humankind:

> Say: If it be Our pleasure We shall render the Cause victorious through the power of a single word from Our presence. He is in truth the Omnipotent, the All-Compelling...However, since Our loving providence surpasseth all things, We have ordained that complete victory should be achieved through speech and utterance, that Our servants throughout the earth may thereby become the recipients of divine good. This is but a token of God's bounty vouchsafed unto them. Verily thy Lord is the All-Sufficing, the Most Exalted.[79] Bahá'u'lláh

God, unlike human beings, is patient:

> He Who leadeth to true victory is come. By the righteousness of God! He is fully capable of revolutionizing the world through the power of a single Word. Having enjoined upon all men to observe wisdom, He Himself hath adhered to the cord of patience and resignation.[80] Bahá'u'lláh

In the following prayer Bahá'u'lláh indicates that God's purpose in not using His supreme powers to gain immediate victory is to separate the sincere from the insincere, the faithful from the unfaithful:

> I know full well Thou [God] hast delayed to manifest Thy triumph in the kingdom of creation...that thereby those who have entered beneath the shadow of Thy transcendent mercy may be separated from those who have dealt disdainfully with Thee, and turned back from Thy presence at the time when Thou didst manifest Thy most exalted Beauty.[81]

God's ways of guiding do not change. How did Jesus gain victory?

> Jesus Christ gave His life upon the cross for the unity of mankind...Only a few were attracted to Him...All of them were men of the least consequence in the eyes of the world ...With this small army Christ conquered the world of the East and the West. Kings and nations rose against Him.

Philosophers and the greatest men of learning assailed and blasphemed His Cause. All were defeated and overcome, their tongues silenced, their lamps extinguished, their hatred quenched; no trace of them now remains. They have become as nonexistent, while His Kingdom is triumphant and eternal.[82]
'Abdu'l-Bahá

The Role of Religious Leaders

The war against God has always been led by religious leaders; this age is no exception. They have more to lose than any other group. God expresses His anger against the shepherds who fail to guide their flock:

> For the idols [revered figures] speak delusion; the diviners [predictors] envision lies, and tell false dreams; ***they comfort in vain***. Therefore the people wend their way like sheep; ***they are in trouble because there is no shepherd***. My anger is kindled against the shepherds [religious leaders], and I will punish the goatherds [those who disobey God]. For the Lord of hosts will visit His flock...
> Zechariah 10:2-3 NKJ

> Alas for the worthless shepherd who abandons the sheep! A sword shall fall on his arm and on his right eye; and his right eye blinded. Zechariah 12:17 NEB

In His *Book of Certitude* Bahá'u'lláh describes the role of religious leaders:

> Leaders of religion, in every age, have hindered their people from attaining the shores of eternal salvation, inasmuch as they held the reins of authority in their mighty grasp. Some for the lust of leadership, others through want of knowledge and understanding, have been the cause of the deprivation of the people. By their sanction and authority, every Prophet of God hath drunk from the chalice of sacrifice, and winged His flight unto the heights of glory. What unspeakable cruelties they that have occupied the

> seats of authority and learning have inflicted upon the true Monarchs of the world, those Gems of divine virtue! Content with a transitory dominion, they have deprived themselves of an everlasting sovereignty.[83]

Islamic Scriptures pass the same harsh judgment on Muslim laity and leaders as do the biblical Scriptures on all the peoples of the world. Consider this prophecy from Muhammad:

> There will come a time for my people when there will remain nothing of the Qur'án except its outward form and nothing of Islam except its name and they will call themselves by this name even though they are the people furthest from it. Their mosques will be full of people but they will be empty of right guidance. The religious leaders (fuqahá) of that day will be the most evil religious leaders under the heavens; sedition and dissension will go out from them and to them will it return.[84]

We should not conclude that all religious leaders deny or deviate from the truth. Bahá'u'lláh asks us to respect those leaders who are just and sincere:

> Respect ye the divines [religious leaders] and learned amongst you, they whose conduct accords with their professions, who transgress not the bounds which God hath fixed, whose judgments are in conformity with His behests as revealed in His Book. Know ye that they are the lamps of guidance unto them that are in the heavens and on the earth.[85]

The Role of Christians

So far Christians as a whole have played no part in the persecution of Bahá'u'lláh or His followers. On the contrary, they have on many occasions offered helping hands. In one city, they aided the dependents of Bahá'í prisoners. Bahá'u'lláh testifies to their assistance and sympathy:

> ...what sin have the little children committed? Hath anyone, in these days, had pity on the dependents of the oppressed?...the followers of the Spirit [Christ]...secretly sent them provisions and befriended them out of utmost sympathy.[86]

Bahá'u'lláh was poisoned three times. On one occasion, the poison made Him gravely ill and bedridden for a month. The doctor who attended Him was a Christian named Shishmán. He found Bahá'u'lláh's condition so alarming that he lost all hope of helping Him. Instead of writing a prescription, he fell at His feet. The offering he made at that instant served its purpose. After leaving, he fell ill. To a disciple whom Bahá'u'lláh sent to see him, he said that his prayer to sacrifice himself for his patient had been answered. His death came in a few days. (That someone sacrifices himself for his Lord is not unusual; that someone who is not even a believer does so is incredible.) Before his death, Dr. Shishmán recommended another doctor to treat his patient. Bahá'u'lláh recovered, but the poison left its mark: He suffered from hand tremors for the rest of His life.

As stated in *Lord of Lords*, the Báb was also treated by a Christian doctor for the injury inflicted on His face. Similarly, a Christian regiment assigned to execute the Báb was miraculously relieved from that burden. When Bahá'u'lláh and His disciples were being banished from Adrianople, many people cried, but it was the Christians who cried the most. Again during the recent persecution of Bahá'ís in Iran, many Christian countries defended the rights of the Bahá'ís and accepted them as refugees to their lands.

According to the Qur'án, Christians also showed more affection toward Muslims than any other group:

> ...thou shalt certainly find those to be nearest in affection to them [Muslims] who say, "We are Christians."
>
> Qur'án 5:85 R

Until now, the general response of Christian clergy has been simply to ignore the challenge that Bahá'u'lláh presents to them. In *The Promised Day Is Come*, Shoghi Effendi states:

> ...the members of the Christian clerical order...for the most part, have ignored the Faith of Bahá'u'lláh, whilst a few among them have, as its Administrative Order gained in stature and spread its ramifications over Christian countries, arisen to check its progress, to belittle its influence, and obscure its purpose.[87]

The time will come when humankind will no longer be able to ignore such a mighty and glorious Revelation from God. Then the leaders will become the followers.

> Grieve thou not at men's failure to apprehend the Truth. Ere long thou shalt find them turning towards God, the Lord of all mankind. We have indeed, through the potency of the Most Sublime Word, encompassed the whole world, and the time is approaching when God will have subdued the hearts of all that dwell on earth. He is in truth the Omnipotent, the All-Powerful.[88] Bahá'u'lláh

Universal Peace

This is the age of peace:

> Nation shall not lift up sword against nation, neither shall they learn war anymore. Isaiah 2:4 NKJ
> Also Micah 4:3

Bahá'u'lláh has not come to wage war but to wage peace. Universal peace is one of His fundamental teachings. This peace can be established not through violence but nonviolence, not through fear but faith. It has taken us several thousand years of pain and suffering and growing up to reach the age of universal peace, justice, and unity. We see some evolution toward peace even in the present age.

The believers in the Báb were allowed to defend themselves. They showed a degree of heroism while defending themselves that is unparalleled in history. (See their stories in *The Dawn-Breakers.*) But when the Báb's dispensation ended, Bahá'u'lláh asked His followers not to defend themselves. Bahá'u'lláh describes the distinguishing features of His followers in these terms:

> By the righteousness of God! Such hath been the patience, the calm, the resignation and contentment of this people... and so great hath been their forbearance, that they have suffered themselves to be killed rather than kill...What could have caused such resignation and serenity?[89]

The time for waging wars has passed. Bahá'u'lláh encourages and urges His followers a thousand times and more to win victories through "goodly deeds:"

> Now is the time for you to put forth your leaves, and yield your fruit. The fruits of the tree of man have ever been and are goodly deeds and a praiseworthy character. Withhold not these fruits from the heedless. If they be accepted, your end is attained, and the purpose of life achieved. If not, leave them in their pastime of vain disputes. Strive, O people of God, that haply the hearts of the divers kindreds of the earth may, through the waters of your forbearance and loving-kindness, be cleansed and sanctified from animosity and hatred...Every cause needeth a helper. ***In this Revelation the hosts which can render it victorious are the hosts of praiseworthy deeds and upright character. The leader and commander of these hosts hath ever been the fear of God, a fear that encompasseth all things, and reigneth over all things.***[90]

Raising the Banner of Search and Love for Truth

The purpose of discussing the topic of rejection at such great length is this: Christians often simplify and minimize their responsibility in finding their expected Redeemer by viewing it in simple terms. Since, they assume, everything will be visible, the faithful need not take any action; when the advent happens, surely they will know it. How could anyone miss the Armageddon? How could anyone miss flying angels? How could anyone miss the dead coming out of their graves? This illusion of visibility creates apathy, self-satisfaction, unawareness, and even avoidance and escape. It destroys any desire to search.

The faithful are told that all they need to do is to be good Christians: go to church every Sunday, pay their tithes, be born again, and make sure they accept no other Lord and Savior except Jesus Christ. If they do all these, they are told, their bodies will be lifted into the sky and saved from all the tribulations that fall on the "unsaved." What about the command that Christians must watch, must be awake and alert? That command, they are told, does not imply that Christians should pay attention to any news that originates outside the church. The command indicates that they should watch the news and be in touch especially with Christian sources: scholars, writers, respected evangelists, Christian universities, Christian radios and TV stations.

Consider this response from Hal Lindsey, perhaps the best known and most popular author of prophecy books, to those who ask, "How can I be sure that when Jesus comes from the sky, I am good enough to be taken to heaven?"

> "But, Hal," you might ask at this point, "how can I be sure I will be one of those taken?" You've got to remember that salvation is a gift of God. All you have to do is be willing to accept it and let His Holy Spirit change your life. I know, I know. You're not ready to change your life. You don't think you can do it. That's not the point. This is not something you can do anyway. Just let God do it. Trust Him. He will change your heart and its desires to conform with His. And He will assure you of eternal life the instant you receive Him and His pardon from sin.[91]

Numerous end-time prophecies point to people's lack of interest in truth. To whom do these prophecies apply? Are Christians exempt from these predictions?

> For the time will come when men will not put up with sound doctrine. Instead, to suit their own desires, they will gather around them a great number of teachers to say what their itching ears want to hear. ***They will turn their ears away from the truth and turn aside to myths.***
>
> II Timothy 4:3-4 NIV

Can people hate the truth and still recognize and love the true One, their new Redeemer?

The abundant evidence presented in this book undermines the prevailing and popular assumption of "Don't do anything. God will do it for you." The Scriptural references indicate that we have a clear responsibility to take the initiative and investigate; otherwise, without knowing, we may remain asleep, dreaming in the dark of our own desires.

Prophecies clearly indicate that waiting and wishing will only lead to a waste of our precious lives. We are given the weapons to break down all barriers and build the glorious Kingdom of God on earth as it is in heaven. What we need to do is to arise, put on our marching boots, and run towards the final victory. While in London, 'Abdu'l-Bahá spoke of raising the banner of the Unity of God and of becoming Celestial Warriors to win the hearts of humanity:

> Some of the people of the earth desire conquest over others; some of them are longing for rest and ease; others desire a high position; some desire to become famous. Thank God our desire is for spirituality and for union with God.
>
> Now that we are gathered here our wish is to raise ***the banner of the Unity of God***, to spread the Light of God, to make the hearts of the people turn to the Kingdom. Therefore I thank God that He is causing us to do this great work.

I pray for all of you, that you may become celestial warriors, that you may everywhere spread the Unity of God and enlighten the East and West, and that you may give to all hearts the love of God. This is my utmost desire, and I pray to God that your desire may be the same.[92]

God's way is radically different from the human way. What did a humble man—Jesus—accomplish?

All the armies that ever marched, and all the navies that were ever built, and all the parliaments that ever sat, and all the kings that ever reigned, put together, have not affected the life of man upon this earth as has that One Solitary Life.[93]

A prayer from 'Abdu'l-Bahá:

O Thou Incomparable God! O Thou Lord of the Kingdom! These souls are Thy heavenly army. Assist them and, with the cohorts of the Supreme Concourse, make them victorious, so that each one of them may become like unto a regiment and conquer these countries through the love of God and the illumination of divine teachings.[94]

Quotations on War and Victory

Quotations about war between God and His enemies are found in abundance throughout the Bible. These are a few examples:

Come near, you nations, to hear; and heed, you people! Let the earth hear, and all that is in it, the world and all things that come forth from it. For the indignation of the Lord is against all nations, and His fury against all their armies; He has utterly destroyed them, He has given them over to the slaughter. Also their slain shall be thrown out; their stench shall rise from their corpses, and the mountains shall be melted with their blood...For My sword shall be bathed in heaven; indeed it shall come down on Edom [symbolic of any rebellious country such as Persia], and on the people of My curse, for judgment. The sword of the Lord is filled with blood, it is made overflowing with fatness, with the blood of lambs and goats, with the fat of the kidneys of rams. For the Lord has a sacrifice in Bozrah [symbolic of any rebellious city, such as Tihrán], and a great slaughter in the land of Edom. The wild oxen shall come down with them, and the young bulls with the mighty bulls; their land shall be soaked with blood, and their dust saturated with fatness. For it is the day of the Lord's vengeance, the year of recompense for the cause of Zion. Isaiah 34:1-3, 5-8 NKJ

Proclaim this among the nations: "Prepare for war! Wake up the mighty men, let all the men of war draw near, let them come up. Beat your plowshares into swords and your pruning hooks into spears…For their wickedness is great." Multitudes, multitudes in the valley of decision!

Joel 3:9-14 NKJ

Then they will cry to the Lord, but He will not hear them; He will even hide His face from them at that time, Because they have been evil in their deeds. Thus says the Lord concerning the [false] prophets who make my people stray; Who chant "Peace"…but who prepare war…

Micah 3:4-5 NKJ

O Lord, how great are Your works! Your thoughts are very deep. A senseless man does not know, nor does a fool understand this. When the wicked spring up like grass, and when all the workers of iniquity flourish, it is that they may be destroyed forever...Your enemies shall perish; all the workers of iniquity shall be scattered.

Psalms 92:5-9 NKJ

Let God arise, let His enemies be scattered; let those also who hate Him flee before Him. As smoke is driven away, so drive them away; as wax melts before the fire, so let the wicked perish at the presence of God. But let the righteous be glad; let them rejoice before God; yes, let them rejoice exceedingly. Psalms 68:1-3 NKJ

Who is this King of glory? The Lord strong and mighty, the Lord mighty in battle. Lift up your heads, O you gates! Lift up, you everlasting doors! And the King of glory shall come in. Who is this King of glory? The Lord of hosts, He is the King of glory. Psalms 24:8-10 NKJ

Now look, God Himself is with us as our head, and His priests with sounding trumpets to sound the alarm against you. O children of Israel, do not fight against the Lord God of your fathers, for you shall not prosper!

II Chronicles 13:12 NKJ

Let them give glory to the Lord, and declare His praise in the coastlands. The Lord shall go forth like a mighty man; He shall stir up His zeal like a man of war. He shall cry out, yes, shout aloud; He shall prevail against His enemies. Isaiah 42:12-13 NKJ

Then the Lord will go out and fight against those nations, as he fights in the day of battle...This is the plague with which the Lord will strike all the nations that fought against Jerusalem: Their flesh will rot while they are still standing on their feet, their eyes will rot in their sockets, and their tongues will rot in their mouths. Zechariah 14:3, 12 NIV

The Lord Almighty is mustering an army for war. They come from faraway lands, from the ends of the heavens—the Lord and the weapons of his wrath—to destroy the whole country. Wail, for the day of the Lord is near; it will come like destruction from the Almighty.

Isaiah 13:4-6 NKJ

God does not conquer the hearts of humankind through violence. He wins victories through His Word.

The Word is the master key for the whole world, inasmuch as through its potency the doors of the hearts of men, which in reality are the doors of heaven, are unlocked.[95]

Bahá'u'lláh

> How vast is the tabernacle of the Cause of God! It hath overshadowed all the peoples and kindreds of the earth, and will, erelong, gather together the whole of mankind beneath its shelter.[96]
>
> Bahá'u'lláh

> The hour is approaching when ye will witness the power of the one true God triumphing over all created things and the signs of His sovereignty encompassing all creation.[97]
>
> Bahá'u'lláh

Questions such as, "Why would God allow good people to suffer?" "Why would God allow His Messengers to suffer?" have puzzled the human race since the dawn of history. The next chapter will shed some light on this topic.

10

That the Souls May Be Edified

Bahá'u'lláh

The Purpose and the Intensity of the Messengers' Suffering

Why did Jesus, the Báb, Bahá'u'lláh, and other great Messengers and Redeemers suffer? How severe were their sufferings? And in what spirit did they bear them?

> We have borne it all with the utmost willingness and resignation, so ***that the souls of men may be edified, and the Word of God be exalted***...My grief exceedeth all the woes to which Jacob gave vent, and all the afflictions of Jacob are but a part of My sorrows. [Emphasis added.][1]
>
> Bahá'u'lláh

> Say: Because He [Bahá'u'lláh] bore injustice, justice hath appeared on earth, and because He accepted abasement, the majesty of God hath shone forth amidst mankind.[2]
>
> Bahá'u'lláh

> ...I have been, most of the days of My life, even as a slave, sitting under a sword hanging on a thread, knowing not whether it would fall soon or late upon him. And yet, notwithstanding all this We render thanks unto God, the Lord of the worlds.[3] Bahá'u'lláh

Why should God's Messengers suffer? They are the perfect models for noble acts and attitudes. Are we not inspired to do the same if we see them keeping their trust in God despite their trials? If we see them living a simple life, in spite of their supreme powers to gain earthly riches, are we not motivated to put more emphasis on the spiritual than the material? It is impossible to identify with and be inspired and elevated by a model who surrounds himself with all the luxuries and pleasures of an earthly life. What would be Jesus' influence on the world, if instead of carrying His cross to His death, He had walked to His castles along with His body guards?

Further, when we learn that our Best-Beloved welcomed His adversities, we develop a more positive attitude about our own inevitable sufferings. Often our attitude about what we experience is more critical than the experience itself.

God's wisdom ordains that every achievement should require efforts and sacrifices, that a price must be paid for every gain. In God's Kingdom nothing is easy or cheap. His Messengers and Redeemers are the first to demonstrate this law. They are the vanguards of the forces of sacrifice. Their suffering is essential. At the end of this passage, Bahá'u'lláh refers to the price He had to pay to crown the world with glory and justice:

> I sorrow not for the burden of My imprisonment. Neither do I grieve over My abasement, or the tribulation I suffer at the hands of Mine enemies. By My life! They are My glory, a glory wherewith God hath adorned His own Self. Would that ye know it!

> The shame I was made to bear hath uncovered the glory with which the whole of creation had been invested, and through the cruelties I have endured, the Day Star of Justice hath manifested itself, and shed its splendor upon men.[4]

The Severity of the Messengers' Sufferings

Because God's Messengers and Redeemers are perfect models, their suffering is also perfect: it covers the full spectrum of pain and anguish, to the deepest level. It has a depth that no human being can ever conceive. They appear whenever it is the darkest and wherever fanaticism, ignorance, and corruption have reached their very depths. Therefore, they encounter ***the worst*** that humans can offer from the vilest of generations:

> All this generation could offer Us were wounds from its darts, and the only cup it proffered to Our lips was the cup of its venom. On our neck We still bear the scar of chains, and upon Our body are imprinted the evidences of an unyielding cruelty.[5]
>
> Bahá'u'lláh

God gives His Messengers special strength to endure more pain than others can, but the strength does not lessen the pain. Because of their knowledge of human potential, they have high expectations, and suffer acutely when people ignore their invitation. They have total understanding and boundless compassion for the suffering of others. They see all, know all, and suffer all.

> Know that if We reveal to thee but a sprinkling of the showers which, through God's decree, and at the hands of the envious and the malicious, have rained upon Us, thou wouldst weep with a great weeping, and wouldst bewail day and night Our plight. Oh, would that a discerning and fair-minded soul could be found who would recognize the wonders of this Revelation—wonders that proclaim the sovereignty of God and the greatness of its power.[6]
>
> Bahá'u'lláh

Can anyone else endure the burden of perceiving the pain and the suffering of ***all*** humanity, even for one instant? Suffering has puzzled humankind since the dawn of history. Many believers cannot understand why a loving God allows good people to suffer. This subject requires a separate and detailed treatment.* Briefly, we should recognize that the removal of suffering would require a complete alteration of the laws of nature. It would lead to a capricious universe in which the supreme Architect, after designing and building His Housc, would need to stand on guard to constantly modify and repair it.

We must make every effort to live in a state of supreme joy and happiness—an achievement that can come only from harmonizing our souls with God. But we must recognize that without adversity, happiness loses much of its depth and wonder. The ecstasy of achievement comes from effort. Contrasts always enrich our lives. They generate a sense of appreciation.

God does not show His involvement in our lives by breaking His laws. He does it in His own unique, subtle, and mysterious ways. Dreams offer the most direct and miraculous way through which our Creator communicates with us and shows His involvement in our lives. To demonstrate God's side of the enduring and emotional puzzle of suffering, let me cite a dream I had many years ago, while afflicted with a deep and long lasting depression. One night I was blessed by seeing Bahá'u'lláh in my dream. We walked together for a long time, perhaps for 20 to 30 minutes. We strolled through many different terrains: streets, deep slopes, high hills, shattered buildings, meadows, and mountains. During this journey we conversed continuously as two intimate friends. It was wonderful, like being in heaven. I felt so intimate with Him that at one point I found myself perhaps a step ahead of Him. Instantly I recognized my fault and exclaimed, "I am walking

---

* For a detailed treatment of this topic, see *Does Your Fish Bowl Need Fresh Water?* by this author.

ahead of my Lord!"✧ I slowed down and let Him catch up. Bahá'u'lláh spoke in a language I had never heard before, yet I understood everything He said. We continued to walk and talk until I saw Bahá'u'lláh suddenly put His hand on His chest and fall to the ground in great pain. I woke up knowing why: ***His*** pain came from ***my*** pain. When I woke up, I could not recall even a single word He had uttered.

This dream did not eliminate the source of my anguish, but it comforted me. What a wonderful feeling to know that Someone knows and cares!

The scenario that follows may give us a glimpse of what God's great Messengers and Redeemers go through; it may portray the depths of their pain and anguish.

Suppose you are placed in a large cage filled with various animals varying from the friendly to the ferocious.* Later, some of them—the gentle ones—find you likable and become your loyal friends. They bring you food and water, and try to defend you against intruders and attackers. You, too, deeply love them and accept them as your only companions. In the cage you also find some harmless animals, like snails, that ignore you, that mind their own business.

But to your dismay, you soon discover that the ferocious animals far outnumber the gentle ones. They are strong, angry, violent, fearful of your presence, and are determined to destroy you. Suppose you are built in such a way that you can be badly hurt but not killed—that is, until your time comes, perhaps years or even decades later. You learn that as long as you live, you remain resilient; you are chewed, torn

✧ And what does the Lord require of you? To act justly and to love mercy and ***to walk humbly with your God***.

* Words such as "ferocious" are used in accordance with human standards and judgment. All animals, whether friendly or ferocious, act according to the natural design of creation. In this sense, all animals are good. Among all creatures, only humans, because of their freedom of choice, can become ferocious.

apart, scraped and scratched, yet you miraculously survive. The animals are astonished by this and they even begin to like your presence; you have become a safe and long-lasting target for their anger, outrage, and violence.

The variety of the vicious animals in that cage astonishes you. Some of them act like snakes. They crawl close, strike quickly, and run away. Others, like wolves, feast on your flesh. Still others, like flies and mosquitoes, seek constant nourishment from your skin. Every animal in that cage prides in its special skills to hurt you.

You wish time and again to leave the cage, to be free. But alas, you are asked to wait, to be patient, to suffer and pray.

Who are you? Are you an ordinary prisoner caught in this cage of destiny? Are you weak and powerless to escape? No, just the opposite, you have the power to subdue and destroy all those animals with one stroke. Indeed, you have the power to rule the whole earth, to live a life of comfort beyond the hope of the most daring dreamers. Yet you decline to use your powers. Why? You have a goal that you see far ahead, you have a dream that you know will prevail centuries after you are gone. Patience and suffering are the price for your dream; adversity the crowning of your goal.

Imagine the frustration of having those incredible powers and not being able to use them to protect yourself, to subdue the violent beasts that hurt you and hunt you. No one can fully conceive of this or comprehend it. Imagine your agony when, time and again, you call them to pause and to listen to your call for one instant, but to no avail.

Your love for all the animals is infinite, even for the vicious ones. You could lead them to greener pastures, you could give them rest and refuge, you could even make them immortal, but alas, they do not heed your call, and you know that their heedlessness will only lead them to suffering and eternal loss.

The animals in the cage also attack your protectors, the people you love. They repeatedly torture them and cut them to pieces before your very eyes. How long could you stay in that cage? How long could you endure the torture? Would not an instant death be a blessing? But alas you are asked to wait, to endure the pain for a dream you see far ahead. You are told to be patient, and pray hard and long. Is this scenario far fetched?

> Witness how We are, at present, living in a nest of serpents.[7]
> Bahá'u'lláh

In both the biblical and Bahá'í Scriptures animals represent various kinds of people. Sheep, lambs, doves, pigeons, peacocks, and gazelles portray beauty and nobility of character. Wolves, vultures, serpents, dragons, dogs, pigs, leopards, scorpions, bats, owls, goats, and beetles represent the depravity of the heart, the destructive forces of evil. Let us look at one animal, the wolf:

> Go, I am sending you out like lambs among ***wolves***.
> Christ (Luke 10:3 NIV)

> ...after I leave, savage ***wolves*** will come in among you and will not spare the flock.
> Acts 20:29 NIV

> Beware that you allow not the ***wolf*** to become the shepherd of God's flock...[8]
> Bahá'u'lláh

The following prophecy, which promises an enduring peace among antagonistic peoples, is yet to be fulfilled:

> The ***wolf*** will live with the lamb, the leopard will lie down with the goat, the calf and the lion and the yearling together...
> Isaiah 11:6 NIV
> See also 65:25

> O ye that are foolish, yet have a name to be wise! Wherefore do ye wear the guise of the shepherds, when inwardly ye have become ***wolves***, intent upon My flock?[9]
> Bahá'u'lláh

> Some people are like bloodthirsty ***wolves***: if they see no punishment forthcoming, they will kill men merely for pleasure and diversion. One of the tyrants of Persia killed

> his tutor merely for the sake of making merry, for mere fun and sport. The famous Mutavakkil, the 'Abbásid [the tenth Caliph], having summoned his ministers, councilors and functionaries to his presence, let loose a box full of scorpions in the assembly and forbade anyone to move. When the scorpions stung those present, he burst forth into boisterous laughter.[10] 'Abdu'l-Bahá

Consider also this passage from Jesus. It compares the cruel deniers to snakes:

> You ***snakes***! You brood of vipers! Matthew 23:33 NIV

The next passage points to the sufferings of the Redeemer of our time:

> My soul is among ***lions***; I lie among the sons of men who are set on fire, whose teeth are spears and arrows, and their tongue a sharp sword. Be exalted, O God, above the heavens; let Your glory be above all the earth.
> Psalms 57:4-5 NKJ

Christian author, J. R. Church believes that "bees and thorns" in the following prophecy "typify the antichrist." "Midrash Shocher Tov described the bees as typical of that final war when God gathers all the nations of the world and brings them against Jerusalem."[11]

> All nations surrounded me, but in the name of the Lord I will destroy them. They surrounded me, yes, they surrounded me; but in the name of the Lord I will destroy them. They surrounded me like ***bees***; they were quenched like a fire of ***thorns***; for in the name of the Lord I will destroy them. Psalms 118:10-12

In the following passage, Bahá'u'lláh names several animals to symbolize His enemies.

> O My friend! Many a ***hound*** pursueth this gazelle of the desert of oneness; many a ***talon*** claweth at this thrush of

> the eternal garden. Pitiless ***ravens*** do lie in wait for this bird of the heavens of God, and the huntsman of envy stalketh this deer of the meadow of love.[12] Bahá'u'lláh

Unlike Jesus who came from a poor family, Bahá'u'lláh was born to gold and luxury. In those days probably only one family in a hundred thousand could have competed with His family in fame and fortune. To give an example, Bahá'u'lláh's father owned a valuable manuscript in the handwriting of the most famous and perhaps the best Persian calligrapher. Muhammad Sháh wanted to buy that manuscript. When he found out the price, he changed his mind. (Bahá'u'lláh's father was a friend of Muhammad Sháh.) Prior to His ministry, Bahá'u'lláh shared much of his father's enormous wealth with the needy. People called Him "the father of the poor." They did not know that someday He too would join the ranks of the poor.

Why, then, did the One who had at His command all earthly blessings and bounties deny Himself the comforts and pleasures of which most people can only dream? Why did He exchange gold and comfort for grief and sorrow? Why did He choose to live in that horrible cage for forty years? Would a man of His wisdom and nobility advance a lie that would lead Him and all His loved ones into a needless arena of pain and torture, imposed by a long procession of cunning and deadly animals? Yes, for Bahá'u'lláh, indeed for anyone who knows there is more to life than meets the eye, this world is but a cage:

> **O SON OF SPIRIT!**
> Burst thy cage asunder, and even as the phoenix of love soar into the firmament of holiness. Renounce thyself and, filled with the spirit of mercy, abide in the realm of celestial sanctity.[13] Bahá'u'lláh

> Hear Me, ye mortal birds! In the Rose Garden of changeless splendor a Flower hath begun to bloom, compared to which every other flower is but a thorn, and before the

> brightness of Whose glory the very essence of beauty must pale and wither. Arise, therefore, and, with the whole enthusiasm of your hearts, with all the eagerness of your souls, the full fervor of your will, and the concentrated efforts of your entire being, strive to attain the paradise of His presence, and endeavor to inhale the fragrance of the incorruptible Flower, to breathe the sweet savors of holiness, and to obtain a portion of this perfume of celestial glory. Whoso followeth this counsel will break his chains asunder...will attain unto his heart's desire, and will surrender his soul into the hands of his Beloved. Bursting through his cage, he will, even as the bird of the spirit, wing his flight to his holy and everlasting nest.[14]
>
> Bahá'u'lláh

Bahá'u'lláh's References to His Sufferings

Before examining a few passages from Bahá'u'lláh about His suffering, it is appropriate to review a description of the way He, His family, and some 60 of His disciples were treated when they entered the desolate city of 'Akká. The description is given by Bahá'u'lláh's daughter, who was interviewed by Myron Phelps from the United States:

> Arrived at the barracks, it was proposed to put the Blessed Perfection [Bahá'u'lláh] and his family on the second floor, and he was sent up; but I fainted from exhaustion and was unable to ascend the stairs. [Here the narrator paused a moment, visibly trembling, and then continued.] Of my own experience perhaps this is the most awful. The horrible sufferings of the voyage had reduced me almost to the point of death. Upon that came the seasickness. When we landed in 'Akká all the people of the town came crowding about us, talking loudly in Arabic, which I understood. Some said that we were to be put in the dungeons and chained; others that we were to be thrown into the sea.

The most horrible jests and jeers were hurled at us as we were marched through the streets to this dreadful prison.

Imagine, if you can, the overpowering impression made by all this upon the mind of a young girl, such as I was then...

When we had entered the barracks the massive door was closed upon us and the great iron bolts thrown home. I cannot find words to describe the filth and stench of that vile place. We were nearly up to our ankles in mud in the room into which we were led. The damp, closed air and the excretions of the soldiers combined to produce horrible odors. Then, being unable to bear more, I fainted. As I fainted, those about me caught me before I fell; but because of the mud and filth there was no place upon which I could be laid. On one side of the room was a man weaving a mat for the soldiers. One of our friends took this mat and I was placed upon it. Then they begged for water, but they could not get it. The soldiers would permit no one to go out. There was a pool of water on the dirt floor, in which the mat-maker had been moistening his rushes. Some of this water was dipped up and strained and put to my lips. I swallowed a little and revived; but the water was so foul that my stomach rejected it, and I fainted again. Then a little of this water was thrown into my face; and at length I revived sufficiently to go upstairs.

In the meantime my brother ['Abdu'l-Bahá] had slipped out and gone down to assist in the landing of the remainder of our company, whom we had left in the boats. When the soldiers discovered that he had disappeared, they at once notified the governor, who had search made for him and found him helping the others ashore. The followers were all brought to the barracks together and lodged on the ground floor. Among them were the women and children, almost dying with hunger and parched with thirst. My brother begged to be permitted to go out for food and water. The soldiers replied: 'You cannot put a foot outside of this room. If you do, we will kill you. Our orders are not to let you leave the barracks under any pretext.' Then he asked permission to send out a servant guarded by soldiers. This was refused.

The above was related to us by my brother, when he at length returned to our family quarters, in reply to our inquiries as to the occasion of his absence. He had been away for hours, and our hearts had been filled with anxiety for his safety.

Then came another time of heart-sickening suffering. The mothers who had babes at breast had no milk for them, for lack of food and drink, so the babes could not be pacified or quieted. The larger children were screaming for food and water, and could not sleep or be soothed. The women were fainting.

Under these conditions, my brother spent the first part of the night in passing about among the distressed people, trying to pacify them, and in appealing to the soldiers not to be so heartless as to allow women and children to suffer. About midnight he succeeded in getting a message to the governor. We were then sent a little water and some cooked rice; but the latter was so full of grit and smelled so badly that only the strongest stomach could retain it. The water the children drank; but the rice only the strongest could eat. Later on, some of our people in unpacking their goods found some pieces of the bread which had been brought from Gallipoli, and a little sugar. With these a dish was prepared for the Blessed Perfection [Bahá'u'lláh], who was very ill. When it was taken to him, he said: 'I command you to take this to the children.' So it was given to them, and they were somewhat quieted.

The next morning conditions were no better; there was neither water nor food that could be eaten. My brother sent message after message to the governor, appealing in behalf of the women and children. At length he sent us water and some prisoners' bread; but the latter was worse even than the rice—appearing and tasting as though earth had been mixed with the flour. My brother also succeeded in getting permission to send out a servant, guarded by four soldiers, to buy food. But before this permission was given, the governor commanded the presence of my brother and told him that neither he nor any of our people—not even a child—was to leave the prison under any circumstances whatever, and that unless this was promised the servant would not be permitted to go out. Under the circumstances my brother was obliged to give this promise.

The servant selected was told that if he spoke to a man or woman except in bargaining for supplies, he would be spitted on the swords of the soldiers.

The servant procured some provisions; yet even thus we were still badly off for food, for we were all so poor that we could buy but little. So the Blessed Perfection requested that the prison allowance for our support should be commuted for money. The governor consented, and gave to my father the amount allowed our family, and to my brother the amount allowed to the others. Then my father gave his own share and that of our family to my brother for the people, the whole being insufficient for them, saying: 'I will eat bread.' Thereafter, when the supply of provisions was insufficient and he learned of it, he would take only bread and water.

When we were first brought to the barracks we had no knowledge as to the manner of life to which we were to be consigned. We feared that the Blessed Perfection, my brother, and perhaps others would be placed in dungeons and chained. The only information we could obtain was that our sentence would be read on Friday—our arrival being early in the week. This uncertainty was an additional horror. When the sentence was read to us, we learned that it stated that we were political prisoners, nihilists, murderers, and thieves; that wherever we went, we corrupted the morals of the people; that we had leagued to overthrow the Ottoman Empire; that we could be given no leniency, and that the orders to keep us under bolt and bar must not be broken. It was because of this evil reputation, which had doubtless been given to the government by those who had reasons for desiring our destruction, and not from any want of humanity on the part of our jailers (who later became very kind and friendly to us) that we were subjected to such stern treatment and were given no more latitude or aid.

The season was summer (1868) and the temperature very high. All our people were huddled together on the damp earth floor of the barracks; with little water to drink...with no water with which to bathe, and scarcely enough for washing our faces. Typhoid fever and dysentery broke out among us. Every one in our company fell sick excepting my brother, my mother, an aunt, and two others of the believers. We were not allowed a physician; we could not procure medicine. My brother had in his baggage some quinine and bismuth. With these two drugs and his nursing, he brought us all through with the exception of four, who died. These were two months of such awful horror as words cannot picture. Imagine it, if you can. Some seventy men, women, and children packed together, hot summer weather, no proper food, bad water, the most offensive odors from purging and excretions, and a general attack of the terrible diseases of dysentery and typhoid.

There was no one with strength to be of any general service but my brother. He washed the patients, fed them, nursed them. He took no rest. When at length he had brought the rest of us—the four who died excepted—through the crisis and we were out of danger, he was utterly exhausted and fell sick himself, as did also my mother and the three others who had been well. The others soon recovered, but 'Abbás Effendi ['Abdu'l-Bahá] was taken with dysentery, and long remained in a dangerous condition. By his heroic exertions he had won the regard of one of the officers, and when this man saw my brother in this state he went to the governor and pleaded that 'Abbás Effendi might have a physician. This was permitted, and under the care of the physician my brother recovered.

For long after our departure from Adrianople none of the friends and followers of the Blessed Perfection in Persia knew our whereabouts. We were not permitted to send any letters. Great efforts were made to find us, and our friends finally traced us to 'Akká; but this whole city was then practically a prison from which strangers were carefully excluded, and they found it impossible to get into communication with us, or even to pass the city gate.

There was a Persian follower of the Báb who some time before, having failed in his business at home, had emigrated to 'Akká. He had not dared to disclose his faith, and no one suspected it. The servant who marketed for us happened one day, as he went about the bazaar, to come to this man's shop; and though he was not allowed to speak with him, he seems to have known intuitively that he was a friend. So thereafter he made most of his purchases of provisions at his shop.

Some of the Persian believers who had come to 'Akká but who had been unable to enter the city, effected communication with this man and arranged with him to send a note to the Blessed Perfection. This the shopkeeper accomplished by concealing the note among some vegetables and giving them to the servant with such a look that the latter understood and afterwards searched for it. The note begged the Blessed Perfection to send out some word; but this seemed to be beyond our power.

The physician who visited my brother, on seeing our condition, had so much sympathy with our distress, and became so fond of 'Abbás Effendi, that he asked him if there was not something which he could do for us. My brother begged him to take a message to the believers who were waiting to hear from the Blessed Perfection. He undertook to do so, and carried a tablet away in the lining of his hat. For two years this physician conveyed tablets and messages to and fro for us in this way.

After this first message had been transmitted from the Blessed Perfection, many believers came here from Persia and remained in the neighborhood with the hope of effecting some communication with him, or at least of getting a glimpse of him. They would go to some prominent point where they could be seen from his window. Some of us, seeing them, would call my brother's attention to them, whereupon he would inform the Blessed Perfection and follow him to the window and wave his handkerchief.

We were imprisoned in the barracks, without any substantial change in our manner of life, for two years. During this time none of us left the prison—not even my brother or any of the children. The Blessed Perfection passed his time in his room, writing tablets, or rather dictating them to my younger brother, who was a rapid penman. 'Abbás Effendi would copy them and send them out by the physician.

It was usual to carry on this work during the evening. One evening towards the end of the second year, my younger brother came, as was his habit, to write for his father. But as he was not very well, and as some others of the family were also ill, the Blessed Perfection told him to go and come later. So he went up to the flat roof of the barracks, where we were accustomed to walk, and which was our only recourse for fresh air and exercise. He was walking up and down, repeating tablets and gazing at the sky, when he stumbled, lost his balance, and fell through the opening to which the ladder from below led up. The room into which he fell had a lofty ceiling; it was the living-room of the family. No one was in the room at the time, but, hearing his cries, some of the family rushed in and found him lying in a heap on the floor with the blood pouring from his mouth. The Blessed Perfection, hearing the commotion, opened the door of his room and looked out. When he saw his son he turned back and reentered his room, saying: 'Mihdí has gone!'

We took him up and laid him on his mat. He was perfectly conscious. Later the Blessed Perfection came and remained with him. The physician was sent for; he said that there was no hope.

My brother lived for about thirty hours. When he was about to pass away the Blessed Perfection said to him: 'What do you desire? Do you wish to live, or do you prefer to die? Tell me what you most wish for.' My brother replied: 'I don't care to live. I have but one wish. I want the believers to be admitted to see their Lord. If you will promise me this, it is all I ask.' The Blessed Perfection told him that it would be as he desired.

So, after much patient suffering, my brother's gentle spirit took its flight. As we could not leave the barracks, we could not bury our dead; nor had we the consolation of feeling that we could provide for him through others the grateful final tribute of a proper and fitting burial, as we had no means wherewith even to purchase a coffin. After some consideration and consultation among ourselves, finding that we had nothing to dispose of, and at a loss how to proceed, we told our Lord [Bahá'u'lláh] of the sad situation. He replied that there was a rug in his room which we could sell. At first we demurred, for in taking his rug we took the only comfort he had; but he insisted and we sold it. A coffin was then procured, and the remains of my deceased brother placed in it. It was carried out by our jailers, and we did not even know whither it was taken.

The death of this youngest and favorite child—of a very gentle and sweet disposition—nearly broke his mother's heart. We feared for her reason. When the Blessed Perfection was told of the condition of his wife, he went to her and said: 'Your son has been taken by God that His people might be freed. His life was the ransom, and you should

> rejoice that you had a son so dear to give to the cause of God.' When our mother heard these words she seemed to rally—knelt, and kissed the Blessed Perfection's hands, and thanked him for what he had said. After that she did not shed a tear.[15]

This is a question we should always ask: Would any person of reason subject himself to a lifetime of torture and suffering? Would a man of His wisdom and nobility advance a lie that would expose Him and all His loved ones to exile, prison, poverty, ridicule, and rejection?

> Had it been in my power, I would have, under no circumstances, consented to distinguish myself amongst men...[16]
>
> Bahá'u'lláh

Bahá'u'lláh's references to His sufferings fill a whole volume. Why did He mention them so often? We can only wonder. Perhaps He wanted to teach us some lessons, perhaps talking gave Him some relief from the unbearable pain. Whatever the reasons, it is essential that we meditate on the depth of His pains and try to understand His plight. For He assures us, no Messenger ever suffered as much as He did:

> I bear witness that the eye of creation hath never gazed upon one wronged like Thee.[17] Bahá'u'lláh

Perhaps other Messengers either did not stay in the cage of cruelty as long as Bahá'u'lláh did, or else they did not encounter creatures as wild and venomous. The following quotations should give us a glimpse of what Bahá'u'lláh went through.

> The cruelties inflicted by My oppressors have bowed Me down, and turned My hair white. Shouldst thou present thyself before My throne, thou wouldst fail to recognize the Ancient Beauty [Bahá'u'lláh], for the freshness of His countenance is altered and its brightness hath faded, by reason of the oppression of the infidels. I swear by God! His heart, His soul, and His vitals are melted!...Before Me riseth up the Serpent of wrath with jaws stretched

> to engulf Me, and behind Me stalketh the lion of anger intent on tearing Me in pieces, and above Me, O My Well-Beloved, are the clouds of Thy decree, raining upon Me the showers of tribulations, whilst beneath Me are fixed the spears of misfortune, ready to wound My limbs and My body...By the righteousness of God! Every morning I arose from My bed I discovered the hosts of countless afflictions massed behind My door, and every night when I lay down, lo! My heart was torn with agony at what it had suffered from the fiendish cruelty of its foes.[18]

In the next passage, Bahá'u'lláh declares that His bed is drenched in tears:

> How numerous the tribulations which have rained, and will soon rain, upon Me! I advance with My face towards Him Who is the Almighty, the All-Bounteous, whilst behind Me glideth the serpent. Mine eyes have rained down tears until My bed is drenched.[19]

Compare Bahá'u'lláh's statement with this prophecy:

> I am worn out from groaning; all night long I flood my bed with weeping and drench my couch with tears. My eyes grow weak with sorrow; they fail because of all my foes. Psalms 6:6-7 NIV

In the next quotation Bahá'u'lláh declares that He is not forced to accept His sufferings. He does so out of His own choosing:

> My God, my Master, my Highest Hope, and the Goal of my desire!...By Thy Beauty, O Thou Whose glory is uncovered to the face of men! I am not impatient in the troubles that touch me in my love for Thee, neither in the adversities which I suffer in Thy path. Nay, I have, by Thy power, chosen them for mine own self, and I glory in them amongst such of Thy creatures as enjoy near access to Thee, and those of Thy servants that are wholly devoted to Thy Self.[20]

Although it is natural for us to feel sad when we see suffering, Bahá'u'lláh asks us not to grieve for His adversities:

> With every piece of bread the Ancient Beauty [Bahá'u'lláh] breaketh is coupled the assault of a fresh affliction, and with every drop He drinketh is mixed the bitterness of the most woeful of trials. He is preceded in every step He taketh by an army of unforeseen calamities, while in His rear follow legions of agonizing sorrows.
>
> Such is my plight, wert thou to ponder it in thine heart. Let not, however, thy soul grieve over that which God hath rained down upon Us. Merge thy will in His pleasure, for We have, at no time, desired anything whatsoever except His Will, and have welcomed each one of His irrevocable decrees. Let thine heart be patient, and be thou not dismayed.[21]

It is human to complain; it is divine to submit. In spite of the incredible tortures Bahá'u'lláh endured, He never complained. In His *Paris Talks* 'Abdu'l-Bahá said:

> None other in prison could have been like unto Him. In spite of all the hardships He suffered, He never complained.[22]

Bahá'u'lláh not only declined to complain of His sufferings, He considered them a blessing:

> By God! Mine head yearneth for the spear out of love for its Lord. I never passed a tree, but Mine heart addressed it saying: 'O would that thou wert cut down in My name, and My body crucified upon thee, in the path of My Lord!' ...By God! Though weariness lay Me low, and hunger consume Me, and the bare rock be My bed, and My fellows the beasts of the field, I will not complain, but will endure patiently as those endued with constancy and firmness have endured patiently, through the power of God, the Eternal King and Creator of the nations, and will render thanks unto God under all conditions.[23]

Sometimes God's way runs opposite to ours. Instead of expecting Him to adjust to our way, we need to adapt to His. We may wonder why He allows His Messengers and Redeemers to suffer. The good that comes from their suffering is incalculable. It manifests itself in such virtues as self-control, strength against adversity, resilience, and trust in God in the lives of countless millions for thousands of years. From their example we learn to set our hearts and hopes on heaven, for we know the earthly pains pass away, but heavenly pleasures endure. We see the One who is our Model and the source of all wisdom and knowledge to be so transformed by the love of His Lord as to declare:

> We render Thee thanks, O our Lord, for all the troubles which have touched us in Thy path. Oh, that the span of my earthly life could be so extended as to embrace the lives of the former and the latter generations, or could even be so lengthened that no man on the face of the earth could measure it, and be afflicted every day and every moment with a fresh tribulation for love of Thee and for Thy pleasure's sake![24] Bahá'u'lláh

Can anything inspire more patience, endurance, hope, trust, strength, and optimism in the face of adversity than the above words? We can relate to our great Teachers only when we see elements in their lives in common with our lives (Hebrews 2:18).

Of course, suffering should never be valued or sought for its own sake, but only as ***an inevitable means*** to a noble purpose: self-development and service to others. What does a kind father wish for his children? Happiness. The same holds true with our heavenly Father. But happiness must be earned; suffering is sometimes the inevitable price.

God sends His Messengers to teach us the art of happiness, the art of overcoming obstacles, the strength and wisdom to cope with suffering. The example of His Messengers is our best guide.

This prayer from Bahá'u'lláh on suffering is a fitting conclusion for this chapter:

> Wherefore, do I plead My grief and My sorrow to Him Who created Me and entrusted Me with His Message. Unto Him do I render thanks and praise for the things He hath ordained, for My loneliness, and the anguish I suffer at the hands of these men who have strayed so far from Him. I have patiently sustained, and will continue to sustain, the tribulation that touched Me, and will put My whole trust and confidence in God. Him will I supplicate saying: Guide Thy servants, O My Lord, unto the court of Thy favor and bounty, and suffer them not to be deprived of the wonders of Thy grace and of Thy manifold blessings. For they know not what Thou hast ordained for them by virtue of Thy mercy that encompasseth the whole of creation. Outwardly, O Lord, they are weak and helpless; inwardly they are but orphans. Thou art the All-Bountiful, the Munificent, the Most Exalted, the Most Great. Cast not, O My God, the fury of Thy wrath upon them, and cause them to tarry until such time when the wonders of Thy mercy will have been made manifest, that haply they may return unto Thee, and ask forgiveness of Thee for the things they have committed against Thee. Verily, Thou art the Forgiving, the All-Merciful.[25]

11

Do Not Put Your God to the Test

Christ (Matt. 4:7 NIV)

Part I, The Role of Miracles in Religion

The Prevailing Misconceptions

> Will none of you ever believe without seeing signs and portents? Christ (John 4:48 NEB)

The followers of many religions—especially Jews, Christians, and Muslims—mistakenly consider miracles the primary proof of their Messenger's Mission. Hal Lindsey, a widely read Christian author, for instance, states:

> He [Jesus] merely set forth his miracles as totally sufficient credentials that he was Messiah...[1]

Those who base their faith on miracles, transfer their belief about the past to an expectation about the future. They assume that if their Redeemer proved Himself through miraculous means, then why would He not follow the same course the next time?

This assumption about the past and its extension into the future suppresses any incentive or desire in the soul of the believers for any knowledge beyond the confines of their inherited beliefs. In this context, evidence and proof become worthless. Searching, reasoning, and understanding lose their honor. All glory goes to visual images. Religion—the supreme expression of God's grace and love for humankind—turns into a magic show! To be convincing, the images must grow more spectacular each time, and the show must become ever more astonishing, more entertaining.

This is one reason why people express no genuine interest in testing any religion other than their own. Investigation loses its relevance to believing. People cling to their own religions because they have been told to believe, all because of ***a visual image*** that a few people happened to see long ago! For this reason, religions have remained separate throughout the centuries. Spiritual segregation is even more widespread than racial segregation. It covers the entire planet. Most people inherit their religious beliefs as if what they were told by their parents is as fixed as the genes and chromosomes they received from them.

This chapter examines the fallacy of basing one's beliefs on miracles and then extending this belief into the future. It demonstrates that the great Messengers and Redeemers have never glorified their supernatural powers and have never displayed them with the intention of advancing their Cause. On the contrary, they have sought to keep their miraculous acts secret, saying:

> See that no one knows about this. Christ (Matt. 9:30 NIV)

> See that you don't tell anyone. Christ (Matt. 8:4 NIV)

Jesus repeatedly asked that His miracles be kept secret (Luke 5:14; 8:56; Mark 1:44; 5:43; 7:36), yet people disobeyed Him:

> But they went out and spread the news [of miracles] about him all over that region. Matthew 9:31 NIV

When the sick implored Jesus to restore their health, His deep compassion would prompt Him to respond. His motive in performing these acts was not to astound or impress the crowds, but to express His deep love for the afflicted. Moreover, the miracles involved only a small number of viewers, and were of such a nature and carried out in such a way as not to compel the masses into believing. Hence those who wished to deny could feel free to rationalize or find "a reason" for refusing to recognize the truth.

Miracles Are Irrelevant to the Messengers' Mission

Is it essential that a Redeemer perform miracles? Can miracles be used as a proof of divine Revelation? Should we expect them from a Messenger before we accept Him? A study of the sacred Scriptures reveals that, although the great Messengers can perform miracles, they refrain from using them as proof of the validity of their Mission.

The reason is this: ***performing supernormal acts is totally irrelevant to the Cause they are inspired to serve!*** The great Saviors do not come to amuse or astound us. Their Mission is to educate us, to elevate our ethical standards, and to give us a new and abundant life. They come not to bring the bread that perishes, but that which bestows eternal peace—the bread that lasts, multiplies, and satisfies the hunger of the spirit.

Ponder the conversation between Jesus and "the tempter:"

***The tempter*:**	If you are the Son of God, tell these stones to become bread.
***Jesus*:**	It is written: "Man does not live on bread alone, but on every word that comes from the mouth of God." Matthew 4:3-4 NIV

Which food is more precious? The ephemeral or the everlasting?

> Do not work for food that spoils, but for food that endures to eternal life... John 6:27 NIV

It is axiomatic that one's claim to competence should be substantiated by an act relevant to the claim. The physician's competence as a physician lies not in his ability to build a marvelous mansion or sing an enchanting song, but rather in his success in healing and comforting the sick. Likewise, the validity of the claims of a Redeemer cannot rest on His ability to raise a dead body, but rather to raise a dead soul, a new society, or "a new race of man." If the divine Educators tried to satisfy the curiosity of the masses for miracles, they would have little time left for teaching spiritual wonders.

> 'Abdu'l-Bahá once gave a very pointed illustration of this subject by telling the story of a sick man, desperately ill and suffering, who called in a physician. He inquired from him if he was a skilled practitioner, and the doctor assured him he was, indeed a genius, and flew round the room to prove it! Although this was no doubt a very interesting experience for the patient, said 'Abdu'l-Bahá, it did not improve his condition; he needed medicine, not miracles![2]

Which miracle is greater and matters more? To save a victim from the belly of a whale or to rescue many millions from the depths of wickedness? A Christian author first quotes this biblical verse from the story of Jonah: "***The people of Nineveh believed God***" (Jonah 3:5). Then he states that the preceding verse is "one of the most remarkable statements in the story. But it never seems to make the impression the whale does. The swallowing of a little man by a big fish is merely a matter of size. The man has only to be small enough and the fish big enough and the job is done. But for that little prophet to walk into New York, Chicago, Philadelphia, London, or any other city and bring that city to repentance and belief in God is some achievement!"[3]

If miracles were to serve as proof of divine Revelation, what, then, would distinguish the Messengers from magicians? If God's great Messengers and Redeemers applied their spiritual gifts to perform earthly wonders, their roles and missions would totally alter. They would no longer be known as Light Bringers and Saviors, but rather as great sorcerers and soothsayers.

God's greatest miracle is His Word, the knowledge He reveals through His Messengers:

> ...through knowledge shall the just be delivered.
>
> Proverbs 11:9

Our sense of justice touched by the divine knowledge generates the force of faith.

God's Respect for Our Freedom

Divine Wisdom ordains that we should find the truth through ***our own*** sincere efforts, and not through miraculous means. It is certainly within God's infinite power to make all His creatures perfect believers, but such an act would imply that He has ***imposed*** His Will upon His most exalted creation—humans. In that state we would no longer be free beings.

Let us assume we have a very precious jewel. We offer it to someone who couldn't care less if he received it. In spite of his attitude, we offer him the jewel. But he refuses to take it. What should we do? Should we force him to accept the jewel by any means within our power, or should we give him the freedom of choice?

The wonders that the Messengers and Redeemers perform do not overwhelm people. ***They might awaken the receptive,***

but will never impose faith on anyone. We have a perfect example in the martyrdom of the Báb that is discussed in the next chapter. It is certain that many of those who observed His "miraculous" martyrdom, could hardly believe what they saw. Yet there is no evidence that they recognized the station of the Báb. The Christian colonel, who was in charge, saw more than others did, and had sympathy for the Báb. Yet he did not become a follower of the new Faith either. Divine Wisdom ordains that people should be allowed to wage their "spiritual battles" with freedom. The unyielding souls are never disarmed.

We can also find many examples in the Christian dispensation. When some of those who had made up their minds against Jesus saw Him perform miracles, they thought of an ingenious way to use what they saw ***to their own advantage***. They said: it was with the aid of demonic powers that He could perform those wonders (Matt. 12:22-24). The human mind is such that it can never fail to find ways of convincing itself of what it wants to believe.

If Jesus' radiant and divine demeanor could not touch the spiritually unripe and unreceptive minds, then, nothing short of a total reshaping of the soul and restructuring of the basic laws of the universe could perform such a miracle.

> If they do not listen to Moses and the prophets they will pay no heed even if someone should rise from the dead.
> Christ (Luke 16:31 NEB)

> There came to you Messengers before me with clear signs and even with what [miracles] ye ask for. Why then did ye slay them, if ye speak the truth? Qur'án 3:183 Y

> Even were We [God] to open above them a gate in Heaven ...they [people] would surely say: It is only that our eyes are drunken: nay, we are a people enchanted.
> Qur'án 15:14-15 R

As it is said, "Convince a man against his will, and he will believe the same still."

'Abdu'l-Bahá indicates why the narratives of miracles do not and cannot serve as proof:

> But these narratives are not decisive proofs and evidences to all; the hearer might perhaps say that this account may not be in accordance with what occurred, for it is known that other sects recount miracles performed by their founders. For instance, the followers of Brahmanism relate miracles. From what evidence may we know that those are false and that these are true? If these are fables, the others also are fables; if these are generally accepted, so also the others are generally accepted. Consequently, these accounts are not satisfactory proofs. Yes, miracles are proofs for the eyewitness only, and even he may regard them not as a miracle but as an enchantment. Extraordinary feats have also been related of some conjurers.[4]

Disloyalty to God's Covenant and Commandment

Asking for miracles shows lack of faith in what ***God*** Himself has established as the evidence of truth. It also proves disloyalty to His eternal Covenant and Commandment that creatures are not given the right to test their Creator:

> Do not put the Lord your God to the test.
>
> Deuteronomy 6:16 NIV
> See also Matthew 4:7

Those who have made their faith dependent on seeing signs and portents have received the harshest and most demeaning response:

> A wicked and adulterous [faithless, disloyal] generation asks for a miraculous sign! Matthew 12:39 NIV
>
> See also I Cor. 10:9-11; Mark 8:12; 15:32; Luke 11:29

In spite of such harsh words, people continue to ignore God's way of establishing the truth, and to insist on their ***own*** way, their ***own*** desire to view displays of power and pageantry.

To use miracles as evidence of validity is extremely demeaning to the supreme station of God's great Messengers and Redeemers. It is like saying to someone: before I can respect you, trust you, or make you my friend, prove to me that you are very powerful and prestigious. Jesus' words clearly show how our Creator perceives those who seek miracles from His Messengers. There is a world of sadness and desperation hidden in these words of Jesus:

> Will none of you ever believe without seeing signs and portents? John 4:48 NEB

> He sighed deeply and said, "Why does this generation ask for a miraculous sign?" Mark 8:12 NIV

What a difference between saying "I believe because I have heard of your miracles," and saying, "I believe because ***you yourself*** are a miracle, a marvelous sign, a manifest wonder." What a difference between saying, "I believe because you have turned stone into bread," and saying, "I believe because I behold in you the glory of God, the splendors of the divine, the heavenly fruits of knowledge and wisdom." How much more reasonable to say "I believe because of the wonders that I see in your Word through ***my own eyes***" than to say "I believe because of what I have seen through the eyes of others who have narrated or recorded the signs."

Finally, why would the divine Messengers ***need*** to resort to miracles? Are not their very Beings, in themselves, manifest miracles? To the discerning and deserving eye, the Messengers' every word, every move, every glance, constitutes a wonder. Nothing about them is ordinary or commonplace; and no one, however astute, can ever fully comprehend the marvels of their acts, the wonders of their transcendent visions. Whatever ***is*** perceived or discerned remains forever confined to the limits of the human potential.

Miracles as Secondary Evidence

Although miracles should never be used as ***primary*** proofs, they can serve as a "sign" or ***secondary*** evidence. Let us assume we listen to a speaker several times and find him capable and competent. By his skill, he proves himself to us ***as a speaker***. Later we learn that he has other talents: he is an accomplished musician, athlete, scientist, inventor, writer, poet, and sculptor. These observations serve to enhance our admiration for him. They may even serve as an evidence of his greatness, ***but not as a proof of his speaking skills***. We continue to judge his speaking ability only by the speeches we have heard, not by his other gifts or talents. Miracles performed by great Messengers are like these ***other*** talents. Their superb gift, indeed the only one they ask us to judge them by, is their ability to produce marvelous "fruits."

'Abdu'l-Bahá refers to wonders that appeared from Bahá'u'lláh continuously as a "sign" of His supremacy,[5] yet He downgrades the significance of miracles as a primary proof. He must have witnessed countless miracles from Bahá'u'lláh, yet He declines to describe them:

> ***I do not wish to mention the miracles of Bahá'u'lláh***, for it may perhaps be said that these are traditions, liable both to truth and to error, like the accounts of the miracles of Christ in the Gospel, which come to us from the apostles, and not from anyone else, and are denied by the Jews. Though if I wish to mention the supernatural acts of Bahá'u'lláh, they are numerous; they are acknowledged in the Orient, and even by some non-Bahá'ís.[6]

In a way, all the acts performed by God's Messengers constitute "miracles," because they are all extraordinary. For these supreme Beings, the ***super***natural is the ***natural*** because their whole lives are nothing less than an accumulation of unusual and miraculous events. But only those acts that are relevant to their missions can be counted as proof of their station. The proofs presented in this work are all of this kind. When "a miracle" passes beyond the acceptable range of the Messengers' mission or purpose, it turns into entertainment and amusement.

Consider this incident. Once when Bahá'u'lláh entered a crowded mosque, the preacher stopped. He forgot his sermon. The audience that was responding to the sermon with words and expression of emotions also stopped. They "were suddenly filled with such awe and wonder that they became speechless." The Muslims spread this news in the city, and called it a miracle. Bahá'u'lláh dismissed the people's response as an illusion. To Him it was not a miracle.[7] What we can learn from this incidence is this: Bahá'u'lláh made absolutely no attempt to perform a miracle. What happened was a ***natural*** consequence of His supreme spiritual powers. He was simply being Himself and doing nothing unusual.

Consider also the way Bahá'u'lláh treated people. In spite of His exalted station, He acted with absolute humility, courtesy, and consideration towards all people, whether rich or poor, powerful or lowly. His love was so sincere, so extraordinary, some people suspected that it was all an act of sorcery, a game, a pretension. They thought He practiced "magical" acts of kindness simply to win or impress the people.[8] As we can see, everything about Bahá'u'lláh was unusual: miraculous and magical. People perceived His distinction and made an effort to explain it in their own way.

Those who obey God's call will use ***His*** established standards—"the fruits"—to find the truth. Prophecies are an integral part of "the fruits." (See *The Glory of the Son*, and *The Glory of the Father* by this author.) As for those who disobey, who set their own standard—miraculous signs—above God's standard, they can in no way discover the truth. And why should they? If they did find the truth, then what would be the difference between them and those who obeyed?

Religion Grows By Pains, Not By Miracles

In spite of the many miracles attributed to Jesus, only a few seekers from the multitudes who were called or exposed to His wondrous works, could set their souls free from earthly bounds. Only a handful were willing to give up their long-cherished and deeply rooted doctrines, traditions, and misconceptions for the gift of eternal life. The multitudes refused to acknowledge the validity of Jesus' claim for three long centuries—an extremely illuminating and instructive fact, yet seldom cited or recognized.

For those who have seen nothing but the triumph and grandeur of Christendom, it is difficult, perhaps impossible, to perceive such an unreasonably long delay on the part of the masses in responding to the divine Call. Every believer would rather assume that the truth of his beliefs was made so plain and evident as to have been readily perceived, even by the most skeptical thinkers.

Many Christians are unaware that, in its early stages, Christianity was called "an Oriental sect." Suetonius, the Roman historian, called it "a new...superstition."[9] Truth always triumphs through the sacrifices and dedicated efforts of the enlightened. That is what caused the seed of Christianity to blossom and enrich the lives of hundreds of millions for centuries.

Bahá'u'lláh's Response to Those Asking for Miracles

It is generally not recognized that God's Messengers have refused to perform miracles at the request of the people. For instance:

> When Herod saw Jesus, he was greatly pleased, because for a long time he had been wanting to see him. From

> what he had heard about him, he hoped to see him perform some miracle. He plied him with many questions, but Jesus gave him no answer. The chief priests and the teachers of the law were standing there, vehemently accusing him. Luke 23:8-10 NIV

Evidently, Herod's questions, to which Jesus did not respond, concerned the performance of miracles. Jesus disappointed both Herod and the religious leaders by refusing even to respond.

Muhammad likewise repeatedly declined to honor requests made for miracles:

> They say, 'Why have signs not been sent down upon him from his Lord?' Say: 'The signs are only with God, and I am only a plain warner.' Qur'án 29:49 A

Bahá'u'lláh made a rare exception to this rule when He was tested by Muslim religious leaders of Iráq.✧ To appreciate fully this significant event, unmatched in religious history, it is helpful to know why it happened. When Bahá'u'lláh lived in Baghdad, His fame grew beyond measure. The brilliance of His glory, as Shoghi Effendi notes, created a combustible mass of hatred, fear, and jealousy in the hearts and minds of many Muslim fanatics. Only a spark was needed. This was provided by a crafty and obstinate Muslim priest named Shaykh 'Abdu'l-Husayn.[10]

Shaykh 'Abdu'l-Husayn's evil character and intentions knew no bounds. Bahá'u'lláh characterizes him as "the scoundrel," "the schemer," and "the wicked one." Shoghi Effendi refers to him as "crafty," and "that vicious plotter."

Shaykh 'Abdu'l-Husayn engaged in many ingenious plots to uproot Bahá'u'lláh and His Revelation. These are five of his plots:

✧ The rule of refusing to respond to requests for miracles was first broken by the Báb. He, like Bahá'u'lláh, offered to perform a miracle, but the Muslim religious leaders found His offer too risky for their own security. See *The Chosen Highway*, pp. 25-26.

- He initiated friendly relations with the Persian consulate to enhance his own powers. With the consul's help he tried to obtain from the governor of Baghdad an order for Bahá'u'lláh's banishment. The first plot failed.
- Then he induced some people to insult Bahá'u'lláh in public to draw retaliation from His followers, which in turn could be used for false charges. The second plot also failed.
- He then hired a man named Ridá (a Turk) to assassinate Bahá'u'lláh. Ridá decided to carry out His scheme while Bahá'u'lláh attended a public bath. He "entered the bath with a pistol concealed in his cloak, and confronted Bahá'u'lláh in the inner chamber, only to discover that he lacked the courage to accomplish his task. He himself, years later, related that on another occasion he was lying in wait for Bahá'u'lláh, pistol in hand, when, on Bahá'u'lláh's approach, he was so overcome with fear that the pistol dropped from his hand; whereupon Bahá'u'lláh bade Aqáy-i-Kalím, who accompanied Him, to hand it back to him, and show him the way to his home."[11] The third plot also failed.
- 'Abdu'l-Husayn, the obstinate plotter, then tried to draw the Persian government to his aid. Through false accusations, he induced that government to recall Bahá'u'lláh to Tihrán. Among his accusations was that Bahá'u'lláh has "won the allegiance of the nomadic tribes of Iráq, and that He is in a position to muster, in a day, fully one hundred thousand men ready to take arms at His bidding."[12] He received a mandate from the sháh of Iran asking religious leaders of Iráq to give him their full support. He instantly sent the mandate to some of those leaders, and invited them to assemble for consultation. His goal was to gain from them a verdict for a "holy war" against the Bahá'ís. By their verdict he intended to gather an army of excited fanatics who would launch a sudden and deadly assault on Bahá'u'lláh and His followers living in Baghdad. He succeeded in bringing the religious leaders together. But after

his intentions became known, the chief religious leader, a pious Mujtahid, whose signature on the verdict was essential, refused to lend him his support. He said he had seen nothing from the Bahá'ís at variance with the teachings of the Qur'án. To the disappointment of most of the assembled leaders, he abruptly left the meeting. The fourth plot also failed.

- The remaining leaders believed that they could invalidate Bahá'u'lláh by asking for miracles that He could not perform. Therefore, they selected and sent a representative—a learned and pious man—to Bahá'u'lláh to present their request for a sign. After attaining the presence of Bahá'u'lláh, the representative stated that the religious leaders and scholars were unanimous in acknowledging His unmatched knowledge and wisdom despite His lack of schooling; they also acknowledged His pure and pious deeds; but they could not regard these as clear and convincing proofs of His Mission. They sought miracles. Bahá'u'lláh replied:

> Although you have no right to ask this, for God should test His creatures, and they should not test God, still I allow and accept this request...The 'Ulamás [religious leaders] must assemble, and, with one accord, choose one miracle, and write that after the performance of this miracle they will no longer entertain doubts about Me, and that all will acknowledge and confess the truth of My Cause. Let them seal this paper, and bring it to Me. This must be the accepted criterion: If the miracle is performed, no doubt will remain for them; and if not, We shall be convicted of imposture.[13]

The representative found Bahá'u'lláh's offer reasonable. He then gathered the religious leaders and gave them the message, but they refused to challenge Bahá'u'lláh. The reason they shared with each other was this:

> This man is an enchanter [sorcerer or magician]; perhaps he will perform an enchantment, and then we shall have nothing more to say.[14]❖

Thus, the fifth plot also failed.

Why did both Jesus and Muhammad decline to comply with requests for miracles, as an evidence of their divine Mission, yet Bahá'u'lláh consented? We can only speculate. Perhaps Bahá'u'lláh knew that His offer would be rejected. Perhaps the doubting people of our age need more evidence. Perhaps ours is the day of divine bounties and we are blessed with many favors not granted to previous generations.

Beyond this highly publicized and well-documented event, Bahá'u'lláh performed many wonders that did not receive publicity. For it was His desire that such events remain unknown to the people. As we noted, Jesus expressed the same desire. One of Bahá'u'lláh's disciples, a prominent historian, is known to have prepared an entire volume on Bahá'u'lláh's miracles. After completing the task of research and writing, the author reportedly offered the book to Bahá'u'lláh, only to be disappointed by His refusal to approve it. It was the eventual destiny of this work—though precious to many Bahá'ís—to be thrown into a river and thus remain forever unknown to future generations. Another man, a Muslim (a Sunnite savant of Baghdad), "wrote a short treatise in which he related certain supernatural acts..."[15]

Although Bahá'u'lláh had wished that His wondrous gifts would not be publicized or emphasized (fearing that they might eventually be regarded as the sole evidence of His divine mission, as has happened in so many other religions), nevertheless a few of His followers proceeded to record and preserve some of the unusual happenings they had witnessed.

❖ For further details of this event, see *Some Answered Questions*, pp. 34-35, *Gleanings from the Writings of Bahá'u'lláh*, pp. 131-132, and *God Passes By*, p. 144.

But the intention of these followers was not to prove the validity of Bahá'u'lláh's Revelation. They simply wished to remain faithful to the history of His Mission, recording and reflecting the events as they unfolded. A few of those wonders are explored in the next chapter.

As stated at the beginning of this chapter, the gravest consequence of putting one's trust in miracles is this: it takes the initiative away from the individual and puts it all in God's Hand. Many Christians today are waiting for a heavenly hand to lift them to heaven. They believe they do not need to do anything except to be good Christians and wait. They do not put their trust in proofs and prophecies. Why then, waste time for prophecies if everything is going to be miraculous? These beliefs and attitudes have created not only apathy but also avoidance.

Because of the supreme significance many believers attach to miracles, we will examine this topic further in the next chapter and will present some examples of signs and wonders in the Bahá'í Revelation.

12

I Will Show Them My Wonders

Micah 7:15 NIV

Part II, Examples of Extraordinary Events in the Lives of the Báb, Bahá'u'lláh, and 'Abdu'l-Bahá

In referring to the supernormal powers possessed by God's Messengers and Redeemers, it may be helpful to differentiate between the acts expressed spontaneously, and the acts displayed deliberately with the clear intention of convincing the doubtful. Communication would improve if we had two separate words for each of these two acts. The word ***miracle***, as often used, implies a deliberate attempt to impress or convince. As stated, such is not and has never been the intent of God's Messengers. Words perhaps free from the undesirable connotation associated with ***miracle*** are ***wonder*** and ***marvel***. Once the distinction is established, communication improves considerably.

Thus in the Bahá'í Faith, we do not speak of miracles as such, but of wonders and marvels—works or attributes that characterize every aspect of the lives of God's great Messengers and Redeemers.

The following is a prophecy about our time:

> As in the days when you came out of Egypt, I will show them my wonders. Micah 7:15 NIV

The following passage applies not only to the Báb but to all the great Messengers:

> He [the Báb] is in truth...endowed with supernatural powers...[1] The Báb

To illustrate the character and magnitude of such wonders, several examples will be cited here. But the purpose in citing them is not to imply in any way that the seeker of truth should use them as proof of the divine mission, as the standard of recognizing God's great Messengers. The accounts are included here for three reasons. First, they are an essential part of the history, and simple curiosity prompts one to want to investigate. Second, many seekers are so accustomed to associating miracles with Messengers that they cannot reconcile themselves to believing otherwise. The absence of such wonders would in itself serve as a stumbling block in their search for truth. Third, the divine Messengers transcend others in every conceivable way. Not only do they transcend the human spirit, but the world of matter as well. Yet in spite of their ascendancy over earthly powers, they never pride themselves therein. Thus their refusal to use their supremacy to fulfill their wishes (whether selfish or unselfish), or to escape adversity, is in itself an evident proof of their sincerity and distinction over others.

The Martyrdom of the Báb

Reasons for Sacrifice

Among the many parallels between Jesus and the Báb was their desire to sacrifice their lives:

> The good shepherd gives his life for the sheep.
>
> Christ (John 10:11)

> ...the Son of Man did not come to be served, but to serve, and to give His life a ransom for many."
>
> Christ (Matt. 20:28 NKJ)

> I have sacrificed myself wholly for Thee; I have accepted curses for Thy sake, and have yearned for naught but martyrdom in the path of Thy love. Sufficient witness unto me is God, the Exalted, the Protector, the Ancient of Days.[2]
>
> The Báb

> …I heard a Voice calling in my inmost being: "Do thou sacrifice the thing which Thou lovest most in the path of God..."[3]
>
> The Báb

> For assuredly ***whatsoever God hath decreed for Me shall come to pass*** and naught else save that which God hath ordained for us shall ever touch us. ***Woe betide him from whose hands floweth evil***, and blessed the man from whose hands floweth good.[4]
>
> The Báb

> Woe to the world because of the things that cause people to sin! ***Such things must come, but woe to the man through whom they come***!
>
> Christ (Matt. 18:7)

The Báb was martyred in July of 1850, a few months short of His 31st birthday. His martyrdom is one of the best documented and most incredible events in religious history. It was observed by an estimated audience of 10,000 and recorded by writers of various religious persuasions, and even by the official historian of the state that ordered the execution.

First, a few words about the reasons behind martyrdom. Why did Jesus and the Báb offer their lives? An essential feature of the design of creation is that every worthy achievement must be preceded or accompanied by self-sacrifice. Whether it is raising well-behaved children, getting a degree, staying healthy, losing weight, or eliminating racism, sexism, and poverty, some degree of sacrifice is required.

To grow and multiply, to bear flowers and fruits, the seed must sacrifice itself:

> Unless a kernel of wheat falls to the ground and dies, it remains only a single seed. But if it dies, it produces many seeds. Christ (John 12:24)

What is by far the greatest achievement? It is educating humanity, elevating the human spirit to everlasting hope and happiness; it is leading the soul from the kingdom of earth to the Kingdom of Heaven. Can such a glorious purpose be achieved without sacrifice?

Human beings are best inspired by models who show their devotion and sincerity through examples. The first ones to offer perfect examples of devotion, nobility, and self-sacrifice are God's chosen Messengers. If they, with all their perfections and powers, submitted themselves to the law of sacrifice, are we not inspired to do the same?

> I have set you an example: you are to do as I have done for you. Christ (John 13:15)

> I am the good shepherd; the good shepherd giveth his life for the sheep. Christ (John 10:11)

For most of us self-sacrifice has negative connotations. It implies giving up something, but that is a misconception. Self-sacrifice involves no loss; it is the process by which short-term interests are exchanged for long-term dividends. It is like exchanging junk bonds for reliable and late-maturing bonds, or junk food for nourishing food. Self-sacrifice is the catalyst of perfection; it is the yeast that elevates the human spirit by breaking down apathy, inertia, complacency, pride, self-glory, and attachment to the world. It is the price that must be paid for lasting and genuine happiness.

God's ways are often opposite to ours. By His standard "We must lose to gain; we must give to obtain; we must be humble to be exalted; we must be least to be greatest; we must die to live."

> ...how can My way accord with thine?[5] Bahá'u'lláh

> Behold how contrary are the ways of the Manifestations of God, as ordained by the King of creation, to the ways and desires of men![6] Bahá'u'lláh

To promote the Cause of God, all great Messengers have endured pain and suffering. The only difference is this: some have accepted martyrdom by death, others have become ***living*** martyrs. Death does not necessarily impose the gravest suffering. In some ways, being tortured and killed can be less painful than a continuing life of suffering. Bahá'u'lláh's life was of this kind. Martyrdom by death attracts our attention because, in addition to being tragic, it is dramatic. The deaths of Jesus and the Báb were of this kind.

In the Báb's death we can discern evidence of a divine power at work. Should we use that evidence as proof of His station? Definitely not! Then what purpose should it serve? Only this: ***It should elevate us from apathy to awareness. It is not an evidence in itself, but a call to investigate the evidence***. For instance, you know you will be asleep at 7:00 a.m. You set your clock to awaken you at that time to be ready for an invited guest. In the state of sleep, you are unaware of the coming of the guest. ***But when you are awakened by the alarm clock, you begin to see and hear your visitor. That is the only purpose miracles should serve***. You do not welcome your guest because of the alarm clock. You welcome him because you see him and recognize him with your own eyes.

With these points in mind, let us proceed with the story of the Báb's martyrdom.

The Story of the Martyrdom

This quotation from *The Dawn-Breakers*, the most comprehensive narrative about the Báb and His disciples, gives us a glimpse of the events prior to the martyrdom:

> That day witnessed a tremendous commotion in the city of Tabríz. The great convulsion associated in the ideas of its inhabitants with the Day of Judgment seemed at last to have come upon them. Never had that city experienced a turmoil so fierce and so mysterious as the one which seized its inhabitants on the day the Báb was led to that place which was to be the scene of His martyrdom. As He approached the courtyard of the barracks, a youth suddenly leaped forward who, in his eagerness to overtake Him, had forced his way through the crowd, utterly ignoring the risks and perils which such an attempt might involve. His face was haggard, his feet were bare, and his hair disheveled. Breathless with excitement and exhausted with fatigue, he flung himself at the feet of the Báb and, seizing the hem of His garment, passionately implored Him: "Send me not from Thee, O Master. Wherever Thou goest, suffer me to follow Thee." [The Báb answered the youth]: "Arise, and rest assured that you will be with Me. Tomorrow you shall witness what God has decreed."[7]
>
> That night the face of the Báb was aglow with joy, a joy such as had never shone from His countenance. Indifferent to the storm that raged about Him, He conversed with us [His disciples] with gaiety and cheerfulness. The sorrows that had weighed so heavily upon Him seemed to have completely vanished. Their weight appeared to have dissolved in the consciousness of approaching victory.[8]

The Persian government wanted to make the execution of the Báb a lesson to all people, especially to His followers. Hence a decision was made to make it a public event. But, as we shall see, God had a different plan.

Just before the time of the execution, the Báb was in prison speaking to a disciple. A government official came to the Báb's prison cell and told Him to come to the public square for the impending execution. The Báb asked for a little time to finish His conversation with the disciple, but the official would not comply. The Báb offered this warning: "Not until I have said to him all those things that I wish to say, can any earthly power silence Me. Though all the world be armed against Me, yet shall they be powerless to deter Me from fulfilling, to the last word, My intention."[9] The official ignored the warning and took the Báb (along with the young disciple who wanted to die with Him) to the public square to be shot by a regiment of 750 soldiers, who stood in three lines ready to fire.

The regiment was headed by an Armenian colonel, Sám Khán, who had no animosity toward the Báb and no interest in executing two young men for their religious beliefs. To absolve himself of responsibility, he went to the Báb and said, "I profess the Christian Faith, and entertain no ill will against you. If your Cause be the Cause of Truth, enable me to free myself from the obligation to shed your blood."[10]

The Báb replied, "Follow your instructions, and if your intention be sincere, the Almighty is surely able to relieve you from your perplexity."[11]

The martyrdom of the Báb and His disciple was planned with precision. To give people a good view of the event, officials suspended the Báb and His disciple above the ground by passing two heavy ropes under their armpits and tying the ropes to a heavy nail driven into a thick wall. The Báb's disciple pleaded to be placed in such a position that his body would shield that of his Master. He was suspended so that his head rested on his Master's chest.

At about 10:00 a.m., the gaze of thousands of onlookers was fixed on the two young men suspended in the air. The first of the three lines of soldiers, 250 of them, was ordered to fire. They fired, then knelt so that the second and then the third lines of soldiers could fire. The firing of 750 bullets created a cloud of smoke that obscured people's vision. (The smoke came from the gun powder used in those days.) For a few minutes, the people could not see, but when the smoke cleared, they saw no trace of the Báb. His disciple was standing unharmed on the ground just below the point of suspension.

It is hard to imagine the uproar, the astonishment, and the confusion that seized the onlookers, especially the government officials. The nervous and puzzled officials searched frantically for the Báb. Where do you think He was found? In His original prison cell where He was completing His unfinished conversation with His disciple.

The man who located Him was the same man who had taken Him for execution. When he arrived, the Báb was ready. His face radiated with unruffled calm. He welcomed the official by saying, "Now you may proceed to fulfill your intention."[12] The guard was so shaken by what he saw that he refused to take the Báb a second time. He left the scene and resigned from his position.

In the meantime, the Christian colonel, who had been looking for any excuse to free himself from the ominous task of executing the Báb, was jubilant. He saw this as a sure sign from God and immediately withdrew his soldiers and swore never again to engage in that task, even if his refusal resulted in death.

A second regiment volunteered for the task. Two hours had passed; it was about noon. Because of the seemingly miraculous event, the Báb now had a more receptive audience. He had a chance to address the people:

> Had you believed in Me, O wayward generation, every one of you would have followed the example of this youth [the disciple who wanted to die with Him]...The day will come when you will have recognized Me; that day I shall have ceased to be with you.[13]

Everything was now ready. The second regiment took position and was ordered to fire. This time the bullets hit their targets. The two bodies were so shattered and riddled with bullets that they were blended into one mass of mangled flesh and bone, except for the face of the Báb, which miraculously remained intact.

"The very moment the shots were fired, a gale of exceptional severity arose and swept over the whole city. A whirlwind of dust of incredible density obscured the light of the sun and blinded the eyes of the people. The entire city remained enveloped in that darkness from noon till night."[14]

> Unto God do I commit my affair and yours, and He verily is the best judge...Naught shall touch Me besides that which God, My Lord, hath pre-ordained for Me. In Him have I placed My whole trust...[15] The Báb

> I am well pleased to lay down My life in Thy path and ere long to return to Thy presence. Unto Thee be praise in the heavens and on the earth.[16] The Báb

> Glory be unto Thee, O my God. Thou art well aware that I have proclaimed Thy Word and have not failed in the mission Thou didst enjoin upon me.[17] The Báb

> I, verily, have not fallen short of My duty to admonish that people, and to devise means whereby they may turn towards God, their Lord, and believe in God, their Creator.[18]
>
> The Báb

The One called the Desire of nations, the Savior and Redeemer of humankind, Lord of Lords and King of Kings, was made a sacrifice for the world. This is the way it has been and may always be:

> You always resist the Holy Spirit! Was there ever a prophet your fathers did not persecute? They even killed those who predicted the coming of the Righteous One.
>
> Acts 7:51-52

> Great spirits have always encountered opposition from mediocre minds. Albert Einstein

The sacrifices made by the Báb and Jesus present us with two dramatic examples by which God teaches us lessons of detachment and dedication. He allows the Ones He loves most to become sacrificial Lambs. The few examples of self-sacrifice by God's chosen Messengers have had and will continue to have far more influence in elevating the human spirit than countless books of commandments and counsels.

Just after the Báb was executed, Sir Justin Sheil, Queen Victoria's Envoy in Tihrán, sent an official letter to the Secretary of State for Foreign Affairs, Lord Palmerston. This is part of his letter:

> He [the Báb] was killed by a volley of musketry, and his death was on the point of giving his religion a luster which would have largely increased his proselytes. When the smoke and dust cleared away after the volley, [the] Báb was not to be seen, and the populace proclaimed that he had ascended to the skies.[19]

Why, we may ask, was such an event allowed to occur? We can be certain that the intention was not to impress or convince the crowds. Had the Báb intended to transform the hearts of the people, it would have been within His power to do so; a miracle would not have been required. So why was the event allowed to happen? The Báb was determined to complete His letter, and as He said, nothing could have prevented Him from doing so. There could have been other reasons as well. Perhaps divine Wisdom ordained that the Christian colonel be relieved from the ominous responsibility placed on him. Perhaps this was God's final testimony, an awakening call, to a doubting and "wayward generation." There could have been other reasons, which we may never know. One thing we ***do*** know: that the event did occur, that it cannot be ignored or overlooked, and that it is now a part of history, which we are entitled to know.

The following prophecy from Zephaniah seems to predict the martyrdom of the Báb. The word "guests" may symbolize thousands of viewers who witnessed God's great sacrifice:

> Be silent in the presence of the Lord God; for the day of the Lord is at hand, for the Lord has prepared a sacrifice; He has invited His guests. Zephaniah 1:7 NKJ

The Báb's brief period of ministry is characterized by many such wonders. Those interested in pursuing the subject further, may wish to consult *The Dawn-Breakers*, a comprehensive account of His dramatic story.

Knowledge of the Unspoken

Let us look at a few records of wonders from Bahá'u'lláh's life. Recorded narratives of Bahá'u'lláh's wondrous powers are numerous and diverse. Among the most common are those relating to His complete knowledge of the thoughts, dreams, and desires of all those around Him. It is repeatedly reported by those attaining His presence that they would suddenly feel as if they had lost the protective guards of their souls. It was as if Bahá'u'lláh was gazing directly into the inmost depths of their beings. It was as if their thoughts, motives, and desires were being unveiled.

> ...wait till the Lord comes. He will bring to light what is hidden in darkness. I Corinthians 4:5 NIV

> On that day ye shall be brought before Him [the promised Redeemer]; none of your hidden deeds shall remain hidden [to Him]... Qur'án 69:18 R

We are told that when believers and unbelievers alike came to visit Bahá'u'lláh, His presence would produce:

> ...such an effect on most of them that they could not utter a word. How many times it happened that one of His most bitter enemies would resolve within himself, 'I will say such and such things when I reach His presence,

> and I will dispute and argue thus with him,' but when he entered the Holy Presence, he would become ***amazed and confounded, and remain speechless***.[20]

> For the earth will be filled with the knowledge of the glory of the Lord...the Lord is in His holy temple. ***Let all the earth keep silence before Him***. Habakkuk 2:14, 20 NKJ

> ***Be silent*** in the presence of the Lord God.
> Zephaniah 1:7 NKJ

Some of those paying a visit to Bahá'u'lláh, have attested that, once in His presence, they could no longer remember their questions. Then unexpectedly, and to their amazement, they would find that their questions were being answered. Such events were commonplace, not only with Bahá'u'lláh but with other Figures of His Faith as well. As we shall see later, the first believer in the Báb and the emissary sent by the king to investigate His Claim, received responses to questions they had conceived but never asked.

His Face Was Like the Sun

Revelation 10:1

Bahá'u'lláh often uses "the sun" symbolically. In this passage, He refers to Himself as "this Sun:"

> Say: O concourse of divines [religious leaders]! Hear ye not the shrill voice of My Most Exalted Pen? See ye not ***this Sun*** that shineth in refulgent splendor above the All-Glorious Horizon? For how long will ye worship the idols of your evil passions? Forsake your vain imaginings, and turn yourselves unto God, your Everlasting Lord.[21]

Several prophecies describe Bahá'u'lláh as ***the sun*** and ***the fire***:

> ...his [Bahá'u'lláh's] face was like ***the sun***...
> Revelation 10:1 NIV

> He [Bahá'u'lláh]—glorified be His mention—resembleth ***the sun***...[22] The Báb

> ...unto you that fear the Lord shall ***the Sun*** of righteousness [Bahá'u'lláh] arise with healing in his wings [teachings]... Malachi 4:2

> Suppose a thousand suns should rise together into the sky: such is ***the glory of...God***...Brilliant like ***the sun***; ***like fire blazing***, boundless.[23] Bhagavad-Gita

> ...his eyes were ***like blazing fire***...His face was like ***the sun*** shining in all its brilliance. Revelation 1:14, 16 NIV

Some pilgrims, who attained the presence of Bahá'u'lláh, have acknowledged their inability to look directly into His face. A pilgrim offers this testimonial:

> Know with absolute certainty that if anyone, whether friend or foe, claims that he was able to look directly into the blessed face of Bahá'u'lláh, he is a liar. I tested this repeatedly and tried time and again to gaze upon His blessed countenance, but was unable to do so. Sometimes, when a person attains the presence of Bahá'u'lláh, he is so enamored and carried away that in fact he becomes dumbfounded, awe-struck, oblivious of himself and forgetful of the world. And whenever he is not carried away, should he try to look into His blessed face with concentration, it would be ***like looking into the sun***. In the same way that the eye is blinded by the effulgent rays of the sun, causing tears to flow, should one persist in gazing upon the countenance of the Blessed Beauty [Bahá'u'lláh], tears will fill the eyes making it impossible to gain any impression of Him.
>
> I myself had this experience. During the seven months that I stayed in Adrianople, I was so carried away and dazzled [by His presence] that I was completely oblivious of myself and all creation.[24]

Another pilgrim also describes Bahá'u'lláh's Face as a brilliant Sun:

> Whenever I attained Bahá'u'lláh's presence I witnessed such wonders and blessings and experienced such joy and radiance that cannot be put in words...Whenever Bahá'u'lláh turned His Face toward the believers in His presence, no one could look at His Face and view ***that brilliant Sun of Oneness***. Therefore, when He spoke, it was His way to look constantly toward the right, so that the friends could gaze at His sacred Face freely. And whenever He looked toward His audience, He would close His eyelids and speak, so that the friends would not be deprived of seeing His blessed Face.[25]

Let us substitute the Arabic translation of ***the Glory of God*** in the prophecy from the Bhagavad-Gita to see how clearly it confirms the two pilgrims' descriptions:

> Suppose a thousand suns should rise together into the sky: such is ***Bahá'u'lláh***...Brilliant like ***the sun***; ***like fire blazing***, boundless.[26]
>
> Bhagavad-Gita

The pilgrim who described Bahá'u'lláh's face as a brilliant Sun of Oneness was asked by some of his Bahá'í friends to remember them and mention them while in the presence of Bahá'u'lláh. He wanted to do this, but he soon discovered that thinking about them would prevent him from focusing on Bahá'u'lláh's words and enjoying the moment. Then suddenly this thought passed through his mind, "If You are aware of our hearts, why mention the names?" He says this thought entered his mind unintentionally. At this point, Bahá'u'lláh suddenly turned His smiling face toward him and uttered the names of the six believers this pilgrim had in mind and wanted to mention before Bahá'u'lláh. After naming them, Bahá'u'lláh concluded, "Yes, yes, your pilgrimage for you and for them is accepted, is accepted, is accepted!"

After witnessing such an expression of divine knowledge from Bahá'u'lláh, the pilgrim lost his composure, his eyes turned dark, and he was about to fall. At this point, Bahá'u'lláh asked His secretary to bring some sweets. He gave one piece to all those present. To this pilgrim, He gave two pieces! When the time came to leave, this pilgrim still had not fully regained his composure and had difficulty walking. He lost his balance once and his friends had to help him.

In a recent dream, I found myself following Bahá'u'lláh at a distance. I saw Him stop at a modest shop with two workers who were barely visible. The place looked bare and filthy, like an empty automobile repair shop.

I thought Bahá'u'lláh was teaching those workers about the Bahá'í Faith. I said to myself, "I should pay close attention to the way He communicates, perhaps I can learn some lessons." But since I was at a distance from Him, I could not hear Him. At one point I saw Him hug the workers to show His love for them.

The shop was rather dark and Bahá'u'lláh's image was barely visible. Then there was a transformation. From that dark background two brilliant eyes suddenly emerged, shining like two small moving lamps. I recognized that the two shining eyes were Bahá'u'lláh's. I knew that no one could focus on those eyes, and decided to test this idea for myself. But since they were moving, I could not focus on them for more than a few seconds at a time.

I felt exhilarated to watch those beautiful piercing eyes shine, to see them gently and consciously move. On the outside they looked like two round, shiny, soft globes of glass that radiated with various shades of soft blue light. At no time was I able to see Bahá'u'lláh's face. His eyes were surrounded by darkness. While basking in this heavenly spectacle, I woke up with the images clearly imprinted on my mind.

The following prophecies indicate that the supreme Redeemer is surrounded with light (a symbol of life) and fire (a symbol of power):

> I saw that from what appeared to be his waist up he looked like glowing metal, as if full of ***fire***...and brilliant ***light***

> surrounded him. Like the appearance of a rainbow in the clouds on a rainy day, so was the radiance around him. This was the appearance of the likeness of the glory of the Lord. When I saw it, I fell face down...
>
> Ezekiel 1:27-28 NIV

> His throne was flaming with ***fire*** and its wheels were all ablaze. A river of ***fire*** was flowing... Daniel 7:9-10 NIV

The metaphors of "the sun" and "the light" are used repeatedly for the great Redeemers. Chapter 19 of Psalms is entirely about the coming of the promised Ones of our time, especially Bahá'u'lláh. Jewish and Christian commentators take it literally, but it also has a prophetic message. Let us first see the verses in sequence, and then study some of their metaphors verse by verse:

> The heavens declare the glory of God; the skies proclaim the work of his hands. Day after day they pour forth speech; night after night they display knowledge. There is no speech or language where their voice is not heard. Their voice goes out into all the earth, their words to the ends of the world. In the heavens he has pitched a tent for the sun, which is like a bridegroom coming forth from his pavilion, like a champion rejoicing to run his course. It rises at one end of the heavens and makes its circuit to the other; nothing is hidden from its heat. The law of the Lord is perfect, reviving the soul. The statutes of the Lord are trustworthy, making wise the simple…May the words of my mouth and the meditation of my heart be pleasing in your sight, O Lord, my Rock and my Redeemer.
>
> Psalms 19:1-7, 14 NIV

Verses 1-2:

> The heavens declare the glory of God; the skies proclaim the work of his hands. Day after day they pour forth speech; night after night they display knowledge.

"Heaven" symbolizes religion; all great religions have declared the coming of Bahá'u'lláh, the Glory of God. "The heavens" here may refer specifically to the Revelations of the Báb and Bahá'u'lláh. The volume of writings and knowledge poured forth by these two Revelations is phenomenal.

Verses 3-4:

> There is no speech or language where their voice is not heard. Their voice goes out into all the earth, their words to the ends of the world.

Since the Bahá'í Faith has come for the entire planet, peoples of all languages will hear the Voice and the Words of the two Redeemers.

Verse 5:

> In the heavens he has pitched a tent for the sun, which is like a bridegroom coming forth from his pavilion, like a champion rejoicing to run his course.

In the heaven of divine Revelation, God has designated a place or a dawning point for Bahá'u'lláh, the Sun of Truth, who radiates with the light and glory of God. The coming of the glory of God from the heaven of divine Revelation is compared to a bridegroom coming from his chamber. We know Jesus compared Himself to a Bridegroom and religion to a Bride coming from heaven. According to *Nelson's Illustrated Bible Dictionary*: "In the New Testament...Christ is the Bridegroom (John 3:29), and the church is His bride (Eph. 5:25-33)."[27]

The New English Bible personifies "the sun" by using the pronoun "who" instead of "which:"

> In them [the heavens] a tent is fixed for the sun [Bahá'u'lláh], ***who*** comes out like a bridegroom from his wedding canopy... Psalms 19:4-5 NEB

Verse 6:

> It rises at one end of the heavens and makes its circuit to the other; nothing is hidden from its heat.

The Sun of Bahá'u'lláh covers the entire planet. Nothing remains beyond His power, His reach and radiance.

Verse 7:

> The law of the Lord is perfect, reviving the soul. The statutes of the Lord are trustworthy, making wise the simple.

Bahá'u'lláh has a Book of laws called *The Most Holy Book (The Kitáb-i-Aqdas).* The laws contained in that Book are perfect. They serve as a source of wisdom to all those endowed with hearts as pure, as simple and as uncomplicated by illusions and prejudice as those of children.

Dreams and Visions

Sometimes, out of His bounty, God awakens or strengthens us through dreams or visions. The prophet Joel was inspired to utter this prophecy about our time:

> In the last days, God says, I will pour out my Spirit on all people. Your sons and daughters will prophesy, your young men will see visions, your old men will dream dreams... And everyone who calls on the name of the Lord will be saved.
>
> Acts 2:17, 21 NIV
> See also Joel 2:28, 32

We find many instances in the rich history of the Bahá'í Faith that confirm or fulfill Joel's prophecy. A disciple of Bahá'u'lláh states that during the earlier stages of his search for truth, he found the evidence for the Bahá'í Faith convincing. But he had doubts until he had a dream in which he saw a divine Being who was pacing up and down among some people. This is what happened in his dream:

> I arrived and spontaneously prostrated myself at His [divine Being's] feet. Graciously, He lifted me up with His own hands and, standing, said 'A person may claim that he has come here wholly for the sake of God, and has truly attained the presence of His Lord, when he is not held back

> by the onslaught of the peoples of the world, who with drawn swords attack him and intend to take his life because he has embraced the Cause of God. Otherwise, he cannot truthfully say that his motive was to seek God.'
>
> On hearing these words, I woke up from my dream and found myself assured, joyous and thankful. All my doubts had completely disappeared. I learnt the mysteries of martyrdom, persecution and sufferings...I was amazed as I looked back upon the doubts I had entertained, my ignorance, low-mindedness, weakness of faith and shallowness of thought...And now, through this dream, I had acquired faith...
>
> ...about fourteen years later I was in the 'Land of Mystery' [Adrianople] where I stayed for seven months. Every day, through His bounty, I used to attain the presence of Bahá'u'lláh once, twice and sometimes more. But during this period, I never thought of my dream...[28]

Then one day, when this pilgrim visited Bahá'u'lláh, he encountered this amazing experience:

> ...I saw the Ancient Beauty [Bahá'u'lláh] pacing in the roofed area of the house. The stream of His utterance was flowing and a few souls were standing. I prostrated myself at His feet, whereupon He lifted me up with His blessed hands. He turned to me and said:
>
> 'A person may claim that he has arrived here wholly for the sake of God, and has truly attained the presence of His Lord when he is not held back by the onslaught of the peoples of the world, who with drawn swords attack him and intend to take his life because he has embraced the Cause.'
>
> These were exactly the words I had heard fourteen years before, and I saw the same incomparable Beauty and the same building as in my dream. I stood by the wall, awestruck and motionless...My purpose in telling this story is

> not, God forbid, to attribute any miracles, but rather to state the facts as they happened...[29]

The following is a similar story about an eminent poet and a distinguished disciple of Bahá'u'lláh named Varqá, who eventually sacrificed his life for his Lord:

> The first time he [Varqá] gazed upon the face of His Lord he was surprised, because he thought that he had previously seen Him somewhere, but he could not remember the occasion or the place. He was puzzled by this until one day after several times coming into His presence, Bahá'u'lláh said to him, 'Varqá! Burn away the idols of vain imaginings!' On hearing these words, Varqá immediately recalled a dream he had had when he was a child. He was in a garden playing with some dolls when 'God' arrived, took the dolls from him and burned them in the fire. When he told this dream to his parents they pointed out to him that no one can see God. However, he had completely forgotten this dream until that day when the words of Bahá'u'lláh, exhorting him to burn the idols, aroused his memory, and he knew that he had seen Bahá'u'lláh in his dream as a child.[30]

The experience of a relative of mine (Hakím Áqá Ján)—a physician and one of the first among the Jews to accept Bahá'u'lláh—is another example. While lying on his deathbed, semiconscious, he suddenly raised himself and exclaimed, "Turn this way and look!" A relative who was tending him, said, "Why?" The dying man responded, "Can't you see Bahá'u'lláh entering?" The relative looked in the desired direction, but could see nothing. The man with the vision then bowed his head, recited a verse from the Torah in Hebrew, lay down and died. About two months later, the surviving relatives received a Tablet (Letter) from Bahá'u'lláh in honor of the deceased man. Near the end of the Tablet Bahá'u'lláh states that He was with him at the time of his death and sought divine forgiveness and blessings for him. The key point is this: no one had informed Bahá'u'lláh about the death of this man. I have a copy of Bahá'u'lláh's Tablet.

Fulfilled Wishes

Among other unusual events attributed to Bahá'u'lláh, the Báb, and 'Abdu'l-Bahá are those relating to the fulfillment of spoken and sometimes unspoken requests, desires, or thoughts of a few individuals who would wish for certain gifts or necessities of life, such as health, wealth, a long life of serenity, or perhaps a child. Here is an eyewitness account:

> One of the most famous merchants of Qazvín was Hájí Muhammad Báqir. Not only was he well known as a merchant, but he was also prominent in his service to the Cause, a service which was much appreciated by all the believers. Once he sent a letter to Bahá'u'lláh asking Him to bestow upon him the bounty of wealth so that he could serve the Cause with greater capacity. Bahá'u'lláh answered that the doors of wealth would be opened to him from all sides, but he must be ever vigilant lest material prosperity become a veil between him and his Creator.
>
> Bahá'u'lláh also said to those in His presence at the time that Muhammad Báqir would soon be drowned in wealth, but material success would close his eyes to the realities of life to such a degree that he would turn his back on the Cause and even deny God. Then he would suffer tremendous losses and would return to his Lord in repentance. Because of his repentance, God would change his losses into ample profits to such an extent as to enable him to become the leading merchant in Tabríz and Constantinople. This time he would become even more proud and would again ignore the Faith, and then his wealth would be gone forever. He would no longer be able to trade and would become helpless. He would then return in repentance once more and remain poor but content. In this state, he would serve the Cause and achieve great success in his service

to God. At the end of His wondrous and ominous statement, Bahá'u'lláh addressed me and advised that I should remember all the events as they unfolded.

After some time, Muhammad Báqir's brother was arrested and thrown into prison because of his Faith. Muhammad Báqir paid a large sum of money to obtain his brother's release. After that, Muhammad Báqir made his way to Constantinople. Upon his arrival, he recanted his faith and approached the court of the sultan and the Persian ambassador, begging them to consider him a true Muslim.

Bahá'u'lláh immediately remarked that this was the starting point of the chain of events he had described before.

I then went to Constantinople, where I stayed fourteen months. There I learned that Muhammad Báqir had purchased great quantities of cotton. All of a sudden, the price of cotton dropped so low that our friend lost his wealth and became submerged in debt. In this deplorable condition, he again remembered his Lord and wrote a letter to Bahá'u'lláh in which he repented and begged Him to come to his aid. Bahá'u'lláh replied, assuring him that he would regain his wealth.

When I was in Egypt I learned that the price of cotton had risen sharply. Muhammad Báqir's wealth grew to ten times more than ever before. Although he had been tested once, he fell a second time into the trap of greed and failed to know his Lord and Provider. Bahá'u'lláh wrote him again and alerted him to the danger of material temptation. He exhorted him to remain steadfast in the Path of God and grateful for His bounties. But once more Muhammad Báqir ignored God and remained heedless.

When after many years I found him again in Tabríz, he told me, "After I received the Tablet, it seemed to me that even the nails and curtains on the walls of my room had ears to hearken and obey. One by one, all of my possessions slipped quietly from me. I was reduced to poverty and was forced to leave Constantinople for Tabríz where I live in this house, which belongs to my wife, and wear clothes that are made by my children."[31]

'Abdu'l-Bahá's Wondrous Gifts

'Abdu'l-Bahá was also endowed with distinct spiritual gifts. We read many stories about Jesus' healing powers. The following story written by an eyewitness about 'Abdu'l-Bahá's healing powers gives us a more detailed picture of how Jesus may have healed the sick:

> At one in the afternoon we arrived at a small village, called Majdal [in the Holy Land].
>
> "Have you any acquaintance in this village?" the Master ['Abdu'l-Bahá] asked.
>
> "Yes, Master, the headman of the village is a good Christian and an acquaintance of mine."
>
> The Master then told me to inform him of His arrival...I went at once to the home of the headman of the village, who was called Khúrí, and told him of the arrival of 'Abdu'l-Bahá. The headman, and many of the notables of the village ran towards the Master's carriage, and with great respect helped Him to alight. 'Abdu'l-Bahá, His attendants, the host, and some of the notables entered the house and sat in the guest room. The Master told Khusraw to make tea and prepare a repast. The food had been brought from Haifa, and the host produced some honey, yogurt, olives, and eggs. 'Abdu'l-Bahá tasted only a few spoonfuls of honey, a little broth, and some olives, and after the meal He slept about an hour. Arising, He washed His hands and bathed His face with cool water, and came again to sit in the guest room. He spoke words of wisdom to the host, and to the notables, and advised them on many of their problems and difficulties caused by the war.

The host thanked 'Abdu'l-Bahá for His advice, and for the great honor bestowed upon his humble dwelling and upon himself by this visit.

"Your visit at such a time of distress...will bring heavenly bounties...to all the dwellers in this village. Now I have one more request to make of you."

"What is your request?" said 'Abdu'l-Bahá. "It will be a happiness to grant it if I have the power."

The Master was always courteous to every creature. He was the symbol of what Bahá'u'lláh had said long ago. "Courtesy is my garment with which we have adorned the temples of our favorite servants."

"The headman continued: "I have only one child, a girl of fourteen, who has been consumptive [has tuberculosis] for two years. All the physicians have pronounced her a hopeless case. Days and nights her mother and I and our relatives can do nothing but weep, wail, and moan. God has not given us another offspring. If your Holiness would pray for the restoration of my only child to health, I feel that a new life would be bestowed upon her, as has been bestowed upon us all by your sympathy and wise advice. We feel sure that the prayers of your Holiness are acceptable to God, and we know that 'Abdu'l-Bahá's bounties shower on all men, regardless of their deserving." At this point the headman burst into tears.

'Abdu'l-Bahá immediately arose from His seat.

"Where is your little girl?"

"In the other room," the headman answered.

'Abdu'l-Bahá went into the other room and saw the young girl lying on a bed on the floor, in the middle of the room. The members of her family were seated about her. Some were acting as nurses, and some only wept. 'Abdu'l-Bahá approached the head of the bed, and sat down beside her. He took the little hand and felt the pulse. The temperature was very high. The child coughed incessantly, and spat blood. She was like a creature of skin and bones. She was in a condition of utter weakness. 'Abdu'l-Bahá laid His blessed hand upon the child's forehead and caressed her. Turning to Jalál, He said, "Bring a cup of tea." This was done at once. 'Abdu'l-Bahá drank some of the tea, and prayed for about five minutes. He Himself gradually poured the rest of the tea with a spoon into the maiden's mouth, and twice placed His hands on her forehead. Once more He prayed, this time for about ten minutes.

Then with a movement of great authority He arose, and turned to the parents, saying in a loud voice of command: "Be assured God will grant a complete cure to your daughter. Do not be perturbed, and neither weep nor moan. With utmost assurance nurse her. Before long she will be in perfect health."

He then returned to the guest room, and comforted the people present with words of great wisdom for half an hour. Then bidding them farewell, He walked out of the house, and stepped into the carriage. Khusraw and I also took our seats.

'Abdu'l-Bahá told Isfandíyár to drive on to Nazareth. All the people of the village, men, women, and children were crowding about the carriage, and until the last second of His remaining there were begging and pleading with the Master for His prayers and blessings.

On the night of that day the maiden perspired a great deal, and gradually the fever abated. According to the word of her father, within two months his daughter was restored to complete health, and in the year 1922 she was married to a Christian man of 'Akká, who is a government official. She is now the mother of three healthy children. Since then, at 'Akká, Haifa, and at Nazareth, the father of the

> girl has recounted this story many times, and always ends his tale with:
>
> "My daughter was given back to me by His Holiness 'Abbás Effendi ['Abdu'l-Bahá]."[32]

The preceding story shows how ineffective miracles are as a means of inducing beliefs. The father firmly believed that 'Abdu'l-Bahá saved his dying daughter, yet this awareness did not convince him to become a Bahá'í.

I have had the privilege of hearing firsthand a number of unusual events about Bahá'u'lláh and 'Abdu'l-Bahá recounted by pilgrims who were blessed by attaining the presence of those divine Beings. A few years ago I conducted and recorded on tape an interview with a rich and extremely generous man (Mr. 'A. Míthãqíyyih) who had attained five wishes he had cherished—but never divulged—while in the presence of 'Abdu'l-Bahá, one being to become rich. (A copy of the tape has been filed in the Bahá'í Archives in the Holy Land.)

The Bahá'í historical records are a rich source of many wondrous events. The purpose in citing a few examples here is not to use them as evidence or proofs of the Bahá'í Revelation. They might, however, be helpful to those who place undue emphasis on personal-spiritual transformations or encounters, who cling unjustifiably to miracles, declining to consider seriously the claims of the Báb and Bahá'u'lláh unless they are confronted with the power of the supernatural.

The True Miracles

As stated, the whole life of God's supreme Messengers and Redeemers consists of no less than an accumulation of unusual or wondrous events and happenings. It seems more reasonable, when looking for evidence of validity, to gaze at the magnificent and majestic Prophetic Profile, which stands supremely above and beyond any man-made or earthly profile. The accumulation of the chief elements of the Profile of a divine Manifestation, if viewed with a keen and perceptive mind, constitutes the most dramatic and the most miraculous event in the history of the world.

Is it not a miracle that God's great Teachers and Messengers reveal teachings that satisfy the needs of so many for so many generations?

Is it not a miracle that they exert the most far-reaching influence on the lives of millions for centuries?

Is it not a miracle that they can tear the dark veil of the future and reveal mysteries far beyond the vision of the wisest and the most learned of people?

Is it not a miracle that so many willingly make sacrifices in their Path, giving their all to attain their presence or partake of the fruits of their love?

Is it not a miracle that they reveal Words so exquisite, so sublime, and with such spontaneity, novelty, grace, and grandeur?

Is it not a miracle that they manifest such a harmony in their teachings and such a constancy in their beliefs and their Missions?

Is it not a miracle that they fulfill distinctly so many prophecies revealed in the Revelations of the past?

Is it not a miracle that the kings and the "high ones of the earth" stand so powerless before their all-pervasive dominion?

Is it not a miracle that they succeed in the most challenging, unyielding, and perplexing task—the changing of the hearts and minds of people?

Is it not a miracle that they manifest deeds so noble and pure—love that knows no bounds, forgiveness beyond measure, humility in its pure essence, detachment beyond human vision, serenity unimpaired?

Is it not a miracle that in spite of their meekness and lack of material means, they attain such an everlasting dominion?

Is it not a miracle that they so willingly make sacrifices and endure so patiently adversities and afflictions far beyond human conception?

Is it not a miracle that in spite of centuries of separation, and the extreme diversity of their cultures, they manifest such a unity of Purpose, always reaffirming and acknowledging the Works and the Missions of those sent before them?

Is it not a miracle that despite their limited or lack of schooling, they unseal and unravel the mysteries and manifest a Knowledge that baffles the minds of the wisest and the most learned?

Is it not a miracle that the opposition of the masses of people, and that of the established religions of the day, is so powerless in the face of their all-pervasive dominion?

To accomplish any of these tasks—unaided, single and alone—is in itself a miracle. How much more is it to accomplish them all? Together they constitute a Supreme Miracle far beyond the vision and comprehension of the human mind.

If these proofs are viewed with justice, with an unbiased and open mind, the distinction of the divine Manifestations and the validity of their claim will become so clear and apparent that no one could fail to recognize them, or hesitate to accept them, even for one short moment.

> Behold Him manifest and resplendent as the sun in all its glory.[33]
>
> Bahá'u'lláh

We are living at the dawning of a new Revelation from God, when the masses of humankind are still sleeping. In their dreams, they think it is inconceivable that they may be among those who deny their Lord. Yet history shows that the inconceivable not only has always been possible but commonplace. The next chapter explains this paradox. It shows how some of the most wonderful people can fail to see the state of their soul at the time of the advent of new Redeemers.

13

Robed in a Cloud

Revelation 10:1 NIV

The Paradox of Anticipation and Denial

A Psychological Explanation

> He [the Promised One] was robed in a ***cloud***...his face was like ***the sun***... Revelation 10:1 NIV

> Indeed the face of ***the sun*** of justice and fairness is hidden behind ***the clouds of idle fancy***...[1] Bahá'u'lláh

A formal prayer recited by the Jews in Israel on Independence Day after a trumpet blast:

> May it be thy will, O Jehovah, our God and the God of our fathers, that as we have been granted the dawn of

> redemption, so may we be granted to hear the trumpet of the Messiah.[2]

Can anything be more astonishing than this: people dream, hope, and pray for their Redeemer; they consider His advent the crowning point in human history. They wish to get a glimpse of the glory of their fondest hopes and dreams, to be mentioned by Him, and to be His humble servant. Yet when they see Him, they ridicule Him, renounce Him, argue with Him, torture Him, and even kill Him. They can respect Him only when separated from Him by a distance of centuries. Why?

> Woe to you...you hypocrites! You build tombs for the prophets and decorate the graves of the righteous. And you say, 'If we had lived in the days of our forefathers, we would not have taken part with them in shedding the blood of the prophets.' Christ (Matt. 23:29-30 NIV)

The paradox of anticipation and denial has not happened just once:

> Was there ever a prophet your fathers did not persecute?
> Acts 7:52 NIV

This paradox needs to be understood. This chapter offers an explanation based on psychological principles. The explanation relates mainly to a prophecy put in a question by the Psalmist:

> ***Why do...the people imagine a vain thing?*** Psalms 2:1

The Power of Fantasy

Fantasy or imagination is a gift from Heaven. It can give birth to creative works in the arts, literature, and science. It can open new and vast horizons to the human mind. But like any other gift, its misuse can lead to disaster. It can lead to separation and remoteness from reality. Some people enjoy specific or multiple fantasies; a few create and live in ***a world*** of fantasy that to them appears in perfect order, solid, and unshaken until a gentle breeze shatters their world.

> We may take fancy for a companion, but must follow Reason as our guide. Samuel Johnson

In many of His Writings, Bahá'u'lláh declares that people for the most part judge their Redeemers by what their own fancy creates and learns from other sources of fancies. The following are some of the words and expressions Bahá'u'lláh presents to portray the critical obstacle that has prevented peoples of all ages, including ours, from seeing the truth:

- idle fancy
- idle thoughts
- idle tales
- idle sayings
- illusions of the embodiments of satanic fancy
- obscuring dust
- vain and obscure thought
- vain fancies
- false imaginings
- fanciful thoughts
- fanciful images
- clouds of idle fancy
- satanic fancy
- fads and fancies
- fleeting fancies
- images that their idle fancy has carved
- mists of idle fancy
- imprisoned in the cage of their fancies
- veils of fancy and false imaginings
- smoke of idle fancy

Bahá'u'lláh also uses the word ***cloud*** to symbolize obstacles:

> These thick ***clouds*** are the exponents ***of idle fancies and vain imaginings***...[3]

> Indeed the face of the sun of justice and fairness is hidden behind the ***clouds of idle fancy***...[4]

Bahá'u'lláh repeatedly encourages seekers of truth to break through the intervening clouds of fancy and to see the light of truth unveiled in all its beauty and splendor:

> **O SON OF MAN!**
> Many a day hath passed over thee whilst thou hast busied thyself with thy ***fancies and idle imaginings***. How long art thou to slumber on thy bed? Lift up thy head from slumber, for the Sun hath risen to the zenith, haply it may shine upon thee with the light of beauty.[5]
>
> **ALAS! ALAS! O LOVERS OF WORLDLY DESIRE!**
> Even as the swiftness of lightning ye have passed by the Beloved One, and have set your hearts on ***satanic fancies***. Ye bow the knee before your vain imagining, and call it truth. Ye turn your eyes towards the thorn, and name it a flower.[6]
>
> O friend, the heart is the dwelling of eternal mysteries, make it not the home of ***fleeting fancies***...[7]
>
> ...when a true seeker determineth to take the step of search in the path leading to the knowledge of the Ancient of Days, he must, before all else, cleanse and purify his heart, which is the seat of the revelation of the inner mysteries of God, from the obscuring dust of all acquired knowledge, and the allusions of the embodiments of ***satanic fancy***.[8]
>
> ...they that thirst for the wine of certitude, must cleanse themselves of all that is earthly—their ears from idle talk, their minds from ***vain imaginings***...[9]
>
> Cast away, O concourse of divines [religious leaders], the things ye have composed with the pens of your ***idle fancies and vain imaginings***.[10]
>
> Fear ye God and follow not your ***idle fancies***...[11]

> Fear God, and be not of the heedless...This is the Cause that hath caused all ***superstitions and idols*** to tremble.[12]
>
> O concourse of divines...We found you behind ***the veils***... measure not the Book of God with your selfish desires.[13]
>
> Arise, O people, and, by the power of God's might, resolve to gain the victory over your own selves, that haply the whole earth may be freed and sanctified from its servitude to ***the gods of its idle fancies***—gods that have inflicted such loss upon, and are responsible for the misery of their wretched worshippers. These idols form the obstacle that impedeth man in his efforts to advance in the path of perfection.[14]

The Báb also asks us to purify our perceptions:

> Reduce not the ordinances of God to ***fanciful imaginations*** of your own; rather observe all the things which God hath created at His behest with the eye of the spirit, even as ye see things with the eyes of your bodies.[15]

Taking "fancy" for "truth," or following "fantasy" instead of "reason" is not new. Fantasy has always been hard at work creating auras of darkness to make the idols of people's desires appear worthy of worship, to make "empty phantoms" look real:

> ...do you see what the elders of Israel are doing in darkness, each at the shrine of ***his own carved image***?
>
> Ezekiel 8:12 NEB
>
> What faults did your forefathers find in me, that they wandered far from me, pursuing ***empty phantoms*** and themselves becoming empty. Jeremiah 2:5 NEB
>
> ...most of them follow nothing but ***fancy***: truly fancy can be of no avail against Truth. Qur'án 10:36 Y

It seems human nature never changes. Krishna, who appeared long before Moses, declares the same message:

> The light [of God] is covered by darkness. This darkness is ***delusion***... Bhagavad-Gita 5:17

> When you have reached enlightenment, ignorance will ***delude*** you no longer. Bhagavad-Gita 4:29

Compare the preceding passage with the following from Bahá'u'lláh:

> ...when thou strippest the wrappings of ***illusion*** from off thy heart, the lights of oneness will be manifest.[16]

This prophecy from the Qur'án points to the prevalence of fantasy in our day:

> Woe that Day to those who practice falsehood, who amuse themselves with their own ***idle fancies***. Qur'án 52:11-12

Living a Life of Fantasy

Fantasy plays a critical role in all phases of human life. Indeed many people judge their whole purpose of living by what their fancy or imagination creates.

> Ye bow the knee before your ***vain imagining***, and call it truth.[17] Bahá'u'lláh

Examples of common fantasies:

- Survival fantasy: terminal disease cannot happen to me; others die, but not me.
- Safety-in-numbers fantasy: do what everybody else does and be safe.
- Wealth fantasy: the richest people are the luckiest.
- Ethical fantasy: everybody cheats on his taxes. I must get even. Besides, the government wastes so much money.
- Moral fantasy: there is no right and wrong. Do everything your way, as long as no one gets hurt.

- Anti-religion fantasy: nothing good ever came from religion. The world would have been a better place without God and faith.
- Racial fantasy: I am glad I am white. I am special.
- Military fantasy: security comes from advanced weapons. Weapons are the best remedy against war.
- Political fantasy: what happens to other countries is not my business. I must be concerned only with my nation.
- Economic fantasy: progress can be measured mainly by industrial growth; the faster the better.
- Education fantasy: education means collecting, memorizing, and transferring information. A good teacher fills students' minds with vast stores of facts and figures.
- Purpose-of-life fantasy: life is too short. What matters most is to cram into every day as much fun as possible.
- After-life fantasy: when I get to the hereafter, then I will worry about the hereafter.
- Marital fantasy: I am a good teacher. I will straighten out my spouse later.
- Parenting fantasy: I don't have enough time to spend with my children. Instead, I buy them everything they want, and more. What more can they expect?
- School fantasy: going to school is a waste of time. The only way to get ahead is to know the right person.
- Ignorance fantasy: what I do not know cannot hurt me.
- Media fantasy: if I need to know something, the news media will tell me.
- Christ fantasy: when Jesus comes I will know for sure. In fact, I will be among the first to be lifted to heaven. (This

is perhaps the shakiest and yet the most consequential of all fantasies.)

- Religion-of-ancestors fantasy: follow the religion of your ancestors. There is no need to investigate other belief systems. Other religions are false or at best half-truths.

- Relegating-responsibility fantasy: I am not smart enough to judge the truth. I will let an expert or authority figure—a rabbi, a priest, a pastor, or a mullá—to lead me and to choose my destiny for me.

- Forgiveness fantasy: when it comes to being saved or not saved, ***what you do does not matter that much***, for it is by grace that you are saved, not by your works. As a sinner you have a lot of company—everyone is with you. The solution to sin is twofold: confession of sin, and a request for forgiveness. These two will wash away your transgressions.

- Faith fantasy: if there is a God, He would not let me suffer.

- Ego fantasy: I am almost perfect.

Some people's whole lives hang on a thread of fantasy. By weaving that thread, they build fantastic mansions that trap all their potential, that becloud all their vision.

How Does Fantasy Work in Reality?

Fantasy initiates and maintains a balance between what an individual desires and what he considers proper; between what his ego demands of him and what his conscience considers fair. The following diagram displays the three forces of fantasy in action:

Fantasy

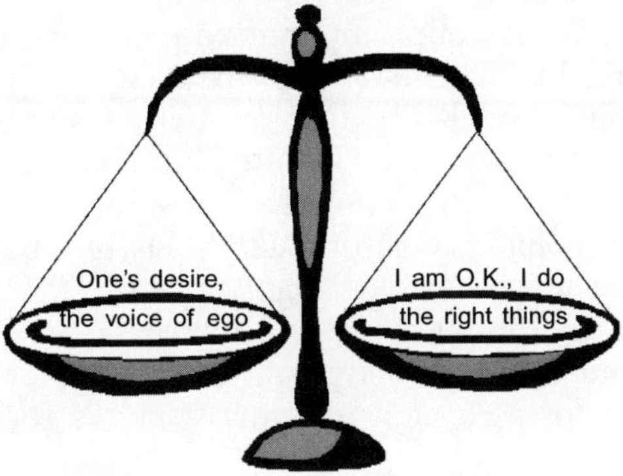

Suppose an individual has a prestigious and lucrative profession and position, and is deeply preoccupied with his work. He knows he must spend more time with his children. His dilemma of trying to maintain a balance makes him anxious. How does he relieve anxiety? By buying more presents for his children and giving them more freedom to please themselves. Then he says to himself: "I am a pretty good father. I must work hard to provide all those extras for my family." His fantasy has helped him to create and maintain a balance between what he desires, and what he considers proper.

Fantasy

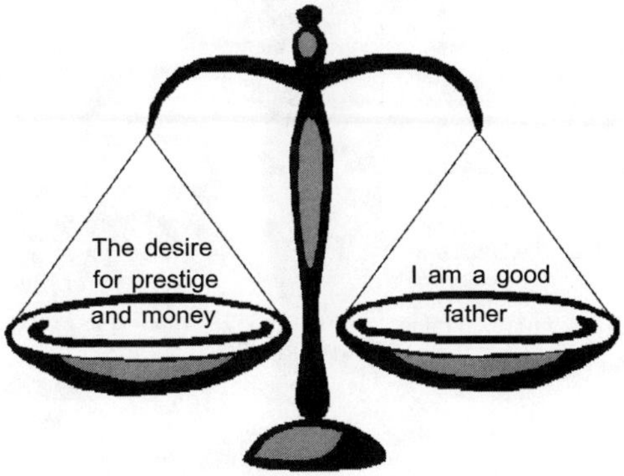

Consider another example, that of a believer who likes to say to himself: other faiths are false; they do not deserve any examination. What can prompt him to think this way? Perhaps fear of losing his own faith. Why take chances? His view of other religions may also be inspired by a desire to protect his position among those who admire him. He knows that an easy way of losing his cherished position is to do or say something unpopular. One obstacle holds him back from fulfilling his desire: he cannot simply ignore other religions or call them false without a "good" reason. He needs a reason to justify and maintain his position. Here as elsewhere, his fantasy goes to work and performs wonders for him.

All he needs is a phrase in his own Scriptures, a simple verse that would confirm his suspicion. With the help of his fantasy, his desire is fulfilled. He reminds himself constantly of that phrase or verse and he associates mostly with people who will reaffirm his fulfilled desire. His fantasy has served a vital purpose: it has protected him from the anxiety of not investigating other faiths. If he is very adventurous, he may risk reading a book about other belief systems, but most likely it will be one written by a recommended author ***from his own religion***. Why? This thought goes through his mind: "When a person of other belief systems writes a book about his own religion, as a rule he is biased. People of my faith are more fair."

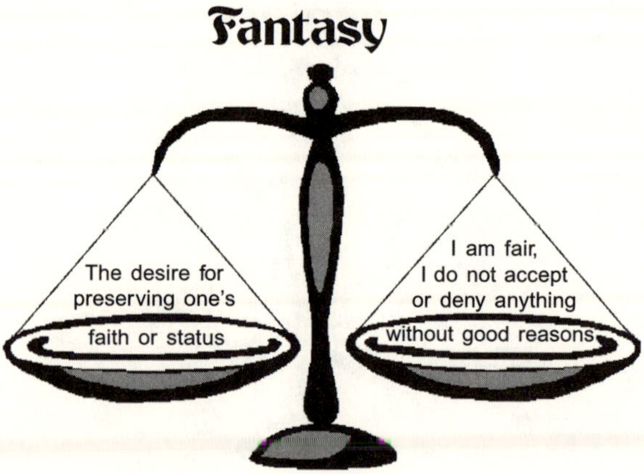

This theory shows the relationship between the heart and the mind; it portrays how humans come to decisions. Think of the heart as a spray bottle and of the mind as eyes. What do the eyes see? They see whatever the heart allows them. If they see something threatening, the heart instantly produces a measured dosage of mist and directs it at the unwelcomed reality, at the new intruder. ***The mists are the forces of fantasy***.

All human beings always carry a spray bottle that can produce vast amounts of mist. What differentiates them is in the size of the spray bottle and the directions the mists may take. For instance, some people are very objective and open-minded about their profession, but the moment they enter the realm of religion, they become a new creation. They see differently, hear differently, and judge differently.

The heart has a vast reservoir of misty notions to direct at that vision of reality that it finds most threatening. Both the reservoir and the mist's pressure are greater for emotionally charged issues, such as family relations, religious, racial, and certain moral questions. Both the force and the reservoir of the mist astonish the mind. Sometimes one spray can conceal mountains of evidence. It can conceal even the Face of God Himself, a Face brighter than the sun.

Prophecies indicate that in this age the mists will become so thick that they will create vast clouds of gloom and darkness:

> That day will be a day of...distress...a day of darkness and gloom, a day of clouds... Zephaniah 1:15 NIV

> How awful that day will be! None will be like it.
> Jeremiah 30:7 NIV

> Woe to you who long for the day of the Lord!...That day will be darkness, not light. Amos 5:18 NIV

Symbolism—the Medium of Fantasy in Religion

Nowhere in the world of reality can fantasy find as much freedom, and command as much power, as it does in the realm of religion. Why? Perhaps the main reason is this: sacred Scriptures contain vast and rich deposits of metaphors, similes, allegories, parables, and codes, from which mansions of fantasy can readily rise:

> These were the words of the Lord to me: Man, speak to the Israelites in ***allegory*** and ***parable***. Ezekiel 17:1-2 NEB

> In all his teaching to the crowds Jesus spoke ***in parables***; in fact he never spoke to them without a parable.
> Matthew 13:34 NEB

> Verily We have propounded for men, in this Qur'án, every kind of ***parable***. Qur'án 30:58 Y

This question comes to mind: God is All-Knowing. He knows people will distort His symbols and parables. Why then does He use them? The abundant use of symbols and parables in sacred Scriptures serves several purposes. Perhaps the most critical among them is God's will to preserve one of His choicest gifts to His children: their freedom of choice.

Symbolism grants people almost unlimited freedom to fashion and choose whatever they wish. The Creator in His Wisdom has provided His children with vast resources of both earthly and spiritual riches. Each individual can select as much or as little of those riches as he may desire. Both God's gift of fantasy and His vast treasuries of symbols and parables work together to create a world of wonders, an ideal level of freedom for all human beings; a freedom by which they are tested; a gift that allows all potential powers to bloom into being.

This question may awaken an awareness of God's Wisdom and ways of accomplishing His goals: Jesus had transcendent knowledge and power. He knew how to convince His adversaries. Why did He choose not to do it?

The Clouds of Fantasy and Selfish Desires

> He [Bahá'u'lláh] was robed in a ***cloud***...his face was like the sun... Revelation 10:1 NIV

> Like the appearance of a rainbow in the ***clouds*** on a rainy day...This was the appearance of the likeness of ***the glory of the Lord*** [Bahá'u'lláh]. Ezekiel 1:28-29 NIV

> He [the glory of God] who is the Lord of Lords is come overshadowed with ***clouds***...[18] Bahá'u'lláh

Symbolic devices—similes, metaphors, analogies, parables—offer the imagination free play. They activate that aspect of the mind that thrives on fantasy and the fantastic. The extreme popularity of science fiction and magic is an evidence of the special need humans have for the free play of their imaginations. Why do people love fantasy? The Psalmist asked this question long ago:

> ***Why do...the people imagine a vain thing?*** Psalms 2:1

Why do they? For many reasons:

- Fantasy, which is a vain thing, entertains the mind. People leave the world of reality temporarily to observe dramatic and fantastic events. This is one reason believers have always loved to see and talk about miracles.
- Fantasy provides an escape from daily pressures. The stressed can temporarily leave their troubles behind.
- Fantasy allows the mind to create heroes with whom to identify. People can then fashion and worship models according to their choosing.
- Fantasy offers instant happiness. Believers can see themselves being uplifted to heaven without any effort.
- Fantasy relieves the individual from responsibility. People do not have to spend time investigating a claim. They

assume that if anything happens, they will be the first to know. How could they be alive, but not see and hear?

- Fantasy allows the individual to justify his desires. It creates mists of darkness to obscure reality.

There are countless theories and interpretations of prophecies about the way Christ will come. Which one is correct? Bahá'u'lláh calls these thoughts and theories "idle tales" and "idle sayings." To recognize the truth, the seeker must set aside every one of them.

> ...he must, before all else, cleanse and purify his heart... from the obscuring dust of all acquired knowledge...[19]
>
> Bahá'u'lláh

The prevailing personal views and theories, like vast and raging dust storms, are preventing the eyes from beholding the Blessed Beauty of God.

God's supreme Messengers and Redeemers always come ***with*** the clouds, ***on*** the clouds, and ***in*** the clouds. ***With*** the clouds may symbolize the degree to which they conceal their great glory due to people's lack of capacity:

> Know of a certainty that in every Dispensation the light of Divine Revelation hath been vouchsafed unto men in direct proportion to their spiritual capacity. Consider the sun. How feeble its rays the moment it appeareth above the horizon. How gradually its warmth and potency increase as it approacheth its zenith, enabling meanwhile all created things to adapt themselves to the growing intensity of its light. How steadily it declineth until it reacheth its setting point. Were it, all of a sudden, to manifest the energies latent within it, it would, no doubt, cause injury to all created things...In like manner, if the Sun of Truth were suddenly to reveal, at the earliest stages of its manifestation, the full measure of the potencies which the providence of the Almighty hath bestowed upon it, the earth of human understanding would waste away and be consumed; for men's hearts would neither sustain the intensity of its

> revelation, nor be able to mirror forth the radiance of its light. Dismayed and overpowered, they would cease to exist.[20]
>
> Bahá'u'lláh

We can see the sun of the solar system, but the spiritual Sun is so awesome, so intense, no human being has the capacity to behold its infinite beauty and splendor without the clouds of concealment.

> O Lord, who has set the sun in heaven, but has chosen to dwell in ***thick darkness***...
>
> I Kings 8:13 NEB

On the clouds may symbolize the illusions, imitations, superstitions, and selfish and sinful barriers and desires that prevent people from seeing the Sun, the things that are contrary to their ways and wishes:

> Consider how men for generations have been blindly imitating their fathers, and have been trained according to such ways and manners as have been laid down by the dictates of their Faith. Were these men, therefore, to discover suddenly that a Man, Who hath been living in their midst, Who, with respect to every human limitation, hath been their equal, had risen to abolish every established principle imposed by their Faith—principles by which for centuries they have been disciplined, and every opposer and denier of which they have come to regard as infidel...and wicked—they would of a certainty be veiled and hindered from acknowledging His truth. ***Such things are as "clouds"***...[21]
>
> Bahá'u'lláh

Notice how clearly this warning from Jesus, as translated in *The New Testament in Modern English*, clarifies the meaning of "clouds," how clearly it shows that "***the clouds***" ***drift in the hearts and minds, not in the skies***:

> Be on your guard—see to it that ***your minds are never clouded*** by dissipation [love for pleasure] or ***drunkenness*** [unawareness and negligence] or the worries of this life...
>
> Luke 21:36

Bahá'u'lláh also uses the metaphor of ***drunkenness***. He states that His divine station shines as brightly as the sun and the exaltation of His Revelation "is such as none can deny save those ***whose eyes are drunken***..."[22]

As the Báb declares, the heavenly Redeemers are "the throne of the ***revelation*** and ***concealment*** of God."[23] Not only do they reveal the Creator, but conceal Him as well—from the "strangers." When the Báb went on pilgrimage to Mecca, thousands saw Him. Did any one of them recognize Him? None! This statement from Him about that visit offers perhaps the clearest meaning of the expression "like a thief:"

> There was a vast concourse of pilgrims from every sect. ***Yet not one recognized Him, though He recognized every one of them***...[24]

The Báb knew every one of those pilgrims better than they knew themselves. He could give every conceivable detail about their lives, yet none of them had the slightest idea who the Báb was. He was the heavenly light concealed in the clouds of glory.

Anyone who cannot see the awesome splendor of God in Bahá'u'lláh is wearing a dark veil of clouds. As it is impossible to see the sun from behind the clouds, so is seeing and recognizing the light of truth from behind the clouds of illusions and unseemly desires.

In the clouds may symbolize the Savior's physical form:

> He makes ***the clouds his chariots*** and rides the wings of the wind. Psalms 104:3 NIV

> In another sense, they [clouds] mean the ***appearance of that immortal Beauty in the image of mortal man***, with such human limitations as eating and drinking, poverty and riches, glory and abasement, sleeping and waking, and such other things as cast doubt in the minds of men, and cause them to turn away. All such veils are symbolically referred to as "***clouds.***"[25] Bahá'u'lláh

Thus we have ***at least three layers of obstacles***. The great Messengers and Redeemers come ***with*** the clouds, ***on*** the clouds, and ***in*** the clouds.

> Even as the clouds prevent the eyes of men from beholding the sun, so do these things hinder the souls of men from recognizing the light of the divine Luminary.[26]
>
> Bahá'u'lláh

> The heart must needs therefore ***be cleansed*** from the ***idle sayings*** of men...so that it may discover the hidden meaning of divine inspiration, and become the treasury of the mysteries of divine knowledge...[27] Bahá'u'lláh

To those below the clouds, the Thief who comes from above remains fully concealed; to those above the clouds He shines with immortal glory, as the lightning that flashes from the East to the West. Should we rest ***below*** the clouds, or rise ***above*** the clouds?

> It behooveth us, therefore, to make the utmost endeavor, that, by God's invisible assistance, ***these dark veils***, ***these clouds of Heaven-sent trials, may not hinder us*** from beholding the beauty of His shining Countenance, and that we may recognize Him only by His own Self. And should we ask for a testimony of His truth, we should content ourselves with one, and only one; that thereby we may attain unto Him Who is the Fountain-head of infinite grace, and in Whose presence all the world's abundance fadeth into nothingness, that we may cease…to cleave unto our own ***idle fancy***.[28] Bahá'u'lláh

Does every human being have the capacity to leave his or her comfort zone of clouds of confusion?

> …all men are endowed with the capacity to see and hear, yet we find them deprived of the privilege of using these faculties.[29] Bahá'u'lláh

> Suffer [allow] not yourselves to be wrapt in the ***dense veils*** of your selfish desires, inasmuch as I have perfected

> in every one of you My creation, so that the excellence of My handiwork may be fully revealed unto men. It follows, therefore, that ***every man hath been, and will continue to be, able of himself to appreciate the Beauty of God, the Glorified. Had he not been endowed with such a capacity, how could he be called to account for his failure?*** If, in the Day when all the peoples of the earth will be gathered together, any man should, whilst standing in the presence of God, be asked: "Wherefore hast thou disbelieved in My Beauty and turned away from My Self," and if such a man should reply and say: "Inasmuch as all men have erred, and none hath been found willing to turn his face to the Truth, I, too, following their example, have grievously failed to recognize the Beauty of the Eternal," such a plea will, assuredly, be rejected. For the faith of no man can be conditioned by any one except himself.[30] Bahá'u'lláh

Jesus said that He would come like a thief, when people are asleep. What do people experience in sleep? They dream. The problem is this: while dreaming, they think they are awake and experiencing reality. The only way they can tell that they are dreaming is to wake up. But how can one awaken a sleeper who thinks he is awake?

How do people conclude that their interpretations are correct? ***They simply assume that what they think or believe cannot be wrong***. Each member of the crowd depends on the others for security. As long as dependency on numbers continues, the individual remains in bondage. As St. Augustine said, "Before God can deliver us, we must undeceive ourselves." It takes courage and spiritual strength to question or rethink the prevailing assumptions.

Some people are architects. They can instantly turn the web of their illusions into magnificent mansions of reality and live in them as permanent residents. Most people protect and cherish their fantasies as if they were priceless antiques. They fear that change may make them less authentic. The elaborate structures of their fantasies at 80 years of age are as authentic as they were at 20, except that they have been embellished and hardened.

The Trap that Will Come on all People

Consider this most critical warning from Jesus:

> But take heed to yourselves and ***be on your guard*** lest your hearts be overburdened and depressed—weighed down—with the giddiness and headache and nausea of self-indulgence, drunkenness, and worldly worries and cares pertaining to (the business of) this life, and that day come upon you suddenly ***like a trap*** or a noose; ***for it will come upon all who live upon the face of the entire earth. Keep awake then and watch at all times*** (that is, be discreet, attentive and ready); praying that you may have the full strength and ability and be accounted worthy to escape all these things [taken together] that will take place, and to stand in the presence of the Son of man. Luke 21:34-36 AB

In the preceding prophecy Jesus speaks of a "trap" that entangles or encompasses all the peoples of the world. What does He mean? Several questions come to mind:

- What is the purpose of a trap? To deceive.
- How does a trap work? By remaining hidden from view.
- Who are the victims who fall into a trap? The ones who do not see it or recognize it. The ones who do not remain awake and aware or who fail to watch their steps.
- When does a trap work best? At night or on a dark or foggy day.

Every false assumption, interpretation, or expectation that we allow to enter and stay in our minds becomes a trap. Every weakness in our soul, such as fear, apathy, and attachment, is a trap. These traps limit our freedom and prevent us from seeking and seeing the truth; they conceal the truth from our view and prevent our rational powers from doing their work. What does Jesus mean by "drunkenness"? He means unawareness. A drunkard is far more likely to stumble and fall into a trap.

Isaiah speaks of a similar trap that falls upon the inhabitants of the earth. He singles out fear as a snare:

> ***Fear*** and the ***pit*** and the ***snare*** are upon you, O inhabitant of the earth. And it shall be that ***he who flees from the noise of the fear shall fall into the pit***, and he who comes up from the midst of the pit shall be caught in the snare…
> Isaiah 24:17-18 NKJ

Bahá'u'lláh often speaks of people who flee from the news of His advent, but there is nowhere to flee to:

> The thing that must come hath come suddenly; behold how they ***flee*** from it![31] Bahá'u'lláh

> There is no place to ***flee*** to, no refuge that any one can seek, except Him.[32] Bahá'u'lláh

The preceding warning from Jesus, if heeded, by itself has the power to rescue every sincere Christian from the endless tangles and traps of illusions and assumptions that have been woven by the fallible imaginations of thousands of theologians over the course of centuries. The trap, Jesus declares, "will come upon ***all*** who live upon the face of the ***entire*** earth" (Luke 21:35). Can Baptists with a good conscience say, "We are out of that trap"? Can Catholics make that claim? Can Mormons or Muslims or Seventh-day Adventists or Lutherans or Jews advance that claim? Can any church or any group claim an exception to that warning? No! Jesus declares that the trap will fall on ***all*** citizens of this planet.

Why does no church or group admit being caught in the prophesied trap? Because if a trap was visible, it would not be a trap! The very fact that people do not admit to being in a trap is evidence of being in a trap!

> There is a way that ***seems right to a man***, but in the end it leads to [spiritual] ***death***. Proverbs 14:12; 16:25 NIV

> ***They hasten to Hell Fire*** [spiritual death]***, and mistake it for light.***[33] Bahá'u'lláh

The way that leads to "death" and "hell fire" is that of false assumptions and fantasies. The only safe path out of this deadly trap is paved with humility, open-mindedness, courage, and passionate love for truth.

The Jews, during the time of Jesus, were also in a trap almost identical to the one that now surrounds all the peoples of the earth. Did they see their traps? Did they see the state of their souls? No! If they had seen the state of their souls, they would have seen the trap.

When people refuse to investigate Bahá'u'lláh's claims, they are hiding or resting in an invisible trap that appears as natural as the air. Ponder all these examples, and see how "innocent" and inviting they look:

- The trap of fear: "I am afraid I will be deceived."
- The trap of complacency: "I like my denomination. I am having a great time."
- The trap of daily demands: "I am too busy."
- The trap of worldliness: "What matters is what you see and what you sense—money and pleasure."
- The trap of conformity: "All my relatives and close friends are Jewish."
- The trap of avoiding responsibility: "My pastor or rabbi will teach me the truth. It is up to him to lead me."
- The trap of apathy: "I don't want to know."
- The trap of ignorance: "I don't know."

- The trap of attachment: "I can't love any other name."

What solutions did Jesus offer to avoid or escape from the trap? Two solutions:

- Keep ***awake*** and ***watch***, pay attention at all times.
- ***Pray*** constantly to become worthy of His grace.

Both of the solutions He offered ***require action***. They indicate that the trap catches believers who make no move, who stay in their previous position, who ***neither investigate nor pray***. ***The soul will only be guided if God is brought into the picture.*** That is the purpose of praying. ***Faith*** always comes from ***the grace of God***.

The honor of knowing the Redeemer of the Age is so glorious, so exalted, so supreme that we must plead with God every moment of our lives to "grant us the favor of the grace." Notice the words "tearful," "fervently," and "repeatedly" in this passage from Bahá'u'lláh:

> ***We should with tearful eyes, fervently and repeatedly, implore Him to grant us the favor of that grace.***[34]
>
> Bahá'u'lláh

Our spiritual birth is in God's hand:

> ***No one can come to me unless the Father who sent me draws him***... Christ (John 6:44 NIV)

> Then you will call, and the Lord will answer; ***you will cry for help, and he will say: Here am I...The Lord will guide you always***... Isaiah 58:9-11

What percentage of people follow both instructions? How many ***both*** investigate ***and*** pray? How many obey this commandment: "***Watch therefore, and pray always***" (Luke 21:36 NKJ)? Perhaps not even one in a thousand. Virtually all people remain entangled in several traps at the same time—those of fear, conformity, complacency, ignorance, tradition, apathy, daily living, and failing to pray to God for an open heart and mind.

Consider the trap of ignorance, the most innocent of all traps. Some of the enlightened truth seekers know "something is wrong." To satisfy their hunger, they go from city to city, from church to church, from cult to cult, but remain dissatisfied:

> "Behold, the days are coming," says the Lord God, "That I will send ***a famine*** on the land, not a famine of bread, nor a thirst for water, but ***of hearing the words of the Lord***. They shall wander from sea to sea, and from north to east; they shall run to and fro, seeking the word of the Lord, but shall not find it. Amos 8:11-12 NKJ

Many people seeking the Word of God lack spiritual capacity. What they fail to do is to go beyond the confines of their churches. They need to love "a new rose" from whatever garden it may grow. They need to taste "a new fruit" from whatever orchard it may come. The attachment to a label or form stifles their souls' freedom. Who is more likely to remain entrapped? The one who investigates with an open mind and a free spirit, and prays for guidance? or the one who neglects to do so? Who has a better chance of discovering the Master? The one who does nothing, or the one who takes action? The one who disobeys the Master's instructions, or the one who obeys? Searching is always essential:

> ...you will find Him, ***if you*** [truly] ***seek Him with all your heart*** (and mind) ***and soul and life***.
> Deuteronomy 4:29 AB

Jesus predicted that at His coming, a "great tribulation or oppression" will encompass the peoples of the earth (Matthew 24:21). Bahá'u'lláh interprets the meaning of the great "oppression" prophesied by Jesus:

> What "oppression" is more grievous than that a soul seeking the truth, and wishing to attain unto the knowledge of God, should know not where to go for it and from whom to seek it? For opinions have sorely differed, and the ways unto the attainment of God have multiplied.[35]

The "oppression" or tribulation predicted by Jesus is a tragedy of unimagined proportions. What a tragedy to starve while the most wholesome food lies within arm's reach. What a tragedy to live in the dark while a touch of desire can flood the heart with the glory of God. What a tragedy to search in vain for love, joy, hope, and peace, while they are as close as our thoughts. What a tragedy to be able to create a world of peace, justice, prosperity, and oneness—and yet live in a world of war, cruelty, poverty, and separation.

We all have a responsibility to proclaim the advent of Bahá'u'lláh to every citizen of our planet. Most people will accept the truth if they are well informed. The reason many are not Bahá'ís is that they just don't know about this outpouring of grace from God or don't know enough about it. If people truly get to know *the Glory of God*, they will embrace His Revelation with all their hearts and souls.

The remedy for lack of knowledge is an independent and passionate search for truth. Ponder the powerful "feeling" or "action" words in this passage from Bahá'u'lláh concerning the traits of a true seeker:

> Only when the lamp of ***search***, of ***earnest striving***, of ***longing desire***, of ***passionate devotion***, of ***fervid love***, of ***rapture***, and ***ecstasy***, is kindled within the seeker's heart, and the breeze of His loving-kindness is wafted upon his soul, will the darkness of error be dispelled, the mists of doubts and misgivings be dissipated, and the lights of knowledge and certitude envelop his being.[36]

How many people do you know whose relationship with truth is characterized by:

- ***earnest striving***
- ***longing desire***
- ***passionate devotion***
- ***fervent love***
- ***rapture***
- ***ecstasy***

The power of the celestial virtues generated by the true seeker moves the heart of God. ***It sets in motion "the breeze of His***

***loving-kindness*.**" ***It brings God into the picture*.** Only then is the seeker able to set himself free from spiritual entrapment. Only then can "the darkness of error" be dispelled. Only then can "the mists of doubts and misgivings be dissipated." Only then can "the light of knowledge and certitude" surround the soul. Bahá'u'lláh continues:

> At that hour will the mystic Herald, bearing the joyful tidings of the Spirit, shine forth from the City of God resplendent as the morn, and, through the trumpet-blast of knowledge, will awaken the heart, the soul, and the spirit from the slumber of negligence. ***Then will the manifold favors and outpouring grace of the holy and everlasting Spirit confer such new life upon the seeker that he will find himself endowed with a new eye, a new ear, a new heart, and a new mind*.** He will contemplate the manifest signs of the universe, and will penetrate the hidden mysteries of the soul. Gazing with the eye of God, he will perceive within every atom a door that leadeth him to the stations of absolute certitude.[37]

Thus Jesus' stern warning to the entrapped peoples of the world makes the examination of Bahá'u'lláh's mission an absolute requirement for every faithful Christian. It unveils the significance and purpose of the "thief in the night." It makes, "seek and ye shall find" a command more urgent than ever before. It makes the instruction, "Watch!" more relevant than ever before. It shows why Jesus emphasized the need for staying awake and alert.

> Blessed the man who stays ***awake***... Christ (Rev. 15:15 NEB)

> Blessed the slumberer who is ***awakened***...[38] Bahá'u'lláh

> **O SON OF MAN!**
> Many a day hath passed over thee whilst thou hast busied thyself with thy fancies and idle imaginings. ***How long art thou to slumber on thy bed?*** Lift up thy head from slumber, for ***the Sun hath risen to the zenith***, haply it may shine upon thee with the light of beauty.[39] Bahá'u'lláh

> ***How long***, O you sons of men, ***will you turn my glory to shame?*** How long will you love worthlessness and seek falsehood?
> Psalms 4:2 NKJ

> **O SON OF DESIRE!**
> ***How long wilt thou soar in the realms of desire?*** Wings have I bestowed upon thee, that thou mayest fly to the realms of mystic holiness and not the regions of satanic fancy.[40]
> Bahá'u'lláh

You may ask, "What about the Bahá'ís? Could they ***also*** be in that universal trap predicted by Jesus?" That is exactly why this book is written. This work is precisely an answer to that concern. If God has allowed all those prophecies to come true in the lives of the Central Figures of the Bahá'í Faith, then we must erroneously assume that God Himself has entrapped the human race. He has deceived the very people He has committed Himself to guide! If God has allowed the Báb and Bahá'u'lláh to speak in His name and to produce the most marvelous heavenly "fruits," then we must assume that God Himself has set a trap for our souls. No, God is not a trapper but One who sifts, separates, and grades the souls! He puts each soul in a "sieve" for the sole purpose of separating and choosing those who obey Him and follow ***His*** standards of knowing a Redeemer rather than ***their own*** selfish desires.

Further, when we read or listen to the stories of those who have become Bahá'ís, we discover that as a whole they are among a few who have followed Jesus' instructions. We find that they are the kind of people who struggled, each in his or her own way "to escape all those things," to disentangle themselves from ***the multiple*** traps that surround every citizen of our planet in this dark night of clouds and confusion. We see that many of them have been helped or guided by dreams, an indication of divine intervention. For examples of such stories—how some people have been guided in their search for truth—read *Once to Every Man and Nation*,[41] and *My Love is My Stronghold*.[42]

Rescuing the Soul from the Trap of Fantasy

Arthur Combs, thc co-founder of perceptual psychology, states that ***for each person, his own particular world is the only world of reality***. Then he adds, "Although this fact seems obvious, the failure of people everywhere to comprehend it is responsible for much of human misunderstanding, maladjustment, conflict and loneliness. Our perceptions of ourselves and the world are so real to us that we seldom pause to doubt them."[43] As the Christian scholar and leader, Bishop John Spong, notes:

> Most of us are too close to our own faith to see clearly, and too invested in the meaning of that faith to have any objectivity about the beliefs that finally undergird our life ...Only when literal truth is challenged are we able to float in the profound and limitless sea of ultimate truth.[44]

Consider this warning:

> ***Be on guard! Be alert!***...If he comes suddenly, ***do not let him find you sleeping***. What I say to you, I say to everyone: "***Watch***!"
> Christ (Mark 13:33, 37 NIV)

Why do we need to "be on guard" and "alert"? Because it is easy to be caught by the trap of denial. ***What*** do we need to "watch" for? The good news of the coming of the Master. ***Why*** do we need to watch for the news? Because it is easy to miss it.

The only way to avoid bondage to our fantasies and to rescue our souls from the traps of complacency, tradition, and conformity is to expand our perception of reality. The only way we can escape the dark and deadly snare of denial is to open all our spiritual channels. How can we do this? By exposing our minds to ***other*** perceptions, especially those different from our own.

People love to associate with and support those who believe and think as they do. Everyone looks to everyone else to get approval for what he thinks or does. To go against the grain takes phenomenal courage. In addition, there is the distrust that people have for new claims. Most believers feel "the tried and true" is the only prudent way, because deceivers are everywhere.

We also need to be aware of human weaknesses and the awesome powers of fantasy to exploit those weaknesses. Human fantasy craves for power, pomp, glamour, and grandeur. People cannot tolerate their Redeemer's humility and apparent helplessness. They would prefer Him to pride Himself on His lust for power than to glory in His poverty, meekness, and love for truth. They find no advantage in Him over themselves:

> ...they all turn their gaze toward their own selves...as they fancifully regard Him as one like unto themselves.[45]
>
> The Báb

People prefer to see their Redeemer in the hazy auras of their dreams rather than in the harsh realities of this world:

> ...if they dreamt of Him they gloried in their dreams; yet now that He hath revealed Himself...they are resting comfortably in their homes...while He at this moment is confined [imprisoned] in the mountain of Mákú, lonely and forsaken.[46] The Báb

People love to reach for the stars, to soar through the vastness of space, and to look down on the unfortunate who are left behind. They like glittering pictures such as those portrayed by their leaders:

> Think about that day when the Lord Jesus Christ breaks through the eastern sky. Think about it over and over. Let it give you something to live for. Could anything be more exciting to contemplate?
>
> Seeing first a small black cloud. Watching it move nearer and nearer till it becomes white and glorious. A cloud like

> none you've ever seen before—a cloud of angels, uncounted angels. Hearing a sound like none you've ever heard before—the sound of a trumpet echoing round the world. Then a voice like none you've heard before. It's the voice of our Lord calling the dead to life.
>
> The earth quivers. Tombs burst open. Angels everywhere carry little children to their parents' eager arms. Loved ones long separated by death reunite with shouts of joy, never to part again! And then, together with those resurrected ones, we who have waited through earth's long night are caught up into that angel starship for the trip to our heavenly home.
>
> I want to be there, and I know you do too! God help us be ready for that great day.[47]

As we can see, when a Redeemer comes, ***everything is set to work against Him***. His soul is infinitely sublime. But a sublime soul is neither visible nor dramatic. The Redeemer does not fit and is not welcomed into people's worlds of fantasy. He bears no resemblance to "the heroic image" that they have carved with their imaginations and immortalized since ancient times. This image has found its way into theology, history, art, music, literature, children's stories, tradition, folklore, even movies. How could anyone alter that deeply ***engraved image***? Even some of those who have recognized Bahá'u'lláh find it difficult to modify that image, to replace the ***conquering*** king with a ***suffering*** King.

There is plenty of pain and misery in everyone's life. Why would anyone want a suffering hero? Why would anyone wish to abandon the joy and glamour of dreaming about the most fantastic drama the human mind could ever conceive? True, time can make anyone a legend, but for now only a few have discovered this, the greatest of all secrets:

> And now here is my secret, a very simple secret:
> it is only with the heart that one can see rightly,
> What is essential is invisible to the eye.
>
> Antoine de Saint-Exupery,
> *The Little Prince*

For now only a few would worship a Hero who says:

> Every morning I arose from My bed, I discovered the hosts of countless afflictions massed behind My door; and every night when I lay down, lo! My heart was torn with agony at what it had suffered from the fiendish cruelty of its foes.[48] Bahá'u'lláh

> I have been, most of the days of My life, even as a slave, sitting under a sword, hanging on a thread...[49] Bahá'u'lláh

> All this generation could offer Us were wounds from its darts, and the only cup it proffered to Our lips was the cup of its venom. On Our neck We still bear the scar of chains, and upon Our body are imprinted the evidences of an unyielding cruelty.[50] Bahá'u'lláh

For now only a few look ***within*** to behold the wonders of the heart:

> ...the Lord seeth not as man seeth, for men looketh on the outward appearance, but the Lord looketh on the heart.
> I Samuel 16:7

For now the masses of people have their eyes on the visible. They judge by what they can see:

> You judge according to the flesh—by what you see...
> Christ (John 18:15 AB)

For now only a few are willing to harmonize their sense of values with that of the Creator:

> What is highly valued among men is detestable in God's sight. Christ (Luke 16:15)

For now only a few wish to give up human standards for the divine, to replace the visible image with the invisible, the tradition with truth:

> You have a fine way of setting aside the command of God in order to observe your own traditions!
> Christ (Mark 7:9 NIV)

> You judge by human standards... Christ (John 8:15 NIV)

For now only a few are willing to search for an almost invisible "thief:"

> ...I shall come upon you like a thief... Christ (Rev. 3:3 NEB)

For now the great masses are waiting for a thunder that every ear shall hear, for a lightning that every eye shall see. They are waiting even as the people of Israel have been waiting for more than two thousand years for a conquering king. This is how people behaved when Noah came. This is how they behaved when Jesus came. And this is how they are predicted to behave again in our time:

> As things were in Noah's days, so will they be in the days of the Son of Man. Christ (Luke 17:26 NEB)

> The coming of the Son of Man will repeat what happened in Noah's time. Christ (Matt. 24:37 NAB)

Noah was present among the people, yet they were unaware of ***His*** presence. To them He was invisible. They kept doing what they would usually do: "they ate and drank and married" (Luke 17:27), "they knew nothing until the flood came" (Matt. 24:37-39).

> That is how it will be when the Son of Man comes.
> Christ (Matt. 24:39 NEB)

And that is how it has been since the dawning of the new Day:

> The world is illumined with the effulgent glory of His countenance. And yet, behold how far its peoples have strayed from His path! None have believed in Him except them who, through the power of the Lord of Names, have shattered the ***idols of their vain imaginings and corrupt desires*** and entered the city of certitude.[51] Bahá'u'lláh

> The light shines in the darkness, but the darkness has not understood it. John 1:5 NIV

The Dawn hath broken, yet the people understand not. The signs have been ushered in, while He Who hath revealed them is overwhelmed with manifest sorrow. Indeed I have endured that which hath caused the world of existence to lament.[52] Bahá'u'lláh

And when, as bidden by Thee [God], I arose and called out, by Thy leave, all Thy creatures, the wayward among Thy servants opposed me. Some turned away from me, others disowned my claim, a few hesitated, while others were sore perplexed, notwithstanding that Thy testimony was set forth before the followers of all religions, and Thy proof demonstrated unto all the peoples of the earth, and the signs of Thy might so powerfully manifested as to encompass the entire creation.[53] Bahá'u'lláh

The accumulations of ***vain fancy*** have obstructed men's ears and stopped them from hearing the Voice of God, and the veils of human learning and ***false imaginings*** have prevented their eyes from beholding the splendor of the light of His countenance.[54] Bahá'u'lláh

For the people are wandering in the paths of ***delusion***, bereft of discernment to see God with their own eyes, or hear His Melody with their own ears...

Thus have their ***superstitions*** become veils between them and their own hearts and kept them from the path of God, the Exalted, the Great.[55] Bahá'u'lláh

Witness how they have entangled themselves with their ***idle fancies and vain imaginations***. By My life! They are themselves the victims of what their own hearts have devised, and yet they perceive it not. Vain and profitless is the talk of their lips, and yet they understand not.[56] Bahá'u'lláh

O friends! It behoveth you to refresh and revive your souls through the gracious favors which in this Divine, this soul-stirring Springtime are being showered upon you. The Day

Star of His great glory hath shed its radiance upon you, and the clouds of His limitless grace have overshadowed you. How high the reward of him that hath not deprived himself of so great a bounty, nor failed to recognize the beauty of his Best-Beloved in this, His new attire.[57]

Bahá'u'lláh

Beware that ye do not deprive yourselves of the grace of God, that ye do not bring to naught your works, and do not repudiate the truth of this most manifest, this lofty, this shining, and glorious Revelation. Judge ye fairly the Cause of God, your Creator, and behold that which hath been sent down from the Throne on high, and meditate thereon with innocent and sanctified hearts. Then will the truth of this Cause appear unto you as manifest as the sun in its noon-tide glory. Then will ye be of them that have believed in Him.[58] Bahá'u'lláh

Cast the ***idle tales*** behind your backs...[59] Bahá'u'lláh

Blessed is that strong one who will shatter the gods of ***vain imaginings*** through the potency of the Name of his Lord...[60] Bahá'u'lláh

Where is your sword...? Draw it and slash ***Delusion*** to pieces. Krishna (Bhagavad-Gita 4:36)

The first teaching of Bahá'u'lláh is the duty...to investigate reality. What does it mean to investigate reality? It means that man must forget all hearsay and examine truth himself, for he does not know whether statements he hears are in accordance with reality or not. Wherever he finds truth or reality, he must hold to it, forsaking, discarding all else; for outside of reality there is naught but ***superstition and imagination***.[61] 'Abdu'l-Bahá

A Prayer from 'Abdu'l-Bahá for Truth seekers:

O seeker of Truth! If thou desirest that God may open thine eye, thou must supplicate unto God, pray to and commune with Him at midnight, saying:

O Lord, I have turned my face unto Thy kingdom of oneness and am immersed in the sea of Thy mercy. O Lord, enlighten my sight by beholding Thy lights in this dark night, and make me happy by the wine of Thy love in this wonderful age. O Lord, make me hear Thy call, and open before my face the doors of Thy heaven, so that I may see the light of Thy glory and become attracted to Thy beauty.

Verily, Thou art the Giver, the Generous, the Merciful, the Forgiving.[62]

Every action has consequences. The next chapter examines the consequences of denying the Redeemer of the age.

14

He That Denieth Me... Shall Be Denied

Christ (Luke 12:9)

> O ye that judge with fairness! If this Cause is to be denied then what other cause in this world can be vindicated or deemed worthy of acceptance?
>
> ...Verily He hath appeared with so great an authority that no man of vision, of hearing, of insight, of justice or of equity can ever deny Him. Unto this beareth witness in this resplendent Hour the Pen of Him Who is the Ancient of Days.[1]
>
> Bahá'u'lláh

In Volume I we discussed three elements of the covenant that binds us to our Creator:

• ***Freedom***
• ***Knowledge***
• ***Responsibility***

One element remains:

• ***Reward and punishment.***

This chapter is written especially for those who read the proofs and prophecies but decline to pursue what God has planned for them, who refrain from making any commitment. They simply respond by saying: this is all very interesting, but it is not for me. They are certainly entitled to that decision. God has granted everyone spiritual freedom. They have every right to stay out of touch with what the Creator has planned for them, but in all fairness they should be well aware of the consequences of their decision. It is to their advantage to know.

It is our Creator's wish that we should pursue a noble life without hope of reward or fear of punishment, that we should be detached from the consequences of our good deeds, so that even if all the rewards were removed, we would continue our acts of kindness and self-sacrifice without hesitation.

> For every act performed there shall be a recompense according to the estimate of God...However, ***unto them that are rid of all attachments a deed is, verily, its own reward.***[2]
> Bahá'u'lláh

But only ***a few*** can attain such a sublime vision. For ***spiritual*** survival, the masses of humanity are as much dependent on reward and punishment as they are on the air for ***physical*** survival. The promise of reward is found in abundance in sacred Scriptures. Consider these examples:

> To him who is victorious [over the selfish desires] I will grant ***a place on my throne...*** Christ (Rev. 3:21 NEB)

> And when the Chief Shepherd appears, you will receive ***the crown of glory*** that will never fade away.
> 1 Peter 5:4 NIV

> ...at the end of time...the righteous ***will shine as brightly as the sun*** in the kingdom of their Father. If you have ears, then hear. Christ (Matt. 13:41-43 NEB)

> The wise leaders ***shall shine like the bright vault of heaven***, and those who have guided the people in the true path ***shall be like the stars for ever and ever***.
> Daniel 12:3 NEB

> As to paradise: It is a reality and there can be no doubt about it, and now in this world it is realized through love of Me and My good-pleasure. Whosoever attaineth unto it God will aid him in this world below, and after death ***He will enable him to gain admittance into Paradise whose vastness is as that of heaven and earth. Therein...the day-star of the unfading beauty of his Lord will at all times shed its radiance upon him and he will shine so brightly that no one shall bear to gaze at him***. Such is the dispensation of Providence, yet the people are shut out by a grievous veil.[3] Bahá'u'lláh

> He that overcometh [the veils of the world] ***shall inherit all things***; and I will be his God, and he will be my son.
> Christ (Rev. 21:7)

> Rejoice and be exceedingly glad, for ***great is your reward in heaven***... Christ (Matt. 5:12 NKJ)

> ***...rejoice, because your names are written in heaven.***
> Christ (Luke 10:20)

Loving and Fearing God. An individual can be motivated by various rewards from the most sublime to the most lowly. These are a few motives with varying levels of nobility:

- Loving God
- Finding joy in good deeds
- The hope of attaining the presence of God
- The joy and comfort of being in heaven
- Fearing God's justice
- Conforming to others

- Obeying blindly
- Seeking short-term and selfish interests

Nearness to God, or attaining His presence, is perhaps among the purest and most powerful motives. Even the most spiritually advanced person is stirred and inspired by knowing that his or her efforts will be consummated by attaining the divine presence. How could the knowledge of attaining the Beloved ***not*** move a true lover to aspire to the noblest deeds? The Qur'án extols this motive:

> ...[he shall be well content in the end] who offers not favors to anyone for the sake of receiving rewards, but only as seeking the face of his Lord. Qur'án 92:18-21

Spiritual advancement requires and always accompanies the refinement of motives. As the individual grows, he finds himself being motivated increasingly by long lasting spiritual goals or incentives. Further, as light dispels darkness, the love of his Lord banishes all fear from his heart:

> A lover feareth nothing...[4] Bahá'u'lláh

> There is no fear in love. But perfect love drives out fear, because fear has to do with punishment. The man who fears is not made perfect in love. I John 4:18 NIV

Whether we like it or not, we must acknowledge that:

> ...self-love is kneaded into the very clay of man, and it is not possible that, without any hope of a substantial reward, he should neglect his own present material good.[5]
> 'Abdu'l-Bahá

It is because of this nature that Bahá'u'lláh declares:

> The structure of world stability and order hath been reared upon, and will continue to be sustained by, the twin pillars of reward and punishment.[6]

> That which traineth the world is Justice, for it is upheld by two pillars, reward and punishment. These two pillars are the sources of life to the world.[7]

Reward is a pleasant word; we like the sound of it. Punishment is negative; from childhood we learn to avoid it. We dislike even thinking about it. Our Creator also does not wish to use the threat of punishment, yet we find the topic in abundance in the words of His great Messengers. Indeed it is one of the most frequently recurring themes of the sacred Scriptures. Why? Since our Creator knows the enduring consequences that the negligent individual must face, it is contrary to His supreme love and wisdom not to use all the means of persuasion at His command. How would a loving and reasonable person respond to a small child who plays with matches, especially if the child is deaf to the voice of reason? Is the spiritual life less significant than the physical? Is the fire of separation from God less painful than the flame of a match? God Himself asks what language He should speak to reach those who are so short-sighted and hard of hearing that they ignore Him:

> What language should He Who is the Mouthpiece of God choose to speak, so that they who are shut out as by a veil from Him can recognize His glory?[8] Bahá'u'lláh

Fear is not necessarily a negative force. It can be both positive and negative, both normal and abnormal. In the Writings of Bahá'u'lláh, fear of God emerges as a positive force. He asks specifically that we live the Law out of our love for the Lord:

> **O SON OF BEING!**
> Walk in My statutes for love of Me and deny thyself that which thou desirest if thou seekest My pleasure.[9]
> Bahá'u'lláh

Perfect love banishes all fear; that is our ultimate goal. For those who cannot attain that goal, fear serves as an inner invisible guard. They need the guard until they grow strong; exactly like a child who cannot avoid the matches simply out of love for his safety, or a student who does not study unless he contemplates the consequences of failing.

Fear is banished not only by love but also by knowledge. The knowledge of God is a haven of safety for every wavering heart. One way that students can diminish their fear of tests is to get to know the teacher and learn the kind of questions he or she asks. Bahá'u'lláh declares that we were made to know and love God. Both true knowledge and love attract us to God. Attraction diminishes our fear and further enhances our love.

"Fear of God" has acquired a bad image. Fearing God means respecting His awesome power; it does not mean being scared of Him like a lamb in the claws of a lion. We are asked to fear God, but not to be terrified of God. Fear is having no desire to touch a tiger; terror is suddenly finding oneself pursued by one. We fear losing an expensive gem, and regard our response as justified caution. As a rule, our fear does not overwhelm us. We fear failure, and consider it healthy. We fear losing our job and displeasing our boss. Why should we not fear displeasing our Lord?

Fear of God gives us another layer of stability and trust. It is said that we should fear only those who do not fear God.

Any given emotion can vary qualitatively over a wide spectrum. Humility can come from self-degradation or self-respect. One person can find nothing but weakness in humility; another nothing but strength. "My power is made perfect in weakness" (II Cor. 12:9 NIV), Paul said. The same is true with love. Love to some people means giving, to others possessing and controlling. Abraham Maslow, the great psychologist, believes that human potential functions on two levels: survival (concern with deficiencies), and self-actualization (concern with growth). He states, "Satisfying deficiencies avoids illness; growth satisfactions produce positive health."

Fear, too, varies qualitatively and covers a wide spectrum. One kind arises out of knowledge, understanding, wisdom, and strength; the other out of ignorance, weakness, and timidity. A house is on fire. One person instantly rushes inside to save a helpless child; another watches and waits. Both of them fear the fire: one out of strength and courage, the other out of weakness. One person overcomes his fear by love, while another submits to his fear. Fear as a positive force makes one's love and courage glow brighter. Isaiah predicted that our Redeemer will "delight in the fear of the Lord:"

> The Spirit of the Lord will rest on him—the Spirit of wisdom and of understanding, the Spirit of counsel and of power, the Spirit of knowledge and of the fear of the Lord—and ***he will delight in the fear of the Lord***.
>
> Isaiah 11:2-3 NIV

Fear of God, if healthy and positive, sets us free from all undesirable fears; it instills courage and self-confidence in our hearts.

> There is a virtuous fear which is the effect of faith, and a vicious fear which is the product of doubt and distrust...
>
> Blaise Pascal

To reach the peak of their potentials, all humans need a well-balanced dose of love and fear. Fear prevents them from evil; love attracts them to virtues.

> By the fear of the Lord men depart from evil.
>
> Proverbs 16:6

Evidently the Creator who is the Essence of Love would wish to be loved, not feared. Bahá'u'lláh glorifies love in many ways and words:

> I belong to him that loveth Me...[10]

> The essence of wealth is love for Me; whoso loveth Me is the possessor of all things, and he that loveth Me not is indeed of the poor and needy.[11]

> Make my love thy treasure and cherish it even as thy very sight and life.[12]

> **O SON OF MAN!**
> I loved thy creation, hence I created thee. Wherefore, do thou love Me, that I may name thy name and fill thy soul with the spirit of life.[13]

> **O SON OF BEING!**
> Thy Paradise is My love; thy heavenly home, reunion with Me. Enter therein and tarry not. This is that which hath been destined for thee in Our kingdom above and Our exalted Dominion.[14]

> **O SON OF UTTERANCE!**
> ...My love is in thee, know it, that thou mayest find Me near unto thee.[15]

Fear, as applied to God, is a positive force. It is a mark of profound respect for His greatness and glory. Fearing God out of respect is a sign of wisdom, of being in touch with reality.

> The essence of wisdom is the fear of God...[16] Bahá'u'lláh

> The fear of the Lord is the beginning of wisdom.
> Psalms 111:10

Appreciation of fear as a positive force requires greater spiritual maturity than the appreciation of fear as a negative force. Each person perceives and interprets "fear of God" according to his or her spiritual maturity.

To be true to God's wisdom and to our own spiritual safety, we need to hear His voice in its fullness. We need to hear it without fear, by allowing our love for Him to stand supreme.

Justice and Mercy. Sacred Scriptures characterize God as both loving and fair, both merciful and just. They also teach that His love and mercy transcend His justice. We have come into being out of divine love. God's grace and forgiveness embrace all humanity like a beautiful rainbow:

> The Lord is compassionate and gracious, slow to anger, abounding in love...As a father has compassion on his children, so the Lord has compassion on those who fear him. Psalms 103:8, 13 NIV

> The greatness of His mercy surpasseth the fury of His wrath, and His grace encompass all who have been called into being...[17] Bahá'u'lláh

> ...verily thy Lord is full of grace to mankind; yet most of them are ungrateful. Qur'án 27:73 Y

> To those who have done evil in ignorance, then afterwards have repented and amended, verily thy Lord is in the end ...gracious, merciful. Qur'án 16:120

> Verily, the breezes of the forgiveness have been wafted from...your Lord, the God of Mercy; whoso turneth thereunto, shall be cleansed of his sins, and of all pain and sickness.[18] Bahá'u'lláh

> O Lord...with you there is forgiveness... Psalms 130:4

> I am Jesus...the Lord replied...I am sending you to open their eyes...that they may receive forgiveness of sins and a place among those who are sanctified by faith in me.
> Acts 26:15-18 NIV

His rainbow of grace encompasses all, but behind the rainbow stand the clouds, the divine justice:

> He who is the Lord of Lords is come overshadowed with clouds...On His [Bahá'u'lláh's] right hand flow the ***living waters of grace***, and on His left ***the choice Wine of justice***...[19✤] Bahá'u'lláh

> O Lord the great and awesome [dreadful KJV] God, who keeps his covenant of love with all who love him and obey his commands. Daniel 9:4 NIV

> Announce to my servants that I am the Gracious, the Merciful, and that my chastisement is grievous.
> Qur'án 15:50-51

✤ As noted in *I Shall Come Again*, Jesus predicts (Matt. 25:31-46) that when He returns He will separate the people. He will send one group to His right, and another group to His left. It was stated that such a simple classification does not seem reasonable unless it is based on this standard: people's response to the new Redeemer, which is either acceptance, or rejection and indifference.

> Vengeance is Mine, and recompense.
> Deuteronomy 32:35 NKJ

> And woe betide him who hath rejected the grace of God and His bounty, and hath denied His tender mercy and authority; such a man is indeed reckoned with those who have throughout eternity repudiated the testimony of God and His proof.[20] Bahá'u'lláh

> Woe to every lying sinner, who heareth the verses of God recited to him, and then, as though he heard them not, persisteth in proud disdain! Apprise him of a painful punishment. Qur'án 45:6

> O Lord God, to whom vengeance belongs; O God, to whom vengeance belongs, shine forth! Rise up, O Judge of the earth; render punishment to the proud. Lord, how long will the wicked, how long will the wicked triumph?
> Psalms 94:1-3 NKJ

> Whoso hath failed to recognize Him will have condemned himself to the misery of remoteness, a remoteness which is naught but utter nothingness and the essence of the nethermost fire. Such will be his fate, though to outward seeming he may occupy the earth's loftiest seats and be established upon its most exalted throne.[21] Bahá'u'lláh

> Terrible, indeed, is God in punishing![22] Bahá'u'lláh

The following passage from the Báb shows that the punishment of the next world may be more difficult to bear than the pains of this world:

> O my God! O my Master! I beseech Thee by Thy manifold bounties and by the pillars which sustain Thy throne of glory, to have pity on these lowly people ***who are powerless to bear the unpleasant things of this fleeting life, how much less then can they bear Thy chastisement in the life to come***—a chastisement which is ordained by Thy justice, called forth by Thy wrath and will continue to exist for ever.[23]

All the words and expressions that describe God's "wrath," "chastisement," and "vengeance" simply refer to His justice. Even God's grace and mercy are sustained by justice.

> ...His favors will He bestow on every one who deserves his favors. Qur'án 11:3

Most of us prefer to look at the rainbow but ignore the clouds and the thunder. For this and other reasons, the divine Teachers try to help us see not only the warm embrace of the rainbow but the thundering clouds as well.

The principle of reciprocity is the backbone of divine justice. It is expressed repeatedly in sacred Scriptures:

> ...with the measure you use, it will be measured to you.
> Christ (Matt. 7:2 NIV)

> But he who denies Me before men will be denied before the angels of God. Christ (Luke 12:9 NKJ)

> **O SON OF BEING!**
> Love Me, that I may love thee. If thou lovest Me not, My love can in no wise reach thee. Know this, O servant.[24]
> Bahá'u'lláh

> Sow ye, and reap. Isaiah 37:30

> And he who reaps receives wages, and gathers fruit for eternal life. Christ (John 4:36 NKJ)

> Whoever sows sparingly will also reap sparingly.
> II Corinthians 9:6 NIV

> Whatsoever a man soweth, that he shall also reap.
> Galatians 6:7

> He who leads into captivity shall go into captivity.
> Revelation 13:10 NKJ

> ...surely the earners of sin shall be recompensed for what they have earned. Qur'án 6:120 A

> Do ye expect [to receive] a reward other than that which ye have earned by your deeds? Qur'án 27:90

> ...whoever is ashamed of me and mine, the Son of Man will be ashamed of him, when he comes in his glory and the glory of the Father and the holy angels.
>
> Christ (Luke 9:26 NEB)

> God will verily do unto them that which they themselves are doing, and will forget them even as they ignored His Presence in His day. Such is His decree unto those that have denied Him, and such will it be unto them that have rejected His signs.[25] Bahá'u'lláh

> My people are destroyed [spiritually] for lack of knowledge [of God]. Because you have rejected knowledge, I also will reject you from being priest for Me. Hosea 4:6 NKJ

> He who does right, it is for himself, and he who does evil—it is for himself. And thy Lord will not deal unfairly with His servants. Qur'án 41:46

Heaven and Hell. The spiritual state of those who are not faithful to God's covenant is expressed in various Scriptures as: "the fire," "the unquenchable fire," or "the everlasting fire." Understanding the meaning of "the fire" is of paramount significance. Misjudgment of this word can undermine not only religion but the very foundation of our faith in God Himself.

Our paradise, our supreme glory and most blessed joy is to draw near to our Creator. That is our ultimate end:

> **O SON OF MAN!**
> Sorrow not save that thou art far from Us. Rejoice not save that thou art drawing near and returning unto Us.[26]
>
> Bahá'u'lláh

> ...no Paradise is more sublime for My creatures than to stand before My face and to believe in My holy Words...[27]
>
> The Báb

The deepest and most enduring depression, deprivation, and emptiness come from denying or opposing God's great Messengers and Redeemers:

...no fire hath been or will be fiercer for them than to be veiled from the Manifestation of My exalted Self and to disbelieve in My Words.[28] The Báb

The most burning fire is to question the signs of God, to dispute idly that which He hath revealed, to deny Him and carry one's self proudly before Him.[29] Bahá'u'lláh

To attain the presence of the Beloved is the most essential and enduring need in every soul; it is the most burning desire of every heart. God's warning of "an eternal fire" is His strongest appeal to save us from "the fire of remoteness." "***The fire*" *is not a scorching flame***; it is only a metaphor that implies a separation, a gulf or chasm between him who desires and the Desired One. Both the Gospel and the Qur'án allude to this:

...there is a great ***chasm*** fixed between us.✣
Luke 16:26 NEB

And a ***gulf*** shall be between them and that which they shall desire. Qur'án 34:53

A ***barrier*** that cannot be passed! Qur'án 25:25

The following is the most clear and complete description of the gulf that separates the selfish and retarded souls from the advanced souls. It presents a warning to those who use popularity as evidence of truth and majority opinion as a safety net:

Someone asked him, "Lord, are only a few people going to be saved?" He said to them, "***Make every effort to enter through the narrow door***, because many, I tell you, will try to enter and will not be able to. Once the owner of the house [the Redeemer] gets up and closes the [heavenly] door, you will stand outside knocking and pleading, 'Sir,

✣ Between Jesus and the rich man who squandered his wealth on himself, without regard for the poor.

open the door for us.' But he will answer, 'I don't know you or where you come from.' Then you will say, 'We ate and drank with you, and you taught in our streets,' 'But I don't know you or where you come from. Away from me, all you evildoers!' There will be weeping there, and gnashing of teeth [anger], when ***you see Abraham, Isaac and Jacob and all the prophets in the kingdom of God, but you yourselves thrown out.*** " Christ (Luke 13:23-28 NIV)

In the following prophecy, our Maker first ***invites*** us and ***encourages*** us to stand humble before our Redeemer. He then ***pleads*** with us, and finally ***threatens*** us, just as did Jesus, that if we fail we will not enter the garden of heavenly rest:

Oh come, let us worship and bow down; ***let us kneel before the Lord our Maker***. For He is our God, and we are the people of His pasture, and the sheep of His hand. Today, if you will hear His voice: "***Do not harden your hearts***, as in the rebellion, as in the day of trial in the wilderness, when your fathers tested Me; they tried Me, though they saw My work. For forty years I was grieved with that generation, and said, 'It is a people who go astray in their hearts, and they do not know My ways.' So I swore in My wrath, '***They shall not enter My rest.***'"
Psalms 95:6-11 NKJ

The following verses concern those who deny the Redeemers of our time, who disregard the divine standards, who exchange the distinctive signs or evidence of God's Message for their selfish desires:

Then he [the Promised One] will say to those on his ***left*** hand...go from my sight to ***the eternal fire***...
Matthew 25:41 NEB

...they who disbelieved our signs, shall be the people of the ***left***. Around them ***the fire*** shall close... Qur'án 90:20

Woe that Day [our Day] to those who practice falsehood, who amuse themselves with their idle fancies. The day

> will come when they will be thrust down to ***the hell-fire***. "This," they will be told, "is the fire whose existence ye denied." Qur'án 52:11-14

The Báb confirms the message of the Bible and the Qur'án:

> ...since thou canst not attain the state of undoubting faith, due to the intervening veils of thy selfish desires, therefore ***thou wilt tarry in the fire, though realizing it not***.[30]
> The Báb

This prophecy from the Qur'án pertains to our time:

> And by troops shall the unbelievers be driven towards Hell [remoteness from God], until when they reach it, its gates shall be opened, and its keepers shall say to them, "Came not Messengers from among yourselves to you reciting to you the signs of your Lord, and warning you of the meeting with Him [God] on this your day?" They shall say, "Yes." But just is the sentence of punishment on the unbelievers. It shall be said to them, "Enter ye the gates of Hell, therein to dwell for ever"...But those who feared their Lord shall be driven on by troops to Paradise, until when they reach it, its gates shall be opened, and its keepers shall say to them, "All hail! virtuous have ye been, enter then in, to abide herein for ever." Qur'án 39:71-73

The first weakness that leads the individual to "the fire" of remoteness from God is the fear of truth. This is a prophecy about our time:

> But ***the fearful***...shall have their part in the lake which burneth with ***fire***... Revelation 21:8

As the following verses declare, it is in our best interest to remove any obstacle that prevents us from attaining the good-pleasure of God, for the consequences of earthly losses are temporary, but those of spiritual losses everlasting. Could a warning be more emphatic than this?

> It is better for you...to enter the kingdom of God with one eye, than to have two eyes and be thrown into hell [remoteness from God] where...the fire [the burning desire to attain the presence of our Creator] is not put out.
>
> Christ (Mark 9:47-48 NIV)

God's Immortal Blessings. Those who remain faithful to God's covenant are promised immortal and immeasurable blessings. This is "the great day of the Lord," and the blessings are equally great. Bahá'u'lláh recounts repeatedly the everlasting gifts and bounties that God has ordained for true seekers and believers:

> Great is the blessedness of him who hath in this Day cast away the things current amongst men and hath clung unto that which is ordained by God...He Who is come from the heaven of eternity through the power of the Most Great Name, invested with so invincible an authority that all the powers of the earth are unable to withstand Him.[31]

> Well is it with him whom the changes and chances of this world have failed to deter from recognizing the Day Spring of the Unity of God...Such a man shall be numbered with the inmates of Paradise, in the Book of God, the Lord of all worlds.[32]

> Great, therefore, is the blessedness of him who hath believed in Thee, and in Thy signs, and hath humbled himself before Thy sovereignty, and hath been honored with meeting Thee, and hath attained the good pleasure of Thy will, and circled around Thee, and stood before Thy throne. Woe betide him that hath transgressed against Thee, and hath denied Thee, and repudiated Thy signs, and gainsaid Thy sovereignty, and risen up against Thee, and waxed proud before Thy face, and hath disputed Thy testimonies...[33]

> He that partaketh of the waters of My Revelation will taste all the incorruptible delights ordained by God from the beginning that hath no beginning to the end that hath no end.[34]

> Blessed are they that remember the one true God, that magnify His Name, and seek diligently to serve His Cause ...The glory of their station, however, is as yet undisclosed.[35]
>
> How regrettable indeed that man should debar himself from the fruits of the tree of wisdom while his days and hours pass swiftly away. Please God, the hand of divine power may safeguard all mankind and direct their steps towards the horizon of true understanding.
>
> Verily our Lord of Mercy is the Helper, the Knowing, the Wise.[36]
>
> Know thou, that I have wafted unto thee all the fragrances of holiness, have fully revealed to thee My word, have perfected through thee My bounty and have desired for thee that which I have desired for My Self. Be then content with My pleasure and thankful unto Me.[37]
>
> He, verily, hath willed for you that which is yet beyond your knowledge, but which shall be known to you when, after this fleeting life, your souls soar heavenwards and the trappings of your earthly joys are folded up.[38]
>
> Glorified art Thou, O Lord my God! Thou hast, in Thine all highest Paradise, assigned unto Thy servants such stations that if any one of them were to be unveiled to men's eyes all who are in heaven and all who are on earth would be dumbfounded. By Thy might! Were kings to witness so great a glory they would, assuredly, rid themselves of their dominions and cleave to such of their subjects as have entered beneath the shadow of Thine immeasurable mercy and sought the shelter of Thine all-glorious name.[39]

Jesus knew the immense obstacles His followers would face in recognizing Him in His second advent. He knew the awesome powers of the invisible trap of tradition, and the passionate desire to be loyal to one's religious heritage. He knew His beloved followers would encounter mountains of illusions and be entangled in unbreakable bonds of attachments. To liberate them and lift them to detachment, humility, and love for truth, He has offered the most magnificent gifts and the most glorious blessings to them and to all those who arise, break the bonds, and climb the mountains with all their might and fervor:

> I am coming soon...Him who overcomes (Rev. 3:11-12 NIV):
>
> - Will ***inherit all things*** (Rev. 21:7).
> - I will be his God and he will ***be my son*** (Rev. 21:7).
> - I will give the right ***to sit with me on my throne*** (Rev. 3:21 NIV).
> - I will give the right ***to eat from the tree of life*** which is in the paradise of God (Rev. 2:7 NIV).
> - I will make ***a pillar in the temple of my God*** (Rev. 3:12 NIV).
> - I will...give him ***the morning star*** (Rev. 2:28 NIV).
> - I...will ***acknowledge his name*** before my Father... (Rev. 3:5 NIV).
> - I will ***never erase his name*** from the book of life... (Rev. 3:5 NIV).
> - I will ***write on him the name of my God***... (Rev. 3:12 NIV).
> - I will write on him...***the name of the city of my God***... (Rev. 3:12 NIV).
> - I will also ***give him a white stone with a new name***... (Rev. 2:17 NIV).
> - ***I will also write on him my new name***. He who has an [spiritual] ear, ***let him hear what the Spirit says to the churches*** (Rev. 3:12-13 NIV).

The Báb promises heavenly glories and honors to the true believers in Bahá'u'lláh:

> Indeed any man whose eye gazeth upon His Words with true faith well deserveth Paradise; and one whose conscience beareth witness unto His Words with true faith

> shall abide in Paradise and attain the presence of God; and one whose tongue giveth utterance to His Words with true faith shall have his abode in Paradise, wherein he will be seized with ecstasy in praise and glorification of God, the Ever-Abiding…[40]

Both the blessings offered to the faithful and the warnings to the unfaithful are extreme; for this reason: at the dawning of a new Revelation, recognizing a new Redeemer is the most marvelous achievement. It is very difficult to recognize a new Redeemer, but very easy to deny Him. The excuses people can find to deny are endless. To move the obstinate and negligent hearts into humility and love for truth, the threats and warnings must be equal in intensity to the prevailing levels of apathy, worldliness, and self-interest.

Our Accountability Before Our Creator

Those who lived at the time of Jesus asked, "What shall we do, that we might work the works of God?" (John 6:28). Jesus answered them:

> This is the work of God, that you believe in Him whom He sent. John 6:29 NKJ

The same holds true today. To do God's work, to please Him and receive His blessings, we must believe in the One He has sent to us.

It is essential that we all recognize and remember what the Scriptures say to those who fail to obey the divine Commandments, who refuse to do God's work, who fail to prepare themselves for the awesome task of seeking the Lord of the last Days:

> Then he [Jesus] will do justice upon those who refuse to acknowledge God and upon those who will not obey the gospel of our Lord Jesus. They will suffer the punishment

of eternal ruin, cut off from the presence of the Lord and the splendor of his might, ***when on that great Day he comes to be glorified*** among his own and adored among all believers... II Thessalonians 1:8-10 NEB
See also Matt. 22:11-14; 25:1-30; Rev. 21:8

Both Christ and Bahá'u'lláh declare that to deny the Redeemer of the Age is to deny ***Him who sent*** the Redeemer:

...whoever accepts me accepts the one who sent me.
Christ (John 13:20 NIV)

He who does not honor the Son does not honor the Father who sent him. Christ (John 5:23 NIV)

And whoever rejects me rejects the One who sent me.
Christ (Luke 10:16 NEB)

For whoever is ashamed of Me and My words in this adulterous and sinful generation, of him the Son of Man also will be ashamed when He comes in the glory of His Father with the holy angels. Mark 8:38 NKJ

Be thou assured in thyself that verily, ***he who turns away from this Beauty*** [Bahá'u'lláh] hath also turned away from the Messengers of the past and ***showeth pride towards God from all eternity to all eternity***.[41] Bahá'u'lláh

In His Olivet Discourse Jesus uttered the parable of the talents (Matt. 25:14-30) to show what will happen to the person who denies Him when He returns. He identified two kinds of followers: the fearful and the enterprising. When the Master returned, He took away the possessions of the fearful servant. This confirms Bahá'u'lláh's pronouncement that whoever denies Him, has also denied and deprived himself of God's past Messengers and Redeemers as well as God Himself. The same parable teaches that the enterprising servants doubled their possessions. They kept the Christ of the first Advent and to that they added the Christ of the second Advent.

The message of the following prophecy is similar to the one enclosed in the parable of the talents, where the adventurous servants are doubly rewarded:

> Turn ye to the stronghold, ye prisoners of hope: even to day do I declare that ***I will render double*** [the reward] ***unto thee***.
> Zechariah 9:12

> Seclude yourselves in the ***stronghold*** of My love.[42]
> Bahá'u'lláh

> My love is My ***stronghold***; he that entereth therein is safe and secure...[43]
> Bahá'u'lláh

While in prison in 'Akká, Bahá'u'lláh wrote an Epistle to one of His disciples. Although it is addressed to an individual, its Message is universal; it concerns every human being on this planet. He refers to Himself by such titles as "that Most Great Beauty," "the Tree of Life," and "the Nightingale." These are a few selections:

> Verily this is that Most Great Beauty, foretold in the Books of the Messengers, through Whom truth shall be distinguished from error and the wisdom of every command shall be tested. Verily He is the Tree of Life that bringeth forth the fruits of God, the Exalted, the powerful, the Great.
>
> ...Thus doth the Nightingale utter His call unto you from this prison. He hath but to deliver this clear message. Whosoever desireth, let him turn aside from this counsel and whosoever desireth let him choose the path to his Lord.
>
> O people, if ye deny these verses, by what proof have ye believed in God? Produced it, O assemblage of false ones.
>
> Nay, by the One in Whose hand is my soul, they are not, and never shall be able to do this, even should they combine to assist one another.[44]

Gaining everlasting life today is as dependent on recognizing Bahá'u'lláh as it was on recognizing Jesus in the past:

> He who believes in the Son has everlasting life; and he who does not believe the Son shall not see life, but the wrath of God abides on him.
> Christ (John 3:36 NKJ)

> No man can obtain everlasting life, unless he embraceth the truth of this inestimable, this wondrous, and sublime Revelation.[45]
>
> Bahá'u'lláh

In an Epistle addressed to a religious leader, Bahá'u'lláh again confirms the principle that denying Him is the same as denying all the Messengers and Redeemers of the past:

> Thou canst excuse thyself no longer. Either thou must recognize it, or—God forbid—arise and deny all the Prophets![46]

What do most people find easier to follow? Truth or tradition? Do they choose their beliefs by an independent search for truth or by conformity and convenience?

> ...the people are wandering in the paths of delusion, bereft of discernment to see God with their own eyes, or hear His Melody with their own ears.
>
> Thus have their superstitions become veils between them and their own hearts and kept them from the path of God, the Exalted, the Great.[47]
>
> Bahá'u'lláh

Why do people uphold their values? What motivates them? This topic has been studied extensively by psychologists. Research shows three levels or kinds of motives:

- Desire for ***reward***, and fear of ***punishment*** or loss of privileges. (Immediate self-interest and pleasure are the prime motives.)
- Desire to please ***authority figures***. (Those on this level are fundamentally conformists and conservatives. They would rather preserve the status quo than risk their security.)
- Desire to uphold the principle of ***justice***. (Those on this level are as a rule detached from self-interest and the influence of authority figures.)

Research indicates that the great majority of people, probably 99 percent, in all cultures function on the first two levels.

Very few reach the third level. Those who do are the heroes and heroines of every nation.

There is no reason to doubt that the preceding classification holds true also with the way people respond to the news of the coming of great Redeemers. History offers the most convincing evidence that this is true.

Our Creator in His Wisdom uses all three motivators. He speaks of rewards and punishment, He expresses His supreme authority in the most awesome words, and He appeals to our sense of justice and love for truth in the most loving and inviting way. Yet during the early years of the advent of all great religions, the first two groups pay little if any attention to the news of the advent of those religions. Fear of losing their own self-interests and their submission to their own authority figures prevent them from looking beyond their security and comfort zone. Only when they see that large numbers are changing course do they take any notice, or find any reason to investigate. Only then do they feel a need to step beyond their comfort and conforming zone. Until then, those who wish to reap the ripened souls of the earth have no choice except search for that one in a hundred who is motivated mostly by justice, who chooses to rise above all obstacles!

Bahá'u'lláh speaks of the ability of each individual to distinguish truth from falsehood, and hence his accountability before his Creator:

> ...I have perfected in every one of you My creation, so that the excellence of My handiwork may be fully revealed unto men. It follows, therefore, that every man hath been, and will continue to be, able of himself to appreciate the Beauty of God, the Glorified. Had he not been endowed with such a capacity, how could he be called to account for his failure? If, in the Day when all the peoples of the earth will be gathered together, any man should, whilst standing in the presence of God, be asked: "Wherefore hast thou disbelieved in My Beauty and turned away from

> My Self," and if such a man should reply and say: "Inasmuch as all men have erred, and none hath been found willing to turn his face to the Truth, I, too, following their example, have grievously failed to recognize the Beauty of the Eternal," such a plea will, assuredly, be rejected. For the faith of no man can be conditioned by any one except himself.[48]
>
> Bahá'u'lláh

That we are all accountable for the choices we make is a fact confirmed in all sacred Scriptures:

> ...every one of us shall give account of himself to God.
>
> Romans 14:12

> And every soul is summoned to a reckoning...
>
> Qur'án 50:20

Notice the authority with which the Báb speaks to those who deny His divine Mission:

> This mortal life is sure to perish; its pleasures are bound to fade away and ere long ye shall return unto God, distressed with pangs of remorse...and will be asked of your doings.
>
> Say, how dare ye flagrantly deny the verses sent down from the heaven of justice, yet ye read the Books of God revealed in the past?...Indeed, by adhering to forms and by following the promptings of your selfish desires, ye have deprived yourselves of the good-pleasure of your Lord, except those whom their Lord hath endowed with knowledge and who in this Day render thanks unto Him for the bounty of being identified with the true Faith of God. Therefore announce ye the Message unto those who manifest virtue and teach them the ways of the One True God, that haply they may comprehend.[49]

Our degree of accountability always depends on our knowledge. This fact is confirmed in sacred Scriptures and acknowledged by Christian authors and scholars:

> In one of His parables, Jesus laid down the principle that those who know what God wants, and refuse to do it, will be punished more severely than those who do not know the will of God, and hence fail to do it (Luke 12:47 ff). So God will be scrupulously fair in His dealings with everyone. People often ask, for example, 'What about the heathens who have never heard of Christ?' The only biblical answer we can safely give to this question is that God knows all about everyone, and that no one will be condemned unfairly. In fact, Paul suggests that those who have never heard the gospel, but who live well in the light of what they do know, may be better off than those who have heard the truth but rejected it! (Romans 2:12-16).[50]

At the end of *The Hidden Words* Bahá'u'lláh declares that the proof of His Mission is well established. He invites us to undo all the attachments that prevent us from stepping into the Kingdom:

> I bear witness, O friends! that the favor is complete, the argument fulfilled, the proof manifest and the evidence established. Let it now be seen what your endeavors in the path of detachment will reveal. In this wise hath the divine favor been fully vouchsafed unto you and unto them that are in heaven and on earth. All praise to God, the Lord of all Worlds.[51]

In the last chapter of Revelation, Jesus invites all hungry and thirsty seekers to the great banquet of the Lord. May our warmest gratitude be offered to our compassionate Creator and His supreme Messengers and Redeemers who do not force us or carry us into the Kingdom. They simply invite us in the kindest and gentlest way:

> Come, gather together for the great supper of God...
>
> Revelation 19:17 NIV

> The Spirit and the bride say, "Come!" And let him who hears say, "Come!" Whoever is thirsty, let him come; and

whoever wishes, let him take the free gift of the water of life. Revelation 22:17 NIV

To everything there is a season, a time for every purpose under heaven... Ecclesiastes 3:1 NKJ

Is there time to wait and waste? Waiting can only retard our spiritual development. It can only prevent us from the joy of reunion with our supreme Beloved, the One for whom we came into this world. It can only add to our accountability before God. It can only prolong the prevailing pain and suffering for all people.

Be dressed ***ready for service*** and keep your lamps [of awareness and wisdom] burning, like men waiting for their master to return from a wedding banquet, ***so that when he comes and knocks they can IMMEDIATELY open the door*** [of their hearts] ***for him***. Christ (Luke 12:35-36 NIV)

Seize your chance...inasmuch as a fleeting moment in this Day excelleth centuries of a bygone age...Neither sun nor moon hath witnessed a day such as this...[52] Bahá'u'lláh

Seek ye the Lord while he may be found, call ye upon him while he is near... Isaiah 55:6

Remember your Creator before the silver cord is loosed, or the golden bowl is broken, or the pitcher shattered at the fountain, or the wheel broken at the well. Then the dust will return to the earth as it was, and the spirit will return to God who gave it. Ecclesiastes 12:6-7 NKJ

Time is pressing. The Divine Charger is impatient, and can tarry no longer. Ours is the duty to rush forward and, ere it is too late, win the victory.[53] 'Abdu'l-Bahá

What more shall I say? What else can my pen recount?... The whole creation...is bursting asunder through the shattering influence of the Divine summons issued from the throne of glory. ***More than this I cannot write***.[54]

'Abdu'l-Bahá

15

The Day of Divine Blessings

The Spiritual Evolution of Humanity

In that day a fountain shall be opened… Zechariah 13:1 NKJ

Everything in the universe is but a token of divine wisdom—progressively manifesting its potential. Nothing attains maturity without growth, and nothing manifests its innate perfections, its capacities, without preparation. Everything exists in a state of constant flow and change. As humans continue to grow progressively toward more advanced states of being, so must the institutions by which they govern themselves. Religion is no exception.

The seed of the spiritual evolution of humanity attained a critical stage at the dawning of the "Adamic Cycle." It has been nourished, cultivated, and refined by the periodic appearance of many divine Messengers and Teachers. Now in our time it has reached the beginning of its final stage of evolution, the Golden Age of maturity and fulfillment. Ours is the most critical era in human history. For we are witnessing, on the one hand, the termination of "the time of the end," the culmination of the age of hope and anticipation, and, on the other, the onset of the harvest time, the glorious millennium of fulfillment.

"The spiritual creation" of humanity, in accord with divine wisdom, continued for an appointed period of time, and now in our age it is attaining the state of maturity. The kingdom of humans has been tested; now the Kingdom of heaven must rule. The days of turmoil, suffering, war, poverty, and injustice are facing their last and final struggle. The citadels of the forces of darkness are fast falling. "The days of creation" have reached their very end. "The Sabbath of rest," the golden day of peace is now upon the horizon.

> For in six days the Lord made the heavens and the earth, the sea, and all that is in them, and rested the seventh day.
>
> Exodus 20:11 NKJ

The divine Message that has guided humanity throughout all of history attests to the gradual unfolding of such a magnificent panorama of evolution. It indicates that the ultimate purpose of God's supreme Messengers and Redeemers has been twofold: first, to release and guide human potential, to educate and elevate us socially and spiritually; and second, to prepare us progressively for the advent of a new day unrivaled in history—***the great day of the Lord***.

As a Christian author notes:

> In Genesis the earth is created; in Revelation it passes away. In Genesis the sun and moon appear; in Revelation there is no need for the sun or moon. In Genesis there is

a garden, the home of man; in Revelation there is a city, the home of the nations. In Genesis we are introduced to Satan; in Revelation we see his doom. In Genesis we hear the first sob and see the first tear; in Revelation we read: "God shall wipe away all tears from their eyes; and there shall be no more death, neither sorrow, nor crying." In Genesis the curse is pronounced; in Revelation we read, "There shall be no more curse." In Genesis we see our first parents driven from the tree of life; in Revelation welcomed back.[1]

The Greater Covenant

It is a prophecy, a promise, and a covenant—the Greater Covenant*—spoken by all the great Ones of the past, that in due time a Universal Manifestation, a great Messenger and Redeemer will arise to mark the end of the age of anticipation and to inaugurate the era of attainment, the millennium of "the Kingdom of God on earth as it is in heaven." This was Jesus' mission:

> I must give ***the good news*** of the kingdom of God...for that is what I was sent to do. Luke 4:43 NEB

The same mission was given to Muhammad:

> We [God] have sent thee not, except ***good tidings*** to bear and warning. Qur'án 25:58 R

> Verily We have sent thee in truth, as a bearer of ***glad tidings***, and as a warner… Qur'án 35:24 Y

> Of what ask they of one another? Of ***the great news***. The theme of their disputes. Nay! they shall certainly know its truth! Again. Nay! they shall certainly know it.
> Qur'án 78:1-5 R

---

* See *God Passes By*, pp. 27-28. ***The Greater Covenant*** has also been used in Bahá'í literature to point to the covenant a Messenger makes with His followers, promising that another Messenger will come.

As Christian author Dr. John White notes:

> Prophecy, that is, predictions of future events, ***occupies approximately one-quarter of all Scripture***. The teaching of the second coming of our Lord is dealt with some 1,845 times in the Bible, 318 of these being in the New Testament. The return of the Lord is the dominant theme of 17 Old Testament books and one epistle in the New. In fact, 7 out of every 10 chapters in the New Testament make reference to the second coming.[2]

Carlyle Haynes confirms:

> This doctrine [of second advent] is one of the fundamental doctrines of Holy Scripture. ***It finds a larger place in the pages of Holy Writ than any other doctrine*** of the church, this glorious event being mentioned more than three hundred times in the New Testament, and fifteen hundred times in the entire Bible.[3]

The Qur'án emphasizes the advent of this great Day no less than the Bible. As with Christians, most Muslims (the Sunni branch) expect the return of Christ at the end of the age.

Never before have so many prophecies pointed to a new Revelation. Why should so much emphasis be given to this one event? As Bahá'í author George Townshend notes in his book *Christ and Bahá'u'lláh*:

> The story of the coming of the Kingdom runs through the whole Bible. It is the climax and consummation of God's grand redemptive scheme. The attainment of the Kingdom at the end is promised in the beginning, and gives to the Bible its note of confident expectation, of success and triumph.[4]

No word is as great as ***Lord*** and no station as supreme as that of the Creator. To show the glory and greatness of our age, our Creator has, out of His infinite bounty, bestowed His own name not only on the twin Redeemers of our time but on the time itself, calling this Day ***the Day of the Lord***. No honor can be greater than this. Yet as Bahá'u'lláh has repeatedly testified, most people are unaware of God's immeasurable blessings destined for our age.

The coming of God stands as a most emphatic theme in both the Bible and the Qur'án, yet it is seldom noted or acknowledged.

> And it shall be said in that day, Lo, this is our God; we have waited for him. Isaiah 25:9

> What can they expect, but that God shall come down to them overshadowed with clouds, and the angels?
> Qur'án 2:206

> ...thy Lord shall come and the angels rank on rank...
> Qur'án 89:23 R

Our age is the realization of the highest hope of the human race, the consummation of the twofold Mission or Covenant for which all the past Messengers and Redeemers have been sent: the age of the maturity of human race and its preparation for a united world civilization, the Kingdom of God on earth as it is in heaven. The following prophecy recorded in both the Old and New Testaments clearly declares such a Covenant and ordained Mission:

> The Spirit of the Lord is upon me, because he hath anointed me to preach the gospel to the poor; he hath sent me to heal the brokenhearted, to preach deliverance to the captives, and recovering of sight to the blind, to set at liberty them that are bruised, to preach the acceptable year of the Lord [to proclaim the year of the Lord's favor, NIV]. Luke 4:18-19
> Isaiah 61:1-2

As the prophecy indicates, Jesus declared two prime Missions for His advent: ***first, offering the good news of spiritual transformation and fulfillment***, so that those held captive by the cares of the flesh may be freed, the poor in heart enriched, and the blind in spirit enlightened; ***and second, declaring the good news of the year of the advent of the Lord***, when God's greatest blessings are bestowed upon the world.

That Jesus fulfilled the first Mission is quite evident; what is not so evident is that He also fulfilled the second. A careful study of the Gospel reveals that during His brief ministry, He repeatedly informed and enlightened the seekers of His Kingdom of His return as the Spirit of truth, the Counselor, the Holy Spirit, the Lord of Lords and King of Kings, the Son sent in the Glory of the Father. Not only did He give the glad tidings of the advent, but the year of the advent as well. The New Testament alone, as we noted previously, contains as many as eleven references to the exact year of the Lord: 1844.

All Messengers and Redeemers have established a covenant concerning this most glorious Revelation:

> ...We have established a separate covenant regarding Him with every Prophet and His followers. Indeed, We have not sent any Messenger without this binding covenant...[5]
>
> The Báb

> The advent of such a Revelation hath been heralded in all the sacred Scriptures.[6] Bahá'u'lláh

> All the...Books of God are adorned with His praise and extol His glory.[7] Bahá'u'lláh

This prophecy from the Qur'án confirms a universal covenant:

> We entered into a firm Covenant with Thee and with Noah, Abraham, Moses, and Jesus, Son of Mary, to test the true believers and punish the deniers [of this Covenant].
>
> Qur'án 33:7

Ours is a unique age referred to in the Gospel as:

> ...the times of restitution of all things, which God hath spoken by the mouth of all his holy prophets since the world began. Acts 3:21

Bahá'u'lláh indicates that the good news of the coming of His Revelation has been the purpose of all previous Messengers:

> The Revelation which, from time immemorial, hath been acclaimed as the Purpose and Promise of all the Prophets of God, and the most cherished Desire of His Messengers, hath now...been revealed unto men.[8]

Jesus clearly confirms Bahá'u'lláh's message:

> I must give the good news of the kingdom of God to the other towns also, for ***that is what I was sent to do***.
>
> Luke 4:43 NEB

> ***He has sent Me...to proclaim the accepted and acceptable year of the Lord***—the day ***when*** salvation and ***the free favors of God profusely abound***. Luke 4:18-19 AB

The preceding translation emphasizes not only the year of the advent but also the outpouring of divine ***favors***, a subject repeatedly proclaimed by Bahá'u'lláh.

The Day of Divine Blessings

Bahá'u'lláh's references to the abundance of blessings ordained for this Day and its awesome supremacy would fill a volume:

> This is the Day in which God's most excellent favors have been poured out upon men, the Day in which His most mighty grace hath been infused into all created things.[9]

> This is the Day whereon the Ocean of God's mercy hath been manifested unto men, the Day in which the Day Star of His loving-kindness hath shed its radiance upon them, the Day in which the clouds of His bountiful favor have overshadowed the whole of mankind.[10]

> The whole duty of man in this Day is to attain that share of the flood of grace which God poureth forth for him.[11]

> Haste ye to win your share of God's good grace and mercy in this Day that eclipseth all other created Days. How great the felicity that awaiteth the man that forsaketh all

he hath in a desire to obtain the things of God! Such a man, We testify, is among God's blessed ones.[12]

Render thanks unto God, the Eternal Truth, exalted be His glory, inasmuch as ye have attained so wondrous a favor, and been adorned with the ornament of His praise. Appreciate the value of these days, and cleave to whatsoever beseemeth this Revelation. He, verily, is the Counselor, the Compassionate, the All-Knowing.[13]

Should the greatness of this Day be revealed in its fullness, every man would forsake a myriad lives in his longing to partake, though it be for one moment, of its great glory—how much more this world and its corruptible treasures![14]

Countless generations have been waiting and praying for the dawning of the great Day of the Lord. Even God Himself has been waiting to shower His bounties on believers:

...the Lord is ***waiting*** to show you his favor...Happy are all who ***wait*** for him! Isaiah 30:18 NEB

Several verses in the Qur'án indicate the impatience of people to witness the promised Day. They were told:

And for thy Lord ***wait*** thou patiently. Qur'án 74:7 R

Will they ***wait*** until God comes to them in shadows of clouds with angels, and the inevitable [His Advent] comes to pass?[15] Qur'án 2:210

The Bible also confirms this impatience:

Wait for the Lord; be strong, take courage, and ***wait*** for the Lord. Psalms 27:14 NEB

Wait quietly for the Lord, be patient till he comes...
Psalms 37:7 NEB

...***wait*** until the Lord comes. I Corinthians 4:5 NEB

Be patient therefore, brethren, unto the coming of the Lord... James 5:7

That blessed Day has now come. The waiting is over. Our greatest glory and honor is to awaken the world.

> Sing to the Lord...***Declare his glory among the nations***... let the trees of the forest shout for joy before the Lord when he comes to judge the earth.
> I Chronicles 16:23, 24, 33 NEB

This is the greatest and most joyous news of this Day:

> And it shall be said in that day, Lo, this is our God we have ***waited*** for him. Isaiah 25:9

Sacred Scriptures have promised that a time will come when God will unveil His face to humanity:

> These, therefore, are the words of the Lord God...No longer will I hide my ***face*** from them... Ezekiel 39:25, 29 NEB

The prophets' desire for the outpouring of God's grace, for the shining of His face upon the world was so strong that they, too, expressed impatience:

> Restore us, O God, and make thy ***face*** shine upon us that we may be saved. O Lord God of Hosts, how long will thou resist thy people's prayer? Psalms 80:3-4 NEB

Both the promise and the desire have now been fulfilled. The Day of the Lord has dawned with the advent of two supreme independent Saviors and Redeemers, both of whom reflect God's great glory to the fullest:

> He Who, from everlasting, had concealed His ***Face*** from the sight of creation is now come.[16] Bahá'u'lláh

> I am the ***Countenance*** of God Whose splendor can never be obscured...[17] The Báb

Bahá'u'lláh confirms the fulfillment of the promise, reminds us of God's everlasting gifts in store for us, and invites all those who wish to enter the banquet of His Kingdom:

> The heights which, through the most gracious favor of God, mortal man can attain, in this Day, are as yet

unrevealed to his sight. The world of being hath never had, nor doth it yet posses the capacity for such a revelation. The day, however, is approaching when the potentialities of so great a favor will, by virtue of His behest, be manifested unto men.[18]

Seize your chance...inasmuch as a fleeting moment in this Day excelleth centuries of a bygone age...Neither sun nor moon hath witnessed a day such as this...It is evident that every age in which a Manifestation of God hath lived is divinely ordained and may, in a sense, be characterized as God's appointed Day. This Day, however, is unique and is to be distinguished from those that have preceded it.[19]

The excellence of this Day is immensely exalted above the comprehension of men, however extensive their knowledge, however profound their understanding...Shouldst thou rend asunder the grievous veil that blindeth thy vision, thou wouldst behold such a bounty as naught, from the beginning that hath no beginning till the end that hath no end, can either resemble or equal.[20]

We have been moved to reveal these words in consideration of the weakness and frailty of men; otherwise, the Cause We have proclaimed is such as no pen can ever describe, nor any mind conceive its greatness.[21]

This is the Day that hath been illumined by the splendors of the light of Our countenance—the Day around which all days and nights circle in adoration. Blessed is the man of insight who hath perceived, and the sore athirst who hath quaffed from this luminous Fountain. Blessed the man who acknowledgeth the truth, earnestly striving to serve the Cause of his Lord, the Powerful, the Almighty.[22]

Great, immeasurably great is this Cause! Mighty, inconceivably mighty is this Day! Blessed indeed is the man that hath forsaken all things, and fastened his eyes upon Him Whose face hath shed illumination upon all who are in the heavens and all who are on the earth.[23]

"This is the King of Days...the Day that hath seen the coming of the Best-beloved, Him Who through all eternity hath been acclaimed the Desire of the World." "The world of being shineth in this Day with the resplendency of this Divine Revelation. All created things extol its saving grace and sing its praises. The universe is wrapt in an ecstasy of joy and gladness. The Scriptures of past Dispensations celebrate the great jubilee that must needs greet this most great Day of God. Well is it with him that hath lived to see this Day and hath recognized its station."[24]

"He that was hidden from the eyes of men is revealed, girded with sovereignty and power!"..."O ye that inhabit the heavens and the earth! There hath appeared what hath never previously appeared. He Who, from everlasting, had concealed His Face from the sight of creation is now come."..."He Who is the sovereign Lord of all is made manifest. The Kingdom is God's"..."All eyes are gladdened, for He Whom none hath beheld, Whose secret no one hath discovered, hath lifted the veil of glory, and uncovered the countenance of Beauty."[25]

In the Book of Isaiah it is written: "Enter into the rock, and hide thee in the dust, for fear of the Lord, and for the glory of His majesty." No man that meditateth upon this verse can fail to recognize the greatness of this Cause, or doubt the exalted character of this Day—the Day of God Himself. This same verse is followed by these words: "And the Lord alone shall be exalted in that Day." This is the Day which the Pen of the Most High hath glorified in all the holy Scriptures.[26]

All glory be to this Day, the Day in which the fragrances of mercy have been wafted over all created things, a Day so blest that past ages and centuries can never hope to rival it, a Day in which the countenance of the Ancient of Days hath turned towards His holy seat.[27]

The onrushing winds of the grace of God...have passed over all things. Every creature hath been endowed with all the potentialities it can carry. And yet the peoples of the world have denied this grace! Every tree hath been endowed with the choicest fruits, every ocean enriched with the most luminous gems. Man, himself, hath been invested with the gifts of understanding and knowledge. The whole creation hath been made the recipient of the revelation of the All-Merciful, and the earth the repository of things inscrutable to all except God, the Truth, the Knower of things unseen. The time is approaching when every created thing will have cast its burden. Glorified be God Who hath vouchsafed this grace that encompasseth all things, whether seen or unseen![28]

This is the Day whereon naught can be seen except the splendors of the Light that shineth from the face of Thy Lord, the Gracious, the Most Bountiful. Verily, We have caused every soul to expire by virtue of Our irresistible and all-subduing sovereignty. We have, then, called into being a new creation, as a token of Our grace unto men. I am, verily, the All-Bountiful, the Ancient of Days.

This is the Day whereon the unseen world crieth out: "Great is thy blessedness, O earth, for thou hast been made the foot-stool of thy God, and been chosen as the seat of His mighty throne." The realm of glory exclaimeth: "Would that my life could be sacrificed for thee, for He Who is the Beloved of the All-Merciful hath established His sovereignty upon thee, through the power of His Name that hath been promised unto all things, whether of the past or of the future."[29]

Verily I say, this is the Day in which mankind can behold the Face, and hear the Voice, of the Promised One. The Call of God hath been raised, and the light of His countenance hath been lifted up upon men. It behoveth every man to blot out the trace of every idle word from the tablet of his heart, and to gaze, with an open and unbiased mind, on the signs of His Revelation, the proofs of His Mission, and the tokens of His glory.

Great indeed is this Day! The allusions made to it in all the sacred Scriptures as the Day of God attest its greatness. The soul of every Prophet of God, of every Divine Messenger, hath thirsted for this wondrous Day.[30]

Forsake your palaces, and haste ye to gain admittance into His Kingdom. This, indeed, will profit you both in this world and in the next. To this testifieth the Lord of the realm on high, did ye but know it.[31]

Take heed lest pride deter you from recognizing the Source of Revelation, lest the things of this world shut you out as by a veil from Him Who is the Creator of heaven. Arise, and serve Him Who is the Desire of all nations, Who hath created you through a word from Him, and ordained you to be, for all time, the emblems of His sovereignty.[32]

Not every sea hath pearls; not every branch will flower, nor will the nightingale sing thereon. Then, ere the nightingale of the mystic paradise repair to the garden of God, and the rays of the heavenly morning return to the Sun of Truth—make thou an effort, that haply in this dustheap of the mortal world thou mayest catch a fragrance from the everlasting garden, and live forever in the shadow of the peoples of this city. And when thou hast attained this highest station and come to this mightiest plane, then shalt thou gaze on the Beloved, and forget all else.[33]

Make haste...that while there is yet time our lips may taste of the immortal draught, for the breeze of life, now blowing from the city of the Well-Beloved, cannot last, and the streaming river of holy utterance must needs be stilled, and the portals of the Ridván [paradise] cannot for ever remain open. The day will surely come when the Nightingale of Paradise [Bahá'u'lláh] will have winged its flight away from its earthly abode unto its heavenly nest. Then will its melody be heard no more, and the beauty of the

> rose cease to shine. Seize the time, therefore, ere the glory of the divine springtime hath spent itself, and the Bird of Eternity ceased to warble its melody, that thy inner hearing may not be deprived of hearkening unto its call. This is My counsel unto thee and unto the beloved of God. Whosoever wisheth, let him turn thereunto; whosoever wisheth, let him turn away. God, verily, is independent of him and of that which he may see and witness.[34]

This is Christ's last invitation to those who wish to come to the banquet of the Kingdom, His last appeal to those who seek His heavenly mansions:

> And the Spirit and the bride say, ***Come***. And let him that heareth say, ***Come***. And let him that is athirst ***come***. And whosoever will, let him take the water of life freely.
>
> Revelation 22:17

Prayers for Divine Blessings

The following parable has a special message for the people of our time:

> Then Jesus told his disciples a parable to show them that they should always pray and not give up. He said: "In a certain town there was a judge who neither feared God nor cared about men. And there was a widow in that town who kept coming to him with the plea, 'Grant me justice against my adversary.' For some time he refused. But finally he said to himself, 'Even though I don't fear God or care about men, yet because this widow keeps bothering me, I will see that she gets justice, so that she won't eventually wear me out with her coming!'" And the Lord said, "Listen to what the unjust judge says. And will not God bring about justice for his chosen ones, who cry out to him day and night? Will he keep putting them off? I tell you, he

will see that they get justice, and quickly. However, when the Son of Man comes, will he find faith on the earth?"

Luke 18:1-8 NIV

Some Christian scholars believe that the widow in this parable symbolizes the church without Christ. The widow may also symbolize an individual who has lost spiritual support. The main message of the parable is this: People of the end-time will live under much pain and suffering, due to a failure to follow spiritual guidance. The way they can escape from the sufferings is by praying; God always answers sincere prayers. At the end of the parable Jesus asks, "However, when the Son of Man comes will he find faith on earth?" When Christ comes, will people have enough faith in God to pray for His help and be comforted? Obviously not. Many other biblical passages also indicate that the people of our time will live in spiritual darkness due to a lack of faith.

For those who wish to follow Christ's admonition to pray, a few prayers from the Báb and Bahá'u'lláh are quoted here. If your heart is not yet fully convinced by the voluminous evidence presented in this work, you may wish to turn to God. Jesus taught us to ask God for help. It is up to you to ask!

Gaining the gift of faith is not cheap. It is more precious than all the other gifts in the universe combined. It requires passionate desire and unwavering determination. Praying should continue until the answer is revealed.

Glory be to Thee, O King of eternity, and the Maker of nations...I pray Thee, by Thy Name through which Thou didst call all mankind unto the horizon of Thy majesty and glory...to number me with such as have rid themselves from everything except thyself, and have set themselves towards Thee...

I have laid hold, O my Lord, on the handle of Thy bounty, and clung steadfastly to the hem of the robe of Thy favor. Send down, then, upon me, out of the clouds of Thy generosity, what will purge out from me the remembrance of any one except Thee, and make me able to turn unto Him who is the Object of the adoration of all mankind...

...O my Lord...deprive me not of the breathings of Thy Revelation at the appearance of the splendors of the light of Thy face. Powerful art Thou to do what pleaseth Thee. Naught can resist Thy will, nor frustrate what Thou hast purposed by Thy power.

No God is there but Thee, the Almighty, the All-Wise.[35]

Bahá'u'lláh

I beseech Thee, O my Lord, by Thy most effulgent splendor, before whose brightness every soul humbly boweth down and prostrateth itself in adoration for Thy sake—a splendor before whose radiance fire is turned into light, the dead are brought to life and every difficulty is changed into ease. I entreat Thee by this great, this wondrous splendor and by the glory of Thine exalted sovereignty, O Thou Who art the Lord of indomitable power, to transform us through Thy bounty into that which Thou Thyself dost possess and enable us to become fountains of Thy light, and graciously vouchsafe unto us that which beseemeth the majesty of Thy transcendent dominion. For unto Thee have I raised my hands, O Lord, and in Thee have I found sheltering support, O Lord, and unto Thee have I resigned myself, O Lord, and upon Thee have I placed my whole reliance, O Lord, and by Thee am I strengthened, O Lord.

Verily there is no power nor strength except in Thee.[36]

The Báb

Praise to be Thee, O Lord my God! I implore Thee, by Thy Name which none hath befittingly recognized, and whose import no soul hath fathomed; I beseech Thee, by Him Who is the Fountain-Head of Thy Revelation and the Day-Spring of Thy signs, to make my heart to be a receptacle of Thy love and of remembrance of Thee. Knit it, then, to Thy most great Ocean, that from it may flow out the living waters of Thy wisdom and the crystal streams of Thy glorification and praise.

The limbs of my body testify to Thy unity, and the hair of my head declareth the power of Thy sovereignty and might. I have stood at the door of Thy grace with utter self-effacement and complete abnegation, and clung to the hem of Thy bounty, and fixed mine eyes upon the horizon of Thy gifts.

...Thou, verily, art the Most Powerful, the Most High, the All-Knowing, the All-Wise.[37] Bahá'u'lláh

Refresh my heart, O my God, with the living waters of Thy love and give me a draught, O my Master, from the chalice of Thy tender mercy...Do Thou graciously forgive me for the things that I have wrought in Thy holy presence, and look not upon me with the glance of justice, but rather deliver me through Thy grace, treat me with Thy mercy and deal with me according to Thy bountiful favors, as is worthy of Thy glory.

Thou art the Ever-Forgiving, the All-Glorious, the Bestower of favors and gifts, the Lord of grace abounding. Verily no God is there but Thee. Thou art the All-Possessing, the Most High.[38] The Báb

I beseech Thee, O my Lord, by this Fire which blazeth and rageth in the world of creation, to rend asunder the veils that have hindered me from appearing before the throne of Thy majesty, and from standing at the door of Thy gate. Do Thou ordain for me, O my Lord, every good thing Thou didst send down in Thy Book, and suffer me not to be far removed from the shelter of Thy mercy.

Powerful art Thou to do what pleaseth Thee. Thou art, verily, the All-Powerful, the Most Generous.[39] Bahá'u'lláh

O My God, my Lord and my Master! I have detached myself from my kindred and have sought through Thee to become independent of all that dwell on earth and ever ready to receive that which is praiseworthy in Thy sight. Bestow on me such good as will make me independent of aught else but Thee, and grant me an ampler share of Thy boundless favors. Verily Thou art the Lord of grace abounding.

I adjure Thee by Thy might, O my God! Let no harm beset me in times of tests, and in moments of heedlessness guide my steps aright through Thine inspiration. Thou art God, potent art Thou to do what Thou desirest. No one can withstand Thy Will or thwart Thy Purpose.[40] The Báb

I beseech Thee...to nourish me with the wine of Thy knowledge and the living waters of Thy love and pleasure. Behold Thy handmaiden, O my Lord, who hath forgotten all else except Thee, and who hath delighted herself with Thy love...Do Thou ordain for her that which Thou didst ordain for such of Thy handmaidens as circle round the throne of Thy majesty, and gaze, at eventide and at dawn, on Thy beauty.

Thou art, verily, the Lord of the Judgment Day.[41]

Bahá'u'lláh

Is there any Remover of difficulties save God? Say: Praised be God! He is God! All are His servants and all abide by His bidding![42] **The Báb**

Appendix

The Origin and the Goals of the Bahá'í Faith

The Origin of the Bahá'í Faith

This work is about proofs of the validity of the claims of the Báb and Bahá'u'lláh, not the history and teachings of the Bahá'í Faith. Those unacquainted with the basics of the new Revelation will find it helpful to begin their search by studying first its history and teachings, and *then* the evidences of its validity. The proofs of a faith are more relevant when one already knows its basic principles. The Message is the goal, and proofs the means for reaching the goal.

For our purposes a brief reference or introduction to the central figures and the supreme institution of the Bahá'í Faith is in order:

- ***The Bahá'í Faith*** literally means ***the Glorious Faith***—the Faith that manifests ***the Glory of God***.

- ***The Báb***. On May 23, 1844, a young man entitled the Báb (the Gate) declared the dawning of a new Day in the religious history of the world. The young man came from southern Persia. He announced that God would soon send a World Teacher and Savior to bring peace and order and to unify all humanity. Within the brief span of His ministry (1844-1850), the Báb attracted many followers, thousands of whom were massacred, mostly by the order of fanatical religious leaders of Islam. The Báb Himself was imprisoned and finally executed in 1850.

- ***Bahá'u'lláh***. In 1863, a nobleman entitled Bahá'u'lláh (Glory of God) announced that He was the World Teacher and Redeemer promised by the Báb and expected by humanity since the dawn of history. Like His Herald, the Báb, Bahá'u'lláh encountered relentless opposition and oppression throughout His ministry. His imprisonment and exile lasted for 39 years. He often refers to His sufferings with both a sense of submission and pride—submission because He welcomed that which was ordained for Him, pride because He suffered for the sake of others to bring hope and love to the heart of humanity and peace and justice to the world. Bahá'u'lláh's Writings equal a hundred volumes. They offer teachings and unveil "all the truth" (John 16:13) that humanity will need for at least a thousand years.

- ***'Abdu'l-Bahá***. Before His passing in 1892, Bahá'u'lláh appointed His eldest Son, 'Abdu'l-Bahá (Servant of Glory), to serve as the Interpreter and Exemplar of His teachings and the Center of His Covenant. 'Abdu'l-Bahá is also known as the Mystery of God. His station is not that of the Báb or Bahá'u'lláh, but of a Perfect Exemplar or Model for all to emulate. 'Abdu'l-Bahá traveled to many countries to spread the teachings of the new Revelation.

- ***Shoghi Effendi.*** Shoghi Effendi did not consider himself one of the central figures of the Bahá'í Faith, yet he occupied a position of preeminence in the development of thc new faith. After the passing of 'Abdu'l-Bahá, he served as the appointed Guardian of the Faith. His chief accomplishment was the building of the Administrative Order of Bahá'u'lláh, which constitutes a pattern for the future World Order—an Order called by Jesus ***the Kingdom of God,*** and ***the Kingdom of heaven,*** meaning the coming of ***the Kingdom of God*** or ***the Kingdom of heaven*** on earth.
- ***The Universal House of Justice.*** Shortly after Shoghi Effendi's passing, the responsibility for leadership in the Bahá'í Faith was delegated to a supreme elected institution called by Bahá'u'lláh ***The Universal House of Justice.*** Its members represent and receive the full support of the entire Bahá'í community living in over two hundred countries and territories around the globe.

The Goals of the Bahá'í Faith

When that time comes...I will gather all the nations together...
Joel 3:1-2 NEB

And I...am about to come and gather all nations and tongues, and they will come and see my glory...they will bring all your brothers, from all the nations...
Isaiah 66:18, 20 NIV
See also Isaiah 10:13-14

Ye were created to show love one to another...Take pride not in love for yourselves but in love for your fellow-creatures. Glory not in love for your country, but in love for all mankind.[1]
Bahá'u'lláh

...the old order of things has passed away...I am making everything new!
Christ (Rev. 21:4-5 NIV)

Soon will the present-day order be rolled up, and a new one spread out in its stead.[2]
Bahá'u'lláh

The Bahá'í Faith seeks to attain these goals:

- To transform our divided planet into a global community crowned with harmony, peace, and justice
- To inspire the heart of humanity with a divine purpose, and an immortal hope
- To raise the ethical standards to levels never achieved before. (For a detailed study of these goals, see any introductory book on the Bahá'í teachings. See also Volume VI of this work—*By My Fruits Ye Shall Know Me.)*

All these goals are pursued in fulfillment of this divine prayer and purpose:

> Our Father in heaven, thy name be hallowed; thy kingdom come, thy will be done, on earth as in heaven.
>
> Matthew 6:9-10 NEB

Many prominent figures of our time have testified to the positive and dynamic influence of the Bahá'í Faith in leading the world toward these goals:

> I sympathize with the Bahá'í Faith with all my heart because it has the Spirit of Christ in it...You hold...the key that will settle all of our difficulties...[3]
>
> Dr. George Washington Carver

> ...the highest and purest form of religious teaching...I know of no other [faith] so profound. Leo Tolstoy

> The philosophy of Bahá'u'lláh deserves the best thought we can give it... Helen Keller

> In our times we can only survive, and our civilization can only flower, if we reorient the conventional wisdom and achieve the new insights...proclaimed by the Bahá'í Faith and...now also supported by the latest discoveries of the empirical sciences. Dr. Ervin Laszlo
>
> Editor of *The World Encyclopedia of Peace,* Renowned Authority on Systems Sciences and World Order

Bahá'u'lláh was...without question one of the supreme spiritual geniuses of history.

Dr. John Holmes
Minister

[The Bahá'í Faith] teaches the essential unity of mankind under one God...That is a force which cuts across politics, trade routes, racial groupings the world around.

It can be made a powerful force in the practical affairs of the world.

Hon. William O. Douglas
U.S. Supreme Court Justice

...the greatest movement working today for universal peace.

Dr. Auguste Forel
Renowned Swiss Scientist

References

A Call To all Peoples of the World

1. *Gleanings from the Writings of Bahá'u'lláh*, p. 42.
2. *Gleanings from the Writings of Bahá'u'lláh*, pp. 319-320.
3. *Gleanings from the Writings of Bahá'u'lláh*, p. 210.
4. *The Proclamation of Bahá'u'lláh*, pp. 5-6.
5. *Gleanings from the Writings of Bahá'u'lláh*, p. 33.
6. *Epistle to the Son of the Wolf*, p. 60.
7. *The Proclamation of Bahá'u'lláh*, pp. 83-85.
8. Shoghi Effendi. *God Passes By,* Wilmette, IL: Bahá'í Publishing Trust. 1957, p. ix.

Chapter 1

1. *Tablets of Bahá'u'lláh*, p. 9.
2. *Tablets of Bahá'u'lláh*, p. 9.
3. Grant, George and Mark Horne. *Unnatural Affections*, Franklin, TN: Legacy Press, 1991, p. 44.

4. Grant, George and Mark Horne. *Unnatural Affections*, Franklin, TN: Legacy Press, 1991, p. 46.
5. Dowley, Tim. *Eerdman's Handbook to the History of Christianity*, Grand Rapids, MI: Eerdman's Publishing Co., 1977, p. 2.
6. Dowley, Tim. *Eerdman's Handbook to the History of Christianity*, Grand Rapids, MI: Eerdman's Publishing Co., 1977, p. 2.
7. France, R.T. *The Evidence for Jesus*, Downers Grove, Illinois: InterVarsity Press, 1986, p. 21.
8. France, R.T. *The Evidence for Jesus*, Downers Grove, Illinois: InterVarsity Press, 1986, pp. 21-22.
9. France, R.T. *The Evidence for Jesus*, Downers Grove, Illinois: InterVarsity Press, 1986, p. 33.
10. *Tablets of Bahá'u'lláh*, p. 10.
11. *Tablets of Bahá'u'lláh*, p. 10.
12. *Tablets of Bahá'u'lláh*, p. 11.
13. *Tablets of Bahá'u'lláh*, p. 11.
14. *Tablets of Bahá'u'lláh*, p. 11.
15. Dyer, Wayne. *You'll See It When You Believe It*, New York: Avon Books, 1989, pp. 166-167.
16. Dyer, Wayne. *You'll See It When You Believe It*, New York: Avon Books, 1989, p. 168.
17. Levine, Samuel. *You Take Jesus, I'll Take God*, Los Angeles: Homoroh Press.
18. *Tablets of Bahá'u'lláh*, p. 11.
19. *Tablets of Bahá'u'lláh*, p. 11.
20. *Tablets of Bahá'u'lláh*, p. 11.
21. *Tablets of Bahá'u'lláh*, p. 11.
22. *Tablets of Bahá'u'lláh*, p. 11.
23. *Tablets of Bahá'u'lláh*, p. 11.
24. *Tablets of Bahá'u'lláh*, p. 11.
25. *Tablets of Bahá'u'lláh*, p. 11.
26. *Tablets of Bahá'u'lláh*, p. 11.
27. *Tablets of Bahá'u'lláh*, p. 11-12.
28. *Tablets of Bahá'u'lláh*, p. 12.
29. *Tablets of Bahá'u'lláh*, p. 12.
30. *Tablets of Bahá'u'lláh*, p. 12.
31. *Tablets of Bahá'u'lláh*, pp. 16-17.

Chapter 2

1. *Gleanings from the Writings of Bahá'u'lláh*, p. 258.
2. *Gleanings from the Writings of Bahá'u'lláh*, p. 332.
3. *The Hidden Words of Bahá'u'lláh* (Persian), no. 37.
4. *The Hidden Words of Bahá'u'lláh* (Persian), no. 40.
5. *The Hidden Words of Bahá'u'lláh* (Persian), no. 42.
6. Riggs, Robert F. *The Apocalypse Unsealed*, New York: philosophical Library, 1981, p. 70.
7. *Epistle to the Son of the Wolf*, p. 24.
8. *Prayers and Meditations by Bahá'u'lláh*, p. 311.
9. *Gleanings from the Writings of Bahá'u'lláh*, p. 120.
10. *Gleanings from the Writings of Bahá'u'lláh*, p. 301.
11. *Tablets of Bahá'u'lláh*, p. 77.
12. *Prayers and Meditations by Bahá'u'lláh*, pp. 240-241.
13. Shoghi Effendi. *The World Order of Bahá'u'lláh*, Wilmette, IL: Bahá'í Publishing Trust, 1980, pp. 146-147.
14. *The Dawn-Breakers*, p. 293.
15. *Gleanings from the Writings of Bahá'u'lláh*, p. 176.
16. *Epistle to the Son of the Wolf*, p. 121.
17. *Gleanings from the Writings of Bahá'u'lláh*, p. 212.
18. *Gleanings from the Writings of Bahá'u'lláh*, pp. 282-284.
19. *The Kitáb-i-Aqdas*, 1992, p. 62.
20. Shoghi Effendi. *God Passes By*, Wilmette, IL: Bahá'í Publishing Trust, 1957, pp. 93-96.
21. Qur'án 7:179.
22. *Gleanings from the Writings of Bahá'u'lláh*, p. 120.
23. *Gleanings from the Writings of Bahá'u'lláh*, p. 258.
24. *Gleanings from the Writings of Bahá'u'lláh*, p. 283.
25. *Prayers and Meditations by Bahá'u'lláh*, p. 286.
26. *Gleanings from the Writings of Bahá'u'lláh*, p. 14.
27. Stein, Jess and Laurence Urdang (eds.). *The Random House Dictionary of the English Language*, New York: Random House, 1973, p. 602.
28. Quoted in *Journal of Bahá'í Studies*, June-Sept. 1992, p. 38.
29. Unger, Merrill, F. *Unger's Bible Dictionary*, Chicago: Moody Press, 1985, p. 409.

30. Gentz, William H. (editor). *The Dictionary of Bible and Religion*, Nashville, TN: Abingdon Press, 1986, p. 394.
31. *The Compilation of Compilations*, vol. 1, p. 461.
32. Hornby, Helen. *Lights of Guidance*, New Delhi: Bahá'í Publishing Trust, 1988, p. 267.
33. *Selections from the Writings of the Báb*, p. 156.
34. *The Proclamation of Bahá'u'lláh*, p. 18.
35. *The Proclamation of Bahá'u'lláh*, p. 19.
36. *The Proclamation of Bahá'u'lláh*, p. 18.
37. *Tablets of 'Abdu'l-Bahá*, p. 1.
38. *The Kitáb-i-Íqán*, p. 248.
39. Smith, Peter. *In Iran*, Los Angeles: Kalimát Press, 1986, p. 163.
40. *Athár-i-Qalam-i-A'lá* (a compilation of the Writings of Bahá'u'lláh in Persian), vol. 6, p. 315.
41. *Gleanings from the Writings of Bahá'u'lláh*, p. 31.
42. *The Proclamation of Bahá'u'lláh*, p. 89.
43. *Epistle to the Son of the Wolf*, p. 63.
44. *Bahá'í Prayers*, Wilmette, IL: Bahá'í Publishing Trust, 1991 edition, pp. 210-212.
45. *Bahá'í Prayers*, Wilmette, IL: Bahá'í Publishing Trust, 1991 edition, pp. 230-231,
46. *Gleanings from the Writings of Bahá'u'lláh*, p. 16.
47. *Gleanings from the Writings of Bahá'u'lláh*, p. 12.
48. *Gleanings from the Writings of Bahá'u'lláh*, p. 27.
49. *Gleanings from the Writings of Bahá'u'lláh*, p. 31.
50. *Gleanings from the Writings of Bahá'u'lláh*, p. 75.
51. *The Hidden Words of Bahá'u'lláh* (Persian), no. 22.
52. For the explanation of the symbols, I wish to acknowledge my debt to Mr. A. Faizi.
53. *Bahá'í Scriptures*, p. 478-479.
54. *Prayers and Meditations by Bahá'u'lláh*, p. 311.
55. *Prayers and Meditations by Bahá'u'lláh*, pp. 48-49.
56. Shoghi Effendi. *The World Order of Bahá'u'lláh*, Wilmette, IL: Bahá'í Publishing Trust, 1980, p. 139.
57. *The Kitáb-i-Íqán*, p. 35.
58. *Epistle to the Son of the Wolf*, p. 57.
59. *Epistle to the Son of the Wolf*, p. 57.

60. Cheney, Elizabeth. *Prophecy Fulfilled*, Wilmette, IL: Bahá'í Publishing Trust, 1968, p. 4.
61. *The Plain Truth*, April 1968, p. 13.

Chapter 3

1. *Tablets of Bahá'u'lláh*, p. 242.
2. Lockyer, Herbert Sr. (ed.) *Nelson's Illustrated Bible Dictionary*, New York: Thomas Nelson Publishers, 1982, p. 424.
3. *Epistle to the Son of the Wolf*, p. 54.
4. *The Hidden Words of Bahá'u'lláh* (Arabic), no. 63.
5. *Tablets of Bahá'u'lláh*, p. 41.
6. *Gleanings from the Writings of Bahá'u'lláh*, p. 325.
7. *Payám-i-Bahá'í* (Persian magazine), January 1997, no. 212, p. 3.
8. Biederwolf, William E. *The second Coming Bible Commentary*, Grand Rapids, MI: Baker Book House, 1985, p. 368.
9. *Tablets of Bahá'u'lláh*, p. 13.
10. *Gleanings from the Writings of Bahá'u'lláh*, p. 12.
11. *Tablets of Bahá'u'lláh*, p. 244.
12. *Tablets of Bahá'u'lláh*, p. 33.
13. *Gleanings from the Writings of Bahá'u'lláh*, p. 250.
14. Esslemont, J.E. *Bahá'u'lláh and the New Era*, Wilmette, IL: Bahá'í Publishing Trust , 1966, p. 23.
15. *Epistle to the Son of the Wolf*, p. 145.
16. Van Kampen, Robert. *The Sign*, Wheaton, IL: Crossway Books, 1992, p. 330.
17. Van Kampen, Robert. *The Sign*, Wheaton, IL: Crossway Books, 1992, p. 331.
18. *Bahá'í News*, October 1968, no. 451, p. 9.
19. *Bahá'í News*, October 1968, no. 451, p. 9.
20. *Gleanings from the Writings of Bahá'u'lláh*, pp. 189-190.
21. *Gleanings from the Writings of Bahá'u'lláh*, p. 203.
22. *Gleanings from the Writings of Bahá'u'lláh*, p. 316.
23. Himes, Joshua V. *Views of the Prophecies and Prophetic Chronology Selected from Manuscripts of William Miller*, Boston: Published by Joshua Himes, 1842, p. 33.
24. Nuqabá'í, H. *Bishárát-i-Kutub-i-Asmání* (Persian), Tihran, Bahá'í Era 124, p. 186.

25. *Bahá'í News*, October 1968, no. 451, p. 10.
26. Taherzadeh, Adib. *The Revelation of Bahá'u'lláh*, Oxford: George Ronald, 1974, vol. 1, p. 34.
27. Shoghi Effendi. *God Passes By*, Wilmette, IL: Bahá'í Publishing Trust, 1957, p. 25.
28. *Selections from the Writings of the Báb*, p. 164.
29. *Bahá'í News*, October 1968, no. 451, p. 8.
30. *Bahá'í News*, October 1968, no. 451, p. 8.
31. *Bahá'í News*, October 1968, no. 451, p. 8.
32. *Bhagavad-Gita*, Translated by Swami Prabhavananda, and Christopher Isherwood, New York: New American Library, 1972, p. 92.
33. Quoted in *The Bahá'í Faith*, a pamphlet published by The Spiritual Assembly of the Bahá'ís of Richardson, Texas, 1991.
34. *The American Bahá'í*, April 1973, p. 14.
35. From a video on Native American prophecies based on a talk by Lee Brown.
36. Dustkhah, Jalil. *The Avesta* (Persian), Tihran, Iran: Morvareed Co., second edition, dated 2535, pp. 290-291.
37. Dustkhah, Jalil. *The Avesta* (Persian), Tihran, Iran: Morvareed Co., second edition, dated 2535, p. 308.
38. Dustkhah, Jalil. *The Avesta* (Persian), Tihran, Iran: Morvareed Co., second edition, dated 2535, pp. 238-241.
39. Mo'ín. *A Persian Dictionary*, p. 2493.
40. Khadem, Javidukht. *Zikrullah Khadem*, Wilmette, IL: Bahá'í Publishing Trust, 1990, p. 304.
41. *Selections from the Writings of the Báb*, p. 41.
42. *Gleanings from the Writings of Bahá'u'lláh*, p. 44.
43. Smith, Peter. *In Iran*, Los Angeles: Kalimát Press, 1986, p. 163.
44. *Gleanings from the Writings of Bahá'u'lláh*, p. 34.
45. *Selections from the Writings of the Báb*, p. 65.
46. *The Plain Truth*, April 1995, p. 7.
47. *The Kitáb-i-Aqdas*, 1992, pp. 80-82.
48. *Epistle to the Son of the Wolf*, pp. 57-58.
49. *The Kitáb-i-Aqdas*, 1992, p. 244.
50. *Tablets of Bahá'u'lláh*, p. 9.
51. *Gleanings from the Writings of Bahá'u'lláh*, p. 258.

Chapter 4

1. *Tablets of Bahá'u'lláh*, p. 156.
2. *The Promulgation of Universal Peace*, p. 6.
3. Biederwolf, William E. *The Second Coming Bible Commentary*, Grand Rapids: Baker Book House, 1985, p. 493.
4. Feyerabend, Henry. *Tearing the Shroud from the Antichrist*, London, Canada: Destiny, 1986, p. 75.
5. Sweeting, George. *Great Quotes & Illustrations*, Waco, TX: Word Books, 1985, p. 17.
6. Pratney, Winkie and Barry Chant. *The Return*, Chichester, England: Sovereign World, 1988, p. 148.
7. *Epistle to the Son of the Wolf*, p. 160.
8. Lady Blomfield. *The Chosen Highway*, Wilmette, IL: Bahá'í Publishing Trust, p. 60.
9. Lady Blomfield. *The Chosen Highway*, Wilmette, IL: Bahá'í Publishing Trust, p. 49.
10. Taherzadeh, Adib. *The Covenant of Bahá'u'lláh*, Oxford: George Ronald, 1992, p. 60.
11. *Epistle to the Son of the Wolf*, p. 175.
12. *Epistle to the Son of the Wolf*, p. 175.
13. *Epistle to the Son of the Wolf*, p. 176.
14. Shoghi Effendi, *God Passes By*, Wilmette: Bahá'í Publishing Trust, 1957, pp. 163-164.
15. *Kitáb-i-Badí'*, p. 292.
16. Lady Blomfield. *The Chosen Highway*, Wilmette, IL: Bahá'í Publishing Trust, pp. 50-52.
17. *The Kitáb-i-Aqdas*, 1992, pp. 86-87.
18. *Tablets of Bahá'u'lláh*, pp. 75-76.
19. *Epistle to the Son of the Wolf*, p. 157.
20. *The Kitáb-i-Íqán*, p. 102.
21. *The Kitáb-i-Íqán*, pp. 151-152.
22. *Gleanings from the Writings of Bahá'u'lláh*, p. 328.
23. *Epistle to the Son of the Wolf*, p. 146.
24. *The Hidden Words of Bahá'u'lláh* (Persian), no. 24.
25. *The Kitáb-i-Íqán*, p. 251.
26. Shoghi Effendi, *God Passes By*, Wilmette: Bahá'í Publishing Trust, 1957, p. 119.

27. Shoghi Effendi. *God Passes By,* Wilmette, IL: Bahá'í Publishing Trust. 1957, p. 120.
28. *The Kitáb-i-Íqán*, pp. 250-251.
29. Hunt, Dave. *How Close Are We?* Eugene, OR: Harvest House Publishing, 1993, p. 121.
30. *Epistle to the Son of the Wolf*, p. 146.
31. Biederwolf, William E. *The Second Coming Bible Commentary*, Grand Rapids: Baker Book House, 1985, p. 67.
32. *Kitáb-i-Badí'*, pp. 335-336 (in Persian).
33. Achtemeier, Paul J. (general editor). *Harper's Bible Dictionary*, San Francisco: Harper and Row, Publishers, 1985, p. 582.
34. *The Hidden Words of Bahá'u'lláh* (Persian), no. 24.
35. Taherzadeh, A. *The Revelation of Bahá'u'lláh*, Oxford: George Ronald, vol. 2, 1977, p. 298.
36. *Ásár-i-Qalam-i-A'lá*, vol. 5, p. 230 (Persian).
37. Stedman, Ray c. *Waiting for the Second Coming*, Grand Rapids: Discovery House, 1990, p. 126.
38. *A Traveler's Narrative*, p. 31.
39. *A Traveler's Narrative*, p. 53.
40. *Mahbúb-i-'Alam*, Canada: National Spiritual Assembly of Canada, 1992-93, p. 54 (Persian).
41. Pratney, Winkie and Barry Chant. *The Return*, Chichester, England: Sovereign World, 1988, p. 157.
42. *Epistle to the Son of the Wolf*, p. 107.
43. Shoghi Effendi, *God Passes By*, Wilmette: Bahá'í Publishing Trust, 1957, p. 163.
44. Church, J.R. *Hidden Prophecies in the Psalms*, Oklahoma City: Prophecy Publications, 1986, p. 313
45. *Gleanings from the Writings of Bahá'u'lláh*, p. 214.

Chapter 5

1. Shoghi Effendi. *God Passes By,* Wilmette, IL: Bahá'í Publishing Trust. 1957, p. 112.
2. Shoghi Effendi. *God Passes By,* Wilmette, IL: Bahá'í Publishing Trust. 1957, p. 112.
3. *A Traveler's Narrative*, p. 55.
4. Taherzadeh, Adib. *The Covenant of Bahá'u'lláh*, Oxford: George Ronald, 1992, p. 67

5. *A Traveler's Narrative*, p. 56.
6. *Laálí'u'l-Hikmat* (Persian), Brasil: Editoria Bahá'í, vol. 3, p. 318.
7. *The Kitáb-i-Íqán*, p. 248.
8. *Epistle to the Son of the Wolf*, pp. 70-71.
9. Pratney, Winkie and Barry Chant. *The Return*, Chichester, England: Sovereign World, 1988, p. 152.
10. Biederwolf, William E. *The Second Coming Bible Commentary*, Grand Rapids: Baker Book House, 1985, p. 535.
11. Hunt, Dave. *How Close Are We?* Eugene, OR: Harvest House Publishing, 1993, p. 112.
12. *The Promulgation of Universal Peace*, p. 6.
13. *Epistle to the Son of the Wolf*, p. 151.
14. *Tablets of Bahá'u'lláh*, pp. 57-58.
15. *Gleanings from the Writings of Bahá'u'lláh*, p. 7.
16. Shoghi Effendi, *God Passes By*, Wilmette: Bahá'í Publishing Trust, 1957, p. 233.
17. Taherzadeh, Adib. *The Covenant of Bahá'u'lláh*, Oxford: George Ronald, 1992, p. 95.
18. Taherzadeh, Adib. *The Covenant of Bahá'u'lláh*, Oxford: George Ronald, 1992, p. 95.
19. Van Kampen, Robert. *The Sign*, Wheaton, IL: Crossway Books, 1992, p. 55.
20. Biederwolf, William E. *The Second Coming Bible Commentary*, Grand Rapids: Baker Book House, 1985, p. 338.
21. Taherzadeh, Adib. *The Covenant of Bahá'u'lláh*, Oxford: George Ronald, 1992, p. 63.
22. Lady Blomfield. *The Chosen Highway*, Wilmette, IL: Bahá'í Publishing Trust, p. 50.
23. *Gleanings from the Writings of Bahá'u'lláh*, p. 286.
24. *The Dawn-Breakers*, p. 583.
25. *Prayers and Meditations by Bahá'u'lláh*, p. 36.
26. *A Travelers Narrative*, p. 31.
27. Taherzadeh, Adib. *The Covenant of Bahá'u'lláh*, Oxford: George Ronald, 1992, p. 61.
28. Taherzadeh, Adib. *The Covenant of Bahá'u'lláh*, Oxford: George Ronald, 1992, p. 64.
29. Lady Blomfield. *The Chosen Highway*, Wilmette, IL: Bahá'í Publishing Trust, p. 51.

30. *A Traveler's Narrative*, p. 53.
31. *Tablets of Bahá'u'lláh*, p. 40.
32. *Gleanings from the Writings of Bahá'u'lláh*, pp. 273-274.
33. *Gleanings from the Writings of Bahá'u'lláh*, p. 274.
34. Lady Blomfield. *The Chosen Highway*, Wilmette, IL: Bahá'í Publishing Trust, p. 50.
35. *A Traveler's Narrative*, p. 38.
36. Annual Report of the National Spiritual Assembly of the Bahá'ís of the United States and Its Agencies, 1996, p. 22.
37. *Prayers and Meditations by Bahá'u'lláh*, p. 132.
38. Shoghi Effendi. *God Passes By*, Wilmette, IL: Bahá'í Publishing Trust. 1957, p. 170.
39. Shoghi Effendi. *God Passes By*, Wilmette, IL: Bahá'í Publishing Trust. 1957, p. 170.
40. *The Kitáb-i-Íqán*, pp. 208-209.
41. *The Kitáb-i-Íqán*, p. 31.
42. *Selections from the Writings of 'Abdu'l-Bahá*, p. 73.
43. *Laálí'u'l-Hikmat* (Persian), Brasil: Editoria Bahá'í, vol. 1, p. 142.
44. Van Impe, Jack. *Everything you always wanted to know about Prophecy but didn't know who to ask!*, Troy, MI: Jack Van Impe Ministries, 1980, pp. 59-61.
45. Van Kampen, Robert. *The Sign*, Wheaton, IL: Crossway Books, 1992, p. 333.
46. *Tablets of Bahá'u'lláh*, p. 87.
47. *Tablets of Bahá'u'lláh*, p. 156.
48. *Selections from the Writings of the Báb*, p. 48.
49. *Prayers and Meditations by Bahá'u'lláh*, pp. 131-132.
50. *Selections from the Writings of the Báb*, pp. 46-47.
51. Yúsuf 'Alí, 'Abdullah. *The Meaning of the Holy Qur'án*, Beltsville, MD, 1989, p. 323.
52. *The Kitáb-i-Íqán*, pp. 249-250.
53. Van Impe, Jack. *Everything you always wanted to know about Prophecy but didn't know who to ask!*, Troy, MI: Jack Van Impe Minisstries, 1991, p. 4.
54. *The Promulgation of Universal Peace*, p. 23.
55. *Tablets of Bahá'u'lláh*, p. 13.

Chapter 6

1. Church, J. R. *The Song of Moses*, Oklahoma City, OK: Prophecy Publications, 1991, p. 81.
2. Feyerabend, Henry. *Tearing the Shroud from the Antichrist*, London, Canada: Destiny, 1986, p. 47.
3. Stedman, Roy C. *What's this World Coming to?* Ventura, CA: Regal Books, 1970, p. 97.
4. *Selections from the Writings of the Báb*, p. 140.
5. *Tablets of Bahá'u'lláh*, p. 10.
6. Van Impe, Jack. *Everything you always wanted to know about Prophecy but didn't know who to ask!*, Windsor, Ontario: Jack Van Impe Ministries, 1980, p. 10.
7. *Gleanings from the Writings of Bahá'u'lláh*, p. 45.
8. *The Kitáb-i-Íqán*, p. 159.
9. *The Kitáb-i-Íqán*, p. 190.
10. *The Kitáb-i-Íqán*, p. 232.
11. *Gleanings from the Writings of Bahá'u'lláh*, p. 103.
12. *Gleanings from the Writings of Bahá'u'lláh*, p. 58.
13. *Epistle to the Son of the Wolf*, p. 161.
14. *Gleanings from the Writings of Bahá'u'lláh*, p. 41.
15. *The Kitáb-i-Íqán*, pp. 15-16.
16. *The Kitáb-i-Íqán*, p. 29.
17. *The Kitáb-i-Íqán*, p. 17.
18. Reagan, David. *The Master Plan*, Eugene, OR: Harvest House Publishers, 1993, p. 217.
19. Biederwolf, William E. *The Second Coming Bible Commentary*, Grand Rapids, MI: Baker Book House, 1985, p. 331.
20. *The Hidden Words of Bahá'u'lláh* (Persian), no. 21.
21. *The Hidden Words of Bahá'u'lláh* (Persian), no. 20.
22. *The Hidden Words of Bahá'u'lláh* (Persian), no. 22.
23. *The Hidden Words of Bahá'u'lláh* (Persian), no. 24.
24. *The Hidden Words of Bahá'u'lláh* (Persian), no. 25.
25. *The Hidden Words of Bahá'u'lláh* (Persian), no. 45.
26. *Selections from the Writings of the Báb*, pp. 51-52.
27. *The Proclamation of Bahá'u'lláh*, pp. 20-21.
28. *The Proclamation of Bahá'u'lláh*, p. 22-23.

29. Khadem, Javidukht. *Zikrullah Khadem*, Wilmette, IL: Bahá'í Publishing Trust, 1990, pp. 286-287.
30. *Memorials of the Faithful*, p. 27.
31. Faizi, M. A. *His Holiness Bahá'u'lláh* (Persian), Tehran, Iran, pp. 234-235.
32. *Paris Talks*, p. 76.
33. Shoghi Effendi. *God Passes By,* Wilmette, IL: Bahá'í Publishing Trust. 1957, p. 71.
34. *Epistle to the Son of the Wolf*, pp. 20-21.
35. Shoghi Effendi. *God Passes By*, Wilmette, IL: Bahá'í Publishing Trust, 1957, p. 72.
36. *Epistle to the Son of the Wolf*, p. 21.
37. Biederwolf, William E. *The Second Coming Bible Commentary*, Grand Rapids: Baker Book House, 1985, p. 28.
38. Church, J. R. *Hidden Prophecies in the Psalms*, Oklahoma City: Prophecy Publications, 1986, p. 47.
39. Lady Blomfield. *The Chosen Highway*, Wilmette, IL: Bahá'í Publishing Trust, p. 60.
40. Lady Blomfield. *The Chosen Highway*, Wilmette, IL: Bahá'í Publishing Trust, p. 60.
41. Shoghi Effendi. *God Passes By,* Wilmette, IL: Bahá'í Publishing Trust. 1957, p. 141.
42. Shoghi Effendi. *God Passes By,* Wilmette, IL: Bahá'í Publishing Trust. 1957, p. 142.
43. Shoghi Effendi. *God Passes By,* Wilmette, IL: Bahá'í Publishing Trust. 1957, p. 186.
44. Shoghi Effendi. *God Passes By*, Wilmette, IL: Bahá'í Publishing Trust, 1957, p. 187.
45. Shoghi Effendi. *God Passes By*, Wilmette, IL: Bahá'í Publishing Trust, 1957, p. 187.
46. *'Abdu'l-Bahá in London*, London, England: Bahá'í Publishing Trust, 1982, pp. 115-116.
47. Lady Blomfield. *The Chosen Highway*, Wilmette, IL: Bahá'í Publishing Trust, p. 66.
48. *Gleanings from the Writings of Bahá'u'lláh*, pp. 119-120.
49. Shoghi Effendi. *God Passes By,* Wilmette, IL: Bahá'í Publishing Trust. 1957, pp. 119-120.
50. Shoghi Effendi. *God Passes By,* Wilmette, IL: Bahá'í Publishing Trust. 1957, p. 147.

Chapter 7

1. Froom, Leroy. *The Prophetic Faith of Our Fathers*, Washington, D.C.: Review and Harold, 1950, vol. 4, p. 527.
2. Froom, Leroy. *The Prophetic Faith of Our Fathers*, Washington, D.C.: Review and Harold, 1950, vol. 4, p. 859.
3. Froom, Leroy. *The Prophetic Faith of Our Fathers*, Washington, D.C.: Review and Harold, 1950, vol. 3, p. 614.
4. Froom, Leroy. *The Prophetic Faith of Our Fathers*, Washington, D.C.: Review and Harold, 1950, vol. 3, p. 614.
5. Froom, Leroy. *The Prophetic Faith of Our Fathers*, Washington, D.C.: Review and Harold, 1950, vol. 3, p. 614.
6. Biederwolf, William E. *The Second Coming Bible Commentary*, Grand Rapids: Baker Book House, 1985, p. 331.
7. *Gleanings from the Writings of Bahá'u'lláh*, p. 163.
8. *Gleanings from the Writings of Bahá'u'lláh*, pp. 323-327.
9. Unger, Merrill F. *Unger's Bible Dictionary*, Chicago: Moody Press, 1966, p. 286.
10. Lady Blomfield. *The Chosen Highway*, Wilmette, IL: Bahá'í Publishing Trust, p. 93.
11. Gottlieb, Randie & Steven. *Once to Every Man & Nation*, Oxford: George Ronald, 1985, pp. 2-3.
12. Gottlieb, Randie & Steven. *Once to Every Man & Nation*, Oxford: George Ronald, 1985, p. 5.
13. Ankerberg, John, John Weldon, Walter C. Kaiser, Jr. *The Case for Jesus the Messiah*, Eugene, OR: Harvest House Publishers, 1989, p. 99.
14. *The Hidden Words of Bahá'u'lláh, (Arabic)*, no. 56.
15. *The Kitáb-i-Íqán*, pp. 236-237.
16. *Selections from the Writings of the Báb*, p. 67.
17. Lindsey, Hal. *The Promise*, New York: Bantam Books, 1984, pp. 92-94.
18. Stedman, Ray C. *God's Final Word*, Grand Rapids, MI: Discovery House, 1991, pp. 74-75.
19. *Some Answered Questions*, p. 65.
20. Shoghi Effendi. *The World Order of Bahá'u'lláh*, Wilmette, IL: Bahá'í Publishing Trust, 1980, p. 204.
21. Shoghi Effendi. *The World Order of Bahá'u'lláh*, Wilmette, IL: Bahá'í Publishing Trust, 1980, p. 205.

Chapter 8

1. *The Kitáb-i-Íqán*, p. 66.
2. *Epistle to the Son of the Wolf*, p. 132.
3. *Epistle to the Son of the Wolf*, p. 46.
4. *Selections from the Writings of the Báb*, p. 141.
5. *Gleanings from the Writings of Bahá'u'lláh*, p. 136.
6. *Epistle to the Son of the Wolf*, p. 46.
7. *The Kitáb-i-Aqdas*, p. 48.
8. Pratney, Winkie, and Barry Chant. *The Return*, Chichester, England: Sovereign World, 1988, pp. 61-62.
9. *Prayers and Meditations by Bahá'u'lláh*, p. 77.
10. *Power of Divine Assistance*, p. 212.
11. *Gleanings from the Writings of Bahá'u'lláh*, p. 41.
12. *Gleanings from the Writings of Bahá'u'lláh*, p. 33.
13. *The Hidden Words of Bahá'u'lláh* (Persian), no. 37.
14. *Epistle to the Son of the Wolf*, p. 142.
15. *The Kitáb-i-Íqán*, p. 23.
16. *The Kitáb-i-Íqán*, p. 205.
17. *The Kitáb-i-Íqán*, p. 215.
18. *Prohibition of Intoxication*, p. 245.
19. *Prayers and Meditations by Bahá'u'lláh*, p. 4.
20. *Prayers and Meditations by Bahá'u'lláh*, p. 299.
21. *The Seven Valleys and the Four Valleys*, p. 28.
22. *Tablets of Bahá'u'lláh*, p. 17.
23. *Tablets of Bahá'u'lláh*, p. 47.
24. *The Proclamation of Bahá'u'lláh*, p. 104.
25. *Epistle to the Son of the Wolf*, p. 52.
26. *Gleanings from the Writings of Bahá'u'lláh*, p. 115.
27. *Prayers and Meditations by Bahá'u'lláh*, p. 68.
28. *Gleanings from the Writings of Bahá'u'lláh*, p. 85.
29. *The Hidden Words of Bahá'u'lláh* (Persian), no. 30.
30. *Tablets of Bahá'u'lláh*, pp. 117-118.
31. *The Kitáb-i-Aqdas*, p. 48.
32. *The Hidden Words of Bahá'u'lláh* (Persian), no. 23.
33. *Prayers and Meditations by Bahá'u'lláh*, p. 166.

34. Hunt, Dave. *How Close Are We?* Eugene, OR: Harvest House Publishers, 1993, p. 26.
35. *Gleanings from the Writings of Bahá'u'lláh*, pp. 45-46.
36. Biederwolf, William E. *The Second Coming Bible Commentary*, Grand Rapids: Baker Book House, 1985, pp. 94-95.
37. *The Proclamation of Bahá'u'lláh*, p. 83.
38. *Gleanings from the Writings of Bahá'u'lláh*, p. 40.
39. *Gleanings from the Writings of Bahá'u'lláh*, p. 44.
40. *Tablets of Bahá'u'lláh*, pp. 237-238.
41. *Prayers and Meditations by Bahá'u'lláh*, p. 97.
42. *Gleanings from the Writings of Bahá'u'lláh*, p. 43.
43. *The Proclamation of Bahá'u'lláh*, p. 92.
44. *The Proclamation of Bahá'u'lláh*, pp. 106-107.
45. *Gleanings from the Writings of Bahá'u'lláh*, p. 203.
46. Toffler, Alvin. *The Third Wave*, New York: Bantam Books, 1981, p. 9.
47. *Epistle to the Son of the Wolf*, p. 132.
48. *Epistle to the Son of the Wolf*, p. 147.
49. *Epistle to the Son of the Wolf*, p. 36.
50. *Gleanings from the Writings of Bahá'u'lláh*, p. 13.
51. *Tablets of Bahá'u'lláh*, p. 12.
52. *Tablets of Bahá'u'lláh*, p. 237.
53. *Selections from the Writings of the Báb*, p. 29.
54. *Tablets of Bahá'u'lláh*, p. 11.
55. *Gleanings from the Writings of Bahá'u'lláh*, p. 9.
56. *Epistle to the Son of the Wolf*, p. 120.
57. *Gleanings from the Writings of Bahá'u'lláh*, pp. 99-100.
58. *Gleanings from the Writings of Bahá'u'lláh*, p. 307.
59. *Epistle to the Son of the Wolf*, p. 92.
60. *Gleanings from the Writings of Bahá'u'lláh*, p. 158.
61. *Gleanings from the Writings of Bahá'u'lláh*, p. 239.
62. *Epistle to the Son of the Wolf*, pp. 78-79.
63. *Gleanings from the Writings of Bahá'u'lláh*, p. 101.
64. *Prayers and Meditations by Bahá'u'lláh*, p. 158-159.
65. *Epistle to the Son of the Wolf*, p. 95.
66. *Prayers and Meditations by Bahá'u'lláh*, pp. 311-313.

Chapter 9

1. Robertson, Norman. *Understanding End Time Prophecy*, Chichester, England: Sovereign World, 1983, p. 95.
2. McKeever, Jim. *The Coming Climax of History*, Medford, OR: Omega Publications, 1982, p. 268.
3. Lindsey, Hal. *Apocalypse Code*, Palos Verdes, CA: Western Front Ltd., 1997, pp. 152-153.
4. Pratney, Winkie and Barry Chant. *The Return*, Chichester, England: Sovereign World, 1988, pp. 53-54.
5. Van Impe, Jack. *Everything you always wanted to know about Prophecy but didn't know who to ask!*, Windsor, Ontario: Jack Van Impe Ministries, 1980, pp. 47-48.
6. *Gleanings from the Writings of Bahá'u'lláh*, p. 296.
7. Shoghi Effendi. *Citadel of Faith*, Wilmette, IL: Bahá'í Publishing Trust, 1965, p. 26.
8. *Tablets of Bahá'u'lláh*, p. 259-260.
9. *Gleanings from the Writings of Bahá'u'lláh*, p. 93.
10. *Crisis and Victory*, p. 153.
11. *Bahá'í Prayers*, Wilmette: Bahá'í Publishing Trust, 1991 edition, p. 215.
12. *Selections from the Writings of the Báb*, p. 163.
13. *Epistle to the Son of the Wolf*, p. 25.
14. *Epistle to the Son of the Wolf*, p. 55.
15. *Epistle to the Son of the Wolf*, p. 29.
16. *Epistle to the Son of the Wolf*, p. 55.
17. *Epistle to the Son of the Wolf*, p. 36.
18. *Tablets of Bahá'u'lláh*, p. 90.
19. *Tablets of Bahá'u'lláh*, p. 123.
20. *Epistle to the Son of the Wolf*, pp. 74-75.
21. Pratney, Winkie and Barry Chant. *The Return*, Chichester, England: Sovereign World, 1988, pp. 233-234.
22. Pratney, Winkie and Barry Chant. *The Return*, Chichester, England: Sovereign World, 1988, p. 198.
23. Lockyer, Herbert Sr. (ed.) *Nelson's Illustrated Bible Dictionary*, New York: Thomas Nelson Publishers, 1982, pp. 98-99.
24. *Epistle to the Son of the Wolf*, p. 32.
25. *Epistle to the Son of the Wolf*, p. 4.

26. *Epistle to the Son of the Wolf*, p. 72.
27. *Epistle to the Son of the Wolf*, p. 159.
28. *Gleanings from the Writings of Bahá'u'lláh*, p. 15.
29. *Gleanings from the Writings of Bahá'u'lláh*, p. 20.
30. *Gleanings from the Writings of Bahá'u'lláh*, p. 21.
31. *Gleanings from the Writings of Bahá'u'lláh*, p. 42.
32. *Gleanings from the Writings of Bahá'u'lláh*, p. 265.
33. *The Hidden Words of Bahá'u'lláh* (Persian), no. 66.
34. *The Kitáb-i-Íqán*, p. 118.
35. *The Kitáb-i-Íqán*, p. 118.
36. *The Proclamation of Bahá'u'lláh*, p. 91.
37. *Prayers and Meditations by Bahá'u'lláh*, p. 152.
38. *Prayers and Meditations by Bahá'u'lláh*, p. 204.
39. *Prayers and Meditations by Bahá'u'lláh*, p. 305.
40. *Tablets of Bahá'u'lláh*, p. 23.
41. *Tablets of Bahá'u'lláh*, p. 90.
42. *Tablets of Bahá'u'lláh*, p. 119.
43. *Tablets of Bahá'u'lláh*, p. 170.
44. *The Kitáb-i-Íqán*, p. 205
45. *Prayers and Meditations by Bahá'u'lláh*, p. 7.
46. *Prayers and Meditations by Bahá'u'lláh*, p. 33.
47. *Prayers and Meditations by Bahá'u'lláh*, p. 69.
48. *Prayers and Meditations by Bahá'u'lláh*, p. 157.
49. *Prayers and Meditations by Bahá'u'lláh*, p. 187.
50. *The Seven Valleys and the Four Valleys*, p. 10.
51. *The Seven Valleys and the Four Valleys*, p. 13.
52. *The Seven Valleys and the Four Valleys*, p. 36.
53. *Tablets of Bahá'u'lláh*, p. 34.
54. *Tablets of Bahá'u'lláh*, p. 88.
55. *Gleanings from the Writings of Bahá'u'lláh*, p. 223.
56. *Gleanings from the Writings of Bahá'u'lláh*, p. 96.
57. *Gleanings from the Writings of Bahá'u'lláh*, p. 38.
58. *Epistle to the Son of the Wolf*, p. 14.
59. *Tablets of Bahá'u'lláh*, p. 156.
60. *Epistle to the Son of the Wolf*, p. 133
61. *Gleanings from the Writings of Bahá'u'lláh*, p. 21.

62. *The Hidden Words of Bahá'u'lláh, (Arabic)*, no. 55.
63. *Prayers and Meditations by Bahá'u'lláh*, p. 76.
64. *Prayers and Meditations by Bahá'u'lláh*, p. 269.
65. *Epistle to the Son of the Wolf*, p. 119.
66. *Epistle to the Son of the Wolf*, p. 21.
67. *Gleanings from the Writings of Bahá'u'lláh*, p. 248.
68. *Tablets of Bahá'u'lláh*, pp. 246-247.
69. *The Kitáb-i-Íqán*, p. 256.
70. Lockyer, Herbert Sr. (ed.) *Nelson's Illustrated Bible Dictionary*, New York: Thomas Nelson Publishers, 1982, p. 351.
71. Lockyer, Herbert Sr. (ed.) *Nelson's Illustrated Bible Dictionary*, New York: Thomas Nelson Publishers, 1982, p. 351.
72. Biederwolf, William E. *The Second Coming Bible Commentary*, Grand Rapids: Baker Book House, 1985, p. 259.
73. *The Amplified Bible*, Grand Rapids, MI: Zondervan Bible Publishers, 1965, p. 196.
74. *The Kitáb-i-Íqán*, p. 112.
75. *The Kitáb-i-Aqdas*, pp. 56-57.
76. *Tablets of Bahá'u'lláh*, p. 57.
77. *Tablets of Bahá'u'lláh*, p. 88.
78. *Tablets of Bahá'u'lláh*, p. 222.
79. *Tablets of Bahá'u'lláh*, p. 197-198.
80. *Tablets of Bahá'u'lláh*, pp. 259-260.
81. *Prayers and Meditations by Bahá'u'lláh*, p. 333.
82. *The Promulgation of Universal Peace*, p. 5.
83. *The Kitáb-i-Íqán*, p. 15.
84. Momen, Moojan. *An Introduction to Shi'i Islam*, Oxford, England: George Ronald, 1985, p. 168.
85. *Gleanings from the Writings of Bahá'u'lláh*, p. 128.
86. Taherzadeh, Adib. *The Revelation of Bahá'u'lláh*, Oxford: George Ronald, 1988, vol. 4, p. 350.
87. Shoghi Effendi. *The Promised Day Is Come*, Wilmette, IL: Bahá'í publishing Committee, 1941, pp. 103-104.
88. *Tablets of Bahá'u'lláh*, pp. 263-264.
89. *Epistle to the Son of the Wolf*, pp. 74-75.
90. *Epistle to the Son of the Wolf*, pp. 25-26.
91. Lindsey, Hal. *Apocalypse Code*, Palos Verdes, CA: Western Front Ltd., 1997, p. 302.

92. *'Abdu'l-Bahá in London*, pp. 46-47.
93. Templeton, John Marks. *Riches for the Mind & Spirit*, San Francisco: Harper Collins Publishers, 1990, p. 172.
94. *Tablets of the Divine Plan*, p. 35.
95. *Tablets of Bahá'u'lláh*, p. 173.
96. *Gleanings from the Writings of Bahá'u'lláh*, p. 92.
97. *Gleanings from the Writings of Bahá'u'lláh*, p. 73.

Chapter 10

1. *Epistle to the Son of the Wolf*, pp. 76-77.
2. *The Kitáb-i-Aqdas*, p. 76.
3. *Epistle to the Son of the Wolf*, p. 94.
4. *Gleanings from the Writings of Bahá'u'lláh*, p. 100.
5. *The Kitáb-i-Íqán*, p. 190.
6. *Gleanings from the Writings of Bahá'u'lláh*, p. 37.
7. *Gleanings from the Writings of Bahá'u'lláh*, p. 344.
8. *Gleanings from the Writings of Bahá'u'lláh*, p. 233.
9. *The Hidden Words of Bahá'u'lláh* (Persian), no. 24.
10. *Some Answered Questions*, p. 270.
11. Church, J.R. *Hidden Prophecies in the Psalms*, Oklahoma City: Prophecy Publications, 1986, p. 327.
12. *The Seven Valleys and the Four Valleys*, p. 41.
13. *The Hidden Words of Bahá'u'lláh* (Persian), no. 38.
14. *Gleanings from the Writings of Bahá'u'lláh*, pp. 320-321.
15. Phelps, Myron H. *The Master In 'Akká*, Los Angeles: Kalimát Press, 1985, pp. 76-90.
16. *Gleanings from the Writings of Bahá'u'lláh*, p. 103.
17. *Prayers and Meditations by Bahá'u'lláh*, p. 312.
18. Shoghi Effendi. *The Promised Day Is Come*, Wilmette, IL: Bahá'í Publishing Committee, 1951, pp. 7-8.
19. *The Proclamation of Bahá'u'lláh*, pp. 59-60.
20. *Prayers and Meditations by Bahá'u'lláh*, p. 278.
21. *Gleanings from the Writings of Bahá'u'lláh*, pp. 119-120.
22. *Paris Talks*, p. 79.
23. *The Proclamation of Bahá'u'lláh*, p. 60.
24. *Prayers and Meditations by Bahá'u'lláh*, p. 18.
25. *Gleanings from the Writings of Bahá'u'lláh*, pp. 274-275.

Chapter 11

1. Lindsey, Hal. *The Promise*, New York: Bantam Books, 1984, p. 86.
2. Rabbani, Rúhíyyih. *Prescription for Living*, Oxford: George Ronald, 1978, p. 149.
3. De Jong, Benjamin R. *Uncle Ben's Quotebook*, Grand Rapids, MI: Baker Book House, 1976, p. 55.
4. *Some Answered Questions*, p. 37.
5. *Selections from the Writings of 'Abdu'l-Bahá*, p. 16.
6. *Some Answered Questions*, p. 37.
7. Taherzadeh, Adib. *The Covenant of Bahá'u'lláh*, Oxford, England: George Ronald, 1992, p. 92.
8. *A Travelers Narrative*, p. 53.
9. Frend, W. H. C. *The Rise of Christianity*, p. 109.
10. Shoghi Effendi. *God Passes By*, Wilmette, IL: Bahá'í Publishing Trust, 1957, p. 141.
11. Shoghi Effendi. *God Passes By*, Wilmette, IL: Bahá'í Publishing Trust, 1957, p. 142.
12. Shoghi Effendi. *God Passes By*, Wilmette, IL: Bahá'í Publishing Trust, 1957, p. 143.
13. Shoghi Effendi. *God Passes By*, Wilmette, IL: Bahá'í Publishing Trust, 1957, p. 144.
14. *Some Answered Questions*, p. 30.
15. *Some Answered Questions*, p. 34.

Chapter 12

1. *Selections from the Writings of the Báb*, p. 45.
2. *Selections from the Writings of the Báb*, p. 59.
3. *The Kitáb-i-Íqán*, p. 232.
4. *Selections from the Writings of the Báb*, p. 15.
5. *The Hidden Words of Bahá'u'lláh, (Arabic)*, no. 56.
6. *The Kitáb-i-Íqán*, p. 57.
7. *The Dawn-Breakers*, New York: Bahá'í Publishing Committee, 1953, p. 507.
8. *The Dawn-Breakers*, New York: Bahá'í Publishing Committee, 1953, pp. 507-508.
9. *The Dawn-Breakers*, New York: Bahá'í Publishing Committee, 1953, p. 509.

10. *The Dawn-Breakers*, New York: Bahá'í Publishing Committee, 1953, p. 512.
11. *The Dawn-Breakers*, New York: Bahá'í Publishing Committee, 1953, p. 512.
12. *The Dawn-Breakers*, New York: Bahá'í Publishing Committee, 1953, p. 513.
13. *The Dawn-Breakers*, New York: Bahá'í Publishing Committee, 1953, p. 514.
14. *The Dawn-Breakers*, New York: Bahá'í Publishing Committee, 1953, p. 515.
15. *Selections from the Writings of the Báb*, p. 27.
16. *Selections from the Writings of the Báb*, p. 28.
17. *Selections from the Writings of the Báb*, p. 166.
18. *Selections from the Writings of the Báb*, p. 156.
19. Ferraby, John. *All Things Made New*, London: Ruskin House, 1957, p. 199.
20. *Some Answered Questions*, p. 34.
21. *The Kitáb-i-Aqdas*, p. 34.
22. *Selections from the Writings of the Báb*, p. 156.
23. *Bhagavad-Gita*, Translated by Swami Prabhavananda, and Christopher Isherwood, New York: New American Library, 1972, p. 92.
24. Taherzadeh, Adib. *The Revelation of Bahá'u'lláh*, Oxford: George Ronald, 1977, vol. 2, p. 9.
25. *The Beloved of the World* (Persian). Toronto, Canada: 'Andalíb Editorial Board, 1992-93, pp. 37-38.
26. *Bhagavad-Gita*, Translated by Swami Prabhavananda, and Christopher Isherwood, New York: New American Library, 1972, p. 92.
27. Lockyer, Herbert Sr. (General Editor). *Nelson's Illustrated Bible Dictionary*, Nashville, TN: Thomas Nelson Publishers,, 1986, p. 192.
28. Taherzadeh, Adib. *The Revelation of Bahá'u'lláh*, Oxford: George Ronald, 1977, vol. 2, pp. 197-198.
29. Taherzadeh, Adib. *The Revelation of Bahá'u'lláh*, Oxford: George Ronald, 1977, vol. 2, p. 199.
30. Taherzadeh, Adib. *The Revelation of Bahá'u'lláh*, Oxford: George Ronald, 1977, vol. 4, pp. 53-54.
31. Faizi, A.Q. *Stories from the Delight of Hearts*, Los Angeles: Kalimát Press, 1980, pp. 20-22.

32. Lady Blomfield. *The Chosen Highway*, Wilmette, IL: Bahá'í Publishing Trust, pp. 202-204.
33. *Gleanings from the Writings of Bahá'u'lláh*, p. 169.

Chapter 13

1. *Tablets of Bahá'u'lláh*, p. 236.
2. Feyerabend, Henry. *Tearing the Shroud from the Antichrist*, London, Canada: Destiny, 1986, p. 61.
3. *Epistle to the Son of the Wolf*, p. 15.
4. *Tablets of Bahá'u'lláh*, p. 236.
5. *The Hidden Words of Bahá'u'lláh* (Arabic), no. 62.
6. *The Hidden Words of Bahá'u'lláh* (Persian), no. 45.
7. *The Seven Valleys and the Four Valleys*, p. 35.
8. *The Kitáb-i-Íqán*, p. 192.
9. *The Kitáb-i-Íqán*, p. 3.
10. *Tablets of Bahá'u'lláh*, p. 211.
11. *Tablets of Bahá'u'lláh*, p. 62.
12. *The Kitáb-i-Aqdas*, p. 80.
13. *The Kitáb-i-Aqdas*, p. 79.
14. *Tablets of Bahá'u'lláh*, p. 86.
15. *Selections from the Writings of the Báb*, p. 146.
16. *The Seven Valleys and the Four Valleys*, p. 24.
17. *The Hidden Words of Bahá'u'lláh* (Persian), no. 45.
18. *The Proclamation of Bahá'u'lláh*, p. 83.
19. *The Kitáb-i-Íqán*, p. 192.
20. *Gleanings from the Writings of Bahá'u'lláh*, pp. 87-88.
21. *The Kitáb-i-Íqán*, p. 74.
22. *The Kitáb-i-Aqdas*, p. 70.
23. *Selections from the Writings of the Báb*, p. 112.
24. *Selections from the Writings of the Báb*, p. 90.
25. *The Kitáb-i-Íqán*, p. 72.
26. *The Kitáb-i-Íqán*, p. 72.
27. *The Kitáb-i-Íqán*, p. 70.
28. *The Kitáb-i-Íqán*, p. 75.
29. *Tablets of Bahá'u'lláh*, p. 171.
30. *Gleanings from the Writings of Bahá'u'lláh*, p. 143.

31. *Gleanings from the Writings of Bahá'u'lláh*, p. 43.
32. *Gleanings from the Writings of Bahá'u'lláh*, p. 203.
33. *Gleanings from the Writings of Bahá'u'lláh*, p. 42.
34. *The Kitáb-i-Íqán*, p. 199.
35. *The Kitáb-i-Íqán*, p. 31.
36. *The Kitáb-i-Íqán*, p. 196.
37. *The Kitáb-i-Íqán*, p. 196.
38. *Tablets of Bahá'u'lláh*, p. 16.
39. *The Hidden Words of Bahá'u'lláh, (Arabic)*, no. 62.
40. *The Hidden Words of Bahá'u'lláh* (Persian), no. 79.
41. Gottlieb, Randie & Steven. *Once to Every Man & Nation*, Oxford: George Ronald, 1985.
42. Foroughi, Tahirih K. *My Love is My Stronghold*, New Delhi, India: Bahá'í Publishing Trust, 1995.
43. Purkey, William and John Novak. *Inviting School Success*, Belmont: California: Wadsworth Publishing Company, 1984, p. 21.
44. Spong, John Shelby. *Resurrection Myth or Reality?* San Francisco: Harper San Francisco, 1994, pp. 39-40.
45. *Selections from the Writings of the Báb*, p. 92.
46. *Selections from the Writings of the Báb*, p. 84.
47. Vandeman, George E. *Showdown at Armageddon*, Boise: Pacific Press Publishing Association, 1987, p. 93.
48. *Gleanings from the Writings of Bahá'u'lláh*, p. 119.
49. *Epistle to the Son of the Wolf*, p. 94.
50. Shoghi Effendi. *The Promised Day Is Come*, Wilmette, IL: Bahá'í Publishing Committee, 1951, p. 11.
51. *Gleanings from the Writings of Bahá'u'lláh*, p. 12.
52. *Gleanings from the Writings of Bahá'u'lláh*, p. 75.
53. *Prayers and Meditations by Bahá'u'lláh*, p. 107.
54. *Tablets of Bahá'u'lláh*, pp. 240-241.
55. *Bahá'í Prayers*, Wilmette, IL: Bahá'í Publishing Trust, 1991 edition, pp. 211-212.
56. *Gleanings from the Writings of Bahá'u'lláh*, pp. 204-205.
57. *Gleanings from the Writings of Bahá'u'lláh*, p. 94.
58. *Gleanings from the Writings of Bahá'u'lláh*, p. 105.
59. *Tablets of Bahá'u'lláh*, p. 242.
60. *Tablets of Bahá'u'lláh*, p. 231.

61. *The Promulgation of Universal Peace*, p. 62.
62. *Bahá'í Prayers*, Wilmette, IL: Bahá'í Publishing Trust, 1991 edition, pp. 61-62.

Chapter 14

1. *Tablets of Bahá'u'lláh*, p. 131.
2. *Tablets of Bahá'u'lláh*, p. 189.
3. *Tablets of Bahá'u'lláh*, p. 189.
4. *The Seven Valleys and the Four Valleys*, p. 9.
5. *The Secret of Divine Civilization*, pp. 96-97.
6. *Gleanings from the Writings of Bahá'u'lláh*, p. 219.
7. *Tablets of Bahá'u'lláh*, pp. 128-129.
8. *Gleanings from the Writings of Bahá'u'lláh*, p. 108.
9. *The Hidden Words of Bahá'u'lláh* (Arabic), no. 38.
10. *Epistle to the Son of the Wolf*, p. 25.
11. *Tablets of Bahá'u'lláh*, p. 156.
12. *The Hidden Words of Bahá'u'lláh* (Persian), no. 32.
13. *The Hidden Words of Bahá'u'lláh* (Arabic), no. 4.
14. *The Hidden Words of Bahá'u'lláh* (Arabic), no. 6.
15. *The Hidden Words of Bahá'u'lláh* (Arabic), no. 10.
16. *Tablets of Bahá'u'lláh*, p. 155.
17. *Gleanings from the Writings of Bahá'u'lláh*, p. 130.
18. *Epistle to the Son of the Wolf*, pp. 46-47.
19. *The Proclamation of Bahá'u'lláh*, p. 83.
20. *Tablets of Bahá'u'lláh*, p. 48.
21. *Gleanings from the Writings of Bahá'u'lláh*, pp. 70-71.
22. *The Kitáb-i-Aqdas*, 1992, p. 32.
23. *Selections from the Writings of the Báb*, p. 204.
24. *The Hidden Words of Bahá'u'lláh* (Arabic), no. 5.
25. *The Book of Certitude*, pp. 256-257.
26. *The Hidden Words of Bahá'u'lláh* (Arabic), no. 35.
27. *Selections from the Writings of the Báb*, p. 87.
28. *Selections from the Writings of the Báb*, p. 87.
29. *Tablets of Bahá'u'lláh*, p. 156.
30. *Selections from the Writings of the Báb*, p. 110.
31. *Tablets of Bahá'u'lláh*, p. 48.

32. *Gleanings from the Writings of Bahá'u'lláh*, pp. 340-341.
33. *Prayers and Meditations by Bahá'u'lláh*, pp. 311-312.
34. Shoghi Effendi. *The World Order of Bahá'u'lláh*, Wilmette, IL: Bahá'í Publishing Trust, 1980, p. 107.
35. *Gleanings from the Writings of Bahá'u'lláh*, p. 110.
36. *Tablets of Bahá'u'lláh*, p. 174.
37. *The Hidden Words of Bahá'u'lláh* (Arabic), no. 70.
38. *The Kitáb-i-Aqdas*, p. 55.
39. *Prayers and Meditations by Bahá'u'lláh*, p. 209.
40. *Selections from the Writings of the Báb*, p. 99.
41. *Bahá'í Prayers*, Wilmette, IL: Bahá'í Publishing Trust, 1991 edition, p. 212.
42. *Epistle to the Son of the Wolf*, p. 49.
43. *The Hidden Words of Bahá'u'lláh* (Arabic), no. 9.
44. *Bahá'í Prayers*, Wilmette, IL: Bahá'í Publishing Trust, 1991 edition, pp. 210-211.
45. *Gleanings from the Writings of Bahá'u'lláh*, p. 183.
46. *Epistle to the Son of the Wolf*, p. 119.
47. *Bahá'í Prayers*, Wilmette, IL: Bahá'í Publishing Trust, 1991 edition, pp. 211-212.
48. *Gleanings from the Writings of Bahá'u'lláh*, p. 143.
49. *Selections from the Writings of the Báb*, p. 162.
50. Pratney, Winkie and Barry Chant. *The Return*, Chichester, England: Sovereign World, 1988, pp. 63-64.
51. *The Hidden Words of Bahá'u'lláh*, pp. 51-52.
52. Shoghi Effendi. *The World Order of Bahá'u'lláh*, Wilmette, IL: Bahá'í Publishing Trust, 1980, p. 107.
53. Shoghi Effendi. *The World Order of Bahá'u'lláh*, Wilmette, IL: Bahá'í Publishing Trust, 1980, pp. 111-112.
54. Shoghi Effendi. *The World Order of Bahá'u'lláh*, Wilmette, IL: Bahá'í Publishing Trust, 1980, p. 112.

Chapter 15

1. De Jong, Benjamin. *Uncle Ben's Quotebook*, Grand Rapids, MI: Baker Book House, 1976, p. 53.
2. White, John Wesley. *Re-entry*, Minneapolis: World Wide Publications, 1971, p. 14.

3. Haynes, Carlyle B. *Our Lord's Return*, Nashville: Southern Publishing Association, 1964, p. 13.
4. Townshend, George. *Christ and Bahá'u'lláh*, London: George Ronald, 1957, p. 14.
5. *Selections from the Writings of the Báb*, p. 46.
6. *Gleanings from the Writings of Bahá'u'lláh*, p. 5.
7. *Tablets of Bahá'u'lláh*, p. 50.
8. *Gleanings from the Writings of Bahá'u'lláh*, p. 5.
9. *Gleanings from the Writings of Bahá'u'lláh*, p. 6.
10. *Gleanings from the Writings of Bahá'u'lláh*, p. 7.
11. *Gleanings from the Writings of Bahá'u'lláh*, p. 8.
12. *Gleanings from the Writings of Bahá'u'lláh*, p. 214.
13. *Gleanings from the Writings of Bahá'u'lláh*, p. 110.
14. *Gleanings from the Writings of Bahá'u'lláh*, p. 197.
15. Translated by the author.
16. *Gleanings from the Writings of Bahá'u'lláh*, p. 31.
17. *Selections from the Writings of the Báb*, p. 12.
18. *Gleanings from the Writings of Bahá'u'lláh*, p. 214.
19. Shoghi Effendi. *The World Order of Bahá'u'lláh*, Wilmette, IL: Bahá'í Publishing Trust, 1980, p. 107.
20. *Gleanings from the Writings of Bahá'u'lláh*, p. 108.
21. *Gleanings from the Writings of Bahá'u'lláh*, p. 99.
22. *Tablets of Bahá'u'lláh*, p. 261.
23. *Gleanings from the Writings of Bahá'u'lláh*, p. 245.
24. Shoghi Effendi. *The World Order of Bahá'u'lláh*, Wilmette, IL: Bahá'í Publishing Trust, 1980, p. 106.
25. *Gleanings from the Writings of Bahá'u'lláh*, p. 31.
26. *Gleanings from the Writings of Bahá'u'lláh*, p. 13.
27. *Gleanings from the Writings of Bahá'u'lláh*, p. 14.
28. Shoghi Effendi. *Guidance for Today and Tomorrow*, London: Bahá'í Publishing Trust, 1953, p. 150.
29. *Gleanings from the Writings of Bahá'u'lláh*, pp. 29-30.
30. *The Proclamation of Bahá'u'lláh*, pp. 111-112.
31. *The Kitáb-i-Aqdas*, p. 50.
32. *The Kitáb-i-Aqdas*, p. 49.
33. *The Seven Valleys and the Four Valleys*, p. 38.

34. *The Book of Certitude*, pp. 23-24.
35. *Prayers and Meditations by Bahá'u'lláh*, pp. 47-48.
36. *Selections from the Writings of the Báb*, p. 180.
37. *Prayers and Meditations by Bahá'u'lláh*, pp. 56-57.
38. *Selections from the Writings of the Báb*, p. 208.
39. *Prayers and Meditations by Bahá'u'lláh*, p. 76.
40. *Selections from the Writings of the Báb*, pp. 209-210.
41. *Prayers and Meditations by Bahá'u'lláh*, pp. 78-79.
42. *Selections from the Writings of the Báb*, p. 217.

Appendix

1. *Tablets of Bahá'u'lláh*, p. 138.
2. *Gleanings from the Writings of Bahá'u'lláh*, p. 7.
3. You will find some of these quotations and many others in *The Bahá'í World*, Volumes viii and ix.

Index

Index of Bible Verses Used in This Book

Sources for Information and Literature

1. Visit these Bahá'í Websites:
   - ***www.globalperspective.org***
   - ***www.bahai.org***
   - ***www.bahai-library.org***
2. To receive information on the Bahá'í Faith, call: 1-800-949-1863 or 1-800-228-6483
3. To communicate with this author, send an Email to: hugh@globalperspective.org

A Few Bahá'í Centers

Alaska

13501 Brayton Drive
Anchorage, Alaska 99516
USA

Australia

Bahá'í Publications
173 Mona Vale Road
Ingleside, NSW 2101
Australia

Canada

7200 Leslie Street
Thornhill, Ontario
L3T 6L8 Canada

England

27 Rutland Gate
London SW7 1PD
United Kingdom

Hawaii

3264 Allan Place
Honolulu, Hawaii 96817
USA

India

Bahá'í House
5 Canning Road
Post Box 19
New Delhi 110 001
India

New Zealand

P.O. Box 21-551
Henderson 1231
Auckland
New Zealand

United States

536 Sheridan Road
Wilmette, IL 60091
USA

Other Books by the Same Author

I Shall Come Again

522 Pages

Volume I

That is the day when I come like a thief. Happy the man who stays awake. ***Christ (Rev. 16:15)***

Do not let Him find you sleeping. What I say to you, I say to everyone: "Watch!" ***Christ (Mark 13:36)***

Did you know that the Bible contains 16 time prophecies concerning the year of the Second Advent? No wonder so many scholars discovered the same date. Did you also know that all those 16 prophecies point to the same year: 1844? ***Bahá'ís believe that the promise of the Second Advent has already been fulfilled, precisely as predicted.*** Christ did return in 1844, "***like a thief,***" in a way that ***the News of His coming did not draw much attention***. And as the Book of Revelation predicts, God gave Him a new name: ***Bahá'u'lláh***, meaning ***the Glory of God***.

Obviously ***we expect you to be very skeptical***, but we invite you ***to stay spiritually awake, to "watch," to pay close attention, and to investigate this most glorious News***. How can you do this? Start your search by examining the evidence presented in ***I Shall Come Again***, the first of a six-volume series on the fulfillment of biblical prophecies by ***Bahá'u'lláh, the Glory of God***.

I Shall Come Again, written after three decades of research, takes you step by step through 16 prophecies that point to 1844, and hundreds of other prophecies, concerning the return of Christ. It proves how these prophecies, without exception, were fulfilled by ***Bahá'u'lláh (the Glory of God)*** and His martyred Herald, ***the Báb (the Gate)***, who appeared in 1844. ***I Shall Come Again*** is one of the most fascinating books of our time. If you have faith in God's promises and a desire to know the truth, you will receive incomparable joy and hope from reading it.

Imagine if the News of the Return of Jesus is true and you choose not to investigate and not to know Him! Imagine also if the News of His Return is true and your investigation leads you to recognize Him!

> ***I shall come again and receive you to myself, so that where I am you may be also.*** ***Christ (John 14:3)***
>
> ***"He, verily, is come with His Kingdom, and all the atoms cry aloud: 'Lo! The Lord is come in His great majesty!'" "Behold how He hath come down from the heaven of His grace, girded with power and invested with sovereignty. Is there any doubt concerning His signs?"***
> ***Bahá'u'lláh (the Glory of God)***

Lord of Lords

634 Pages

Volume II

This volume presents hundreds of biblical prophecies concerning the Central Figures of the Bahá'í Faith—the Báb, Bahá'u'lláh, 'Abdu'l-Bahá—as well as Shoghi Effendi (the

Guardian of the Bahá'í Faith), the Universal House of Justice (the supreme administrative body in the Bahá'í Faith), the Bahá'ís (the followers of Bahá'u'lláh), the Bahá'í teachings, and the Book of Bahá'í Laws (*The Kitáb-i-Aqdas*).

Lord of Lords presents six fulfillments for Daniel's prophecy of 1335, and shows their connection to the Bahá'í Faith. The book also presents ***86 similarities between Jesus and the Báb***, who is called "***One like a Son of Man***."

Christian scholars often apply the statistical laws to the prophecies of Hebrew Scriptures to prove the divine station of Jesus. ***Lord of Lords*** applies the same laws to the prophecies of both Hebrew and Christian Scriptures to prove the divine station of the Báb and Bahá'u'lláh.

Lord of Lords shows that the probability of biblical prophecies coming true in the Bahá'í Faith by chance alone is about 1 in 10^{80}. The number 10^{80} is equal to the number of atoms in the known universe! What does this evidence indicate? ***It indicates that if anyone could pick a specific atom in the universe by chance, he could then claim that the biblical prophecies fulfilled in the Bahá'í Faith also happened by chance!*** The proof presented in this volume is so compelling it can convince even the most skeptic seeker!

> ***...the desire of all nations shall come...*** ***Haggai 2:7***

> ***He who is the Desired One is come in His transcendent majesty...Better is this for you than all ye possess.***
> ***Bahá'u'lláh (the Glory of God)***

> ***For the Son of man shall come in the glory of his Father.***
> ***Christ (Matt. 16:27)***

> ***I have come in the shadows of the clouds of glory, and am invested by God with invincible sovereignty.***
> ***Bahá'u'lláh (the Glory of God)***

What do others say about:

I Shall Come Again, Lord of Lords, King of Kings?

A scholarly work of meticulous research. Appealing to reason and applying the scientific method to prophetic scripture, it demonstrates that God has once again revealed Himself to humankind and has provided hope for unity and peace on this planet. **John Paul Vader, M.D.**
Author of *For the Good of Mankind*

A book with a message of hope and fulfillment, a message that can transform our planet into a place of peace, into a kingdom that has been the dream and hope of humanity since the dawn of history...a scholarly, comprehensive, and fascinating work that has been long overdue. No wonder it took over three decades to complete it.
Hon. Dorothy W. Nelson
Judge, U.S. Court of Appeals, 9th Circuit

A story with an incredible ending that is made credible by the sheer weight of evidence. It is a must for anyone interested in the proofs of the advent of the Promised One of all ages. **John Huddleston**
Former Chief of Budget and Planning Division, International Monetary Fund,
Author of *The Earth Is But One Country*

...a treasure house of great value for both Bahá'ís and seekers. **Adib Taherzadeh**
Author and Scholar

I am in awe at the extent of research you have undertaken! **Waldo Boyd**
Writer and Editor

Your work never fails to astound me. The effort and breadth of your knowledge both of the Bible and other

literature as well as the depth of your understanding of Bahá'í Scripture is truly amazing. Also, a hallmark of your work is your thoroughness. Anyone who believes in biblical prophecy, and reads these volumes with an open mind, cannot fail to be convinced. **Dr. Tom Rowe**
Professor of Psychology

Your work is the best I've seen on biblical prophecies and proofs of Bahá'u'lláh's Revelation. You offer so much information in relatively few pages. Your many references prove clearly the book's central claim. Your language is simple and exciting. You take the reader through a complete spiritual and prophetic adventure. Your approach is modest, yet dynamic. I pray it will excite all your readers as it has excited me. **Joe Killeen**
Bible Scholar, with a Degree in Eschatology and Soteriology

There are few works by a single author that can rival Dr. Motlagh's in their sheer scope, depth and thoroughness of scholarship. Without doubt, future Bahá'ís will thank Dr. Motlagh for his achievements, that are, in my opinion, not only astonishing—they are heroic.

An important work that will be referenced by future Bahá'í scholars for millennia to come. **Robert F. Riggs**
Aerospace and Marine Scientist, Inventor,
Author of *The Apocalypse Unsealed*

By writing these volumes Dr. Motlagh has made a momentous contribution to our understanding of biblical prophecy. As a former Baptist minister, I urge all Christians to investigate the news of the return of our Lord as presented in *I Shall Come Again, Lord of Lords,* ***and*** *King of Kings.* ***"Arise, shine, for your light has come, and the glory of the Lord rises upon you" (Isa. 60:1).***
Mel Campbell
Former Baptist Minister

Come Now, Let Us Reason Together

286 Pages

This book is written in response to the objections raised by a pastor against the Bahá'í Faith. It removes all the main obstacles that prevent Christians from recognizing the return of the Son in the glory of the Father, from acknowledging the promised Redeemer of our time—***Bahá'u'lláh, the Glory of God***. Once you start reading this book, you will find it hard to put down.

On Wings of Destiny

274 Pages

On Wings of Destiny is based on a dialogue between two friends. Reading it is like joining a circle of friends and participating in a "fireside chat."

The prime purpose of the book is to inspire you—and anyone else who values his soul and spiritual life—to recognize that ***in this world you have an awesome responsibility: you must choose your everlasting destiny. That choice has unimaginable consequences that will endure beyond death for all eternity***. Failing to make a choice is also a choice. This book invites you to make every effort to discover God's plan for you and to follow that plan.

On Wings of Destiny shows that the only way you can attain true joy and happiness in all the worlds of God is to cultivate your spiritual potential and to draw nearer and nearer to God.

If you value your soul and wish to choose your destiny in the light of knowledge and freedom, take the time to listen to this inspiring "fireside chat" to discover how the Bahá'í teachings can help you attain contentment, fulfill your life's purpose, and discover your divine destiny: Heaven's most glorious gift to you.

A Messenger of Joy

112 Pages

A Messenger of Joy is the most comforting and positive book ever written on death and the afterlife. In consoling and uplifting the souls of the grieving, it sets a standard that is not likely to be surpassed for a long time.

This book portrays death as a message of joy and hope, and not as the news of sorrow and despair. It lifts the veil to show that death is not the end of life, but the beginning of an everlasting and most glorious journey toward God.

Choosing Your Destiny

375 Pages

Most people leave their destiny to "chance." Whatever their parents happen to believe, they believe. This book shows that our "destiny" is God's most precious gift to us. Should we throw this gift to the wind? Should we allow "chance" rather than "choice" determine our destiny?

The Bahá'í Faith has come to give us spiritual insight and to help us choose our destiny in the light of reason and true knowledge, rather than in the darkness of tradition and conformity. The knowledge contained in ***Choosing Your Destiny*** can liberate us from past prejudices and illusions and set our souls free. It can help us become spiritual by developing "the divine image" in our soul.

One God, Many Faiths; One Garden, Many Flowers

290 Pages

One God, Many Faiths; One Garden, Many Flowers shows that in God's garden there are many fragrant flowers, planted and nourished by the same Gardener. The Bahá'í Faith has come to help us recognize the beauty of the garden, the harmony of the flowers, and the oneness of the Gardener.

When we realize that we are all one people, on one planet, under one God, with one common destiny, the walls of prejudice that divide God's beautiful garden will crumble. Only true knowledge and love can reveal this beauty and bring about this wonder. The Bahá'í Faith is that knowledge and that love. It penetrates the hearts and souls of humankind to dispel all shadows of prejudice and separation. It connects our hearts and reveals the beauty and splendor of our souls in the light of oneness. ***One God, Many Faiths, One Garden, Many Flowers*** offers you the knowledge that can change your destiny.

Forthcoming Books

The Glory of the Son

It is absolutely essential to know why we believe in Jesus. Where can we find the answer? Only in the Words of Jesus Himself. ***The Glory of the Son*** offers a brief summary of all the reasons Jesus—not His followers—gave to substantiate His claim. This is a book that every Christian should read. It will also be of great value to those of the Jewish faith who have a desire to know the evidence for their glorious King and Redeemer: Jesus Christ.

The Glory of the Father

This is the sequel to ***The Glory of the Son***. It applies the same standards to Bahá'u'lláh that ***The Glory of the Son*** applies to Jesus Christ.

The book presents 35 standards by which the seeker of truth can compare ***the Glory of Jesus*** with ***the Glory of Bahá.*** It also contains a brief summary of some of the prophecies about the advent of the Báb and Bahá'u'lláh as presented in ***Lord of Lords***, and ***King of Kings***.

True seekers will find this book very convincing, because it shows the absolute oneness of ***Jesus Christ, the Anointed***

One of God; ***Bábu'lláh, the Gate of God***; and ***Bahá'u'lláh, the Glory of God***. It proves that they are identical Celestial Roses, a Bouquet of beauty and fragrance sent as a gift from heaven to humankind.

Will Jesus Come from the Sky or as a Thief?

***Be always on the watch!* Luke 21:36**

***The day of the Lord will come like a thief in the night.* I Thess. 5:2**

In the mid-19th century many Christian scholars had discovered that, according to numerous biblical prophecies and promises, Christ would return in 1844. Thousands of Christians around the world expected His Return in that year. Why did so many discover the same date? And what piece of "the prophetic puzzle" did they miss? Let us explore this critical question.

Jesus declared that He would return "***like a thief***." He also repeatedly warned us to "***Watch!***" How does a thief come? Secretly. A thief does not want to draw attention to himself. This is his foremost concern. How can we catch a thief? By being awake and "***watchful***," by "***paying attention***" to his coming. Jesus' warning that He would return "***like a thief***," and His recommended strategy for recognizing Him by staying ***awake*** and by "***watching***" for Him, are complementary:

The warning: I shall come like a thief!

The way to recognize me: Watch, pay close attention! Do not be complacent!

What, then, did Jesus mean by warning us repeatedly and emphatically to "***Watch!***"? He meant: "***Pay close attention to the news of My coming!***"

How did Jesus come the first time? Like a thief. He walked among the Jews. He knew every one of them, but with a few exceptions, they did not know Him. Jesus concealed His supreme glory from "the strangers," from all those who were unworthy of seeing the Spirit of God in Him (John 12:40), from all those who "***may look and look but see nothing***" (Mark 10:12). ***Only the spiritually-sighted paid close attention to Him***, only they "watched" with their hearts and souls, and only they saw the glory of God in Him. Jesus did not allow the spiritually blind to witness His divine glory.

By the vivid expression "***like a thief***" Jesus instructs us to expect a repetition of the way He came the first time. He further confirms this fact by predicting that ***people will respond to the News of His coming the same way that they responded to the News of the coming of Noah***. They will be complacent, non-attentive, negligent, and spiritually asleep!

What piece of "the prophetic puzzle" did Christians (who expected the Return of Christ in 1844) miss? The same "piece" that the Jews had missed 18 centuries earlier and are still missing! That piece is the word "***SPIRIT:***"

The "missing piece" for Jews:

He will come as a "***king***" means: "***His Spirit*** will come as a king."

The "missing piece" for Christians:

He will come from ***heaven*** means: "***His Spirit*** will come from heaven."

Jesus Himself decoded the word "sky" or "heaven" several times. Compare the following two verses, one from ***Jesus Christ, the Anointed One of God***; the other from ***Bahá'u'lláh, the Glory of God***:

> ***I [the Spirit of God, Christ] have come down from heaven.*** ***Christ (John 6:38)***
>
> ***He [the Spirit of God, Bahá'u'lláh], verily, hath again come down from heaven, even as He came down from it the first time.***
>
> ***Bahá'u'lláh (the Glory of God)***